Woolf Editing / Editing Woolf

Virginia Woolf. Diaries. Saturday, 21 June 1924 (Reel Two D19-1924). Reproduced by permission of the Society of Authors on behalf of the Virginia Woolf Estate and by the Henry W. and Albert A. Berg Collection of English and American Literature, the New York Public Library (Astor, Lenox and Tilden Foundations). Cf. *The Diary of Virginia Woolf*, vol. 2, ed. Anne Olivier Bell (New York: Harcourt, 1978) 304.

Woolf Editing / Editing Woolf

Edited by Eleanor McNees and Sara Veglahn

Every effort has been made to trace all copyright-holders, but if any have been inadvertently overlooked, the publisher will be pleased to make the necessary arrangement at the first opportunity.

Copyright 2009 by Clemson University
ISBN 978-0-9796066-9-4

Published by Clemson University Press in Clemson, South Carolina

Editorial Assistants: Bridget Jeffs, Jordan McKenzie, and Charis Chapman

To order copies, please visit the Clemson University Press website: www.clemson.edu/press.

Cover portrait (etching) of Virginia Woolf by Helene Orr.

Frontispiece: Virginia Woolf. Diaries. Saturday, 21 June 1924 (Reel Two D19-1924). The Henry W. and Albert A. Berg Collection of English and American Literature, The New York Public Library (Astor, Lenox and Tilden Foundations). Cf. *The Diary of Virginia Woolf*, vol. 2, ed. Anne Olivier Bell (New York: Harcourt, 1978) 304.

Endpiece: Virginia Woolf. Diaries. Thursday, 20 June 1940 (Reel Three D35-1940). The Henry W. and Albert A. Berg Collection of English and American Literature, The New York Public Library (Astor, Lenox and Tilden Foundations). Cf. *The Diary of Virginia Woolf*, vol. 4, ed. Anne Olivier Bell (New York: Harcourt, 1982) 323.

Contents

Eleanor McNees and Sara Veglahn • *Introduction* vii
Acknowledgments xiii
List of Abbreviations xiv

Julia Briggs Memorial Lecture

Brenda Silver • *Editing Mrs. Ramsay: or, "8 Qualities of Mrs. Ramsay That Could be Annoying to Others"* 1

Editorial Revision and Censorship

Joyce Kelley • *"Corrected in Red Ink": Septimus Warren Smith, the First World War, and the Culture of Erasure* 11
Meghan Fox • *"The vision must be perpetually remade": An Examination of Ethical and Aesthetic Revisions in* To the Lighthouse 18
Susan Solomon • *Editorial Deletion: Presenting Absence in* To the Lighthouse 25
Courtney Carter • *The World with and Without a Self:* Between the Acts *as a Revision of* The Waves 29
Alice Lowe • *Editing* A Writer's Diary: *Leonard Woolf as Censor or "Keeper of the Flame"* 37
Nicole Coonradt • *Editing Memory: Virginia Woolf's Memoir Identity and her Re-Presentation of the Traumatized Self* 43

Woolf and the Presses

Diane Gillespie • *The Hogarth Press and "Religion": Logan Pearsall Smith's Stories from the Old Testament* 50
Brenda Helt • *Bright Young Editor: John Lehmann at the Hogarth Press* 57
Beth Rigel Daugherty • *Virginia Stephen, Book Reviewer: or, The Apprentice and her Editors* 63
Elisa Bolchi • *Virginia Woolf within Italian Literary Periodicals under Fascism* 70

Silent Editing: Woolf and Other Authors

Roberta Rubenstein • *Reading over her Shoulder: Virginia Woolf Reads* Anna Karenina 76
Joanne Campbell Tidwell • *Straightening the Scraps and Scratches: Editing the Diaries of Virginia Woolf, Vera Brittain, and Katherine Mansfield* 84
Erica L. Johnson • *Adjacencies: Virginia Woolf, Cora Sandel, and the Künstlerroman* 90
Cheryl Hindrichs • *Reading the Other, Editing the Self: Mentoring in Woolf and Welty* 96
Nephie Christodoulides • *On Not Being Able to Paint: Writing Inhibitions and Self-Editing in Virginia Woolf's and Sylvia Plath's Fiction* 104
Luke Ferretter • *"The Influence of Somebody Upon Something":* To the Lighthouse *in Sylvia Plath's Work* 111

Editions of Woolf in the Classroom

Beth Rigel Daugherty • *Editions in the Classroom: Does it Matter?* 117
Karen L. Levenback • *Wielding One's Own Pen: Virginia Woolf's Holographs in the Classroom* 123

Adaptations as Editing

Leslie Kathleen Hankins • *Complicating Adaptation: Virginia Woolf's 1925 novel,* Mrs. Dalloway, *and Abel Gance's 1918-1919 film,* J'accuse 129

Justyna Kostkowska • *Cinematic Editing of Virginia Woolf:* Mrs. Dalloway *and Stephen Daldry's* The Hours *as Reflective Ecosystems* 138

Carol Samson • *After Tea: Adapting Virginia Woolf's* A Writer's Diary *for Stage Performance* 144

Danaë Killian-O'Callaghan • *Wave to the Depths: A Performance of* The Waves' *Hidden Music* 151

Editing and Visual Arts

Maggie Humm • *Editing Virginia Woolf and the Arts: Woolf and the Royal Academy* 154

Elisa Kay Sparks • *Bloomsbury West: London Bohemians Find a New World in the American Southwest* 160

Pamela Hall Evans • *Biography, Portraits, and the Fine Spirit: Dorothy Brett, Artist* 166

Evelyn Haller • *The Botanical Works of Marianne North (Painter, Writer, Traveler) Edited by Absorption into Virginia Woolf's Writing* 174

Documentary and Scholarly Editing

Stuart N. Clarke • *"A Few Cigarettes in Lilian's Ash Tray": Woolf's Revisions to her Essays* 182

Jane Goldman • *Who is Mr. Ramsay? Where is the Lighthouse?: The Politics and Pragmatics of Scholarly Annotation* 189

Anne E. Fernald • *Semi-Colons and Major Changes: Editing* Mrs. Dalloway 196

Linden Peach • *Editing* Flush *and Woolf's Editing in* Flush 201

Woolf in the Public Sphere

Milena Radeva • *Re-visioning Philanthropy and Women's Roles: Virginia Woolf, Professionalization, and the Philanthropy Debates* 206

Virginia Brackett • *The Artist/ Intellectual as Politician* 215

Bonnie Kime Scott, Brenda Silver, Georgia Johnston, Vara Neverow • *Modernist Archives and Issues of Intellectual Property* 221

Robert Spoo • *"For God's sake, publish; only be sure of your rights": Virginia Woolf, Copyright, and Scholarship* 227

Plenary Lecture

James Haule • *Reading Dante, Misreading Woolf: New Evidence of Virginia Woolf's Revision of* The Years 232

Notes on Contributors 245

Introduction

by Eleanor McNees and Sara Veglahn

Editing played a crucial role in Virginia Woolf's career beginning with the inheritance of her father's editorial legacy. Leslie Stephen edited *Cornhill Magazine* from 1871 to 1882, publishing, besides his own series of literary and occasional sketches, such major Victorian authors as Matthew Arnold, Thomas Hardy and ex-patriot Henry James. In 1882, the year of Woolf's birth, Stephen commenced the largest editorship of his life—the *Dictionary of National Biography*—resigning that position in 1891 after compiling some 378 entries.[1] Woolf began publishing book reviews in British periodicals in 1904, the year following her father's death, and, as Beth Rigel Daugherty points out in an essay included in this volume, Woolf's apprentice years as a writer owe much to the editors of those various journals and newspapers. When she and Leonard Woolf established the Hogarth Press in 1917, her editing of others' works became a daily activity. Editing—from both sides—was Woolf's vocation.

The theme of the 18th Annual Conference on Virginia Woolf, *Woolf Editing / Editing Woolf*, held June 19-22, 2008 at the University of Denver, was timely for several reasons. New technologies, demonstrated most dramatically at the opening of the conference by Nicholas Hayward's lecture/demonstration "Digitizing Woolf: An Electronic Edition and Commentary on Virginia Woolf's 'Time Passes,'" on which the late Woolf scholar Julia Briggs was working, are shifting our traditional definitions of editing and rendering the old distinction between substance and accidents of the copy text almost obsolete. Woolf's manuscripts from the University of Sussex's Monks House collection and the New York Public Library's Berg collection are now available on microfilm enabling scholars to investigate and compare each deleted word, each mark of punctuation from holograph to typescript to published version. Many of Woolf's holograph manuscripts have been meticulously transcribed and published. Source materials including Brenda Silver's edition of *Virginia Woolf's Reading Notebooks* and Vara Neverow's and Merry Palowski's digital *Reading Notes for Three Guineas* have provided readers and researchers with a deeper understanding of the background materials for the novels. British editions of Woolf's works proliferated in the United Kingdom between 1991 when the copyright expired and 1997 when copyright was extended by 20 years. After a conference on editing Woolf in March 1991 at the University of Toronto, Blackwell's commenced the scholarly Shakespeare Head Press Edition of Woolf's novels. Currently Cambridge University Press, under the general editorship of Jane Goldman and Susan Sellers, is publishing new scholarly editions of the novels, three of whose editors are represented in this conference collection. In the United States, Harcourt launched its annotated editions of Woolf's works.

Consequently, many of the selected papers in this volume reflect a significant return to close textual analysis of Woolf's work coupled with a recovery of the lost voices of writers published by the Woolfs' Hogarth Press. The University of Denver, home to one of the oldest doctoral programs in Creative Writing and the *Denver Quarterly*, a preeminent literary journal now in its forty-first year of continuous publication, was hence an appropriate venue for a conference dedicated to editing in a broad sense of the word. Of the 106 papers delivered in 32 panels at the conference we are pleased to present a representative sampling of most of the panels. We are fortunate to publish in full both Brenda Silver's keynote address, "Editing Mrs. Ramsay: or, '8 Qualities of Mrs. Ramsay That Could Be Annoying to Others,'" in honor of the late Julia Briggs, who was to have been one of the plenary speakers, as well as veteran editor James Haule's plenary talk, "Reading Dante, Misreading Woolf: New Evidence of Virginia Woolf's Revision of *The Years*." Silver's lecture on readers' responses to Mrs. Ramsay over three decades pondered the reasons why generations of students alternately identify with and oppose themselves to Woolf's powerful mother figure. Silver suggests that a new focus on matraphobia (fear of being like one's mother) particularly affected the middle generation of students in the 1980s. In a previously published essay, Silver had redefined editing as "versioning," and in her conference talk, she extended that idea of versioning to examine students' and colleagues' versions of Mrs. Ramsay.[2] In his lecture, James Haule humorously sketched the history of editing to illustrate the old debate between textual scholars and literary theorists before introducing a new reading of *The Years* to illustrate how Woolf structurally and thematically incorporated Dante's *Purgatorio* into successive revisions of the novel. These two lectures serve as bookends to this collection. The two other plenary talks, Mark Hussey's "'W.H. Day Spender' had a sister: Joan Adeney Easdale," and Jane Lilienfeld's "'Truth in Circumference Lies': Editing the War in *Mrs. Dalloway*," while not included in the *Selected Papers*, extended discussion of the conference theme in different directions—Hussey's exploration of Hogarth Press's decision to publish the work of a young, relatively unknown poet, and Lilienfeld's examination of Woolf's self-editing of World War I in *Mrs. Dalloway*. Finally, Andrew McNeillie's interleaving of Julian Bell's poetry with some of his own poems at the Saturday banquet brought two distinct voices together from across a century.

We have collapsed some of the categories under which the conference papers were grouped and "elastically defined" editing (to borrow Haule's and Stapes's term) to allow for eight chapter headings: 1) Editorial Revision and Censorship, 2) Woolf and the Presses, 3) Silent Editing: Woolf and Other Authors, 4) Editions of Woolf in the Classroom, 5) Adaptations as Editing, 6) Editing and Visual Art, 7) Documentary and Scholarly Editing, 8) Woolf in the Public Sphere.[3] These chapters, we hope, indicate the ways Woolf scholars and artists continue to range over the entire corpus of Woolf's work from holograph to published texts to Woolf's texts in conversations with other authors and other media to the legal implications of copyright.

Editorial Revision and Censorship begins with Joyce Kelley's examination of Britain's postwar "Culture of Erasure" that forced the "editing out" of potentially subversive voices like that of Septimus Smith in *Mrs. Dalloway*. Meghan Fox explores how Woolf applies the technique of defamiliarization in revisions of *To the Lighthouse*, particularly in regard to the idea of death, while Susan Solomon redefines Woolf's use of brackets on both semantic and visual levels in capturing death and loss in the same novel. Borrowing psychologist Les Fehmi's distinction between narrow and open focus as applied to self-awareness, Courtney Carter discusses the move from characters' narrow focus in *The Waves* to a more open focus in *Between the Acts*. The last two papers in this chapter mine Woolf's autobiographical works to offer examples of editing as manipulation of other and self. Alice Lowe reads Leonard Woolf's edition of *A Writer's Diary* as "cautious but conscientious" in its view of the potential reading public, and Nicole Coonradt looks at how memory, particularly in regard to traumatic events, becomes self-editing in Woolf's late memoirs.

Chapter Two, **Woolf and the Presses**, moves outward to investigate the role of Hogarth Press and the periodical presses in the United States, United Kingdom and Italy in relation to editorial decisions and public reception. Diane Gillespie and Brenda Helt both deal with Hogarth's decision to publish works either topically or aesthetically outside of the Press's typical list. Gillespie queries both Logan Persall Smith's motives for writing *Stories from the Old Testament* and the Woolfs' subsequent decision to publish the work in 1920 before they initiated their "Religion" category. Helt acknowledges the significance of John Lehmann's partnership with the Woolfs in introducing the press to a new generation of poets—Spender, Isherwood and Auden—but focuses on the conflicts between Lehmann and Leonard Woolf as exemplifying the movement from "'Old Bloomsbury'" to these "'Bright Young Things.'" Beth Rigel Daugherty's paper examines Woolf's early relationships with a variety of editors from *The Guardian* to the *Times Literary Supplement* during Woolf's "apprentice years" (1904-1912) as a book reviewer. Elisa Bolchi sheds valuable new light on Woolf's reception in Italian periodicals as well as on the editorial relationship between Leonard Woolf and editor Arnoldo Mondadori, publisher of Woolf's works in Italian translation.

Chapter Three, **Silent Editing: Woolf and Other Authors,** collects six papers that view editing as authorial interpretation and absorption of others' works. We have termed this "Silent Editing" since in many cases neither Woolf herself nor other authors directly acknowledge allusions or influences. The exception to this silent editing is Roberta Rubenstein's paper which draws on Woolf's unpublished reading notes for *Anna Karenina* to discuss Tolstoy's profound and admitted influence on Woolf's philosophy of writing. Joanne Tidwell tackles the dilemma of how one might approach editing personal diaries for public consumption, comparing shorter versions to their un-silenced longer volumes. Her study includes Woolf, Brittain, Mansfield and Nin. Both Erica Johnson and Cheryl Hindrichs employ Woolf's works, especially those that deal with the creation of the self, as lenses through which to discuss Norwegian novelist Cora Sandel and American writer Eudora Welty respectively. Johnson's essay focuses on issues of autobiographical presentation while Hindrichs's paper looks at the significance of mentorship. The final two papers in this section, by Nephie Christodoulides and Luke Ferretter, interrogate the complicated influence of Woolf on Sylvia Plath. Christodoulides performs a Kristevan reading of the writing inhibitions of both authors while Ferretter considers Plath's experience of Woolf's work first through her Smith professor Elizabeth Drew and later through Plath's ambivalent markings of Woolf's novels. He asks why Plath never acknowledges "the feminist content of Woolf's fiction" pointing to a troubling silence, possibly a legacy of Drew's pre-feminist lectures.

The small but significant chapter on **Editions of Woolf in the Classroom** analyzes students' responses to specific editions of Woolf's works in both published and holograph form. Beth Rigel Daugherty's paper presents the results of a survey of students in a Woolf seminar to determine whether or not editions with specific editorial apparatuses such as annotations, scholarly introductions and footnotes guide or obstruct undergraduate reading of Woolf. Karen Levenback highlights new technologies that allow digital access to Woolf's holographs both to demonstrate aspects of Woolf's self-editing and to assess student responses to the writing process.

Three of the papers in Chapter Five, **Adaptations as Editing**, were based on performances at the conference and demonstrate how readily Woolf's work has lent itself to interpretation by other media. Leslie Hankins presented her comparison of Woolf's *Mrs. Dalloway* to Abel Gance's 1918-1919 anti-war film, *J'accuse*, at the opening-night reception at the Tattered Cover Bookstore in downtown Denver. Screening a section of the film, Hankins suggested an intriguing possible influence of the war-traumatized poet-soldier in the film on Woolf's depiction of Septimus Smith in *Mrs. Dalloway*. Justyna Kostkowska's paper offers an ecocritical comparison of Stephen Daldry's film adaptation of Michael Cunningham's novel *The Hours* to *Mrs. Dalloway*. Both works focus, she suggests, on "an ecosystem where nothing exists in isolation." Carol Samson and Danaë Killian-O'Callaghan provided conference attendees with two spectacular performances—*After Tea*, a dramatic rendition of *A Writer's Diary*, and a musical composition inspired by *The Waves*. Killian-O'Callaghan performed this piano piece at a tea just prior to Samson's play. Samson chaired a panel the following morning with the two actors—younger and older portrayals of Virginia Woolf—offering their interpretations of Woolf's character. The papers in this collection detail the conception and performance of both pieces. Samson recalls the rationale for cuts and repetitions she made in adapting the diary for the stage while Killian-O'Callaghan discusses her interpretation of the musical score, "Wave to the Depths," written by Eve Duncan in response to Woolf's novel.

Chapter Six, **Editing and Visual Art**, brings together Maggie Humm, chair of the panel "Virginia Woolf and the Arts," and all three members of another panel, "Artists and Artifacts." Humm, currently editing *The Edinburgh Companion to Virginia Woolf and the Arts*, explores Woolf's Bloomsbury-informed antipathy for such established institutions as the Royal Academy and asks why in her 1919 review of the Annual Summer Exhibition Woolf appeared to ignore both the larger issues of trauma and post war restoration as well as works by women artists in the exhibit. Elisa Sparks and Pamela Evans investigate parallels between Woolf and transplanted Bloomsbury associates, specifically Dorothy Brett and D.H. and Frieda Lawrence. Sparks's work (lavishly illustrated in her conference talk) is based on an extensive analysis of the holdings in the O'Keeffe library in Santa Fe, New Mexico and the trans-Atlantic aesthetic influences these holdings suggest. Evans's paper charts her progress in writing a biography of Brett and, not unlike Woolf, attempting to "rediscover...the all but lost voice and work of a woman...who was determined to do her work in a world that alternately prevented and encouraged her." Evelyn Haller introduces us to the possible influence of botanical painter Marianne North "edited by absorption" into Woolf's essay on Walter Sickert. Woolf would, Haller argues, have seen the 832 botanical paintings in the gallery at Kew Gardens as well as her great aunt Julia Margaret Cameron's photograph of North in Ceylon, and she may also have read Mrs. John Addington Symonds's edition of North's autobiography.

Documentary and Scholarly Editing perhaps most closely aligns itself with the original definition of the conference theme in the grouping of the new editor of Woolf's *Essays*, Stuart Clarke, with three of the editors of the new Cambridge University Press's edition of Woolf's works. In all four papers, close textual editing again achieves prominence, especially now with the accessibility of a number of "versions" of Woolf's writings from holograph transcriptions through various published editions. The Hogarth University Press *Essays* and the Cambridge editions of Woolf promise to offer the paratextual materials essential to scholarly study of Woolf's work. Taking over the two final volumes in the Hogarth series from Andrew McNeillie who had meticulously edited the first four volumes, Stuart Clarke considers in his conference paper three of Woolf's essays published in his new Hogarth volume and interrogates Woolf's "imaginative handling of facts" in her revision of the essays for *The Common Reader: Second Series*. Jane Goldman, general editor (with Susan Sellers) of the Cambridge University Press edition of Woolf's novels and editor of *To the Lighthouse*, enunciates the dilemma of the editor caught between "objective" and "interpretive" scholarly annotation. She and the other editors of the individual works tread a fine line between "politics and pragmatics" in their preparation of the texts for 21st century scholars for whom many of Woolf's allusions to British history and culture have become increasingly recondite. Goldman's paper presents as a test case of this editorial practice the multivalent surnames and place names in *To the Lighthouse*, the only one of Woolf's novels to be set in Scotland. She demonstrates how Woolf's own reading at the time may have influenced the particular choices of these names, and she further reveals how tracing the complex origin of names like "the Pope's nose" belies the old criticism of Woolf as a visionary aesthetic. Anne Fernald's account of the textual emendations to the page proofs of *Mrs. Dalloway* juxtaposes the major revision of Septimus's contemplation of suicide to the many minor but, when taken-together, significant shifts in punctuation at this final stage of revision. Linden Peach's discussion of the intertextual challenges of editing *Flush* addresses both the textual variants in punctuation that Fernald examines as well as the larger historical and cultural context that Goldman addresses. And, like Stuart Clarke, Peach probes Woolf's creative use of biographical materials.

The final chapter, **Woolf in the Public Sphere**, moves outward from textual editing to consider Woolf's ambivalent engagement in philanthropic and political issues. The final two papers draw Woolf into the 21st century by considering problems of archival access and copyright. Milena Radeva examines Woolf's rhetorical responses to the "old" versus "new" philanthropy debates in the British press as Britain moves toward a welfare state. Radeva argues that both in her fiction and nonfiction Woolf evinces an understanding of this transition from private self-interest to public duty. A similar debate as to the role of the artist-intellectual in the public arena informs Virginia Brackett's reading of Woolf's biography of Roger Fry especially in light of Woolf's argument with Benjamin Nicolson who believed the Bloomsbury artists too elitist to make a lasting impression on the British public. The final two papers by Woolf scholars who have had considerable experience with accessing, editing and publishing archival materials seek to inform readers and researchers about the practical steps and potential pitfalls of such work especially in regard to issues of intellectual property. These issues, burgeoning since Woolf's archives have become available on-line, are now, as the co-authored paper by Bonnie Kime Scott, Brenda Silver, Georgia Johnson and Vara Neverow asserts, a central part of the editor's work. Negotiating with curators to access delicate manuscripts and subsequently with the Society of Authors for permission to publish archival materials are just two of the time-consuming tasks invisible to readers / viewers who encounter the edited text in published form. In Neverow's and Pawlowski's digital project, *Reading Notes for Three Guineas: An Edition and Archive*, negotiations with librarians and the representative of the Woolf Estate proved fruitful and led to only modest copyright permission costs though tracing permissions for visual images was more difficult and problematic. As a crucial coda to the panel on Modernist

Archives and Issues of Intellectual Property from which the first paper is drawn, Robert Spoo offers an indispensable legal perspective on the concerns attending copyright of Woolf's works. As a copyright lawyer and modernist scholar Spoo ranges the difficulty of securing permissions on a scale from friendly to hostile—from Pound (friendly) to Joyce (hostile)—and places Woolf's estate "somewhere between these extremes." Though he applauds the Society of Authors as a valuable "clearing house" for securing permissions, he urges scholars to familiarize themselves with fair use laws that allow more leeway in quoting from copyrighted works. Spoo's paper sheds authoritative light on the discrepancy in copyright laws among different English-speaking countries. In Woolf's case, Canada is the only country to hold her unpublished work as of 1997 in the public domain.

The 18th Annual Virginia Woolf Conference ended with a plenary panel chaired by Bin Ramke, University of Denver professor, poet, and editor of the *Denver Quarterly*, and composed of three of the plenary speakers, Mark Hussey, James Haule and Jane Lilienfeld. In addition, we were pleased to have a fourth panel participant, distinguished Woolf editor and current literary editor for Oxford University Press, Andrew McNeillie. The panelists responded informally to questions on all aspects of editing--from preparing new editions of works from the 17th to the 21st centuries to the future of digital editing of Woolf's work. Judging by the animated questions from a sizeable audience (it was by then Sunday afternoon) the topic, Woolf Editing / Editing Woolf is as relevant today as it was when Hogarth and Harcourt Presses first published Woolf's writings or when over a century ago Woolf ventured into print at the behest of editors of literary periodicals.

Notes

1. See John W. Bicknell, ed. *Selected Letters of Leslie Stephen. Vol. 1*. (Columbus, OH: Ohio State UP, 1996) 378.
2. See Brenda Silver, "Textual Criticism as Feminist Practice: Or, Who's Afraid of Virginia Woolf Part II," in *Representing Modernist Texts: Editing as Interpretation*, ed. George Bornstein (Ann Arbor: U of Michigan P, 1991): 193-222.
3. See J.H. Stape and James M. Haule's introductory chapter, "Introduction: Editing and Interpreting the Texts of Virginia Woolf," in *Editing Virginia Woolf: Interpreting the Modernist Text* (New York: Palgrave, 2002): 1-10.

Acknowledgments

In addition to the individuals and sponsors acknowledged in the Conference Program, we would like to thank the following people for their generous assistance in making this volume of the *Selected Papers from the 18th Annual Conference on Virginia Woolf* aesthetically, editorially and financially possible: Helene Orr, designer of both the conference brochure cover and the cover of this volume; Christina Cain and Nicole Coonradt, doctoral candidates in English at the University of Denver, for their careful and insightful editing of a number of the papers in this collection; University of Denver Arts, Humanities and Social Sciences Dean Anne McCall for permission to use some of the Woolf Conference funds for publication costs; Wayne Chapman and his assistants at Clemson University Digital Press for their attention to all editorial and copyright questions; and Elisa Kay Sparks for her generous contribution. Finally, we offer our thanks to our contributors for their prompt responses to our editorial suggestions and for making this volume possible.

Virginia Woolf
Standard Abbreviations
(as established by *The Woolf Studies Annual*)

AHH	*A Haunted House*
AROO	*A Room of One's Own*
BP	*Books and Portraits*
BTA	*Between the Acts*
CDB	*The Captain's Death Bed and Other Essays*
CE	*Collected Essays* (ed. Leonard Woolf, 4 vols.: *CE1, CE2, CE3, CE4*)
CR1	*The Common Reader*
CR2	*The Common Reader, Second Series*
CSF	*The Complete Shorter Fiction* (ed. Susan Dick)
D	*The Diary of Virginia Woolf* (5 vols.: *D1, D2, D3, D4, D5*)
DM	*The Death of the Moth and Other Essays*
E	*The Essays of Virginia Woolf* (ed. Andrew McNeillie, 6 vols.: *E1, E2, E3, E4, E5, E6*)
F	*Flush*
FR	*Freshwater*
GR	*Granite and Rainbow: Essays*
HPGN	*Hyde Park Gate News* (ed. Gill Lowe)
JR	*Jacob's Room*
JRHD	*Jacob's Room: The Holograph Draft* (ed. Edward L. Bishop)
L	*The Letters of Virginia Woolf* (ed. Nigel Nicolson and Joanne Trautmann, 6 vols.: *L1, L2, L3, L4, L5, L6*)
M	*The Moment and Other Essays*
MEL	*Melymbrosia*
MOB	*Moments of Being*
MT	*Monday or Tuesday*
MD	*Mrs. Dalloway*
ND	*Night and Day*
O	*Orlando*
PA	*A Passionate Apprentice*
RF	*Roger Fry*
TG	*Three Guineas*
TTL	*To the Lighthouse*
TW	*The Waves*
TY	*The Years*
VO	*The Voyage Out*
WF	*Women and Fiction: The Manuscript Versions of* A Room of One's Own (ed. S. P. Rosenbaum)

Editing Mrs. Ramsay: or, "8 Qualities of Mrs. Ramsay That Could Be Annoying to Others"

by Brenda Silver

In her 1923 essay "Jane Austen at Sixty," Virginia Woolf described one group of Austen's admirers as the "twenty-five elderly gentlemen living in the neighborhood of London who resent any slight upon her genius as if it were an insult offered to the chastity of their aunts." If we substitute "mother" for "aunt," and imagine how devoted readers might respond to any critique of that figure, we begin to get a sense of the aura surrounding Mrs. Ramsay when I started teaching *To the Lighthouse*. The year was 1973; I was a newly hired assistant professor, and I was team teaching the course on Twentieth-Century British Fiction with a senior male colleague. He was a mild man, a tolerant man, who had studied with Lionel Trilling and saw his role as encouraging his junior partner rather than competing with her; but when, in my lecture on *To the Lighthouse*, I implied that perhaps Mrs. Ramsay was not the idealized vision of womanhood, motherhood, unity, continuity, fertility that critics at that time painted her to be, and that in fact she dies, he became apoplectic. "How dare you question Mrs. Ramsay's sanctity" is a fair translation of his response. I was floored—and scared; it was clear I had just committed an act of matricide. Summoning my wits, I also summoned Geoffrey Hartmann, whose essay "Virginia's Web" had influenced my thought. Look, I said, here's an eminent critic, and a man, an older man, who makes just this point; if my hands aren't clean, the guilt at least is shared. The moment passed, though I don't think he ever quite forgave me for upending his Mrs. Ramsay.

I begin with this anecdote because it introduces my topic: the shifting attitudes towards Mrs. Ramsay over the thirty-five years that I've been teaching the novel and what it tells us about shifting attitudes towards the figure of the mother, particularly among women. This is in many ways a generational story, one that those of you who have been around as long as I have will be familiar with; those who came to Woolf more recently might be surprised at the passions swirling around the topic, especially at the time I gave my initial talk. My impetus was an article that appeared in the *New York Times* in June 2007 under the headline "Mommy is Truly Dearest"; in it the writer argued that for many women in their 20s and 30s their mothers are their closest confidants, and they talk to them at least once a day (Rosenbloom). Shortly after, while teaching *To the Lighthouse*, I mentioned that someone should study whether changes in the mother-daughter relationship translate into changes in the reading of the novel, so when Eleanor McNees invited me to speak at the Virginia Woolf conference in Denver, I thought, why not me?

Originally, I planned to use the introductions to successive editions of the novel as my primary source, but I soon realized that the project far exceeded what I could present. Instead, I have concentrated on the period around my original lecture in 1973 when feminism and other critical trends were radically reframing—or editing—not only Mrs. Ramsay but the mother-daughter relationship itself. In addition, I'll be interspersing my comments with those by a number of other readers and teachers of Woolf. From the start

I realized that my own experience would not be enough, so I sent emails to Woolf scholars from different generations asking if they remembered their initial responses to Mrs. Ramsay; whether their readings had changed over the years; what their students' responses had been and were; whether these had changed. When the replies began arriving, I knew they had to be included: in part because they were so fascinating, but for the most part because this talk, oh so sadly, is in memory of Julia Briggs. I began to feel that the best way to honor Julia was to incorporate as many voices as I could: to make this tribute a conversation among individuals and generations. This is exactly the kind of conversation Julia was so brilliant at starting, whether in the talks she gave or the conferences she helped organize or her extensive writings, and exactly the kind of conversation she would have relished.

Back, then, to winter 1973. Oddly, I don't remember what my reactions to Mrs. Ramsay were when I read the novel in 1965 at age 22; nor do I remember re-reading it until I began to teach it. At this point my memories become very clear, for my encounter with my colleague paled before my next experience of the outrage directed toward my so-called feminist distortion of the text by two far younger men at Middlebury College when I served as an outside reader for a senior thesis on the novel. I, of course, was not alone. As Carolyn Heilbrun wrote that same year, "One criticizes Mrs. Ramsay at one's peril. One of the first critics to suggest in print that Mrs. Ramsay was less than wholly admirable was Mitchell Leaska, whose study of the voices in *To the Lighthouse* was greeted with howls of protest" (155). This was also the experience of at least one of the leading women scholars at the time who, she wrote me, faced opposition to her questioning of Mrs. Ramsay both from the male readers of her dissertation and when she tried to get her first articles published.

In order to understand this rage, one needs to look at the critical discourse about Mrs. Ramsay that framed that moment. As Annis Pratt described it in 1972, "A survey of critical assessments of the relationship between Mr. and Mrs. Ramsay reveals a range of opinion from one extreme of sexual politics to the other. . . . At one extreme we have those who see Mrs. Ramsay as Prototypal Mother and Mr. Ramsay as Tyrannical Male; at the other extreme those who see her as Devouring Female and him as her Victim. We have those who see the marriage as an anatomy of complementary male and female attributes" and "those who take it as an anatomy of sexual warfare" (417).

Joseph Blotner's 1956 essay "Mythic Patterns in *To the Lighthouse*," reprinted in Murray Beja's 1970 collection of essays on the novel, lays out the argument for Mrs. Ramsay, a "symbol of the female principle in life," as ideal and idealized woman/goddess, a figure who is not only perfection in herself but Woolf's and his model of what a woman should be. "In this novel Virginia Woolf's concept of woman's role in life is crystallized in the character of Mrs Ramsay, whose attributes are those of major female figures in pagan myth. The most useful myth for interpreting the novel 'is that of the Primordial Goddess, . . . threefold in relation to Zeus: mother (Rhea), wife (Demeter), and daughter (Persephone).'" In her guise as Rhea, Mrs. Ramsay is "the completely good and loving mother"; as Demeter, "symbols of fruitfulness cluster around" her, and she becomes an embodiment of "complete femininity," a femininity that stands in contrast to male sterility, just as she is more perceptive if less analytic than men. "There is little doubt," he writes, "that these sentiments are inherent in Virginia Woolf's feminism." "As Mrs Ramsay gives love, stability, and fruitfulness to her family and those in her orbit, so the female force should always function. It serves to ameliorate or mitigate the effects of male violence, hate, and destructiveness" (172, 169, 173, 176, 177, 186-187). Mr. Ramsay, it should be noted, is absent from this reading; Prue and Lily appear as doubled embodiments of Persephone, and Lily's role as artist enacts her fertility.

For the archetypally antithetical view of Mrs. Ramsay, we can turn to Glenn Pedersen's 1958 essay "Vision in *To the Lighthouse*":

> "Someone had blundered." The vision of Lily Briscoe reveals that it was Mrs. Ramsay.
>
> Superficially Mrs. Ramsay is a beautiful, positive creature, but gradually . . . she is revealed as the negative force which usurps the lighthouse and thus prevents the integration of the family while she lives. Only after her death can James and Cam go to the lighthouse, and thus symbolically to their father. . . . [I]n the beginning the reader is influenced to believe that Mr. Ramsay is a villainous character, a father who prevents his son from fulfilling his desire. Essentially Mrs. Ramsay is the negating influence. . .
>
> "Yes, of course, if it's fine tomorrow," she says, but the Ramsay weather is never fine as long as she lives, fundamentally because Mrs. Ramsay refuses to subordinate her individuality to community, to become one with Mr. Ramsay, to share with him the forming of the family into a unity, with the father as head and the mother as heart. . . .She demands dominion and exacts it. (585)

Pedersen's examples of Mrs. Ramsay's destructiveness extend to almost every detail in the novel, though much of it is focused on the mothering that sacrifices Cam to James and hurts them both. In this reading Lily's role is not to reaffirm the mother's fertility but to recognize and restore what has been missing before, Mr. Ramsay's intelligence, and ensure the integration of the family.

As Murray Beja noted in his email to me, "the assumption . . . that Mrs. Ramsay was, well, ideal: the wife and the mother anyone would want," was "very common" when he edited his volume in 1970. "I can remember graduate professors invariably comparing her to Mrs. Moore in *Passage to India*. My own view was . . . more complex . . . , so it was a relief to see exceptions to that idealization appear, some of them quite balanced and sensible. An earlier attempt, by Glenn Pedersen . . . , had gone much too far and ended up making Mrs. Ramsay villainous, even monstrous."[1] In the introduction to his volume Beja recommends instead Josephine Schaefer, who in her 1965 study makes two significant moves: first, her claim that neither Mr. nor Mrs. Ramsay are the one-sided stereotypes critics made them out to be; and next, her insistence that we understand Mrs. Ramsay as trapped within the narrow confines of the "strict codes of rules" and "demarcations between the sexes" that she passes on to her children, making her daughters "in particular feel dissatisfaction with the simple scheme of things." Mrs. Ramsay, she continues, "cut off from the wider world of action available to men, . . . finds no range for the exertion of her powers and inevitably employs them in personal domination. . . . Lily Briscoe recognizes how Mrs. Ramsay's pity for men is related to her desire for a suitable arena for her own activities" (117, 123). Reading Schaefer one wonders whether Stuart Clarke's teacher, Mrs. Judith Kirman, had read her as well when in 1965 she evoked the "8 qualities of

Mrs. Ramsay that could be annoying to others," including "She was too sure, too drastic"; "perhaps her masterfulness"; "She upset the proportions of one's world." Nevertheless Schaefer's reading leaves Mrs. Ramsay as the light that "illuminates a space of life even after her death." In this reading Lily has yet to come into her own: "Since the reader cannot take [her 'artistic'] activities seriously, Lily Briscoe on the shore is the one real weak spot in the novel" (124, 133-134).

The other dominant reading of Mrs. Ramsay in 1970 presented her as the feminine complement to the masculine Mr. Ramsay. More than just husband and wife, Thomas Vogler argues that year, they are "supplementary components of the life force and the human imagination. Alone, neither is representative of life or capable of grasping it completely" (18). Woolf's vision, he notes, is essentially androgynous.

Women critics, or some of them, begged to differ, not only with the androgynous union of the married couple but with each other. Annis Pratt's 1972 "Sexual Imagery in *To the Lighthouse*: A New Feminist Approach" locates the androgyny not in the married relationship but in Mrs. Ramsay herself. Using two scenes characterized by their strong and highly unconventional use of sexual imagery—the one where Mr. Ramsay comes to Mrs. Ramsay for comfort, and the one where Mrs. Ramsay has an orgasmic union with the long beam of the lighthouse—Pratt reads the first as illustrating Mrs. Ramsay's "taking on both male and female sexual characteristics in response to Mr. Ramsay's infantile sexuality. We might consider Mrs. Ramsay's erection, then,—the "column of spray"–"as an act of androgynous creativity in which the hero calls upon the fullest reach of her internal nature—including motions and forces usually allocated to males alone—to respond to her marital situation." Her subsequent union with the lighthouse becomes a symbol of her androgyneity and a mark of her "preferring tranquility or solitude (and, implicitly, death) to a world which impinges excessively upon her autonomy" (425, 429).

In contrast, Carolyn Heilbrun, in her classic 1973 *Toward a Recognition of Androgyny*, follows her statement that "*To the Lighthouse* is Mrs. Woolf's best novel of androgyny" with the surprising statement that the novel "enables us to see that, just as Flaubert said: 'I am Emma Bovary,' so Virginia Woolf has, in a fashion, said, 'I am Mr. Ramsay.'" What follows is one of the sharpest critiques of Mrs. Ramsay's roles as perfect wife, beautiful woman, and earth mother you're likely to read, including their destructive impact on herself and others. To give just one example: after acknowledging that "as the mother of young children, at certain moments"—and her example is the nursery scene—"Mrs. Ramsay is perfection," Heilbrun comments drily, "This is not the sort of act of which it is possible to make a lifetime's occupation" (156, 160).

I want to pause here to note one of things that emerged from the responses I received: the role of teachers or mentors or friends in one's reading of Mrs. Ramsay, and Heilbrun played that role for many women over the years. Both Mary Ann Caws and Lyndall Gordon evoked Heilbrun's attitude toward Mrs. Ramsay during the memorial panel for her four years ago and again in their notes to me. "I did talk about Mrs. Ramsay frequently with Carolyn," Caws wrote, "and very much disagree with her point of view, but then Carolyn didn't like making Thanksgiving dinner, didn't like making dinner, period, and to me the around the tableness of Mrs. Ramsay . . . was a big part of the point." Gordon's story is, I think, more typical of women of our generation—hers and mine: her recollection of "not responding to the novel when I first read it as a set text . . . in 1962; then the terrific impact it made on me rereading it at the age of 28 when I was a graduate at Columbia," where she worked with Heilbrun. "I was reacting against domesticity and saw/taught Mrs. Ramsay as blinkered to be saying to others 'Marry . . . marry.'" Twenty-some years later, in 1992, Heilbrun's teaching gave Victoria Rosner a Mrs. Ramsay who "represented the dead past, an old way of life that young women were casting off as fast as they could. . . . For Carolyn, the great hope of the novel was Cam, whose fierce energy would propel her into the future, away from the limiting traditions that Mrs. Ramsay represented and that ultimately killed Prue."

Returning to 1973, I want to say a word about the article that influenced me most in my original lecture: Geoffrey Hartmann's "Virginia's Web." Usually evoked as one of the first deconstructive readings of the novel, what moved me was his statement, "Resistance is the major theme of this novel. . . . Mr. Ramsay, an enemy of the sea that becalms his boat, is a stronger resister than Mrs. Ramsay who lives towards the sea"; "Mrs. Ramsay thinking to affirm life really affirms death" (72, 79). Strongly attracted to the existential reading, I found Hartmann's emphasis on the necessity to fill the spaces, resist the flow, irresistible—and a way to focus my nagging discomfort with Mrs. Ramsay. See, I could say, as I did to my senior colleague, she doesn't survive; she dies. Moreover, what she so carefully knits in the first section is, ultimately, her own shroud.

In my original copy of Hartmann's essay I put a big star next to the phrase "her identification with death" (80). What I wanted was a woman who was a survivor; what I wanted was Lily, who tended to be absent from the critical discourse or portrayed as a means to the restoration of Mrs. and/or Mr. Ramsay's powers in the third section of the novel. I didn't have to wait long; in the next few years Lily more than came into her own, and she did so as part of an emerging discourse about mothers and daughters that spanned disciplines and was one of the most significant interventions of the feminist movement in both the academic and non-academic realms.

In reconstructing the history of this phenomenon, I turned first to Nancy Chodorow's 1974 essay on "Family Structure and Feminine Personality," the basis for her 1978 book *The Reproduction of Mothering* that in turn generated innumerable studies of the mother-daughter relationship in both literature and life. Chodorow set out to rewrite the psychoanalytic theories used to explain the "differences that characterize masculine and feminine personality and roles" ("Family Structure" 43). Her starting point was succinct and to the point: "Women mother" (*Reproduction* 3), and the fact that women are responsible not only for early child care but the later socialization of their daughters "points to the central importance of the mother-daughter relationship for women." The results are "feminine personalities founded on relation and connection, with flexible rather than rigid ego boundaries," as well as a "lack of self-differentiation," "boundary confusion or equation of self and other," and a "sense of inescapable embeddedness in relationships to others" that lead women to experience a "loss of self in overwhelming responsibility for and connection to others." This experience, she adds, "is described particularly acutely by women writers," including Virginia Woolf ("Family Structure" 43-44, 58, 59).

The second crucial text appeared two years later, in 1976: Adrienne Rich's *Of Woman Born: Motherhood as Experience and Institution*. "The cathexis between mother and daughter," Rich writes in one of the most widely cited statements to come out of the women's movement, "—essential, distorted, misused—is the great unwritten story" (225). Appearing in the chapter called "Motherhood and Daughterhood," it prefigures her reading of *To the Lighthouse*, in which, Rich asserts, "Virginia Woolf created what is still the most complex and passionate vision of mother-daughter schism in modern literature." In Rich's reading Mrs. Ramsay emerges as "a kaleidoscopic character, [who] in successive readings of the novel . . . changes, almost as our own mothers alter in perspective as we ourselves are changing"; "she is no simple idealization." Lily becomes the daughter who wants what she cannot have because Mrs. Ramsay "doesn't like women very much" and spends her life "in attunement to male needs," making her unavailable to Lily, perceptions she attributes to Jane Lilienfeld. "The scene," Rich writes of Lily with her head in Mrs. Ramsay's lap, "has a double charge: the daughter seeking intimacy with her own mother, the woman seeking intimacy with another woman, not her mother but toward whom she turns those passionate longings. Much later she understands that it is only in her work that she can 'stand up to Mrs. Ramsay.'" Ultimately, Rich concludes, the novel stands as "testimony not merely to the power of [Woolf's] art but to the passion of the daughter for the mother, her need . . . to understand, in all complexity, the differences that separated her mother from herself" (227-228). Recalling in her note to me the impact of reading Rich in 1978, Sybil Oldfield put it this way: "She alerted me not only to Lily Briscoe as the daughter, Virginia Stephen, yearning for more mothering than could be granted to her, but also to Lily Briscoe as Virginia Woolf (and me), as a woman loving another woman—as well as to Lily Briscoe/Virginia Woolf, the grownup, independent woman artist."

But like many other women struggling to create new roles of ourselves in the mid-1970s, what spoke to me most in Rich's book was her evocation of the concept of matrophobia, defined by Lynn Sukenick, Rich tells us, as "the fear not of one's mother or of motherhood but of *becoming one's mother*. Thousands of daughters," Rich notes, "see their mothers as having taught a compromise and self-hatred they are struggling to win free of, the one through whom the restrictions and degradations of a female existence were perforce transmitted." "Matrophobia can be seen as a womanly splitting of the self, in the desire to become purged once and for all of our mothers' bondage, to become individuated and free." "Many daughters live in rage at their mothers for having accepted, too readily and passively, 'whatever comes.' A mother's victimization does not merely humiliate her, it mutilates the daughter who watches her for clues as to what it means to be a woman" (235, 236, 243).

I cannot overemphasize how powerfully Rich's emphasis on the mother-daughter relationship and the concept of matrophobia resonated at the time, manifesting itself in all aspects of women's lives. To take just one example: my women students in the late-1970s who, having watched their divorced mothers struggle to support themselves and their children with no training to call on, said, "not me; never; I'm going to have a career." This spilled over into their readings of Mrs. Ramsay, who embodied everything they felt they had to reject. During this period I found myself not so much questioning Mrs. Ramsay in the classroom as defending her, pointing out her positive attributes, insisting she is not one thing only. As Gillian Beer recalls this moment:

> I well remember the shock I felt when one of my students—a thoughtful, intelligent young woman—wrote an essay denouncing Mrs. Ramsay as an oppressive and life-leeching figure. This would have been in the late 1970s. Perhaps be-

cause I had always been very close to my own mother who brought me up alone I had tended to see Mrs. Ramsay as benign if sometimes wrong headed. So this heartfelt diatribe pulled me up short and made me think hard about the traps that custom laid for women who wanted to do well by their families.

I also want to emphasize that the denunciation of mothers at the time was not necessarily shared by women of color, a point that Christine Stansell made in a talk she gave this past winter called "The Revolt of the Daughters: Matrophobia and 1960s Feminism." As a poster on Slate.com's Fray forum put it, "Stansell convincingly argued that mommy-bashing was a key feature of second-wave feminism, not incidental to it (and, by the way, severely impeded coalition-building between feminists/womanists of color). It took 'In Search of Our Mothers' Gardens' by Alice Walker to inspire a reappreciation of motherhood for many' (lola_44). Walker, of course, rewrites *A Room of One's Own* in her 1974 essay "In Search of our Mother's Gardens"; more to my point, she calls her essay on her ambivalence about mothering and writing, where she disagrees with her own mother, "*One* Child of One's Own."

Looking back now, it seems to me that Rich's book, with its desire to give voice to both the mother and the daughter, anticipated, ironically, a split within the women's movement between those who focused more on mothers and mothering and those who focused more on the daughters' need to break free. This statement, I am well aware, is not without controversy. Two articles on *To the Lighthouse*, both published in 1977, chart the fissures, part of which were generational, in the emerging discursive terrain: Sara Ruddick's "Learning to Live with the Angel in the House" and Jane Lilienfeld's "Love and Hate in *To the Lighthouse*." Both essays make use of Woolf's memories of her own mother in her then recently recovered memoirs; both strongly influenced future criticism of the novel, in part by making it impossible to read Lily simply as a pale imitation of or understudy for Mrs. Ramsay or as a link to Mr. Ramsay. From this point on, Lily's central place, the importance of her perspective in even the first section of the novel, not to mention her role as artist, became a given, at least for those not rigidly resistant to any feminist reading of the text. Where the two essays differ, and where they indicate divergent trends in feminist scholarship, is in their representation of Lily's, the daughter's, attitude toward the mother.

For Ruddick, who provides a nuanced reading of Mrs. Ramsay's mothering that ranges from her "maternal perfection" to the problems it creates for her daughters, Lily's relationship to the mother, the central one in the novel, is characterized most of all by longing, a longing for an emotionally or physically absent mother that is mitigated by her turning to her art, a turn that allows her to "paint her way to peace with Mrs. Ramsay." Woolf, she writes, "claims to have killed" the Angel in the House, "but if we think back through our mothers . . . we must also learn to live with them" (185, 194, 190). For Lilienfeld, the daughter's attitude toward the mother is one of "anger and hurt." Lily is a portrait of a "daughter, angry at her mother's commitment to others, a daughter who sustains her mother's death, and who lives beyond it to grow into her own personhood. . . . More than a celebration of the wonderfulness of Mrs. Ramsay, *To the Lighthouse* is plotted to take the reader and characters through a successful reconsideration and rejection of Mrs. Ramsay's mode of life" (346). At the risk of oversimplifying, Ruddick's perspective, with its focus on mothering, anticipates her 1989 book on *Maternal Thinking: Towards a Politics of Peace* and can be read in conjunction with that strand of scholarship that emphasized women's differences from men. Lilienfeld's perspective, one might say, is more that of the daughter who envisioned difference as difference from the mother and the traditional roles, with an emphasis on how women themselves construct and can therefore demystify the feminine archetypes, including that of wife and mother, that have limited them in the past.

Over the next decade, the mother-daughter relationship ceased to be an unwritten story, and *To the Lighthouse* often served as the exemplary text. But judging from the responses I got to my query, the story continues to resonate powerfully for women, coloring their reading of Mrs. Ramsay and Lily. These readings varied widely, and I wish I could include them all; instead, I want to start some conversational threads, beginning with the observation that one's reading of a novel, to paraphrase Woolf, is very much attached to material things like age; family circumstances, past and present; the context in which the novel is read—on one's own, for example, or in a class; and, when it comes to our students' reactions, where we teach.

For one thing, a woman's initial response to Mrs. Ramsay is often compared or contrasted to her feelings about her own mother, and this crosses generations. Maria DiBattista, for example, writes that "My initial identification with Mrs. Ramsay was in itself odd, since my mother was more talkative than Mrs. Ramsay, more open, less guarded . . . But my mother inspired the same kind of overwhelming love and trust." Andrea Adolph, whose mother died when she was 14, found herself empathizing with Lily, whose "longing" for Mrs. Ramsay, "the ur-mother," was also the longing of someone who "has no map, no understanding of how to be a woman in her culture." For AnneMarie Bantzinger, "Mrs. Ramsay . . . was the 'universal' mother, an institution I was not particularly happy about. The reason being—to stay close at home—because of my difficult relation with my own mother." Jane Goldman, who identified with Lily and saw Mrs. Ramsay through Lily's eyes, notes that "my own mother was an artist . . . and I grew up with her ambivalence re maternal/artist roles." For Natania Rosenfeld, "My mother *was* my best friend, so to me, Mrs. Ramsay has always seemed a rather old-fashioned model of mother—cut off from her children's psyches despite acute curiosity about them." Rebecca Walkowitz thinks "my first response to Mrs Ramsay was warmth . . . but also distance. She didn't resemble my mother in any way, I thought, and I wouldn't have wanted my mother to be like her—someone who put up with Mr Ramsay." And, although Mrs. Ramsay wasn't anything like her own mother, a senior professor who works on Bloomsbury tells me, "we all disliked her; she was the bossy Mom." Finally, Douglas Mao, who has always felt "intense admiration" for Mrs. Ramsay, "a feeling of powerful affection and of wishing I knew her in real life," has also always imagined her as looking not like his mother, "admirable in a different way," but "a little like . . . Katherine Hepburn."

Equally notable, Rich got it just right when she argued that Mrs. Ramsay changes in successive readings "almost as our own mothers alter in perspective as we ourselves are changing." Here, generational divides do come into play. Although Maren Linett reported the shift from a "quite positive and idealized" response to Mrs. Ramsay to a more wary one that was common to my generation, most women who came to novel after the 1970s described initial feelings of annoyance or rejection, followed by a shift in attitude toward empathy and respect, particularly when they became mothers themselves. For Erica

Johnson, Mrs. Ramsay changed "between my first readings (as a 20-something graduate student in the mid-90's) and my more recent readings as a mother. . . . I am somewhat appalled when I think about how unsympathetic I was to Mrs. Ramsay when I read as a daughter but I suspect that it had to do with my own relationship with my mother, which followed what I think was a pretty typical pattern of breaking away and then seeking out a friendship with her once I had asserted my independence. . . . But now, reading as a mother . . . I am much more attuned to Mrs. Ramsay . . . . I wouldn't say that I identify with her—the mere fact that she had eight children keeps one at arm's length—but I am pulled into the complexity of her failings and the quiet magnificence of her skills." Rishona Zimring simultaneously acknowledges this shift and questions it. Now forty-five and the mother of two, she writes, "Surely I identify with Mrs. Ramsay? Or do I identify with Mr. Ramsay because I am a professor? Or with Carmichael, because I published some new things recently? . . . Now the identifications seem all too easy . . . the before and after motherhood, that are mixed together in this self, the 'I' who is both Lily and Mrs. Ramsay. The artist and the mother . . ."

Johnson's reservation about identifying with Mrs. Ramsay introduces a third thread that is very clearly generational: younger women, who have grown up with more options and with mothers who had already taken advantage of them, tend to find Mrs. Ramsay not so much a threat to their independence as out-of-date, even as they grow to understand her more. Several people noted a similar response in their students. Andrea Adolph attributes her students' indifference to Mrs. Ramsay to "what they collectively seemed to find . . . an antiquated version of maternal femininity. . . . [S]he represented to them something that seems long gone already, and not something that can be missed." Leslie Hankins' students "now seem much more impatient with the Mrs. Ramsay angel role—they find it, I think, incomprehensible." Although Hankins finds herself thinking "how some aggressively professional women students . . . have missed out on something in their self-absorbed me-first barracuda-like training," she quickly adds, "Not that I would want the angel to reassert her control!" Instead, teachers and students alike tend to respond more to Lily than to Mrs. Ramsay. Urmilla Seshagiri, who herself initially read the novel "principally as a story about Lily," notes "that almost all of my students identify with Lily, even though she is so much older than they are. . . . I find that my undergraduate students don't understand Mrs. Ramsay as well as they understand Lily, and they often react negatively to her investment in marriage." Jessica Berman has "students who respond well to the book, but . . . fewer of them fall in love with Mrs. Ramsay than I would expect"; they are "much more interested in Lily." Madelyn Detloff compares her students' reactions to her own early readings of the novel: "They don't get the novel's emotional resonance, but they are gung-ho to read the novel as a critique of patriarchal marriage." And in Anna Snaith's experience "students gravitate to the marriage question;" "I'm not sure I've noticed a real change in [their] reactions."

Anne Fernald provides a somewhat different view. Because her students are young, female, straight, and expect to have children, she writes, "they have trouble thinking of a mother, any mother, as difficult or pernicious—especially when she's not actively unkind or abusive." But only two responses evoked students whose identification and sympathies resided unequivocally in Mrs. Ramsay. Mary Childers encountered this when teaching at a Catholic university, where the students "were not at all bothered by [Mrs. Ramsay's] sacrifices for her tetchy husband and her compulsion to impose the fate of marriage even on a woman as self contained as Lily. They were enraptured by the evocation of Mrs. Ramsay and the references to her beauty and saw Lily as pinched and sad." And Jane Garrity found that "several . . . young women really rallied around Mrs. Ramsay [feeling] she was 'devalued' (their word) by the men in the novel; . . .I have long felt that one cannot really appreciate the representation of Mrs. Ramsay until you are around 40, but my students did surprise me in their passionate defense of her tyrannical views. I'm not sure if this is a sign of 'enlightenment' or post-feminist entrenchment. Perhaps you know the answer?"

I don't; if anything, my research and the responses I received have increased my questions, questions that are shared by other scholars as well. Christine Stansell's talk, for example, was described as exploring "the implications" of the matrophobia that characterized the 1960s, defined more broadly than just fear of becoming one's mother, "for today's third-wave granddaughters and the future of gender politics" (Mast), a timely concern indeed: the post about Stansell's talk on Slate.com was part of a heated online forum about Hillary Clinton and mothers. And Alice Walker's daughter Rebecca Walker's recent attack on her mother and the whole of second-wave feminism for devaluing traditional motherhood set off a furor of debate. While studies support the *New York Times'* article about the current closeness of mothers and daughters, who, researchers say, no longer fear growing up to be like their mothers (Carpenter, Shaw), most of the women surveyed were older, suggesting perhaps, that no matter how often they may talk to their mothers our students' responses to Mrs. Ramsay are still framed by their need to define a space of their own. As my research assistant, a junior, told me, it's fashionable to say your mother is your best friend, and performative.

Julia Briggs wrote of *To the Lighthouse* that it "sets up a dialectic between the ideal and the real, reiterated in the final lines of Shakespeare's sonnet ('As with your shadow I with these did play') and embodied in the figure of Mrs. Ramsay" (viii). All I can say with certainty is that Mrs. Ramsay's shadow continues to color both our reading of the novel and our lives.

Note

1. This and all subsequent emails are cited with the permission of their authors; I wish to thank them for participating in this project.

"Corrected in Red Ink": Septimus Warren Smith, the First World War, and the Culture of Erasure

by Joyce Kelley

England's involvement in the First World War began in early August 1914 when Germany, promising aid to Austria-Hungary, invaded neutral Belgium to reach France. Thousands of British troops were prepared for deployment when Germany thus violated the Treaty of London, a pact between Belgium and Britain which Germany famously dismissed as just "a scrap of paper."[1] The treaty became one of the many "scraps of paper" which would prove so instrumental in understanding and characterizing the war as those at home and those on the Western Front fought over the control of written language.

The First World War was primarily a war of distance; not only was there great separation between the English soldiers in the trenches and those they fought, but there was also a notable gap in communication between these soldiers and the civilians at home. This made written communication crucial and powerful in negotiating these gaps. Newspapers reporting the war relied heavily on positive framings, romantic language, and euphemism. As Paul Fussell puts it, events had to be "tidied up for presentation" (178). Soldiers' letters were often censored and pre-printed postcards sent home from the Front allowed for only cryptic expression. Nonetheless, many "soldier-poets" fought back against the censoring of language, producing works showing the true horrors of war, knowing too well that their culture of repression only bred greater trauma. It is in an historical moment still reeling from battle and still repressing war's ills that Virginia Woolf creates the shell-shocked veteran Septimus Warren Smith, *Mrs. Dalloway*'s own "soldier-poet." Significantly, the language of Septimus's war-inspired illness becomes a threat to the ordered world around him, until Septimus himself must be edited out.

Paul Fussell and other war scholars have asserted that modernist authors such as Woolf knew and wrote little of the Great War simply because they were not directly involved in it; they argue that one must look to those who actually experienced the fighting first-hand to recover the veracity of war experience (Fussell 314). Woolf critics such as Mark Hussey, Helen Wussow, and Karen Levenback respond that, though Woolf perhaps did not know the fighting from the Front intimately, she was personally affected by the war and wrote often about what Hussey terms its "private and public violence" (3). Levenback has shown in *Virginia Woolf and the Great War* that Woolf was made aware of the mental ravages of war through the misfortune of her brother-in-law, Philip Woolf, who returned from the war injured by the same shell that killed his brother, Cecil.[2] Woolf also was keenly cognizant of the distance between her own world at home and the action taking place abroad, a space bridged only by war journalism. At the war's outset, on August 3, 1914, Woolf remarks in a letter to her sister on the difficulty of obtaining a newspaper:

> We are just (4. P.M.) off to Lewes to get a paper. There were none at breakfast this morning, but the postman brought rumours that 2 of our warships were sunk—however, when we did get papers we found that peace still exists—save

for a stop press message that England had joined in. It is rather like Napoleonic times I daresay, and being Bank holiday of course makes us more remote from life than ever. (*L2* 50)

Woolf's frustration reveals the powerlessness that comes from being so "remote" that printed news is slower and less trustworthy than gossip. The stop-press news revision particularly demonstrates how quickly printed matter becomes irrelevant or erroneous.

More menacing than the necessary revision of news due to continually changing events is the intentional manipulation of public consciousness through filtered language. Like Woolf, the majority of the British public relied on newspapers for their information and, naturally, those reporting on the war could spin the information they received in whichever way they pleased. War reporting was a tool of political power and as propagandistic as the pro-war posters produced by the Parliamentary Recruiting Committee at this time. As Modris Ecksteins writes in *Rites of Spring: The Great War and the Birth of the Modern Age*, "Defeats were presented as victories, stalemate as tactical maneuvering. Truth became falsehood, falsehood truth. As euphemism became the official order of the day, language was turned upside down and inside out" (233). The British government even asked well-known writers to help fight this war on words; David Roberts has explored how "The Secret War Propaganda Bureau" recruited civilian writers such as Thomas Hardy, H. G. Wells, Arnold Bennett, John Galsworthy, Robert Bridges, J. M. Barrie, and Arthur Conan Doyle to produce poetry and journalism that would help maintain morale and validate the government's military decisions.[3]

Only those at the Front could report with accuracy the actual daily events of the war, yet letters home would often be censored. Many soldiers relied on the postcard as a means of communication, a public form which allowed for brief messages and abridged emotion; some such postcards were pre-printed, imposing further restrictions, like the example made well-known by Fussell's *The Great War and Modern Memory* (see below).[4] The directions at the top of the "Field Service Post Card" state: "Nothing is to be written on this side except the date and signature of the sender. Sentences not required may be erased. <u>If anything else is added the postcard may be destroyed</u>." The sentences to choose from included:

I am quite well.

I have been admitted into hospital
{sick / wounded}   and am going on well
                     and hope to be discharged soon.

A quick look at the postcard's message reveals that it allows for only the most general and optimistic communication; a soldier cannot write, for example, "I have been admitted into hospital, feel terrible, and may die." The only hope for communication on the card exists in its permission to erase unnecessary lines. Anything *added* to the card will lead to the card's destruction, so to communicate, a soldier has to *subtract*. For instance, one can only say "not well" by censoring the line "going on well." As a result, language becomes rationed, just as sugar, meat, and butter were rationed at home by the war's end. While this censorship was also a safety measure, it implies that there was only so much that was "proper" to say of the war experience, and what was said would ideally be declared, as in the example of this postcard, through another's language.

Other significant "scraps of paper" from the Front were the poems produced by the soldiers fighting there. In earlier years, war poetry was largely produced by civilians. The First World War became one of the first moments in British history when those witnessing the battle described it in their own poetry, causing the term "soldier-poets" to become popular (Lyon 30). Despite the unifying label, a rift developed between the glorified Georgian poetry of the early war, poems such as Rupert's Brooke's "The Soldier" which re-encodes death in a foreign field as something heroic, everlasting, and "forever England" (line 3), and the more modern poems of Siegfried Sassoon and Wilfred Owen who write in unapologetic terms of war's physical and psychological ravages. In 1918 Woolf noted such a schism in her essay for the *Times Literary Supplement* "Two Soldier-Poets"; while Geoffrey Dearmer layers the war scenes with poetic language and metaphor, Sassoon "effectually" reveals, in Woolf's words, "the terrible pictures which lie behind the colourless phrases of the newspapers" (*E2* 269-270). Woolf thus champions Sassoon as a breaker of euphemism and an awakener of anesthetized language.

Sassoon's poem "They," for example, challenges head-on the inadequacy of current war rhetoric. In the poem's first stanza the Bishop tells a group of boys that the soldiers returning from battle "will not be the same; for they'll have fought / In a just cause: they lead the last attack / On Anti-Christ; their comrades' blood has bought / New right to breed an honorable race, / They have challenged Death and dared him face to face" (2-6). Here Sassoon satirizes the traditional heraldic language and chivalric imagery of war reflected in propaganda posters of the era. Two popular posters particularly illustrate this; one bearing the cry-to-arms "Britain Needs You at Once" depicts St. George on a white steed slaying a dragon. Another shows a toga-clad Lady Justice, in a pose reminiscent of the Lady of the Lake, rising out of the Atlantic with the "Sword of Justice" held above the reaching hands of the dying passengers from *The Lusitania* (see Figure 1).[5] In Sassoon's poem, the pen becomes mightier than the sword: in the poem's second stanza the boys agree that "We're none of us the same" (7), but reinterpret the Bishop's assertion by pointing out how "George lost both his legs; and Bill's stone blind; / Poor Jim's shot through the lungs and like to die" (8-9).[6] The poem "They" and the "Sword of Justice" propaganda poster thus function as opposites: while old-fashioned

Figure 1: Poster of the Parliamentary Recruiting Committee, June 1915.

Lady Justice replaces and obscures the fragmented bodies from the wreckage, Sassoon's poem fights euphemism by replacing traditional chivalric ideas of war with images of death and dismemberment.

In her 1925 novel *Mrs. Dalloway*, Woolf is intent on revealing the tension between the artist and the post-war culture of erasure by placing shell-shocked war veteran and soldier-poet Septimus Warren Smith into a society which has no room for him. As Elaine Showalter has suggested, Septimus Smith may be inspired by Siegfried Sassoon, whom Woolf refers to as "S.S." in her diary (Showalter 192); both share "fantastic" first names, a characteristic which Showalter notes was thought to be a sign of "family degeneracy" that could lead to shell-shock (Showalter 179). When Sassoon wrote an anti-war letter to his commanding officer, he was diagnosed with "shell-shock" and rushed off to a military hospital; in this example, institutionalization becomes literally a kind of censorship. But Septimus is not quite so outspoken; he is a character who scribbles in margins instead of writing letters and who mutters rather than yells. Septimus's name is also curiously akin to that of Septimus Scott, a popular British illustrator who drew illustrations for book covers, advertisements, and even propaganda posters.[7] Thus in him we find layered both the artist caught up in a movement to restrict language and the modern poet intent on releasing it, a duality that reveals Septimus's own struggles with self-expression in a society relying on repression for stability.

Woolf is quick to note the lingering effects of war in her novel, even as English society struggles to restore normalcy by moving on. In the opening pages of *Mrs. Dalloway*, Clarissa Dalloway asserts that:

> The War was over, except for some one like Mrs. Foxcroft at the Embassy last night eating her heart out because that nice boy was killed and now the old Manor House must go to a cousin; or Lady Bexborough who opened a bazaar, they said, with the telegram in her hand, John, her favourite, killed; but it was over; thank heaven—over. (5)

This is 1923: the very fact that Clarissa must remind herself that the war is "over" five years after its conclusion suggests how much it persists. Just as Woolf's characters contain layers of memory, strata of their past for Woolf to "tunnel" into,[8] the war remains an ever-present memory, a wound lingering beneath the scar tissue of society and ready to resurface even in the most celebratory moment, as we see in Clarissa's climactic line, "in the middle of my party, here's death" (183). As Clarissa's early comment about Mrs. Foxcroft and Lady Bexborough makes clear, the war may be "over," but its influences remain in the everyday lives of its citizens. As the novel states, the era "bred in them all. . . a well of tears" (9). In this "well," this place of storage and repression, society keeps its fears and emotions hidden; through this repository of hidden suffering it can keep itself "well" on the surface. Nonetheless, the emotions do not always stay in their assigned place; though Lady Bexborough retains what Clarissa calls "a perfectly upright and stoical bearing" (9-10), Mr. Bowley, like an unread letter, is "sealed with wax over the deeper sources of life but could be unsealed suddenly, inappropriately, sentimentally" (20).

Septimus Warren Smith's name implies the extent to which he has kept the "war in" him. Yet, as a character who articulates his unconventional ideas in both written and verbal language, Septimus becomes the most "unsealed" of them all; he is a reminder, a visual symbol that life cannot just go on in a stoical manner after the war, and as such he is an embarrassment both to his wife Lucrezia and to the society around him. His legibility exists in contrast to other soldiers we see in the novel, "Boys in uniform, carrying guns," who march by like a propaganda poster, bearing a shared legible expression "like the letters of a legend written around the base of a statue praising duty, gratitude, fidelity, love of England" (51). For Woolf, Septimus represented freedom of language: writing in her diary of the "mad scene in Regents park," she confided, "I feel I can use up everything I've ever thought" (*D2* 272). For the other characters, however, Septimus is too free with his speech. Lucrezia is understandably distressed by Septimus's remark that he will kill himself, but she is alarmed moreover by the fact that someone else might hear him ("Suppose they had heard him?" [16]). She feels adamant that "he must not talk aloud to himself out of doors" (26). To put something into language makes it real; the signifier of Septimus's madness must be hidden: "failure one conceals. She must take him away into some park" (16). For Rezia, the true Septimus is the soldier who "was brave" and thus did not articulate his distress (23). When Septimus and Rezia first met, Septimus remained successful in repressing war's trauma; she recalls with admiration how he was "suffering sometimes through this terrible war, but even so, when she came in, he would put it all away" (146). Memory and suffering are conceptualized as tangible objects that should be hidden from society's eyes. Now that Septimus has begun to articulate his distress, Septimus's writings must, in turn, be tied up and "put. . . away" by Rezia (148).

Septimus, like so many, has been changed by the war. Similar to Rupert Brooke, or at least the Brooke the public came to celebrate, he went off to war to defend a conception of England that was both literary and romantic: "He went to France to save an England which consisted almost entirely of Shakespeare's plays and Miss Isabel Pole in a green dress walking in a square" (86). A passionate young man in love with a scholar, he "wrote poems to her, which, ignoring the subject, she corrected in red ink" (85). Editing a love poem seems a bit cruel, an act stripping emotion and context from expressive language. By the time Septimus leaves the war, he, too, has been "corrected in red ink," changed, stripped of emotion until he cannot feel even the death of his closest war companion, Evans: "The War had taught him" (86), with the word "taught" underscoring that pedagogical correction.

In Woolf's novel, Septimus's writing is the only way for him to express himself. But Septimus does not write an organized autobiography. He notes his revelations "on the backs of envelopes" (24). To "make it known," he "wrote it down" (24); through inscription, his inner thoughts on life, love, human nature, and death become real. Crucially, though, he never seems to use a whole sheet of paper for his ideas. As he "muttered, gasping, trembling, painfully drawing out these profound truths which needed, so deep were they, so difficult, an immense effort to speak out," we see him "fumbling for his card and pencil" (67). Later in the novel, we find Septimus noting his thoughts "on the back of a postcard" (92), a means of communication which strikingly evokes the postcards sent from the Front. This time, however, there is something subversive about this soldier's words as he writes in the margins of the paper provided him by his society.

The other collector of scraps of paper in the novel is the doctor Sir William Bradshaw, who can be glimpsed at several moments writing notes about Septimus "with his pencil on a pink card" (98, also 95, 96), presumably notecards which he keeps with his patient files. Both Septimus and Bradshaw have their "card and pencil." For Bradshaw, when something is "serious" or significant about Septimus's condition, it is "to be noted on the card" (96); Septimus's notes are equally important to him, and record what he senses to be the "truths" and ailments of modern society. Yet there is a tension in the text between Septimus's cards and Bradshaw's own: Septimus's represent his private thoughts; Bradshaw's turn these private thoughts into something needing correction. Septimus seems more like the writer of the text, the misunderstood visionary, with Bradshaw representing the practical but unimaginative editor. Aligned with the regulators of society, Bradshaw removes out-of-place individuals to rest homes and champions euphemism: "he never spoke of 'madness'; he called it not having a sense of proportion" (96). He is even there to fix the mistakes caused by lesser doctors such as Holmes: "It took half his time to undo their blunders. Some were irreparable" (95).

Bradshaw, who "never had time for reading" and who holds "a grudge" against educated men (97), functions as the poet's antithesis. Clarissa, imagining Septimus with the "passion" of the "poets and thinkers" (184), cringes to think of Holmes's effect upon him. Bradshaw works by "worshipping" Proportion and Conversion, close cousins of Censorship, and through his techniques he "not only prospered himself but made England prosper" (99): like a government regulator or a member of the Propaganda Bureau, he "made it impossible for the unfit to propagate their views" until they share his own (99). Most tellingly, Bradshaw's methods consist of linguistic revision: when men come in with "a message, as they mostly have, . . . you invoke proportion; . . . silence and rest" (99). Indeed, after merely standing in the presence of Bradshaw, Septimus cannot remember "his message" (98).

Septimus believes that if he can "confess" or "communicate" he might be released from his punishment, but Sir William has no real desire to hear his stammered declaration (98). On learning that he is going to be taken away to one of "Holmes' homes" (a phrase which, in itself, the doctor sees as an inappropriate play on written language) Septimus tries in desperation to censor himself by burning the writings which Rezia keeps in the table drawer. Minutes earlier, Septimus and Rezia share a beautiful moment in which Rezia takes the scraps, ribbons, and beads from her workbasket which she "tumbled. . . out on the table" (143) and Septimus creates a hat from these fragments. The same thing cannot be done, however, with the scraps of writing and illustrations which Rezia "tumbled. . . out on to the sofa" (147) in a strikingly similar manner. They cannot make an acceptable art object, and instead must be destroyed.

Septimus's suicide is one of simultaneous communication and erasure. Yelling "'I'll give it you'" (149), he jumps from the window "on to Mrs. Filmer's area railings" (149). As Clarissa later imagines the fall or experiences it vicariously, the rusty spikes go "though him" as Septimus is literally crossed out (184). But, as Clarissa later understands, this is his last "attempt to communicate" (184). Septimus discovers that, as with the war postcards, sometimes one can only find expression through erasure.

Notes

1. For instance, a recruitment poster of the time published by the Parliamentary Recruiting Committee proudly depicts the signed and sealed treaty under the ironic heading "The 'Scrap of Paper.'"
2. See Levenback, 32-35. Leonard Woolf also discusses the tragedy of Cecil's death and Philip's difficult recovery on pages 179-183 of *Beginning Again: An Autobiography of the Years 1911-1918*. London: The Hogarth P, 1964.

3. David Roberts, *Minds at War: The Poetry and Experience of the First World War*. Quoted in Philippa Lyon, Ed. *Twentieth-Century War Poetry*. New York: Palgrave Macmillan, 2005: 41.
4. The "Field Service Post Card" appears on p. 184 of Fussell's landmark study. Roger Poole also makes use of this postcard in "We All Put Up with You Virginia: Irrecievable Wisdom about War" in discussing the parenthetical narrative remarks of *To the Lighthouse*. His essay appears in Mark Hussey's *Virginia Woolf and War: Fiction, Reality, and Myth*. Syracuse: Syracuse University Press, 1991.
5. *The Lusitania* was a British luxury ocean liner torpedoed by the Germans in May 1915. This Parliamentary Recruiting Committee poster appeared in June 1915.
6. Note the disjuncture between the poster's St. George and Sassoon's George; while one is England's conquering hero, the other has been defeated and disabled in battle.
7. For instance, Septimus E. Scott drew the 1917 National Service Poster depicting one man punching another and bearing the lines, "Germany means to starve us out / There is only one answer / A blow straight between the eyes."
8. I refer here to Woolf's famous diary entries about the "tunnelling process" she discovered when writing *Mrs. Dalloway* (*D2* 272) and the "caves" she can "dig out" behind her characters (*D2*: 263).

Works Cited

Brooke, Rupert. "The Soldier." *The Norton Anthology of English Literature*. Vol. F. 8th ed. Ed. Stephen Greenblatt and M. H. Abrams. New York and London: W. W. Norton & Company, 2006. 1955.

Ecksteins, Modris. *Rites of Spring: The Great War and the Birth of the Modern Age*. New York: Doubleday, 1989.

Hussey, Mark. "Living in a War Zone: An Introduction to Virginia Woolf as a War Novelist." *Virginia Woolf and War: Fiction, Reality, and Myth*. Syracuse, NY: Syracuse UP, 1991. 1-13.

Fussell, Paul. *The Great War and Modern Memory*. Oxford, OH: Oxford UP, 2000.

Levenback, Karen L. *Virginia Woolf and the Great War*. Syracuse, NY: Syracuse UP, 1999.

Lyon, Philippa, Ed. *Twentieth Century War Poetry*. New York: Palgrave Macmillan, 2005.

Sassoon, Siegfried. "They." *The Norton Anthology of English Literature*. Vol. F. 8th ed. Ed. Stephen Greenblatt and M. H. Abrams. New York and London: W. W. Norton & Company, 2006. 1960.

Showalter, Elaine. *The Female Malady: Women, Madness, and English Culture, 1830-1980*. New York: Penguin, 1987.

Woolf, Virginia. *The Diary of Virginia Woolf*. Vol. 2. Ed. Anne Oliver Bell. New York and London: Harcourt Brace Jovanovich, 1978.

—. *The Letters of Virginia Woolf*. Vol. 2. Ed. Nigel Nicolson. New York and London: Harcourt Brace Jovanovich, 1976.

—. *Mrs. Dalloway*. 1925. New York and London: Harcourt Brace & Company, 1990.

—. "Two Soldier-Poets." *The Essays of Virginia Woolf*, Vol. 2. Ed. Andrew McNeillie. London: The Hogarth P. 269-272.

"The Vision must be perpetually remade": An Examination of Ethical and Aesthetic Revisions in *To the Lighthouse*

by Meghan Fox

On June 18, 1925, Virginia Woolf wrote that Lytton Strachey, a fellow Bloomsbury member, disliked her latest novel, *Mrs. Dalloway*, and suggested that she write something "wilder and more fantastic, a framework that admits of anything, like *Tristram Shandy*" (*AWD* 77). Interestingly, the Russian Formalist Victor Shklovsky utilized this particular work to demonstrate his concept of defamiliarization. Although Woolf would not have known Shklovsky or his Formalist terminology, she, like many other modernists, nevertheless intuits the value of this literary technique, using it often within her own work and indirectly defending its necessity in a post-war era of stagnation and barbarity.

In this paper, I examine the formal revisions that Woolf made to her subsequent novel *To the Lighthouse*, focusing upon the middle section of her book entitled "Time Passes." In my study of the original holograph draft edited by Susan Dick in tandem with the 1927 Hogarth Press Edition, I argue that Woolf's use of brackets in the published form dramatically alters one's reading of the novel by demanding a reconsideration of death as it is re-contextualized by typography. By definition, brackets enclose a portion of text for the purpose of supplying some type of clarification or explanation (*OED*); however, their insertion in *To the Lighthouse* disrupts a fluid reading of the novel by eliciting careful consideration of the isolated text. The omission of many war references in the published form likewise transforms the role of death in the novel by diminishing much of the original emphasis placed upon destruction. Paradoxically, by limiting and re-contextualizing images of war and death, their appearance in the novel is all the more startling. Although the Russian Formalists defined defamiliarization as a strictly aesthetic technique for prolonging a reader's perception, I argue that Woolf deploys this literary technique to expose substantial ethical implications left unexamined by the formalists. Her defamiliarized representations of fatality begin to dismantle the implicit disparity between life and death.

In Woolf's 1927 published edition, death is nearly elided, as it has been relegated to bracketed text. Woolf writes, "[Mr. Ramsay stumbling along a passage stretched his arms out one dark morning, but Mrs. Ramsay having died rather suddenly the night before he stretched his arms out. (sic) They remained empty]" (*TTL* 199-200). Within a few succeeding pages, the deaths of Prue and Andrew also appear within brackets as if they were insipid details, deserving no more than minimal attention. Uncerimoniously we learn, "[Prue Ramsay died that summer in some illness connected with childbirth, which was indeed a tragedy, people said. They said nobody deserved happiness more]" (*TTL* 205). Moments later, we brusquely discover: "[A shell exploded. Twenty or thirty young men were blown up in France, among them Andrew Ramsay, whose death, mercifully, was instantaneous]" (*TTL* 207).

In earlier passages of this published text, parenthetical notes consistently intimate extraneous or superfluous details, such as a reference to James's sleeping habits or Mrs. Ramsay's musings throughout the dinner party. Woolf's use of the brackets as a similar typographical device would thereby seem to consign these deaths to the realm of the commonplace. Unfortunately, during the war and thereafter, death and news of death were common occurrences. Therefore, a straightforward depiction of these fatalities, such as the one present in the holograph draft, presumably would have elicited minimal attention from the reader. Observing a considerable shift from the Victorian to the Modernist treatment of death, Alan Warren Friedman speaks to this point: "Modern novels are replete with characters of uncertain mortal (and moral) status, 'grave' voices, revenants. No longer natural and culturally acceptable, fictional death became attenuated, denied, or horrific: initiatory or evaded rather than climactic" (18). Hence, in place of detailed descriptions of Victorian mourning rituals, modern readers encounter one of two extremes—a nearly elided death, as is the case with Woolf's Mrs. Ramsay, or a grotesque depiction of rotting flesh, as is present in Faulkner's *As I Lay Dying*. Therefore, despite the presence of widespread casualties in Europe, a fictional death may still shock its readers.

This is precisely the desired effect of defamiliarization. As Victor Shklovsky asserts, "The technique of art is to make objects 'unfamiliar,' to make forms difficult, to increase the difficulty and length of perception because the process of perception is an aesthetic end in itself and must be prolonged" (12). Modifying the form and positioning of the familiar enables a previously unremarkable entity or concept to be perceived in a new way.

In her posthumously published memoir, "A Sketch of the Past," Woolf notes her propensity for receiving "sudden shocks" during exceptional moments of her life that likewise increase her perception of the moment. Although a "peculiar horror and a physical collapse" accompany these instances, Woolf deems them "particularly valuable" and declares, "the shock-receiving capacity is what makes me a writer" (*MOB* 72). Through her writing, Woolf transforms such moments so that her readers, too, may experience a portion of the impact. By taking a regrettably familiar event and altering its presentation and its context via typography and juxtaposition, Woolf skillfully captures and maintains her audience's attention.

In "Time Passes," physical darkness and images of nature's destruction of the Ramsay's home pervade the narrative, but the deaths of Mrs. Ramsay, Prue, and Andrew are nevertheless unexpected. These events do not gesture toward a narrative crescendo, and the preceding sections of the text offer no real anticipatory indications to warn the reader of their imminence.

These characters' tragic ends are no more foreseeable in the holograph form than the published text. In the manuscript, however, Woolf does not use the bracketed form to address death; she simply writes their fatalities into the body of the text without substantial attention. Rather than devoting individual moments to each of the deceased, Woolf conveys the news in rapid succession, separating their names and deaths only by a semicolon and a conjunction. Their individual lives are further diminished by the reported widespread losses occurring as a result of the war. In the holograph text, Woolf writes, "many families lost their dearest. So Mrs. Ramsay was dead; & youn Mr. Andrew killed they said & Miss Prudence, who had married, she had died too, with her first bady baby they said, but Everyone w had lost someone, in these years" (*TTLhd* 225). A very similar collection of sentences appears in the published work. In the 1927 edition, however, this disclosure occurs after the initial shock of the terse and bracketed accounts of these deaths, discussed earlier in this paper. In both versions of the text, when the deaths appear consecutively in the plain typography above, they are followed by an aloof comment regarding the recent rise in commodity prices. Here, death and inflation become equated as mere matters of fact.

These death notices are admittedly unsettling on account of their brevity and disconcertingly nonchalant delivery, but they are banal in contrast to the grotesque images of dead or dying fish offered in a later section of the novel. The published 1927 edition reads: "[Macalister's boy took one of the fish and cut a square out of its side to bait his hook with. The mutilated body (it was alive still) was thrown back into the sea]" (*TTL* 277-278). Here, the death of a fish has taken the same bracketed form as the text's first intimations of human death. Grammatically, brackets are "used for enclosing a word or number of words [...] so as to separate it from the context" (*OED*). Hence, use of this typographical device disrupts a fluid reading of the passage. The bracketed sentences become distinct from the surrounding text thereby eliciting additional attention and consideration.

Immediately preceding and following this zoological abuse, we find Lily's desperate cries for Mrs. Ramsay's return. The juxtaposition of Lily's grief and this violent depiction connects the dying fish to the loss of Mrs. Ramsay in the published version. Although the holograph draft evades any direct linkage between the two, Woolf's diary entries suggest that she had been attempting to work through a similar metaphor. In holograph form, Cam empathizes with these tortured creatures: "She had imagined them dying, like these fish, beating their tails up & down in a pool of water on the bottom of the boat; She had imagined the drowning men swirling round & round" (*TTLhd* 354-355). Despite the looser connection of this strange representation of death with the loss of loved ones, the image of dying fish had always been connected in Woolf's mind to certain individuals. In a diary entry on May 14, 1925, Woolf writes of *To the Lighthouse*: "This is going to be fairly short; to have father's character done complete in it; and mother's; and St. Ives; and childhood; [...] But the centre is father's character, sitting in a boat, reciting We perished, each alone, while he crushes a dying mackerel" (*AWD* 75). Indeed, Woolf's initial vision was most theatrical; her textual revision, however, is more aesthetically refined, and perhaps delivers a more prudent account of her father.

Like Cam and James, Woolf ultimately softened her antagonistic feelings toward her parents by the conclusion of the novel. A year after the publication of *To the Lighthouse*, Woolf writes:

> Father's birthday. He would have been 96, 96, yes, today; and could have been 96, like other people one has known: but mercifully was not. His life would have entirely ended mine. What would have happened? No writing, no books;—inconceivable.
>
> I used to think of him and mother daily; but writing the *Lighthouse* laid them in my mind. And now he comes back sometimes, but differently. (I believe this to be true—that I was obsessed by them both, unhealthily; and writing of them was a necessary act.) (*AWD* 135)

From her personal writings, it becomes evident that the significance of revision for Woolf cannot be reduced simply to a part of the writing process. Clearly, the act of re-envisioning plays a large role in her aesthetic practices, but it also figures into the way that she lives her life. Defamiliarization may thereby offer more than mere aesthetic ends achieved by making objects "unfamiliar"; it may, in fact, offer a modern philosophical and ethical imperative for leading an ethically conscious life. Shklovsky explains, "[...] as perception becomes habitual, it becomes automatic [...] Habitualization devours words, clothes, furniture, one's wife, and the fear of war [...] And art exists that one may recover the sensation of life" (11-12). When art, literature, and life become routine and mechanical, they must be re-contextualized and re-imagined; otherwise, they will no longer hold one's attention, which is both aesthetically and ethically dangerous.

This concept finds its parallel in Woolf's memoirs. In "A Sketch of the Past," she defines those moments of habitual perception as the "cotton wool" of life, or the "non-being" (*MOB* 70). Although Woolf laments that much of our lives are spent in "non-being" without conscious attention to what we are doing, she asserts that these non-exceptional moments are still significant: "behind the cotton wool is hidden a pattern" (*MOB* 72). The aesthetic moment thereby provides an opportunity for prolonged perception, for one's consciousness to be awakened, and for one's place in the world to be considered.

Fixating upon the overriding presence of war within her novel likely would have elicited a perfunctory perception, for much of the world still felt the devastation of the Great War that had ended less than a decade before. Although the novel still maintains traces of war, many references in the holograph draft have been omitted in published form. For example, Woolf's marginal note, "the mindless warfare, the soulless bludgeoning" (*TTLhd* 202), does not appear in the final edition, nor does the violent grass cutting metaphor embodied in the inarticulate, yet aggressive man in the yard (*TTLhd* 232). Woolf writes, "He [...] resumed again that rhythmic singsong stroke, which was advanced like the sweep of an invincible army over the insugr insurgents rioting" (*TTLhd* 232). James M. Haule—who has analyzed the holograph draft, the published edition, and an intermediary version of "Time Passes" published as a French translation by Charles Mauron—focuses primarily upon the omission of war references. He argues that the holograph draft conveys Woolf's "feminist convictions" (Haule 178) as well as her contention that the history of war is always written from a man's perspective (a stance expressed by Woolf in 1919 in a *Times Literary Supplement* review of D. Bridgman Metchim's *From a South London View*). However, the brash critique of war and male aggression that appears in Woolf's holograph draft did not align itself with her aesthetic agenda. Haule considers the holograph draft to be a more personal statement, one that was "clearly too intense" (177). Yet in an act of refinement, Woolf's forthright portrayal of war transforms into one of subtlety, one that conveys the more ordinary lived experience that she believed was lacking from historians' recorded accounts (Haule 165). The novel thus focuses primarily upon the domestic motions and concerns generated indirectly by the war rather than the motions of the war itself.

While the presence of war has been greatly reduced in the published edition, so has the power of human agency to combat the devastation wrought upon the Ramsays' home. Within the holograph draft, Mrs. McNab exhibits more restorative power over the havoc caused by war and nature. While criticized for her witlessness in both versions, she does receive validation within the holograph draft, as her revelation is termed "more profound, but confused, but more profound" (*TTLhd* 216) than any of the other visionaries mentioned in this portion of the text. But despite her revelation and her restorative presence, certain things appear to be beyond repair. Woolf writes, "Let the ch broken china be & all beaut civilisation lie like broken china to be tangled over with the blackberries & grass" (*TTLhd* 228). Although the Ramsays' home may be slowly mended, hope for the nation and the world is much dimmer. The devastation of war has resulted in more than broken china and an infestation of rodents. Civility and progress have been mocked by violence and bloodshed, with nature mirroring and condoning this barbarity. Yet, in the passage of time between the holograph draft and final publication, Woolf's literary response changed. In the 1927 edition, her remark about the dilapidation of civilization has been excised, leaving only the china and glass destroyed, and allowing for the possibility of a greater faith in humankind to prevail.

Although the final words of "Time Passes" in the holograph draft are not bleak, they do not resonate with the same vigor and renewed liveliness as in the published text. In holograph form, Woolf concludes this section of the novel with the following image: "[…] another emotion half waking them at the moment, sleepy, & mixing & mighty, & making their hands leap, even as they fell over the edge of the cliff into sleep, with a the stab & stir & wild expectation & desire of the com coming day" (*TTLhd* 237). Evidently, life has not been halted. There is a stirring experienced even by the sleepers, who retain their desire to persist in this war-torn universe. Still there is a more palpable vitality in the final words of the published edition: "[…] Lily Briscoe stirring in her sleep clutched at her blankets as a faller clutches at the turf on the edge of a cliff. Her eyes opened wide. Here she was again, she thought, sitting bolt upright in bed. Awake" (*TTL* 221). The verb "Awake" appears within the text without a given subject. Although it is clear that Lily Briscoe is awake in bed, this sentence may also resonate as a directive intended for Woolf's readers. As the last word of this section of the text, "Awake" reverberates with renewed vibrancy, suspending the gloom of devastation and decay, breaking the stagnation of routine behavior, and anticipating the light of day to come. We, too, are reminded of the necessity to awaken from our own stupors and to live our lives with intention rather than drift through a habitual existence.

In her preface to *Virginia Woolf and the Bloomsbury Avant-Garde,* Christine Froula writes, "This book situates Virginia Woolf and Bloomsbury within a modernity understood as a 'permanent revolution'" (xi). She posits this statement in the context of Thomas Jefferson's democratic vision, one never to be set in stone, but rather "creatively transformed by the living" whenever necessary (Froula xi). It is evident from Froula's assessment that this revolution entails more than just aesthetics. In fact, she observes an effort to renew the promises of the Enlightenment project, the "unfinishable struggle for human (including economic) rights, democratic self-governance, world community, and peace," which can only be striven for after first acknowledging the "barbarity *within* Europe and the West" (Froula xii). Mass atrocities should not be familiar images for a literary audience. Certainly, the fact that death has been fictionally elided or presented grotesquely demands our further reconsideration.

Such ethical imperatives resound within the greater realm of human rights, but also in the context of one's individual responsibility to live and act daily with conscious intention. In his journal, Tolstoy relates the regrettable consequences of automatism; he states, "If […] no one was looking, or looking on unconsciously, if the whole complex lives of many people go on unconsciously, then such lives are as if they had never been" (qtd. in Shklovsky 12).

Although Mrs. Ramsay's family and friends could testify to her vigorous physical presence and her aura, Mrs. Ramsay's reflections upon her own identity and outlook on life paint a rather different portrait. We learn that she considers life to be an "antagonistic" force (*TTL* 124), one which has exacted its demands upon her mind and body, slowly subtracting her piece by piece,[1] until "there was scarcely a shell of herself left for her to know herself by; all was so lavished and spent" (*TTL* 63). In examining this metaphor of subtraction, coupled with the frequent appearance of Mrs. Ramsay in the text after her passing, we observe a conflation of life and death. These enigmatic moments suggest that Mrs. Ramsay's death was not merely a single event but a process that began during her life. Tolstoy warns of a meaningless life dominated by unconscious existence. Overextended, Mrs. Ramsay finds it her responsibility to ensure the happiness of others, yet her own life is substantially deficient. Woolf writes, "But she wanted something more, though she did not know, could not think what it was that she wanted" (*TTL* 181). Despite rare moments of transcendence, such as the experience at the dinner party, Mrs. Ramsay's vision often was static and her life habitual. This same lack of consciousness perpetuated by way of a mechanical existence was a palpable fear for Virginia Woolf herself. In her diary she expresses genuine concern that all too frequently life and death are problematically conflated in our world.

In an entry from 1928 Woolf writes, "So the days pass and I ask myself sometimes whether one is not hypnotised, as a child by a silver globe, by life; and whether this is living" (*AWD* 135). Lily, too, is confronted by this problem within the novel, but is ultimately released from the bondage of habitualization by her ability to re-envision the ordinary and the commonplace:

Notes

1. "She looked down the railway carriage, the omnibus; took a line from shoulder or cheek; looked at the windows opposite; at Piccadilly, lamp-strung in the evening. All had been part of the fields of death. But always something—it might be a face, a voice, a paper boy crying *Standard, News*—thrust through, snubbed her, waked her, required and got in the end an effort of attention, so that the vision must be perpetually remade" (*TTL* 279). Thus, in the midst of the monotony of existence, it is the remaking of the vision that restores vitality to life. Like the line drawn in the center of Lily's painting, Woolf's revisions provide the desired formalist effect to solidify her work. These adjustments meld the first section of the text to the final section, thereby creating the "corridor" that she imagined from the beginning.[2] In her diary as well as her fiction, Woolf impressively demonstrates the power of revision—both in life and in art—to break through the habitualization of everyday life, and to offer redemptive opportunities for experiencing all things anew. Friedman makes use of a metaphor of subtraction, as well. He utilizes the metaphor, however, to account for the absence of Mrs. Ramsay as the text fails to provide physical evidence of her passing. See Friedman 224.
2. In her preliminary notes for the novel, Woolf envisioned the form of *To the Lighthouse* as "Two blocks joined by a corridor," and sketched a block letter "H" below (*TTLhd*, Appendix A 11). "Time Passes" enacts the ideal corridor between "The Window" and "The Lighthouse," with brackets reinforcing the aesthetic disjunction yet paradoxical union established by the larger structure of the novel. The brackets perform a similar corridor on the level of typography.

Works Cited

Friedman, Alan Warren. *Fictional Death and the Modernist Enterprise*. Cambridge: Cambridge UP, 1995.
Froula, Christine. *Virginia Woolf and the Bloomsbury Avant-Garde: War, Civilization, Modernity*. New York: Columbia UP, 2005.
Haule, James M. "To the Lighthouse and the Great War: The Evidence of Virginia Woolf's Revisions of 'Time Passes.'" *Virginia Woolf and War: Fiction, Reality, and Myth*. Ed. Mark Hussey. Syracuse, NY: Syracuse UP, 1991. 164-179.
Oxford English Dictionary. 1989. Oxford UP. 19 October 2008. <http://dictionary.oed.com>.
Shklovsky, Victor. "Art as Technique." Trans. Lee T. Lemon and Marion J. Reis. *Russian Formalist Criticism: Four Essays*. Ed. Paul A. Olson. Lincoln: U of Nebraska P, 1965. 3-24.
Woolf, Virginia. *Moments of Being*. Ed. Jeanne Schulkind. 2nd ed. San Diego: Harcourt, 1985.
—. *To the Lighthouse*. London: Hogarth, 1927.
—. *To the Lighthouse: the original holograph draft*. Ed. Susan Dick. Toronto: U of Toronto P, 1982.
—. *A Writer's Diary*. Ed. Leonard Woolf. New York: Harcourt, 1954.

Editorial Deletion: Presenting Absence in *To the Lighthouse*

by Susan Solomon

The seven passages enclosed in brackets in *To the Lighthouse* have puzzled readers since its publication. An article from as early as 1927 notes what must have been a common contemporary reading of them: that they serve to marginalize the content they surround. Frank M. Patterson writes in the *English Record*, "Each of the isolated statements [set off by brackets] deals with such earthly concerns as birth, marriage, death, booksellers, and fishing trips. This ordinary stuff of life had been the primary subject matter of novelists preceding Virginia Woolf, but it was to play a small part in this highly symbolic and psychological novel" (28). Though Woolf's brackets operate differently from her parenthesis marks, Patterson here describes them as performing a straightforwardly parenthetical function. On the other hand, modern scholars agree that Woolf places the important matter in brackets, but they understand that move as an oblique reversal of center and margin. Tucked away in what Marianne Dekoven calls "throwaway asides" (149), square brackets present death and historical trauma by "veiled representation." More recently, Michele Barrett notes that brackets present their importance "obliquely," "cautiou[sly]," and with "deliberate buri[al]." Woolf's use of them dramatizes her "disposition to regard the marginal as central, by placing that which is crucial in the position of heavy parenthesis" (195). This scholarship still makes the same mistake as Patterson by conflating the purpose of square brackets with curved parenthesis marks and ignoring the distinction between the two according to their editorial functions and uses in the novel.

Woolf's parentheses perform the action the scholars just cited attribute to brackets. Their digressive insertion transforms the sentence, and they scrutinize the categories of center and margin. Since its development punctuation has provided vocal and bodily gesture to disembodied or *lifeless* texts, and the curved parenthesis is the most bodily and intimate mark of punctuation. The direct address it often contains carries privacy and intimacy, like the "aside" in theater. Woolf's parentheses designate an intimate space—like a curved hand directing a whisper—and unify the varied points of views revealed in her prose through the voice of a knowing, detached narrator's address to the reader. Woolf also surrounds identifying, clarifying phrases in parentheses. Often they attribute speech or thought to a particular character, or as is even more interesting, they insert simultaneous gesture or physical presence into the sentence. These parentheses visually and literally return the disembodied text to the materiality of the human subject.

Reading Woolf's bracketing as ironic understatement is unnecessary if we look at its institutional purpose, of which—as an editor—Woolf was certainly aware. Style manuals contemporary to Woolf agree that it is used for three main purposes: as providing explanation, as an *editorial* rather than an *authorial* interpolation, and as marking a correction or omission. That is to say, in contrast to parentheses, brackets enclose the straightforwardly *necessary* insertion. In translations, brackets supply the original language as that which is already replaced and rendered readable. Editors bracket language to be removed. When the writer brackets the language he adds to a quote, he designates precisely what is not quoted. This is to say brackets present and memorialize what is absent. This is crucial to understanding Woolf's brackets, since the content of her novel is so engaged with empty space and loss.

The first passage I'd like to treat comes late in the novel: the sixth chapter of "The Lighthouse," which is entirely in brackets. It interrupts chapters five and seven, in which Lily Briscoe discovers her grief for Mrs. Ramsay: "For how could one express in words these emotions of the body? express that emptiness there? (She was looking at the drawing-room steps; they looked extraordinarily empty.) It was one's body feeling, not one's mind" (178). Lily, as she grapples to represent the space of Mrs. Ramsay's world without Mrs. Ramsay on the canvas, struggles also with a bodily grief that extends beyond words. At the close of the chapter Lily is still occupied by the empty space on the drawing room steps. The pain she struggles to articulate, comes through in the shape of the brackets that surround the interrupting chapter:

"[Macalister's boy took one of the fish and cut a square out of its side to bait his hook with. The mutilated body (it was still alive) was thrown back into the sea.]" (180).

The visual continuity between the square-shaped wound in the fish's body and the pair of brackets suggests that the cut figuratively reenacts the work of the bracket on the novel. Macalister's boy cuts into the body of the fish, just as Woolf cuts into the narrative with brackets to represent in a manner that words cannot, the empty space left behind by the bodies of the dead. In this passage, brackets are interrupted with parenthesis marks, which enclose the literally vital information: despite the mutilation, the fish remains painfully alive and the text moves on. The living body is located in the parentheses, and its parts removed and mutilated with the square brackets.

In this way, brackets perform the editorial excision style handbooks attribute to them when used to announce Mrs. Ramsay's death:

"[Mr. Ramsay, stumbling along a passage one dark morning, stretched his arms out, but Mrs. Ramsay having died rather suddenly the night before, his arms, though stretched out, remained empty.]" (128)

The next sentence, following in the fourth chapter, returns to the vacation home: "So with the house empty and the doors locked [...]" (128-9). The bracket, like the fact of death, is composed of uncompromising lines, which shut away the living Mrs. Ramsay. Involved in the architecture of textual construction, it represents both the emptiness housed by the walls of the vacation home and the faraway, outstretched and empty arms of Mr. Ramsay. The spatial articulation of loss *invites* the reader to take notice of the visual character of the brackets on the space of the page. James Krasner calls Mr. Ramsay's stumbling feet and empty arms an embodied grief—a grief experienced in bodily and spatial terms, comparable to amputees' experience of phantom pain (218-219). Like Lily Briscoe's "body feeling," Mr. Ramsay's grief is articulated by means of this spatial description. Rather than representing the body itself, the brackets' editorial function presents the absence that other bodies still feel. The bracket does not evoke for us the extended and empty arms of Mr. Ramsay, but the round parenthesis marks that would so suitably represent them were they embracing a living body. It marks a nostalgia for the intimate parentheses of "The Window" in which Mr. and Mrs. Ramsay could momentarily merge.

Like Mr. Ramsay's encounter with the absence and space left empty by her death, the reader must navigate this strange marked-off space on the page. He or she stumbles over the narrative loss and spatial rupture of this passage. Thus, embodied grief might be enacted not only through the narration of the scene, but also through the materiality of the brackets on the printed page, which incite a textual phantom pain for the reader. Its physicality supplements verbal modes of signification as it communicates "body, not mind feeling." Like music, in which performance and expression are one and the same, the bracket's meaning is posited not propositionally, but contiguously with its own movement. This is to say it acts on its own; it is simultaneously subject and verb. This subjectless action aligns it with the editorial. It also offers clues about the nature of Woolf's representation of World War I.

Brackets also represent the lost bodies and lives of Prue and Andrew as they enclose the information of their deaths a few pages later: "[Prue Ramsay died that summer in some illness connected with childbirth, which was indeed a tragedy, people said, everything, they said, had promised so well.]" (132). Directly opposite on the facing page is: "[A shell exploded. Twenty or thirty young men were blown up in France, among them Andrew Ramsay, whose death, mercifully, was instantaneous.]" (133). These brackets ominously present the absence left by the two children's deaths by invoking the editorial use of brackets to mark words and the bodies they represent for removal. This deletion takes on a disturbing resonance when it is read in conjunction with the military use of the word, in which—according to *Oxford*—it refers to "the (specified) distance between a pair of shots fired, one beyond the target and one short of it, in order to find the range for artillery" ("bracket"). This suggests that Andrew has been bracketed both by the enemy shooter and by the author-editor who desires to represent his death. The grouping of Andrew and Prue's deaths together in visual symmetry on facing pages also brings the private and intimate mourning of one family member for the other together with the public military death, the almost anonymous death of Andrew Ramsay, who dies in a group of twenty *or* thirty. To bracket also means to classify or group. Prue's and Andrew's deaths are bracketed interchangeably by their symmetrical arrangement on the pages as well as the circumstances of their deaths: World War One England celebrated motherhood as the feminine form of military service. In this sense, all seven passages are bracketed together by the enemy: the passing of time and war. Mr. Ramsay's loss, grouped with the period including the war, becomes bound to those public losses. Like the square window of the first book, brackets provide a threshold between public and private worlds, losses, conflicts, and actions. All are conflated and equated by the leveling work of time.

Having understood that the bracket not only marks loss in a material way, but performs translation between public and private, and establishes an interchangeability among bracketed passages, we can read the first bracketed passage in the novel differently in light of the passages we just analyzed. It takes place early in "Time Passes," and chronologically and thematically belongs equally to the world of the "The Window." Leading into the passage, we are offered a scene in which the vague united forces of time that have just entered the structure are disrupted and forced to a halt as the entranceway to another passage of the house is closed off: "At length, desisting, all ceased together, gathered together, all sighed together; all together gave off an aimless gust of lamentation to which some door in the kitchen replied; swung wide; admitted nothing; and slammed to" (127). With this the chapter is closed with the bracketed sentences: "[Here Mr. Carmichael, who was reading Virgil, blew out his candle. It was midnight.]" At the stroke of midnight, the day is concluded, as well as the world of "The Window," a world prior to the vacancy of the house, loss, and disruption to follow in the next chapter. The kitchen door shuts itself, which is followed by the closed passage of the bracket, in which Mr. Carmichael's book presumably is closed and the space enclosed in darkness. The visual aspect of the bracket echoes and repeats the content of the passage it frames and closes. Because it is grouped together with the other bracketed passages in the novel, we recognize this closing off in more momentous, historical terms. A private, individual action becomes the emblem of an historical and narrative turning point. Insofar as the vacation home and the novel's form share architectural structures (as we've seen in the "two blocks connected by a corridor" plan for the novel), they become figurative counterparts; the invading airs, as they invade the house, also invade the novel.

Read collectively, we see that the bracket *publicizes* the parenthetical round bracket and extends the import of events beyond the domestic space as it changes the voice from the whisper of a direct address to the metallic tone of a loudspeaker. Most scholars have read literary punctuation as a tool of authorial control, but in Woolf's case the bracket emblematizes the transformative editorial hand of history. The bracket as an *editorial*, not *authorial* tool is noteworthy, even as it is used by the author herself. Woolf displaces authorship to the institutional authority of the state and military, whose hand has intruded into and corrupted the domestic space of the novel. It is more than coincidental that Woolf's revision of "Time Passes," the section including most of the brackets, removed overt references to the war and inserted instead the bracketed sentences.[1] The war is presented through literal excision in this editing process, and the isolated bracketed events, not integrated into the narratives they rupture, act as memorials of a war that once had its presence in an earlier published version. History becomes a force that inserts itself with the brackets and edits out the characters whose deaths they enclose. Rather than representing war and loss propositionally, the bracket actually *performs* the movement of war on the text.

Note

1. I'm referring to the version of "Time Passes" translated into French that was first brought to light by James Haule.

Works Cited

Barrett, Michele. "Virginia Woolf Meets Michel Foucault." Chapter 11. *Imagination in Theory: Essays on Writing and Culture*. Cambridge: Polity P, 1999. 186-204.
"Bracket, n." *Oxford English Dictionary Online*. 2nd ed. 1989. Oxford: Oxford UP, 2007.
"Bracket, v." *Oxford English Dictionary Online*. 2nd ed. 1989. Oxford: Oxford UP, 2007.
DeKoven, Marianne. "History as Suppressed Referent in Modernist Fiction." *ELH* 51.1 (1984): 137-152.
Haule, James M. "'Le Temps Passe' and the Original Typescript: An Early Version of the "Time Passes" Section of *To the Lighthouse*." *Twentieth Century Literature* 29.3 (1983): 267-278.
Krasner, James. "Doubtful Arms and Phantom Limbs: Literary Portayals of Embodied Grief." *PMLA* 119.2 (2004): 218-232.
Patterson, Frank M. "The Brackets in *To the Lighthouse*." *The English Record*. 16 (1927): 28-29.
Woolf, Virginia. *To the Lighthouse*. San Diego: Harcourt Brace Jovanovich, 1990.

The World with and Without a Self: *Between the Acts* as a Revision of *The Waves*

by Courtney Carter

The sun had not yet risen. . . . Gradually as the sky whitened a dark line lay on the horizon dividing the sea from the sky and the grey cloth became barred with thick strokes moving, one after another, beneath the surface, following each other, pursuing each other, perpetually. (*TW* 7)

It was a summer's night and they were talking, in the big room with the windows open to the garden, about the cesspool. . . .

A bird chuckled outside. "A nightingale?" asked Mrs. Haines. No, nightingales didn't come so far north. It was a daylight bird, chuckling over the substance and succulence of the day, over worms, snails, grit, even in sleep. (*BTA* 3)

Both *The Waves* and *Between the Acts* have inspired sharply contrasting critical responses. Many view *The Waves* as Woolf's "masterpiece"; to James Naremore, it is an "interesting" failure (Hussey, *Woolf A to Z* 356; Naremore 189). For some, *Between the Acts* is Woolf's darkest novel; to Gillian Beer, it is her "most mischievous and playful" (Hussey, *Woolf A to Z* 29; Beer 395). One of the most extreme contrasts has been voiced by Mark Hussey, who (in his 1986 study of Woolf's "philosophy") defined *The Waves* as an "aesthetic failure"[1] and viewed *Between the Acts* as a "brilliant union of design and substance that holds within it the clearest exposition of [Woolf's] faith in 'reality'" (*Singing* 81, 129). These differing responses indicate that questions concerning the artistic value and thematic significance of these novels have not been resolved.

In an attempt to understand critical responses to these two novels, I turn to the work of Les Fehmi, a psychologist and pioneer in the use of neurofeedback. In *The Open-Focus Brain: Harnessing the Power of Attention to Heal Mind and Body*, Fehmi argues that "styles of attention"–"the way we shape and direct our awareness"—create our sense of both self and world, that a "narrow focus of attention" leads to rigidity and anxiety, to a sense that we are walled in and threatened by that which exists outside the walls. A shift to a more "open" focus of attention generates a more "flexible" and "accepting" attitude to both self and world (11-14).

In this paper, I use Fehmi's distinction between "narrow" and "open" styles of attention as a template through which to observe Woolf's two novels and argue that, in both *The Waves* and *Between the Acts*, Woolf evokes a sense of the world both with and "without a self."[2] In *The Waves*, however, Woolf views the world, primarily, from the perspective of her characters; she identifies with those who are struggling to create and maintain a self. In *Between the Acts*, on the other hand, she observes her characters from a far more "open" perspective. She sees beyond the very limited characters she observes to the creative possibilities of the "world without a self." The opposition between self and non-self appears in each novel. But the focus of attention (on the self and its limitations) has been "edited out" of the later novel. And this shift in focus gives rise to a shift in both tone and thematic implications that helps to explain some of the striking differences between these two novels.

In *The Open-Focus Brain,* Fehmi argues that attention is "all-encompassing in our lives," but the "issue is not *wha*t we attend to. Far more critical is *how* we attend, *how* we form and direct our awareness, and *how* we adhere–rigidly or flexibly–to a chosen style of attention"(11-13). To explain how "the brain creates and dissolves our personal reality," Fehmi introduces the image of stones being dropped into a pond: dropping one stone causes ripples; dropping two creates waves that collide and form what physicists call "an interference pattern" (169).

Consciousness, according to Fehmi, consists of "three primary elements": "attention," the "contents of our attention, and "the witness of both": the "contents of attention are represented by activity in one or more sensory . . . regions of the brain, and attention (awareness) is represented by activity in . . . the rest of the brain." If activity between these regions is "out of phase," an "interference pattern" (between internal and external content) gives rise to a sense of "self." If we shift, however, into a more "diffuse-immersed" attention style, the self tends to merge into attention and its contents and can, at its "most profound level," expand to a "universal embrace, resulting in ecstatic experience, a sense of complete oneness" (169-70). Thus, according to Fehmi, "simply by admitting into consciousness the space, silence, and timelessness that pervades [*sic*] our experience," we "can create a far different reality than the one we normally inhabit" (137, 168).[3]

We observe in all of Woolf's novels an oscillation between narrow and diffuse awareness. In *Mrs. Dalloway,* for example, when Peter Walsh focuses on his failure as lover or civil servant, his world contracts and he reaches for his pocket knife—as a defense against the world that threatens his sense of self (250). When, on the other hand, he muses on the bench next to the "grey nurse," his world expands into a universal embrace, into the embrace of a figure so imbued with "compassion, comprehension, absolution" that Peter longs to "mount . . . on her steamers and . . . blow to nothingness with the rest" (85-87). This ability to move from a narrow to a more open focus is in fact the defining characteristic of Woolf's most complex (and most representative) characters. Both Mrs. Dalloway and Mrs. Ramsay contract in fear and self-doubt: when, for example, Mrs Dalloway recalls that "Lady Bruton, whose lunch parties were said to be extraordinarily amusing, had not asked her" (45) or when Mrs. Ramsay acknowledges that to Mr. Carmichael "all this desire of hers to give, to help, was vanity" (65). Each understands that, because every carefully constructed sense of self is threatened continually, it is "very, very dangerous to live even one day" (*MD* 11). Yet each attains at moments a sense of calm, even ecstasy, when they experience a "sense of oneness" with the world that transcends the self.[4]

In both *The Waves* and *Between the Acts,* Woolf presents characters suspended between a narrow sense of self and an awareness of the world that lies beyond—and threatens—that self. And in each novel she presents characters who illustrate distinctly different ways of focusing their attention, of creating and experiencing both self and world. In *The Waves,* however, Woolf focuses on the mystery of individual consciousness and the tragedy of its dissolution. She traces the process each character undergoes in order to maintain a relatively stable sense of self and create a distinctly different experience of the world. And most of the characters oscillate throughout the novel between a fear of losing this carefully constructed self and the fear of being enclosed within it. Each character attempts what Woolf attempts in this novel, to capture "reality" in an image or pattern of images—a "loop of light"(9), a "ring of steal" (40), a pool with marble columns "where the swallow dips her wings" (105). And all acknowledge, what Rhoda and Bernard enunciate, that an attempt to focus narrowly on any image of reality leaves something "outside," that all stories are constructed over a vast sea of possible stories and that, in fact, all stories are false.[5]

As critics have acknowledged, the reality that haunts this novel is the reality of death, the death of the "self." And because the attention of both characters and narrator is so narrowly focused on the preservation of self, the tone, imagery, and rhythm of the novel communicate a sense of tension and helplessness. (In the interludes the narrating consciousness seems obsessed by the process of death and dissolution: Birds "intensely conscious of one thing, one object in particular. . . . fixed their gaze on the small bright apple leaves. . . . Then one of them . . . spiked the soft, monstrous body of the defenceless worm" [74].) Since the emphasis is on the fragility of each separate self and the need to snatch "joy . . . quickly now at this instant" (73), there is no release—for characters, narrator, or reader— from fear and failure. We, along with the narrator and the characters, are trapped within a state of mind that knows "it is very, very dangerous to live even one day" (*MD* 11). We are trapped within a landscape where the waves beat upon the shore and, ultimately, no self can escape the ravages of time.

The entries in Woolf's diary relating to *The Waves* (or *The Moths*, her original title), make it clear that in this novel she is attempting to capture the implications of that troubling and elusive image, the "fin in the waste of water," that appeared to her shortly after she completed *To the Lighthouse* (*AWD* 100, 165), to capture in "this angular shape" (the novel itself) the "essence of reality" (*AWD* 165, 139, 100). Thus, the characters in *The Waves* reflect the metaphysical problems Woolf struggles with as she composes the novel: Is life "solid" or "shifting"? Does it last forever or is it "transitory"? "I shall pass like a cloud on the waves. . . . yet we are somehow . . . continuous we human beings, and show the light through. But what is the light?" (*AWD* 138). Each character, like Woolf, acknowledges two "realities": that narrow, focused ring of light (or steel) that each has constructed to maintain a sense of self (the "real" life—which consists of each character's struggle to live—and Woolf's struggle to design the novel) and a world that goes on "for ever," even when the self vanishes.[6] In this novel, both Woolf and her characters focus on the difficulty of maintaining that narrow, carefully constructed sense of self (or "angular shape"). And, because of this focus, the author, characters, and readers feel the strain.

In *Between the Acts* Woolf presents, once again, a world inhabited by characters who exhibit very different habits of "attention."[7] And both works, I would argue, present portraits of the world both with and "without a self." But in *Between the Acts*, Woolf's narrator adopts a more "open" focus. Many of the characters are trapped within a "narrow" view of the world: Isa, for example, is obsessed by the burden of playing wife and mother while dreaming of the "gentleman farmer" (13-14); her husband Giles is enraged by his Aunt Lucy's indifference to conditions in Europe (53), while his father, Bart Oliver, dreams of "youth and India" (17-18). The narrating consciousness, however, is not trapped. She sees what Fehmi advises us to see: "all the space, silence, and timelessness that pervades our experience" (137). She maintains an awareness of the "three-dimensional space [that passes in reality,] between, around, and through objects . . . [the] space that permeates everything" and an awareness of the "background space against which everything is highlighted" (Fehmi 137).[8] Each of the characters, like those in *The Waves,* exhibits the need to create a "self and the fear of losing it. Even Lucy "flush[es]" when Bart "str[ikes]" at her faith. When she said 'pray,' he added 'umbrellas.'. . . She shrank; she cowered. . ." (23-24). Yet each character, from the perspective of the narrator, serves as an illustration of the miracles that arise from the fecundity of the "world without a self." The narrator recognizes (like Lucy as she stares into the fish pond) that "the sea on which we float" (the underlying "reality") gives rise to all selves: the "speckled, streaked, and blotched . . . [the] beauty, power, and glory in ourselves" (205). And, like Miss La Trobe, as the "starlings attacked the tree behind which she had hidden. . . . [and] the tree became a rhapsody, a quivering cacophony. . . syllabling discordantly life, life, life, without measure," she recognizes that, though the play has ended, another play will begin: "It was strange that the earth, with all those flowers incandescent . . . should still be hard. From the earth green waters seemed to rise over her. She took the voyage away from the shore, and, raising her hand, fumbled for the latch of the iron entrance gate" (209-11). Images throughout the novel–the earth from which "green waters" rise, the pond where "something moved"(205), and the tree that sings of "life"—all point to the underlying reality, the "fertile" mud (212) that gives rise to all selves.

The sharpest contrast between these two novels relates to the differing attitudes the narrators adopt toward the "world without a self." Whereas in *Between the Acts* the narrator retains a "diffuse-immersed" awareness of the whole that gives rise to all selves, the narrator of *The Waves* seems to reside within the consciousness of characters who, like Bernard, oscillate throughout the novel between the desire to retain a relatively limited sense of self in order to "fight" (to participate in the "adventure" of living)—"Must go, must sleep, must wake, must get up–sober merciful word which we pretend to revile" (234)—and the desire to see beyond and escape the compulsions and limitations of that self. This oscillation reaches a climax in Bernard's brief encounter with the world without a self:

For one day as I leant over a gate that led into a field, the rhythm stopped....I saw through the thick leaves of habit. (283)

The scene beneath me withered. It was like the eclipse when the sun went out and left the earth. . .withered....(284)

How then does light return to the world after the eclipse of the sun? Miraculously. So the landscape returned to me....I walked alone in a new world, never trodden; brushing new flowers, unable to speak save in a child's words of one syllable....

But how describe the world seen without a self? There are no words....How describe or say anything in articulate words again?—save that it fades...becomes... habitual–this scene also. Blindness returns....Loveliness returns....

But for a moment I had sat on the turf somewhere above the flow of the sea and the sounds of the woods, had seen the house, the garden, and the waves breaking. The old nurse who turns the pages of the picture-book had stopped and had said, "Look. This is the truth." (283-287)

Bernard moves from depression to clarity ("This is the truth"), and then to a perception of the beauty of the world glimpsed "without a self." But he cannot sustain the vision. The world of "Must, must, must–detestable word"(293)—calls him back to "fight," the fight he can engage in only if he maintains a narrow, focused sense of his own identity. Bernard has glimpsed the world beyond his stories. He sees it as "truth," but he flees back to the world of "I, I, I" and continues to confront "the enemy"—the enemy that is both the "other" (any other) and death (296). Perceiving for an instant the beauty of the world "seen without a self," he flees from it, unable to sustain more than a glimpse: because he fears the death of the self, he is unable to maintain any awareness of the miracle that underlies and gives rise to all selves.

In *Between the Acts*, on the other hand, images of the pond "on which we float," of mud that is "fertile,"of starlings pelting the tree give Lucy, Miss La Trobe, and the reader some glimpse of that which lies beyond and gives rise to all selves, cows, starlings, and stories. Here the narrating consciousness seems to reside in a more "open" psychic space, aware of the anguish and anger of individual characters, of Europe arming and planes flying, but never focusing narrowly on any of these perceptions. Here all characters are viewed with both sympathy and comic irony. We might, for example, contrast the portrait of La Trobe as artist with that of Lily in *To the Lighthouse:* "O to write a play without an audience—*the* play. But here she was fronting her audience. Every second they were slipping the noose. Her little game had gone wrong. . . . Panic seized her. Blood seemed to pour from her shoes. This is death, death, death, she noted in the margin of her mind; when illusion fails (180). Lily suffered fear of failure, but here the exaggerated diction suggests that, in a world of birds that chuckle, cows that cough, and tears that rain down from the sky to save a pageant, even the artist's failure is comic. This narrator is not trapped within the narrow focus of selves struggling to sustain their roles. She sees beyond all roles—and laughs.[9]

Almost every reference in Woolf's diary to her experience of composing *The Waves* suggests difficulty, tension, anxiety,[10] the same anxiety her characters experience as they struggle to maintain a narrow image of self and world while acknowledging, subliminally, that the task is impossible. Most references in the diary to *Between the Acts* (or *Pointz Hall*, its original title) suggest release, freedom from strain: She speaks of the "immense relief and peace I have gained and enjoy at this moment. . . . I am an outsider. I can take my way: experiment with my own imagination in my own way. The pack may howl . . . . I'm free" (282).[11] The war and its terrors, the "real" threat that hangs over her civilization, seems to have freed Woolf from the compulsion to capture for an audience that "essence of reality" and placed her, perhaps, where Bernard stood when he looked over the fence and the "rhythm stopped." Of course, for Woolf, as for Bernard , the rhythm begins again, "blindness" and "loveliness" return. But this time Woolf (unlike Bernard) maintains an "open" focus of awareness and achieves that "brilliant union of design and substance that holds within it the clearest exposition of [Woolf's] faith in 'reality'" (Hussey, *Singing* 129). She acknowledges, with calmness and detachment, the reality that though all passes (we will follow the mastodons), the curtain rises—and it all begins again.

We can, Fehmi argues, "create a far different reality than the one we *normally inhabit*" (my emphasis). *The Waves*, I would argue, is the artistic embodiment of the state of mind most of us live within most of the time; it is narrowly focused on survival and on the reality of death; it is defined by a sense of anxiety, and a compulsion to compete with other egos, other selves. In this novel Woolf does fail to evoke in us that "faith in 'reality'," that "singing of the real world" explicated so convincingly by Mark Hussey. I believe, however, that Woolf herself is aware of that failure, that the failure becomes, in fact, the "content" of the novel. And, to use Fehmi's terminology, since the content of the novel and Woolf's awareness of her original intention are "out of phase," an "interference pattern" creates both her sense of anxiety as artist and the sense of anxiety we experience as readers. Still, at the end of the process, like Lily when she completes her painting, Woolf says, "I have netted that fin in the waste of water. . ." (*AWD* 165). Like Lily, she senses that she has achieved something she needed to achieve; and like Lily, after she completes the work, she attains a sense of release. She is released by that effort into a new state of mind and a new view of the artist, the view expressed in "Anon."[12]

Both novels paint a portrait of the world without a self and the selves that arise from that "world." But in *The Waves* we are trapped inside the consciousness of those who are attempting to create and maintain a self whereas, in *Between the Acts*, we are observing those narrow worlds from a perspective that reminds us, continually, of the infinite potential of the source ("reality" or "nothingness")[13] from which all selves arise and to which they return, leaving others to replace them as they replaced the dinosaurs. *Between the Acts* emphasizes the miracle that such limited, imperfect creatures ("Liars most of us. Thieves too" [187]) can in fact come together and create a world, can build both self and society, both art and history. This narrator focuses, not on the fragile selves who are continually threatened but on the source of creativity itself, on the world without a self that Rhoda glimpses as she plunges to her death and Bernard fears even as he uses it to create another fiction--which he then inhabits.

By the time Woolf turns to *Between the Acts,* her prototype of the artist is not Lily or Bernard (or even Miss La Trobe) but the voice of the community she evokes in "Anon." She is no longer attempting to capture reality in an "angular . . . sharply cornered" work (*AWD* 139). She is allowing "reality" to flow through her consciousness–the reality that includes (and gives rise to) mammoths and mastodons, cows and starlings, and human beings. She has adopted a more open focus of attention. She has attained the state of mind that Mrs. Dalloway and Mrs. Ramsay attained at moments and that Bernard glimpsed after his brief encounter with the "world without a self." By altering her focus, she has opened herself to the reality that we are all surrounded and permeated by atoms of energy: all flows, all passes away and rises again. In this "world," even death is no longer "the enemy."

Notes

1. In a personal e-mail to the author (1 Nov 2008), Mark Hussey confirms that he has qualified his 1986 opinion and now believes that *The Waves* should be viewed as an "aesthetic failure" only "if read as a continuation of the aesthetic developed in" *To the Lighthouse*. He now believes that *The Waves* is "not a continuation but something entirely new." See *Virginia Woolf: A to Z* for a reference to this more recent judgment (361).
2. See Naremore's study of Woolf's novels as an expression of the conflict between "the world of the self" and the "world without a self": according to Naremore, Woolf's entire body of work reflects this conflict, and in *The Waves* "as elsewhere Virginia Woolf sees death as a kind of victory and a kind of defeat–a loss of the self, but at the same time an ecstatic embrace" (188).

3. To achieve this state of awareness, Fehmi advises the reader: "Be aware of the three-dimensional space [that passes, in reality,] between, around, and through objects. [Attend] to all your senses: seeing, hearing, feeling, taste, smell, mental activity, and time. Include both objects and space. Imagine an awareness of space that permeates everything. Imagine feeling the background space against which everything is highlighted" (137).
4. See *Mrs. Dalloway*: "Quiet descended on her, calm, content. . . .So on a summer's day waves collect, overbalance, and fall . . . and the whole world seems to be saying 'that is all' . . . until even the heart in the body which lies in the sun on the beach says too, That is all" (58-59). See also *To the Lighthouse*: "Losing personality, one lost the fret, the hurry, the stir; and there rose to her lips always some exclamation of triumph over life when things came together in this peace, this rest, this eternity. . ." (96).
5. See Rhoda, the character who has "no face" (43) and finds it impossible to sustain any stable sense of self, who asks "what is the thing that lies beneath the semblance of the thing?" and consoles herself with the notion that the "players take the square and place it upon the oblong. . . .they make a perfect dwelling-place. Very little is left outside" (163).
6. "Directly I stop writing I feel that I am sinking down, down. And as usual I feel that if I sink further I shall reach the truth. . . . I shall make myself face the fact that there is nothing–nothing for any of us. . . . [and in reference to *The Moths*] There must [in this novel] be great freedom from 'reality.'" Yet everything must have relevance. Well all of this is of course the 'real' life; and nothingness only comes in the absence of this" (*AWD* 140-41).
7. As critics have acknowledged, the women in *Between the Acts* seem far more capable of "merging" with the whole and accepting, even embracing the world beyond themselves. See, for example, Eileen Barrett, "Matriarchal Myth on a Patriarchal Stage."
8. See note 3 above.
9. See Carubia on chaos, women, and laughter (267, Note).
10. See *AWD* 139, 143, 149, 159, 161.
11. See also *AWD* 279, 298, 323, 331, 347.
12. See Eisenberg 263, Minow-Pinkney 195, Silver 285.
13. See Gough, Kane, Minnow-Pinkney, and Hussey (*Singing* 40-41) on Woolf's "ironic" relationship to mysticism.

Works Cited

Barrett, Eileen. "Matriarchal Myth on a Patriarchal Stage: Virginia Woolf's *Between the Acts*." *Twentieth Century Literature* 33 (Spring 1987): 18-37.

Beer, Gillian. "Introduction" to *Between the Acts*. Ed. Julia Briggs. Virginia Woolf: *Introductions to the Major Works*. London, Virago, 1984. 395-424.

Carubia, Josephine M. "'The Higgledy-Piggledy' Puzzle: A Fractal Analysis of the Patterns in Virginia Woolf's Fiction." *Virginia Woolf and the Arts*. Selected Papers from the Sixth Annual Conference on Virginia Woolf. Ed. Diane F. Gillespie and Leslie K. Hankins. Pace UP, 1997. 260-68.

Eisenberg, Nora. "Virginia Woolf's Last Words on Words: *Between the Acts* and 'Anon.'" *New Feminist Essays on Virginia Woolf*. Ed. Jane Marcus. Lincoln: U of Nebraska P, 1981. 253-66.

Fehmi, Les, and Jim Robbins. *The Open-Focus Brain: Harnessing the Power of Attention to Heal Mind and Body*. Boston: Trumpeter, 2007.

Gough, Val. "With Some Irony in Her Interrogation: Woolf's Ironic Mysticism." *Virginia Woolf and the Arts*. Selected Papers from the Sixth Annual Conference on Virginia Woolf. Ed. Diane F. Gillespie and Leslie K. Hankins. Pace UP, 1997. 85-90.

Hussey, Mark. *The Singing of the Real World: The Philosophy of Virginia Woolf's Fiction*. Columbus: Ohio State UP, 1986.

——. *Virginia Woolf A to Z*. New York: Oxford UP, 1995.

Kane, Julie. "Varieties of Mystical Experience in the Writings of Virginia Woolf." *Twentieth Century Literature* 41.4 (Winter 1995): 328-49.

Minow-Pinkney, Makiko. "'How then does light return to the world after the eclipse of the sun? Miraculously, frailly': A Psychoanalytic Interpretation of Woolf's Mysticism." *Virginia Woolf and the Arts*. Selected Papers from the Sixth Annual Conference on Virginia Woolf. Ed. Diane F. Gillespie and Leslie K. Hankins. Pace UP, 1997. 90-98.

Naremore, James. *The World without a Self: Virginia Woolf and the Novel*. New Haven: Yale UP, 1973.

Silver, Brenda R. "'Anon' and 'The Reader': Virginia Woolf's Last Essays." *Twentieth Century Literature* 25. 3/4 (Fall/Winter 1979): 356-441.
Woolf, Virginia. *Between the Acts*. 1941. New York: Harvest/Harcourt, 1969.
—. *Mrs. Dalloway*. 1925. New York: Harcourt/Harvest, 1953.
—. *To the Lighthouse*. 1927. New York: Harcourt/Harvest., 1955.
—. *The Waves*. 1931. New York: Harvest/Harcourt, 1951.
—. *A Writer's Diary*. Ed. Leonard Woolf. 1953. New York: Harcourt/Harvest, 1981.

Editing *A Writer's Diary*: Leonard Woolf as Censor or "Keeper of the Flame"

by Alice Lowe

The purpose of this paper is not to enter into the debate about Leonard Woolf's positive or negative role in Virginia Woolf's life and work, but rather to explore his excerpting and editing of her diaries, published as *A Writer's Diary – Being Extracts from the Diary of Virginia Woolf* in 1953.

As her literary executor, Leonard was committed to preserving and protecting Virginia's name and reputation. And as the proprietor and publisher of the Hogarth Press, he was in a position to do this. Her books had been the mainstay of the Press in the 1920s, so continuing publication of her work would accomplish both his personal and business goals. He and his business partner, John Lehmann, planned the publication of Virginia Woolf's posthumous work soon after her death, starting with *Between the Acts* (1941), and followed by collections of essays and short stories. These publications served to keep Virginia Woolf in the public eye in spite of a deflection of interest from literary and cultural activities to the war and its aftermath and launched what became the Bloomsbury industry, the focus of Regina Marler's *Bloomsbury Pie*.

By the 1950s Leonard was receiving growing numbers of inquiries about Virginia's life and work and some pressure to make her diaries public. *A Writer's Diary* includes about one-fifth of the complete diaries. The methods Leonard employed in abridging 30 manuscript volumes into one have been criticized as haphazard. He had them transcribed and typed out, keeping the original intact, and using a carbon copy for this project. From this he literally cut out the passages he wanted to use and assembled them for printing (Bell 10).

In his preface, Leonard Woolf anticipates many of the criticisms that followed publication concerning his abridgement of the diaries, selections and omissions. He contends that the diaries could not be published in their entirety during the lifetime of many people referred to in them though he acknowledges the risk of publishing extracts from diaries or letters, in that omissions may "distort or conceal the true character of the diarist…" (Preface vii). He has included "practically everything" (Preface viii) that referred to her writing. He also included passages in which she experiments with her writing style or comments on what she's reading, along with scenes and sketches that give a sense of her source material. As published, he said, it "throws light upon Virginia Woolf's intentions, objects, and methods as a writer" (Preface ix).

He chose not to make note of omissions, but he cautions that the book represents a small and specific portion of the diaries (Preface ix). He included similar caveats relative to omissions and corrections in the earlier essays and stories, and again in the Virginia Woolf and Lytton Strachey letters that he edited with James Strachey in 1956.

A Writer's Diary garnered a mixed reception both for itself and for Leonard's decisions as editor and publisher. Elizabeth Bowen remarked in the *New York Times Book Review* that it "gives no impression of having been stripped down…nor is mood absent…" Rather than presenting a distorted portrait, she thought that Leonard's editing corrected any imbalance there might have been. W.H. Auden commented in a *New Yorker* review that he felt it a good idea to confine it to her reflections on her writing, noting that, "Henry James...may have said more interesting things about literary technique, but I have never read any book that conveyed more truthfully what a writer's life is like..." (*Forewords & Afterwords* 412).

Negative reception was more likely to reflect the current hostility to Bloomsbury, both in Britain and in the U.S. The *Times Literary Supplement* noted that "Virginia Woolf's reputation suffered, and is still suffering" (quoted in Marler 24) from attacks on Bloomsbury, and the Bloomsbury bashers pointed to evidence of arrogance and snobbery in *A Writer's Diary* to bolster their claims.

But there is no question that the publication of *A Writer's Diary* led to increased interest in Virginia Woolf and the Bloomsbury circle, unleashing a torrent of books and articles, each with its own perspective on Virginia's life and work. Victoria Glendinning writes in her biography of Leonard Woolf, "Bloomsbury, as myth and idea, had moved into the public domain... They were harvesting the past, unsure what to display and what to lock away" (380).

Leonard called in Virginia's letters from her correspondents, so that he, rather than they, could edit and publish them as he deemed timely and appropriate. Vita Sackville-West wanted to publish the letters between herself and Virginia letters to each other, believing that they would undo damage done to Virginia's reputation by *A Writer's Diary* and the Virginia/Lytton letters, but Leonard wouldn't allow it, objecting to "too much washing of intimate Bloomsbury linen" (quoted in Marler 33), given the anti-Bloomsbury climate at that time.

Fast forward to the 1970s, when, after Leonard's death, the Woolf wave was building anew, highlighted by Quentin Bell's 1972 biography of Virginia Woolf. Leonard chose Quentin to write Virginia's biography and provided him with the complete diaries, but gave him the same carbon copy he had used himself, now cut into ribbons for his own extractions. Anne Olivier Bell organized the diaries for Quentin's use, and later edited the complete diaries, which were published in five volumes between 1977 and 1984.

In 1990, she gave us an account of her painstaking work in deciphering, editing, and annotating the diaries. She obtained photocopies of the original diaries from the Berg Collection—2,317 pages—and found that Leonard and/or his transcriber had in some instances misread and thus misstated portions that were difficult to read. She acknowledges Leonard's concerns about excerpting the diaries, but felt that "although it reveals a moving and absorbing self-portrait of a true artist at work, its publication probably did a good deal to create or reinforce that popular journalistic image of Virginia Woolf, the moody, arrogant, and malicious Queen of Bloomsbury" (Bell 7).

The publication of the diaries, along with the flood of work on Virginia Woolf and Bloomsbury, triggered additional dialogue about Leonard's impact on Virginia's life and work. Some criticism focused on the inherent bias of family members' contributions. Anne Olivier Bell noted that these "home-produced books, launched a veritable avalanche of studies... [some] purporting to demonstrate that both Leonard and Quentin had completely misrepresented her, and by concealing or cooking the evidence to which only they had access, had been able to present *their* preferred image—and one in which Leonard himself figured as hero" (22). Cynthia Ozick wrote that Leonard's "deliberately truncated" (30) diary was self-serving and misleading.

In her biography of Virginia Woolf, Hermione Lee discusses how Leonard's "husbanding" of the work would set the terms for her posthumous reception and reputation, noting specifically his decisions, "that the diary should be produced in severely edited form…that the essays should be published in selections without dates or annotations; [and] that the first biography should be written by a member of the family" (754). In addition, Brenda Silver devotes a chapter of *Virginia Woolf Icon* to *A Writer's Diary*, citing it as the first notable event in Virginia Woolf's reemergence. She writes that Leonard's presenting Virginia "as a writer, period, introduces into my narrative the family's desire both to disseminate and to control Virginia Woolf's image" (97).

With this background, I set about making some comparisons between *A Writer's Diary* and the five volumes of the complete diaries. As they say on the London Tube, "Mind the gap," and indeed the first thing that caught my attention was a number of seemingly significant gaps—periods of time in which there are no entries in *A Writer's Diary* but sometimes frequent entries in the diaries. In each of these intervals, Virginia Woolf's diary entries include regular comments about her writing and reading, as well as the kinds of character and travel sketches included elsewhere in *A Writer's Diary* and believed to serve as material for her writing. Leonard Woolf thought that noting omissions might worry readers (Preface ix), but I found that not knowing was more troublesome. *A Writer's Diary*, according to Leonard, included *most* entries pertaining to her writing between 1918 and her death in 1941. Perhaps including them all would have resulted in too much material for a single volume, but he doesn't say. While condensing 300,000 words into 40,000 clearly resulted in some difficult decisions about what would stay and what would go, one has to wonder if these intervals, without any explanation, might be misleading in themselves.

In *A Writer's Diary*, I found 51 intervals of more than one month, 20 of those two months or more. Yet in only six of those instances did the same gap appear in the full diaries, and then it was explained as generally due to illness, travel, or absorption in other writing. Virginia was inclined to chastise herself in her diaries for neglecting them for any period of time, and these reflections themselves demonstrate the significance of her diaries and offer insights into her approach to writing. The following example appears in her diary in the middle of a six-week gap in *A Writer's Diary* in early 1919:

> What a disgraceful lapse! Nothing added to my disquisition, & life allowed to waste like a tap left running. Eleven days unrecorded. Still I think if I were a painter I should only need a brush dipped in dun colour to give the tone of those eleven days. I should draw it evenly across the entire canvas. But painters lack subtlety; there were points of light, shades beneath the surface, now, I suppose, undiscoverable (*D1* 239).

There is no 1923 entry in *A Writer's Diary* until June, and yet in January she recorded the death of Katherine Mansfield. She says, "When I began to write, it seemed to me there was no point in writing. Katherine won't read it" (*D2* 226), and she continues with one of her remarkable character sketches.

In a nine-month period between October 1923 and August 1924, there was only a single entry in *A Writer's Diary*, and yet there were more than 20 diary entries during this time. While she explained that she had been working diligently on *Mrs. Dalloway*, she did, in fact, write in her diary too, setting forth her progress and plans. And again, one entry bridged the weeks between April 26 and August 7, 1939 in *A Writer's Diary*, while there are 18 entries in the diaries, which include comments on her ongoing work on Roger Fry, and ruminations on her diary itself as it related to her other writing.

I was also curious about the X's and Y's—the names omitted to protect the living—but few of them appear. They include references to John Collings Squire (his mediocrity), Desmond McCarthy, who destroyed a Saturday walk, and her niece Ann, after a difficult visit. The most interesting was revealed in the diaries as being about Vita (*D3* 126), the observation that, "X's prose is too fluent. I've been reading it and it makes my pen run. Had I been writing "Y__" [*Passenger to Teheran*] I should have run off whole pools of this coloured water; and then (I think) found my own method of attack" (*AWD* 102). Encounters with illegible words and blanks in the manuscript were infrequent as well and tended to be equally perceived in both *A Writer's Diary* and the diaries. In only a few instances was Anne Olivier Bell able to figure them out where Leonard couldn't. Misdated entries, corrected by Bell, appear insignificant.

My next step was to take a year at random and compare *A Writer's Diary* and the diaries entry by entry for that year. Virginia Woolf turned 40 in 1922. She had finished writing *Jacob's Room*, and it was published in October; she saw the publication of *Monday and Tuesday*; and she started working on *Mrs. Dalloway*. The diary from that year revealed a number of entries missing from *A Writer's Diary*.

A Writer's Diary begins the year on February 15, but Virginia Woolf talked in her diary about her writing plans on January 3. On January 22 she observes: "Why do I trouble to be so particular with facts? I think it is my sense of the flight of time…I try to stop it. I prod it with my pen. I try to pin it down" (*D2* 158). A gap in *A Writer's Diary* from February 18 to June 23 is broken in the diaries by several March entries speaking of her resumption of writing after some illness, her work on *Jacob's Room*, her lack of attention to the diary. She writes only once in April and not at all in May, starting her June 11 entry with "Disgraceful! disgraceful! disgraceful!" (*D2* 176) and some musing on her current state of mind.

July and August are well represented in *A Writer's Diary*, but not an August 3 entry that included two significant notes: First, "Mrs Nicolson thinks me the best woman writer—& I have almost got used to Mrs Nicolson's having heard of me" (*D2* 187). This happens to be the first mention of Vita Sackville-West. And then, "I must broach a new page to announce the beginning, the true not spurious beginning, of *Reading* this morning" (*D2* 188), marking the start of what became the first *Common Reader*.

On August 22 she comments at length in her diary on the depression that's getting in the way of Dalloway. From "writing off the fidgets" to "Slowly the cloud withdraws" (*D2* 192), she has drawn an extraordinary picture of her mental processes, absent from *A Writer's Diary*, which picks up near the end of this self-reflection (47). And *A Writer's Diary* omits her delightful rumination of September 3 on nibs and pens, when, she says, "I should be reading the last immortal chapter of Ulysses…" (*D2* 197).

Her diary writing flows smoothly through the last months of the year and into 1923, yet *A Writer's Diary* ends the year on October 29, right after the publication of *Jacob's Room*, and does not resume until the following June. In November and December, she is eagerly following and reacting to the reviews and sales of *Jacob*, but at the same time is moving forward and hard at work on essays, criticism, and *Mrs. Dalloway*.

So, there are indeed gaps and omissions in *A Writer's Diary*, but I do not believe that they do any real harm to the portrait of Virginia Woolf as a writer or that there is any reason to object to the limitation in an abridged diary to that aspect of her life. In fact, there is so much of her there—her wit, her curiosity, her humanity. If I have any argument with *A Writer's Diary*, it is that I would have liked it to include these additional passages and others that pertain, directly and indirectly, to her writing, going further back to the years 1915-1918 and even to the early journals of *A Passionate Apprentice*. I think that long intervals could have been bridged with meaningful entries or explained without resorting to too much editorial notation.

Wayne Chapman presented and published a paper that considers the posthumous editing of Virginia Woolf and Sylvia Plath by their literary executor husbands and how it perpetuated or altered the writers' intentions. He found Ted Hughes to be self-serving in his editing, noting specifically *Ariel*, from which he cut 11 poems and rearranged the remaining collection from the deliberate order Plath had specified to a less controversial and revealing chronological order. Alternately, Chapman concluded that Leonard Woolf's preservation of Virginia's work and perpetuation of her reputation as a writer were generally salutary. He felt the publications in the 1940s and 50s, *Between the Acts*, the essays, stories, letters and *A Writer's Diary*, gave Virginia Woolf an "afterlife that enjoins us today as her public" (66).

By way of comparison Ted Hughes, as consulting editor, saw posthumous publication of his wife's journals. In editing Sylvia Plath's journals, published in 1982 and representing approximately one-third of her total diaries, Frances McCullough noted that her goal was to include that which related most to Plath's work, her inner life, and her struggle to find herself and her voice. The "nasty bits," as she called them (Editor's Note ix), derogatory references to the living, were omitted, similar to some of the editing of *A Writer's Diary*. Hughes, however, forthrightly admits that he had destroyed the last notebook because he didn't want their children to read it (Foreword xiii).

Mark Hussey provides another view on Leonard Woolf as editor and publisher in a paper presented at this conference last year, in which he questioned whether or not *Between the Acts* should have been published. Virginia herself had said that it needed revision and wasn't ready to be published, and Hussey concluded that Leonard's decision to publish along with his specific editorial choices were hasty and influenced by economic pressures.

In drawing conclusions about Leonard Woolf's editing of *A Writer's Diary*, one needs to determine if such an abridged work, and indeed the premise of a "writer's diary," was appropriate and of value, not just at the time of publication, but also today.

Gail Godwin recently published a volume of her journals and credits Joyce Carol Oates as having suggested the format. Oates suggested to Godwin that she might edit her journal, "in the way that Leonard Woolf shaped the wonderful book titled *A Writer's Diary*" (quoted in Godwin, Preface ix). Upon rereading it, Godwin said that "…its immediacy and charm were still fresh for me. Like any apprentice writer, I have been—and continue to be—avid for information about how others became writers, what they tried, what worked, what didn't…" (Preface xiv).

In 1988, Joanne Trautmann Banks edited *Congenial Spirits: The Selected Letters of Vir-*

ginia Woolf, commenting in her introduction that while "condensing a life usually falsifies it," it's possible too that it "distils an essence that the whole disguised" (xiv). She found the Virginia Woolf who emerged to be different – more vulnerable and more admirable. The letters were not only excerpted from the six published volumes, but most individual letters were abridged as well.

In the same respect, it can be said that a different portrait of Virginia Woolf emerges from *A Writer's Diary* as compared to the complete diaries—we see, as we are intended to, the writer, with the writer's strengths and weaknesses. She appears vulnerable, uncertain about the value of her work and sensitive to responses and reviews. The Virginia Woolf of *A Writer's Diary* is also admirable, perhaps in a heightened sense, in her dedication and determination to pursue and perfect her art.

In *The Virginia Woolf Writers' Workshop*, Danell Jones extracts from the diaries (notably *A Writer's Diary*), as well as the letters, fiction and essays, to imagine Virginia Woolf teaching a writing class. I think we recognize, in this age of sound bites and text messaging, and in a culture that increasingly values action over contemplation, that educators and artists are looking for new ways to reach audiences. *The Hours* (both the book in 1998 and the film in 2002) is an example, and whether we liked it or not, it did fulfill that goal with extraordinary success, and in so doing brought new readers and new scholars to Virginia Woolf.

A Writer's Diary may be a flawed work, but its worth and importance are immeasurable. And perhaps someday it will be separated from the pro- and anti-Leonard debate and recognized for its true and timeless value. I believe that if Leonard Woolf hadn't produced it in 1953, someone would have had to do it for readers and writers today.

Works Cited

Auden, W.H. "A Consciousness of Reality." *The New Yorker*, 6 March 1954. Rpt. in *Forewords & Afterwords*. New York: Random House, 1973.
Bell, Anne Olivier. *Editing VW's Diaries*. London: The Bloomsbury Workshop, 1990.
Bowen, Elizabeth. "The Principle of Her Art Was Joy." *New York Times Book Review*, 21 Feb. 1954. 15 April 2008, <http://www.nytimes.com/ads/thehours/woolf-diary.html>
Chapman, Wayne. "Last Respects: The Posthumous Editing of VW & Sylvia Plath." *The South Carolina Review* 38.2 (2006): 65-71.
Glendinning, Victoria. *Leonard Woolf, A Biography*. New York: Free Press, 2006.
Godwin, Gail. Preface. *The Making of a Writer*. By Godwin. New York: Random House, 2006.
Hughes, Ted. Foreword. *The Journals of Sylvia Plath*. Ed. Frances McCullough. New York: Dial Press, 1982.
Hussey, Mark. "Should *Between the Acts* Have Been Published?" Virginia Woolf: Art, Education & Internationalism. Miami University of Ohio, Oxford Ohio. 8 June 2007.
Jones, Danell. *The Virginia Woolf Writers' Workshop*. New York: Bantam Books, 2007.
Lee, Hermione. *Virginia Woolf*. New York: Vintage Books, 1999.
Marler, Regina. *Bloomsbury Pie*. London: Virago Press, 1997.
McCullough, Frances. Editor's Note. *The Journals of Sylvia Plath*. Ed. McCullough. New York: Dial Press, 1982.
Ozick, Cynthia. "Mrs. Virginia Woolf: A Madwoman and Her Nurse." *Art & Ardor*. New York: Knopf, 1983.
Silver, Brenda. *Virginia Woolf Icon*. Chicago: U of Chicago P, 1999.
Trautmann Banks, Joanne. Intro. *Congenial Spirits, The Selected Letters of Virginia Woolf*. Ed. Banks. San Diego: Harcourt Brace Jovanovich, 1989.
Woolf, Leonard. Preface. *A Writer's Diary*. Ed. Leonard Woolf. San Diego: Harcourt Inc., 1953.
Woolf, Virginia. *The Diary of Virginia Woolf*. Ed. Anne Olivier Bell. 5 vols. Middlesex: Penguin Books, 1979-85.

EDITING MEMORY: VIRGINIA WOOLF'S MEMOIR IDENTITY AND HER RE-PRESENTATION OF THE TRAUMATIZED SELF

by Nicole Coonradt

This paper examines previously ignored details of Rose Pargiter's Lamley outing in Woolf's *The Years* as an important example of editing and Woolf's coded style of re-presenting the trauma to self that she first explored in her earlier work and that continued to haunt her until her death. The details hinge on Woolf's sexual abuse at the hands of her half-brothers, George and Gerald Duckworth, that she first records overtly as such in "A Sketch of the Past." This memoir, and hence, Woolf's attempt to employ memory to record the important "moments of being" that shaped her conception of self, is obviously important to our understanding of both the woman and the author. Since she did not write this until she was 57, just two years before her suicide, and when the Duckworth half-brothers both were dead already (George in 1934 and Gerald in 1937), we need to examine the trauma of sexual abuse as she re-presents it in her earliest writing and as she revisits it in her later work. Louise DeSalvo notes that "it [was] impossible to write honestly and forthrightly about sexual abuse. The law prevent[ed] it" (188). In "A Sketch of the Past," Woolf wanted her remembrances to include the present as she re-presented the "I then / I now," where "this past is much affected by the present moment" (*MOB* 75). In a weird way, her work prior to writing memoir, is an attempt to edit her experience in order to re-present the traumatized self in a series of writings in which she could not express openly what really had happened to Virginia Stephens in her girlhood.

As my guide, I have relied most heavily on DeSalvo's important work on Woolf. DeSalvo's "In the House of the Paterfamilias" explores more fully the link between the ten-year-old Virginia Stephen's juvenile story, *Pater-familias*, and the abuse and neglect in the Stephen household. See especially the dinner party incident and DeSalvo's claim that it is a coded portrayal of sexual abuse (157-61).

DeSalvo's work establishes particulars connected with Woolf's work-- recurring images that readers must notice if Woolf's meaning is to be understood. This nexus of meaning includes water and drowning, ledges, cages and confinement, animals, the looking glass, and, as particularly concerns my own study here, duck-related diction: duckweed, duck-pond, and a box of ducks in a window. Because we know of Woolf's abuse retrospectively from her memoir identity, we can see that any overt mention of her abuse or neglect could not be articulated *prior* to the death of the abusers. Therefore, all re-presentations of that abuse must be revealed through indirection. In her 1995 essay on Woolf titled "'My Boldness Terrifies Me': Sexual Abuse and Female Subjectivity," Diana L. Swanson notes Woolf's artistic methods of indirection, which include "'ways of telling it slant,' such as allusion, symbol and metaphor (often heavily coded), humor, hints, irony, and understatement to express feminist critique and to handle the problem of 'telling the truth about [her] own experiences as a body' ("Professions" 241)" (284-85). Importantly, Swanson notes that "The responsibility of the critic toward such a writer is twofold: [firstly,] to help the writer's cryptic and coded messages to be heard—to re-member her text—and [secondly,] to explore *why* [Woolf] felt compelled, apparently to censor herself" (285). Both DeSalvo and Swanson document that, "as Woolf revised earlier drafts with an eye toward publication, she consistently cut or made more obscure material concerning sexual abuse, feminist critique, [. . .] as well as autobiographical material" (Swanson 286). It is my goal in this essay to fulfill those critical responsibilities, filling a gap in the current scholarship on the Rose Pargiter Lamley incident by connecting it to Woolf's coded references to sexual abuse in one of many instances of her life-long attempt to break the silence about the Duckworths' incest. But first, let us recall Woolf's unambiguous revelation of her earliest memory of sexual abuse from her memoirs.

In "A Sketch of the Past," Woolf recounts the looking-glass, in which she used to steal furtive glimpses of her young self, about which she remarks, "I must have been ashamed or afraid of my own body" (*MOB* 68). She immediately connects this to "Another memory, also of the hall, [which] may help to explain this" (*MOB* 68-69). "This" refers, of course, to her feelings of fear and shame in connection with her body as a direct result of the 19-year-old Gerald Duckworth's abuse of the six-year-old Virginia as she sat trapped on the slab in the hall. She also recounts the "puddle" moment, when some inexplicable fear paralyzes her and she "could not step across the puddle" (78). Then, she relates the moment of "the idiot boy [who] sprang up with his hand outstretched mewing, slit-eyed, red-rimmed" (78) and how she later that night, *in the bath*, was overcome again with "dumb horror" (78) about the event. She calls these moments "hopeless sadness; that collapse I have described before; as if I were passive under some sledge-hammer blow; exposed to a whole avalanche of meaning that had heaped itself up and discharged itself upon me, unprotected, with nothing to ward it off, so that I huddled up at my end of the bath, motionless. I could not explain it; I said nothing even to Nessa sponging herself at the other end" (78).

The recurrence of the previously noted images grew out of these events-- as well as the general incestuous liberties the Duckworth brothers took with the Stephen girls. In "22 Hyde Park Gate," Woolf writes, "Sleep had almost come to me. The room was dark. The house silent. Then, creaking stealthily, the door opened; treading gingerly, someone entered. 'Who?' I cried. 'Don't be frightened', George whispered. 'And don't turn on the light, oh beloved. Beloved—' and he flung himself on my bed, and took me in his arms. Yes, the old ladies of Kensington and Belgravia never knew that George Duckworth was not only father and mother, brother and sister to those poor Stephen girls; he was their lover also" (*MOB* 155).

DeSalvo notes that Woolf's early writings reveal the importance of imagery. "Drowning metaphors are frequently used by incest victims. Woolf wrote of being left an orphan 'in a sea of halfbrothers'; of being 'drowned in kisses'; of feeling, around George like 'an unfortunate minnow shut up in the same tank with an unwieldy and turbulent whale.' In one of the most important extant works that we have from her adolescence, . . . [Woolf] describes nearly drowning in a pond covered with duckweed and she signed her work, 'One of the Drowned.'" (111)[1]

That text, "The Terrible Tragedy in a Duckpond," is related as a news story, written in 1899 when Woolf was 17. DeSalvo calls this Woolf's "adolescent counterpart to [*The Pater-familias*]" and it is of interest because of the fear of drowning it portrays as well as the "repetition of duck imagery throughout the extract" (256). Even more significant is the fact that Woolf sent this story to Emma Vaughan with a note that read, "Do you see? You must read my work carefully—not missing my peculiar words" (qtd. in DeSalvo 258). As DeSalvo notes, "This letter makes it clear that Virginia was trying to communicate something of more than passing importance to Emma and that she was telling her reader where to look for meaning—look at the peculiar words, the words that seem out of place, out of context" (258). Furthermore, in *editing* the account, Woolf adds "more 'ducks' and 'duckweed' to the original text. She describes herself as 'One of the Drowned' . . . The reason for her death by drowning is that she is shrouded in . . . 'duckweed,' in 'slimatica.'" (258)[2]. DeSalvo notes that the last syllable of Virginia's half brothers' name has been changed from "worth" to "weed," noting "that they are noxious growths" (258). Even more revealing is that this document was hidden from view in "the pages of a book [Virginia] had bought for that purpose" (DeSalvo 260). This seems to be the start of a pattern Woolf continued throughout her life—that of using particular, "peculiar" words to communicate an otherwise forbidden subject. Her half-sister Laura provided a frightening example of what might be the fate of a girl who attempts to speak or act out about abuse[3].

One point of interest is that the important pioneer we see in Woolf as a writer—her experiments in form, style, and genre—often seem to be in direct reaction to her abuse; a result of abuse; necessitated by abuse. Some have argued that psychologically Woolf may have been effecting much of this coded communication subconsciously, but it makes far more sense that her genius found a way around censorship, allowing her to beat patriarchal control on her own terms as a writer, just as the example of the "Terrible Tragedy in a Duckpond" demonstrates. She knew exactly what she was doing in editing the truth and this is one aspect of her life where she maintained control-- not of her physical body, but of her body of work—her life's *corpus*.

In *The Pargiters, The Novel-Essay Portion of The Years*, we find an important discussion of what Woolf labels "street love," but which leads to her views on the novelist and censorship, though she does not name it as such. Worth quoting at length, Woolf writes:

> This instinct to turn away and hide the true nature of the experience, either because it is too complex to explain or because of the sense of guilt that seems to adhere to it and make concealment necessary, has, of course, prevented [. . .] the novelist from dealing with it in fiction [. . .] and if the novelists ignore it, this is largely because the biographers and autobiographers also ignore it, and thus reduce the material which the novelist has to work upon to a minimum. In addition, there is, as the three dots used after the sentence, "He unbuttoned his clothes . . ." testify, supported by law, which forbids, whether rightly or wrongly, any plain description of the sight that Rose, in common with many other little girls, saw under the lamp post by the pillar box in the dusk of that March evening. All the novelist can do, therefore, in order to illustrate this aspect of sexual life, is to state some of the facts; but not all; and then to imagine the impression on the nerves, on the brain; on the whole being, of a shock which the child instinctively conceals, as Rose did; [I 62] and is also too ignorant, too childish, too frightened, to describe or explain even to herself, as again Rose was. (51)

Importantly, these ellipses Woolf notes—the "three dots"—are later changed to a period end-stop in *The Years* and so that important suggestion of the forbidden, unarticulated information is censored further. Clearly Woolf, for her whole life, had "hid the true nature of her experience" of abuse and was even forbidden to write about it—by law—in any form. And yet she finds ways to "illustrate this aspect of sexual life [by] stat[ing] some of the facts; but not all" (51). Sadly, Woolf did not have "to imagine" any of it because she lived it. She is speaking about and against censorship and abuse here and her peculiar words are important. In this way we see that as Swanson queried, the reasons "*why* [Woolf] felt compelled, apparently to censor herself*" (285) have to do far more with the law and patriarchal societal convention than any personal feelings. Indeed, all of Woolf's work seems to battle against repressive conventions in one way or another. If she ever hoped to get a "cryptic" message about her abuse noticed, it had to be published first, and to achieve that, she had to find a way around the legal obstacles as the law forbid certain truths to be voiced.

Furthermore, Woolf clearly attempts to distance herself from Rose's experience at the beginning of that essay portion of *The Pargiters* by claiming that it is a usual occurrence in London streets, which she labels "common" (50), and is the reason for "The actual fact— that children of Rose's age are frequently assaulted, and sometimes far more brutally than she was—it is familiar to anyone who reads the Police Court news; so that, even today, a mother in the poorer parts of London will make an effort that her small daughter shall not run round to the grocer's shop after dark [alone]" (50). Notice the irony of claiming that such "assault" was "frequent" and that it was "familiar" in "the Police Court news" and was especially prominent in "poorer parts of London" when in truth the "far more brutal" assault that she suggests happened to her own young self within the supposed safety of her upper-middle-class home. Rose and her sisters, like the Stephen sisters, are forbidden to leave the house unaccompanied, and yet the greater damage occurs *in the home*, which as has been documented, turns out to be a far more sinister place to Victorian children, especially girls, than we are meant to believe. It is this abuse that Woolf is forbidden, by law, to address openly in any written, published form. It is this psychologically and emotionally crippling system that forces people like Woolf, her half-sister Laura, and Rose Pargiter, to repress their experiences. Even more tellingly, Woolf continues:

> The principle itself—that love of this kind raged everywhere *outside the drawing room*—is of far greater importance, in considering the lives of the Pargiters: not only did it restrict their lives, and to some extent poison their minds—lies of all sorts undoubtedly have a crippling and distorting effect, and none the less if the liar feels that his lie is justified—but [these lies] also helped to bolster up, to burden, and substantiate a conception of the utmost importance about conduct, not only in the minds of the Pargiter sisters, but in the minds of their brothers. [. . .] [*each of them required an attitude, according to . . . temperament, a conception of the right attitude to adopt toward sex and the wrong attitude to adopt toward love, which was not natural but highly artificial*]. (52)

One cannot help reading this in the context of Woolf's incestuous abuse by the Duckworths. Note the repetition of the word "lie." The "principle"—"the lie" she references—is that such assault "raged outside the drawing room." Such lies—in general and in particular—poison minds and damage lives. The lie "bolsters," "burdens," and "substantiates" "a conception of the utmost importance about conduct" which is an "[un]*natural and highly artificial*"—Woolf can only be referring to her personal experiences of abuse at the hands of her Duckworth half-brothers where sex and love breach nature.

Of course none of this essay portion made it into *The Years*—not directly, of course. How could it? It was far too inflammatory, too provocative, and thus forbidden by law and convention. However, Woolf does continue to address the issue of her own traumatic abuse, importantly, though Rose's trip to Lamley's. The details to examine that have passed critical notice and which offer further support of Woolf's autobiographical intent to reveal her own abuse include the lamp, the pillar-box, and the box of ducks in the window.

In this subversively, disturbingly, sexually-charged passage in *The Years*, Rose sees "The lamplighter . . . poking his stick up into the little trap-door" (27). Significantly, the man who exposes himself will be illuminated under a gas lamp near a decidedly phallic pillar-box. "Poking his stick up into the little trap-door" in context, seems to employ *peculiar* words, the kind to which Woolf had alerted Emma Vaughan regarding "The Terrible Tragedy in a Duckpond" account. According to *OED*, "poke" was originally used as slang for sexual intercourse in 1602. The date charts then place it squarely in the Victorian period with examples from 1868 and 1890. "Stick" is clearly phallic. Being confined or trapped, is common in Woolf's coded language alluding to abuse, and doors are known Freudian images of female private parts, such as a "little trap-door"—the kind Gerald Duckworth explored in the six-year-old Virginia as she sat trapped on the slab outside the dining room in the lie of the "safety" of her home.

Also of interest, the lamp is referenced eight times in the brief three-page passage, further linking the abuse at which Woolf hints with the lamp's "trap-door," into which the lamplighter is "poking his stick" (27-29), and Woolf's attempts to illuminate the truth about abuse. The lamp posts, which could be considered phallic as well, "stood at great distances apart, and there were pools of darkness between them" (29). The inversion in associating darkness with pools—rather than the more common "pools of light" —also draws attention to the image. Furthermore, the "pool," as water imagery, recalls the paralyzing "moment of the puddle in the path" account from Woolf's memoir noted above. Most importantly, in addition to the phallic pillar-box, is the box of ducks in the window—the object of Rose's solo mission to Lamely's. In *The Pargiters*, as Spilka notes, Woolf specifies that Rose wants them for her bath, suggesting that this links to the paralyzing idiot-in-the-park episode, especially as the leering man reaches for Rose when he "put out his arm as if to stop her" (28) and later makes "a mewing noise" (29) when she passes him on her return trip. Spilka writes, "Certainly [Woolf's] dumb horror in the bath reminds us of Rose Pargiter's quest for bathtub toys in *The Years* and of her inability to tell her older sister what had happened at the pillar-box. . . . As their functional fusion suggests, these episodes carry a heavy overload of psychic meaning" (679). But no one, neither Spilka nor DeSalvo, connects the box of ducks in the window to Woolf's caution of privileging her "peculiar words." Recall that she told Emma Vaughan in reference to the Duckpond incident: "Do you see? You must read my work carefully—not missing my peculiar words" (qtd. in DeSalvo 258).

"'I want the box of ducks in the window,' Rose at last remembered" (*TY* 28). Important to the scene and Woolf's message, Rose is portrayed in an act of re-membering, just as Woolf, through Rose, re-members her own experience with the Duckworths. The box suggests other images of confinement, of trapping, of repression, of "the wrong box" or a [bad] predicament (1884 *OED*)[4], and may also link to the letter box, which was the pillar-boxes' function, further suggesting the phallic imagery. In 1880, "box" was also used for "witness box" or "jury box"—1880 being the important year of Rose's traumatic event, and perhaps further links matters to the deleted "Police Court" records noted in *The Pargiters* and the acts of witnessing and judgment that the law forbid the novelist, biographer, or autobiographer to record. The "window" is again another Freudian sexual image for female private parts—like "the little trap-door" of the lamp—and the "ducks" are a clear reference to the Duckworths, just as Woolf had used the duck image repeatedly in "Terrible Tragedy" so many years earlier[5]. Importantly, but cryptically, as Swanson might realize, the ducks are *in the box / in the window*. A window is also for looking through or framing and further suggests "exposure"—"Do you see?"—just as Gerald Duckworth exposed little Virginia, and George exposed himself to her later and repeatedly after her mother's death, as the leering man exposes himself to Rose, and as those who were abused were forbidden to expose their abusers by telling the truth about their traumatic experiences. These are the liars who "distort the relationship between the liar and the lied to" about that which is "unnatural" and "highly artificial." Here, seemingly innocuous objects—box, lamp, window, trap-door, poking stick, pool, pillar-box, ducks, etc.—become Woolf's "'ways of telling it slant,' [through] [heavily coded] allusion, symbol and metaphor . . . hints, irony, and understatement . . . to handle the problem of 'telling the truth'" (Swanson 284-85). The irony is heightened further through Woolf's use of the child's bath toy—the ducks— which exposes the lie of her Victorian childhood, a childhood which was neither innocent nor protected, but exploited and abused by the Duckworths. This is a further, poignant mark of the author's genius. How sad to think that Woolf's genius was, in many ways, born of necessity, merely a survival tactic and a desperate cry for help and justice.

Woolf's later-in-life, honest memoir identity, revealed with "absolute frankness," provides the careful reader with the blueprint of trauma and a better understanding for what the writer was forced to do throughout her troubled life to *re-present* the experiences about which she was forbidden to speak. Editing memory, Woolf shares her abuse through her life's work as she re-members the past.

Notes

1. She also mentions running into George later in life and thinking him a dangerous alligator and she being shut up in a glass tank with him. (DeSalvo 109).
2. Ironically, duckweed, the common name for Lemna Minor, or Lemna Disperma, looks similar to human sperm, especially as found in nature drawings, of which Victorian's were fond. This might explain Woolf's invention of the word "slimatica," which DeSalvo connects to Duckworth sperm, and forced oral sex (258-59)—Virginia drowning on duckweed.
3. In addition to DeSalvo, see Nancy Cervetti's *Scenes of Reading*, "Virginia Woolf in Her Father's Library" (89-108).
4. The slang use of "box" for "female genitalia" is not in use, according to *OED*, until 1942, and so cannot be considered here among Woolf's possible coded meanings, though for modern readers, it is tempting to do so.

5. Freud's work, with which Woolf eventually was familiar, had been translated by James Strachey—the younger brother of Lytton Strachey—both members of the Bloomsbury Group. James had also been editor of *The Spectator*. See *The Interpretation of Dreams* for the door image as female genitalia (241-242). Freud also notes sleepers "disappearing 'through an invisible trap door" (6). James Strachey's "agency" led to Hogarth publication of the *International Psychoanalytical Library* (D4 Appendix 367).

Works Cited

Cervetti, Nancy. *Scenes of Reading: Transforming Romance in Brontë, Eliot, and Woolf.* New York: Peter Lang, 998.
DeSalvo, Louise. *Virginia Woolf: The Impact of Childhood Sexual Abuse on Her Life and Work.* Boston: Beacon, 989.
Freud, Sigmund. *The Interpretation of Dreams.* (1899) A. A. Brill trans. New York: Macmillan, 1913.
Oxford English Dictionary On-line. http://0-dictionary.oed.com.bianca.penlib.du.edu
Spilka, Mark. "The Robber in the Bedroom; Or, The Thief of Love: Woolfian Grieving in Six Novels and Two Memoirs." *Critical Inquiry* 5.4 (1979): 663-82.
Swanson, Diana L. "'My Boldness Terrifies Me': Sexual Abuse and Female Subjectivity in The Voyage Out." *Twentieth Century Literature* 41.4 (1995): 284-309.
Woolf, Virginia. *The Diary of Virginia Woolf. Vol. 4. 1931-1935.* Ed. Anne Oliver Bell. New York: Harcourt, 1982.
—. *Moments of Being.* Ed. Jeanne Schulkind. New York: Harcourt, 1976.
—. *The Pargiters.* The Novel-Essay Portion of The Years. Ed. Mitchell A. Leaska. NewYork: Harcourt, 1978.
—. *The Years.* (1939) New York: Harcourt, 1956.

THE HOGARTH PRESS AND "RELIGION": LOGAN PEARSALL SMITH'S
STORIES FROM THE OLD TESTAMENT

by Diane F. Gillespie

This essay is a small portion of a longer one on Leonard and Virginia Woolf's avant-garde Hogarth Press[1] and several books from the 1920s and 30s that fit a category the Press, by 1934, had conventionally labeled "Religion." To the Woolfs and their liberal audience, however, neither the "Religion" category nor the authors and titles within it were conventional. Instead, the Press published analyses of, or challenges to, entrenched ideas and institutions, or they documented or advocated change—all anathema to uncritical believers. True, the books published under the "Religion" heading in the Complete Catalogues (through 1934) were few: R. B. Braithwaite's *The State of Religious Belief* (1927), Sigmund Freud's *The Future of an Illusion* (1928), Rose Macaulay's *Some Religious Elements in English Literature* (1931), and John Charleton Hardwick's *A Letter to an Archbishop* (1932). Added to the list in 1939 was Freud's *Moses and Monotheism*. Anticipating the "Religion" category, but published under "New Publications" or "General Literature," then listed by Spring 1925 as out of print, was Logan Pearsall Smith's *Stories from the Old Testament* (1920). As this early publication is an anomaly, it is easy to discuss on its own.

Neither Leonard nor Virginia Woolf, it is generally agreed, was "religious" in any dogmatic or institutional sense. Their awareness of the Judeo-Christian religion as part of human history and literature, however, may explain, in part, their curiosity about Logan Pearsall Smith's[2] Old Testament stories which he first showed to Virginia in May of 1919 (*L6* 496-7). The Woolfs clearly liked the stories well enough, and they published them in April of 1920. By then, Pearsall Smith (1865-1946) had published a small collection of short prose sketches and, in 1918, had combined some of them with others written later for Desmond MacCarthy, literary editor of the *New Statesman*, under the title *Trivia*.[3] MacCarthy, in an obituary notice, recalls that Pearsall Smith's original audience greeted the book with "angry contempt," and found his "self-delighting, self-conscious preciosity [...] irritating" (147). Virginia Woolf, who had reviewed *Trivia* when it appeared, was kinder. David Porter sees her comments as damning with faint praise the book's "lack of substance" (12). She does describe it as "a handful of chosen flowers, a dinner of exquisite little courses, a bunch of variously coloured air balloons" designed for "pleasure alone" (*E2* 250). Yet she adds that Pearsall Smith's "purpose is as serious as" that which "fulfils itself in other books of more ambitious appearance." He wants "to catch and enclose certain moments which break off from the mass, in which without bidding things come together in a combination of inexplicable significance." She calls these experiences "moments of vision" (*E2* 250-1), a phrase that becomes the title of her review and a central tenet of her own creative process.[4]

Early in their relationship, therefore, and early in her career as a writer, editor, and publisher, Virginia Woolf felt some affinity with Pearsall Smith. Porter thinks that, more pragmatically, they saw each other as mutually beneficial, in part as reviewers of each other's work.[5] To Virginia, Logan also was a man whose reputation, social and literary connections, and advice could benefit the Press; to Logan, Virginia and Leonard also were potential publishers of his work (Porter 13).

Stories from the Old Testament was one of nine books printed during the first four years the Press existed and one of three appearing in 1920.[6] In length (53 pages) and unconventional treatment, it fit the Press's "object, [...] to produce and publish short works which commercial publishers could not or would not publish" (L. Woolf, *Downhill* 66). Although the Woolfs disclaimed any interest in "fine binding" (L. Woolf, *Downhill* 80), they often used "gay, striking, and beautiful papers" for their early covers (L. Woolf, *Downhill* 74). The copy of *Stories from the Old Testament* remaining in the Woolf's library at Washington State University sports one of these papers, a geometric design of tan, criss-crossing diagonal lines forming diamonds, each with a tan dot in the center, against a background of horizontal tan and orange stripes.

A month after the publication of this small, visually attractive book, however, Virginia Woolf noted in her diary that *Stories from the Old Testament* "flags & we run the risk of losing money by it. A bad review in the Times, another in the Athenaeum; no rush of orders" (*D2* 39-40). In June, Virginia confided to Lady Robert Cecil that "we don't altogether think Stories from the O. T. up to the very very highest standards of prose composition" (*L2* 433). Yet, of those original publications, Leonard retrospectively reported, *Stories from the Old Testament* had the third highest net profit (after Maxim Gorky's *Reminiscences* and Virginia Woolf's *Kew Gardens*) (*Beginning* 253).

The reviews were more ambiguous than Virginia Woolf made out, although they do hint at something sophomoric about Pearsall Smith's tone and superficial about his method that she may have thought reflected on his publishers. In a short note in *The Athenaeum,* the anonymous reviewer was not ill-disposed towards the author but, rather, towards the Biblical subject matter: "The Old Testament is such an easy prey that we are surprised that so witty a writer as Mr. Pearsall Smith should waste his time in sniping at it." Parodying the style of Biblical commentary, says the reviewer, Pearsall Smith "glosses the crude text with those sentimental, 'psychological' explanations so dear to the heart of a certain class of religious writers. The result is a little dull" ("List" 653).

An unidentified *Times Literary Supplement* reviewer, who gives the book a more respectful column and a half, looks at it as an example of the "Humour of Anachronism." When anachronisms make us feel superior to an earlier age, the reviewer says, or when they show up our own age as inferior to a previous one, they can be funny. The "real fun," especially on stage in plays like Shaw's *Caesar and Cleopatra*, is when anachronisms show "men as alike always with the same trivialities, the same little undignified problems" ("New" 298). Although Pearsall Smith achieves some of that "real fun," and his method requires educated readers, the reviewer thinks he could have done more than the formula required: he might have made the stories "cumulative," linking them as indications of "the rationalizing process." To be "a little disappointed" ("New" 298), however, is not to dismiss the book.[7]

Logan Pearsall Smith was prepared to write his version of Old Testament stories by his own religious background. Born in America to Quaker parents, business people who became revivalist preachers and tract writers, Logan was converted at an early age and taken on a revivalist tour of England (Basu 242, Porter 4-6).[8] He lost his faith, but turned to literature and fine writing with equal zeal, as Virginia Woolf realized. He was prone, she notes, to quoting bits of Charles Lamb and Thomas Browne, having "several of these sentences always on his person, and read[ing] them aloud in a high nasal chant, which again suggested the priest, and the eunuch" (*L2* 359).[9]

Indeed, Pearsall Smith treats English literary texts far more reverently than traditionally sacred ones. In the case of the Old Testament stories, Porter thinks, Pearsall Smith "undercut[s] with irony and anachronism whatever passion and sweep there is in these ancient tales" (30). Yet his audience, Pearsall Smith says in his ironic and misleading introduction, is church-goers: Sunday School children, their teachers, and their parents. He acknowledges a debt to Biblical scholars, but names among them "A. Bugg and F. Pott." More seriously, he says he intends to introduce a "modern and psychological portrayal" of the "Old Testament worthies" (*Stories* 5). However light-hearted and sometimes heavy-handed, the emphasis on "moments of vision" of an individual consciousness, as in *Trivia*, must have caught Virginia Woolf's attention. Pearsall Smith sums up Joshua's making the sun and moon stand still, for example, as "a miracle of psychology and imagination, rather than [...] a so-called supernatural occurrence" (*Stories* 10). Similarly, Jonah's periodic "strange and sudden [prophetic] outbreaks" were possibly "mere phenomena of morbid psychology" (*Stories* 43-5). Two of the stories focus on David who, Pearsall Smith emphasizes in ways sympathetic to Bloomsbury, always emerges as poet and artist, aware, as he remembers the amazing day when he slew the giant Goliath (I Sam. 17:49), that "action in itself was nothing" compared to "states of consciousness" (*Stories* 13). When two she-bears tear apart forty-two children who have mocked the prophet Elisha's bald head (II Kings 2: 23-24), however, Pearsall Smith alludes to Freud's work by speculating too coyly that perhaps they had "little anti-baldness complexes in their little insides, Oedipus complexes, quite beyond their control, against bald fathers" (*Stories* 38-40).[10]

Stories from the Old Testament further departs from its sources by highlighting women's roles and perspectives. Pearsall Smith's recreation of the viewpoint of Michal, David's wife, is primarily an example of anachronistic writing. When she is curious about the Ark he wants returned to Jerusalem, she consults an encyclopedia, and reads not only "Ark," but also "Alkali, Arctic Exploration, Arbitration, and Arizona" as well as biographies from "Arius" to "William Archer." Michal, as the Old Testament does indicate (II Sam. 6: 16), is horrified to see that David, celebrating the return of the Ark, "had thrown off his royal garments, and was leaping and gyrating in public with practically nothing on but a pair of white spats!" (*Stories* 18-19). Contemporary Anglican clergymen, Pearsall Smith notes, denounce Michal for lack of "wifely sympathy," but these same clergymen make excuses for David as "an Oriental," and inconsistently excuse themselves from following his exuberant example (*Stories* 20-1).

The best instance of Pearsall Smith's focus on women, however, is his reinterpretation of Jezebel of I Kings as a blue-stockinged feminist. Even the *Times* reviewer thinks this apology for Jezebel is not only amusing but also serious and that Logan Pearsall Smith re-envisions her as "the only person we can admire in the story" ("New" 298). From "a cosmopolitan and highly-cultured society" at Tyre, where she served tea to "Plotinus and William James," conversed with Schliemann about his discoveries, with Renan about "Saint Paul and with Holman Hunt about Pre-Raphaelitism," and where she sang in a Bach choir, Pearsall Smith's Jezebel suddenly finds herself in "little provincial," boring

Samaria. What could she do, he asks, but get interested in the local religion with its picturesque "temples of the rustic Baals or fertility gods"? How could she not sympathize with the "kindly old clergymen" cast out by "a fanatical monotheistic cult"? It would be an "absurd anachronism," Pearsall Smith says (ironically scrutinizing his own method), to expect the "licence" of the old "fertility rites and vintage festivals" to have shocked her, even had she known about them (*Stories* 28-9). Finally, how could a "strong feminist" like Jezebel not be intrigued by a religion that included Astoreth, a goddess? Pearsall Smith admits that some of her acts were brutal, but certainly, he says, we can understand her making "away with a party of evangelical missionaries" who hated her, denounced her to her husband, and slaughtered the elderly clergymen she had befriended. What were her sins compared "to Elijah's record of bloodshed and unprovoked slaughter" and to the horrible "slaughter of Jezebel" herself by the Jahvists? One cannot help but wish, he concludes, "to revise that cruel verdict of history under which, for three thousand years, Jezebel has so unjustly suffered" (*Stories* 30-31).

On their positive side, then, stories like this one must have diverted both Woolfs, especially Virginia, with their playful psychology, learned references, and irreverent revisions. The Woolfs must have appreciated the humanizing treatment of Old Testament characters, not only women but also other minor ones like Ammiel whose little-known story concludes Pearsall Smith's book. Mentioned only once in the book of Numbers (13:12) as one of twelve spies sent ahead into the Promised Land to report back to Moses, Pearsall Smith's much embroidered Ammiel is a writer who reports his findings in a personal, but now fragmentary journal. The way Pearsall Smith cites this historical artifact, including Ammiel's complaints about his "wretched stylographic pen" (*Stories* 47), anticipates the biographer/narrator's elliptical quotations from surviving fragments of a diary and a letter in Chapter Three of Virginia Woolf's *Orlando* (126-29).

Pearsall Smith imagines that Ammiel and his fellow spies infiltrate Palestine disguised as "Cook's tourists," each wearing a "check suit of large pattern, the cork hat, the red hair and weeping whiskers of the English milord" (*Stories* 47). A guide shows them tourist sites, some of which Ammiel knows his people will invade and destroy. Feeling alienated from it all, he fears his costume actually is turning him into an English gentleman, contemptuous of the natives (*Stories* 52), an insight that anticipates Woolf's more complex questions about clothes and their relation to identity in *Orlando*. Do they "change our view of the world and the world's view of us," Orlando asks; do they define or reflect sexual differences, or do they mask androgyny? (*O* 187-89).

The Old Testament Ammiel is one of ten who died of plague for bringing back an "evil report upon the land" (Num. 14:37-8), a fact Pearsall Smith does not mention but one that may explain why *Stories from the Old Testament* ends with Ammiel pondering the state of his belief in the monotheistic "Omnipotence, [...] His whims and freaks and fancies, His frenzied megalomaniac boastings....' Here, and perhaps not too soon," Pearsall Smith writes, "the last of these fragments ends" (*Stories* 53). In his introduction, he may use the words "reverent," "sacred," and "hallowed" to describe his treatment of the Old Testament characters and events, but this ironic claim also turns out be a more serious acknowledgment that every individual, major or minor, male or female, has a unique and important point of view.

Virginia Woolf's deteriorating relationship, over the years, with Logan Pearsall Smith is documented in her diaries, in their letters to each other, and in various critical and biographical treatments.[11] Although, in retrospect, Leonard Woolf includes Pearsall Smith among "good writers" like "Virginia and the other authors whom we published during the first five years of the Hogarth Press" (*The Journey* 125), both Woolfs increasingly found his personal affectations and literary rituals off-putting (cf *Downhill* 99-100). Problems between Virginia and Logan surfaced in July 1924 over his response to her article "Character in Fiction." He agrees that "the whole tendency of the time [...is] the discovery and exploration of our consciousness," but does not agree that "we are [...] 'trembling on the verge of one of the great ages of English literature'" (*Chime* 20-21). Then, in 1925, Virginia rightly thought Logan criticized her for stooping to write, for money, articles for popular women's magazines like *Vogue*. Almost everyone who writes on Woolf and *Vogue* details their disagreement.[12] Jane Garrity argues well, however, that Woolf's contributions resist and "disrupt the magazine's overt valorization of mass-produced womanliness" (209).[13] Finally, in 1932, reports of Logan's mocking comments about Bloomsbury and Virginia's equally mocking remarks about Chelsea triggered a series of superficially conciliatory and ironic, but also tense and hurtful letters (*L5* 115, 118, 131, 133-4 and n.1; and *Chime* 61-64). The resulting social rift was never repaired (e.g. *D4* 145, 162).

Still, in 1932, Logan wrote to Virginia to compliment her on her *Common Reader: Second Series* essays and to circle back to his out-of-print *Stories from the Old Testament*. He would like to republish the stories because, he boasts ironically, "I find they have helped many to find salvation, and I have thus been carrying on my family trade of saving souls, and hope to wear these diamonds in my heavenly crown" (*Chime* 61). Already he has earned rubies, he teases, since his father once printed a tract called *How Little Logan Was Brought to Jesus* recounting his conversion "at the age of four." The tract was popular, he declares, and had "an especially powerful effect on the Red Indians of the West, who were quite unable to withstand it" (*Chime* 61). The Woolfs actually seem to have read this tract when Logan sent it, and Virginia responds in the ironic tone she usually uses with him. It is amusing, she claims, and "edifying in the extreme; and the portrait is delightful." If Logan would write an introduction, she'd even hand print it, she promises, "if only to carry on the work of conversion and find a shorter way to Heaven myself" (*L5* 131 and n. 1, 290 and n. 1). When the tract appeared elsewhere (*L5* 290 n. 1), Virginia put her initials in a copy and, writing to thank him, noted that she would put it "on my shelves in the hope, as you suggest, that I may profit by it" (*L5* 420).[14]

Logan Pearsall Smith's *Stories from the Old Testament* was not reprinted. It constitutes a small, curious chapter in the early history of the Hogarth Press. Once the Woolfs engaged more professionally with the world of letters and cultural debate, the later writers advertised in the "Religion" category adopted more serious tones and methods. Possibly, however, Virginia Woolf learned a lesson from the *TLS* reviewer's criticism of Logan's anachronisms as formulaic and lacking cumulative structure. In *Orlando*, she may show individuals of different historical periods "as alike always with the same trivialities, the same little undignified problems," as the reviewer says Logan does ("New" 298). Instead of proliferating anachronisms, however, she creates a single character whose life crosses centuries and transcends sexes, who piles one facet of her personality on top of another "as plates are piled on a waiter's hand" (*O* 308). Woolf retains the fun of playing with historical figures and texts. At the same time, she finds a way to create a much more complex and cumulative view of human psychology and personality than Pearsall Smith did in *Stories from the Old Testament.*

Notes

1   "'Woolfs' in Sheeps' Clothing: The Hogarth Press and 'Religion'" has been accepted for a collection of essays on the Hogarth Press edited by Helen Southworth.
2   I will refer to Logan Pearsall Smith, as Woolf herself does, as "Pearsall Smith," or "Logan."
3   These were followed by *More Trivia* in 1922, *Afterthoughts* in 1931, and an omnibus collection, *All Trivia*, in 1933 (Basu 242).
4   Edmund Wilson, in 1950, concluded that Pearsall Smith will be remembered for his reminiscences and for *Trivia* which, Wilson says, "is wistful with immortal longings, but it knows its best achievements are tiny" (105).
5   Logan reviewed Virginia's *Kew Gardens* positively in 1919 and praised *Jacob's Room* in 1922. While the Woolfs were producing *Stories from the Old Testament*, Virginia reviewed Logan's *A Treasury of English Prose* for the *Athenaeum*. She gives him high praise as "Anthologist Royal to the English-speaking races" (*E3* 171), but she casts her lot with novelists rather than the poets he favors (*E3* 175).
6   The other eight were Leonard and Virginia Woolf's *Two Stories* (1917), Katherine Mansfield's *Prelude* (1918), Virginia Woolf's *Kew Gardens* (1919), T. S. Eliot's *Poems* (1919), J. Middleton Murry's *Critic in Judgment* (1919), Hope Mirrlees' *Paris* (1919), E. M. Forster's *Story of the Siren* (1920), and Maxim Gorky's *Reminiscences of Tolstoi* (1920).
7   Knowing who reviewed for what periodicals, and reviewers themselves, the Woolfs may have detected more negativity.
8   There is evidence that Logan's parents' evangelical activities had a significant sexual component (Porter 5, 33 n. 39; *D3* 282).
9   Similarly, Wilson, who refers to Pearsall Smith's "devotion to" and "worship of" literature, says he "consecrated his life to writing" (100, 105).
10 Freud defined the "Oedipus complex" in the last of four essays published in *Totem and Taboo* which appeared in German in 1913 and in English translation in 1918.
11 See Porter for a good summary of their history and of these sources. Others see influences on Virginia Woolf's writing. Whitworth, for example, thinks Nick Green in *Orlando* echoes some of Pearsall Smith's theories of literature.
12 See, for example, Luckhurst, Garrity, and Brosnan.
13 When the Hogarth Press published Pearsall Smith's *The Prospects of Literature* in 1927, he returned to his arguments with Virginia Woolf. See especially 5, 10, and 14.
14 The pamphlet is no longer among the Woolfs' books at Washington State University.

Works Cited

Basu, Sayoni. "Smith, (Lloyd) Logan Pearsall." *Oxford Dictionary of National Biography.* Ed. H.C.G. Matthew and Brian Harrison. Oxford: Oxford UP, 2004. 241-43.
Brosnan, Leila. "'Whoring after Todd': *Vogue* and the Question of Value." *Reading Virginia Woolf's Essays and Journalism: Breaking the Surface of Silence.* Edinburgh UP, 1997. 49-58.
Garrity, Jane. "Virginia Woolf, Intellectual Harlotry, and 1920s British *Vogue.*" *Virginia Woolf in the Age of Mechanical Reproduction.* Ed. Pamela L. Caughie. New York: Garland, 2000. 185-218.
"List of New Books": *Stories from the Old Testament* by Logan Pearsall Smith. *The Athenaeum* (May 14, 1920): 653.
Luckhurst, Nicola. *Bloomsbury in Vogue.* London: Cecil Woolf, 1998. "New Books and Reprints." *Stories from the Old Testament* by Logan Pearsall Smith. *Times Literary Supplement* (13 May 1920): 298.
MacCarthy, Desmond. *Memories.* London: MacGibbon & Kee, 1953. 145-48.
Porter, David. *Virginia Woolf and Logan Pearsall Smith: 'an exquisitely flattering Duet'.* London: Cecil Woolf, 2002.
Smith, Logan Pearsall. *A Chime of Words: The Letters of Logan Pearsall Smith.* Ed. Edwin Tribble. New York: Ticknor & Fields, 1984.

—. *The Prospects of Literature*. Hogarth Essays, 2nd Series, no. 8. London: Hogarth Press, 1927.
—. *Stories from the Old Testament*. Richmond: The Hogarth Press, 1920.
Whitworth, Michael. "Logan Pearsall Smith and *Orlando. Review of English Studies* 55 (Sept. 2004): 598-604.
Wilson, Edmund. "Books: Virginia Woolf and Logan Pearsall Smith." *The New Yorker* 26 (May 27, 1950): 99-105.
Woolf, Leonard. *Beginning Again: An Autobiography of the Years 1911-1918*. New York: Harcourt Brace Jovanovich, 1963.
—. *Downhill All the Way: An Autobiography of the Years 1919 to 1939*. New York: Harcourt Brace Jovanovich, 1967.
—. *The Journey Not the Arrival Matters: An Autobiography of the Years 1939 to 1969*. New York: Harcourt Brace Jovanovich, 1969.
Woolf, Virginia. *Diary of Virginia Woolf*. Ed. Anne Olivier Bell. 5 vols. New York: Harcourt, Brace and Jovanovich, 1974-84.
—. *The Essays of Virginia Woolf*. Ed. Andrew McNeillie. 4 vols. London: Hogarth and San Diego: Harcourt Brace Jovanovich, 1986-94.
—. *Letters of Virginia Woolf*. Ed. Nigel Nicolson and Joanne Trautmann. 6 vols. New York: Harcourt Brace Jovanovich, 1975-80.
—. *Orlando: A Biography* (1928). New York: Harcourt Brace Jovanovich, 1956.

BRIGHT YOUNG EDITOR: JOHN LEHMANN AT THE HOGARTH PRESS

by Brenda S. Helt

In *Expert Modernists, Matricide, and Modern Culture*, Lois Cucullu points out the way Virginia Woolf transformed the feminine domestic space into a feminist professional one when, in 1917, the Woolfs installed their first hand-press in the drawing room at Hogarth House, Richmond. Equally remarkable about the Woolfs' attitude toward what soon became the "Hogarth Press," however, is that not only did they professionalize domesticity by installing a printing press in the drawing room—"that symbolic locus of middle-class domesticity" (Cucullu 31)—but when the Hogarth Press as a business outgrew the immediate confines of their home and required employees and its own professional space, Leonard especially continued to think of it in part as a domestic enterprise, almost a hobby. At the same time, however, he was proud of the Press's professional success and of his own business acumen. This schizophrenic attitude towards the Press is visible in Leonard's discussion of it in his autobiography, where he vacillates between denying having any interest in making Hogarth a successful business venture and boasting of its financial success:

> We never considered it in any way as a means of making a living. I had always treated it as a half-time, or, more strictly, quarter-time occupation and we deliberately fought against its expansion into a larger scale business. We were determined to publish only books which we thought worth publishing and our aim was to limit our list to a maximum of round about 20 new books a year. . . . The Hogarth Press was by 1935 a successful business financially. . . . my income from it was annually over £1,000. . . . but in fact Virginia and I did not need (or want) to make £1,000 a year by publishing. We made enough from writing to live the kind of life we wanted to live without bothering about money. We knew the kind of life we wanted to live and we would not have altered it however much money we might make. (*Journey* 98-99)

In *Bloomsbury Rooms*, Christopher Reed has documented this Bloomsburian modernist trend of merging the professional and the domestic in ways that re-imagined and transformed domesticity, constructing new forms of domestic tranquility that facilitated contemplation and creativity, intellectual and artistic interaction with others, and the physical labor of productivity—the painting of canvases, walls, fabrics, or storage boxes, or, in the case of the Woolfs, the writing, printing, publication, marketing, and distribution of books. These working arrangements that were also living arrangements fought against other modern trends: large-scale capitalist business trends, especially, as well as heteronormativity, lassitude, and what Leonard most feared for the Press, "mental sclerosis."[1] In the case of the Hogarth Press, though, the Woolfs' desire to keep it small "in house" and their desire to maintain the avant-garde professional reputation that made it a venue encouraging of new writing by young authors eventually became irreconcilably different goals. Nothing more clearly illustrates that fact than the unhappy dissolution of the eight year partnership between Leonard Woolf and John Lehmann in 1946, which immediately resulted in Leonard's sale of the Hogarth Press to Chatto and Windus.

❧

John Lehmann first came to the Press as a manager in 1931, through his friends at Cambridge, Julian Bell and George "Dadie" Rylands. As an undergraduate, Lehmann was a protégé of Rylands, who was by then a fellow at King's College. Rylands had worked briefly as manager at the Press in 1924, and in 1930 he introduced Lehmann's poetry to the Woolfs, who then published his first book of poems, *A Garden Revisited*, in 1931. Knowing that Lehmann wanted to break into publishing, both Dadie and Julian recommended him to Leonard, though both also warned John that Leonard was difficult to work for, Julian writing: "Leonard has had very little success as an employer . . . he's apt to lose his temper, and also to be rather interfering and overbearing, also obstinate and argumentative" (qtd. in Glendenning 262). Fairly warned, in 1931 John took a job as manager and partner-in-training at the Hogarth Press.

John Lehmann was bright, eager, hard-working, competent, and full of initiative. He had a profound gift for recognizing talented new work and encouraging it. Perhaps more importantly, he could also edit it. Though he stayed only eighteen months this first time before joining his friends Christopher Isherwood and Stephen Spender in Berlin and then in Vienna, during that short time he did much for the Press—not the least of which was to introduce to it the work of the two friends just named, and, through Isherwood, also the work of Auden. It was also during this first short stint that Lehmann brought the important anthology *New Signatures* to the Press. Edited by Michael Roberts and published in the spring of 1932 as a volume of the Hogarth Living Poets series for which Dorothy Wellesley was general editor, *New Signatures* is still considered by many to have initiated the thirties poetic movement whose most ardent members were referred to as the "Pylon School" or, more commonly and less accurately today, the "Auden Group." *New Signatures* contained a manifesto type preface by Michael Roberts, poems by Julian Bell, Cecil Day Lewis, and John Lehmann, all of whom had previously published with Hogarth, as well as poets new to the Press: Wystan Auden, Richard Eberhart, William Empson, William Plomer, Stephen Spender, and A.S.J. Tessimond.[2] It was continued in 1933 by a second anthology edited by Roberts titled *New Country*, again containing poems by Lehmann, Auden, Spender, Plomer, Day Lewis, and Tessimond, but now also containing poems by Richard Goodman, Charles Madge, Rex Warner, and Roberts himself, as well as essays and short stories by Isherwood, Day Lewis, Plomer, Roberts, John Hampson, Edward Upward, G.F. Brett, and T.O. Beachcroft. Many of these authors continued to publish with Hogarth for years to come and became major literary figures—most obviously: Auden, Spender, Plomer, Day Lewis, Isherwood, and Upward. The works collected in *New Signatures* and *New Country* were revolutionary-minded, anti-fascist, socialist, and communist.

Though Lehmann's difficulties working with Leonard Woolf have been given considerable attention by scholars, John's own accounts of his first experience at the Press primarily express the need of a young poet for life experience and the desire to play an active role in the dangerously exhilarating politics of the thirties. Daily structured office work was a problem for the upper-middle-class, Cambridge educated, would-be political revolutionary poet John was in his mid-twenties. And so, in 1932 he left for the Continent, and spent four years traveling, working as a journalist, and developing his poetry.

Lehmann returned to England in 1936, and with the help of Spender and Isherwood began to collect contributions for a project he called "New Writing," the various versions of which he is still perhaps best known for today. Similar in format to *New Country* and adhering to the tenets set forth in *New Signatures*, *New Writing* was a periodical in book format. Its contributors are remarkably international, a trend Lehmann continued in most of his anthologies and periodicals. The first three volumes of *New Writing* feature authors from England, Scotland, Poland, Germany, Spain, Austria, India, Trinidad, Russia, the Ukraine, France, Italy, and the U.S. From 1936 to 1939 it was published twice yearly in London by John Lane at The Bodley Head, and then by Lawrence and Wishart, and simultaneously published by Knopf in the States. By 1938, though, with the war looming and publishers wary about taking on new projects, Lehmann was looking for a new home for *New Writing*.

Meanwhile, the Woolfs were becoming frustrated with the Hogarth Press, which seemed to be acquiring a will of its own—becoming too successful, threatening the carefully controlled environment Virginia especially needed for her writing, and becoming too much work for both Leonard and Virginia. They again began to look for a full partner, or even for a buyout that would enable them to retain some control over publishing decisions and to continue to give priority to the publication of Virginia's work, while also maintaining the Press's reputation as a small and independent publisher. Further, they were concerned that Hogarth continue to attract and publish young authors with new ideas.3 It was therefore fortuitous that, having heard of the Woolfs' difficulties and imagining the Press as a stable home for New Writing, John Lehmann presented to Leonard the possibility that he, Stephen Spender, and Christopher Isherwood—"the young Brainies," Leonard and Virginia called the trio—might buy the Press. Leonard named the price: 6,000 pounds. In the end, his friends unable to raise the money, John bought Virginia's share for 3,000 pounds, and on April 1, 1938, at the age of thirty-one, he became full partner at the Hogarth Press. Leonard had his partner and John had a home for New Writing that put him in control of its publication—or so it seemed.

John's tenure at the Hogarth Press was predominantly a wartime one, and the importance of the war in posing and aggravating problems in the partnership that have often been blamed on one partner or the other cannot be overemphasized. The difficulties of maintaining production during the Blitz, especially, were enough to finish off many publishers, if the bombing itself hadn't already destroyed them—which it did, in many cases. Now housed in Mecklenburgh Square, the Hogarth Press too was badly damaged by bombing in 1940, and had to be moved to the suburbs, to Letchworth. What was hardest on the partnership, though, was the paper rationing.

The Ministry of Supply began rationing paper in 1940, restricting small presses like Hogarth to 40% of the paper they had used in 1939. It was fortunate, then, that Lehmann joined the Press in 1939, because he immediately expanded its list and production with his young thirties writers, and consequently the restrictions of the next year were not quite as damaging as they otherwise would have been. Nevertheless, keeping the Press solvent during the rationing was extremely difficult and stressful. It took all the ingenuity and business acumen both men possessed.

In 1940, the first year of the paper restrictions, much of the paper allotment went to Virginia Woolf's *Roger Fry*. A significant percentage also went to *Pack My Bag*, an autobiography by one of Lehmann's discoveries, Henry Yorke, who published under the pseudonym "Henry Green." Stephen Spender's only novel, *The Backward Son*, also took a sizeable share.4 Since there was not enough paper to continue to produce *New Writing* at its pre-war length, Lehmann devised a wartime compromise periodical, *Folios of New Writing*, which was half as long. He also introduced the New Hogarth Library series. These books were small, thin volumes—nineteen by twelve centimeter octavos, forty-five to sixty-five pages in length—and so were conservative of paper. They usually featured the work of a single poet and contained a combination of new and previously published poems. Poets published in the series included Vita Sackville-West, Cecil Day Lewis, William Plomer, Terence Tiller, Rainer Maria Rilke, new translations of Lorca and Rimbaud, Robert Graves, Laurie Lee, and John Lehmann himself. Their uniform size and limited production appealed to collectors, so they could be priced on the high end. "A small enough venture," Lehmann later said of the series, "but I think the aesthetic vitamin-content was high, and it gave me almost more pleasure than anything else the Press undertook during the war" (*I Am My Brother* 40).

Additionally, hoping greatly to expand readership of a large number of new authors, Lehmann contracted with Allen Lane at Penguin to publish much of the material already published in New Writing in a periodical that would be attractive to a much larger group of people. During the war, this meant each number had to be cheap, easy to carry, and had to appeal to many different types of readers. The resulting periodical was *The Penguin New Writing*. The issues were sized to fit in the pocket of a military uniform and contained a variety of genres and authors. They were produced as paperbacks, printed on low quality stock, and included advertisements. These were not meant to be collected, but bought by the masses, read and passed around, then disposed of or lost on the battlefield. So popular was *Penguin New Writing* that it outlasted the war: it was published from 1940 to 1950.

Early in 1942, Lehmann merged two of his periodicals, *Folios of New Writing* and *Daylight*, to form *New Writing and Daylight*, which Hogarth published from 1942 to 1946. Again it was paper supplies that prompted Lehmann's decision, which was a judicious one. By featuring mostly Eastern European authors, Lehmann had procured paper from a Czech source for *Daylight*. Merging the two periodicals enabled him to justify the use of this paper to publish not only Czech authors like Jiří Mucha and Egon Hostovsky, but also British ones: Edith Sitwell, Terence Tiller, Roy Fuller, Philip Toynbee, and, of course, himself and old friends like Stephen Spender.

During the war, Lehmann also saw numerous books through the Press. If reprints are included in the tally, Hogarth managed to publish an average of about thirty-five books a year from 1939 to 1946. After Virginia Woolf's death in 1941, it was Lehmann who was primarily responsible for the daily management of the Press as well as for acquisition and publishing decisions. Leonard lived primarily at Rodmell, though he drove up a few times a week, and consulted—or commandeered, depending on one's perspective—from a distance via phone and letter.

In 1946, it all became too much for Lehmann. He felt that if he was going to do the majority of the work, he should have full control over decisions, but after Virginia's death, Leonard had exercised his right to veto Lehmann's publication choice on more than one occasion. The partnership contract contained a stipulation that either partner might at any time dissolve the partnership by requesting a buyout. John issued an ultimatum, hoping Leonard would let him buy the Press. Disturbed by what he understood as Lehmann's plans for "expansion," Leonard instead bought out John by selling Hogarth to Chatto and Windus, retaining control over publishing decisions for the duration of his life.

༶

I have focused on Lehmann's periodicals here because it was through the various iterations of *New Writing* that Lehmann made his most concerted attempt to promote the new writers in whose work he believed. With production limited both by paper rationing and by the very premise upon which the Hogarth Press was founded—a premise one might term "modernist domestic professionalism"—Lehmann's use of periodicals to promote, encourage, and help financially to support such a large number of these writers during the war seems extraordinary.

From the beginning, John and Leonard had irreconcilably different goals with regards to the Press. Though both wanted to encourage new young authors, Leonard hoped to maintain Hogarth's small size and to continue to publish the staple authors who had established its reputation and whose steady-selling books kept it financially stable even during the war. Partnership negotiations between the Woolfs and Lehmann had established that publication priority would be given first to the work of Virginia Woolf, then to that of Freud, Sackville-West, and other Hogarth staple authors like Rilke.5 Though *New Writing* was also to be given priority, with its variable content it could be shortened more easily when paper supplies were rationed. As full partner, John, too, was invested highly in devising ways to keep the Press functioning and profitable during the war, so the decisions to alter *New Writing* were his as much as they were Leonard's.

If Lehmann wanted to expand somewhat to increase capital and production, as Leonard later alleged in his autobiography,6 his purpose in doing so was to publish more new authors and thereby to encourage them and to publicize their work—a goal the Woolfs also embraced. Leonard's attempts to keep the Hogarth Press small and domestic, while both maintaining the old guard and ushering in the vanguard at a time when the means of production were limited by uncontrollable outside forces, were self-contradictory and thus destined to fail. It seems clear, then, that the Press only survived the war because of John Lehmann's efforts and business acumen. The sale to Chatto and Windus may have been the end of the Hogarth Press as a domestic professional enterprise, but without John Lehmann there would have been nothing to sell.

Rather than understanding the outcome of the partnership in terms of a personal conflict between John and Leonard—an understanding that encourages unproductive scholarly side-takings—we need to think of the sale of Hogarth as the inevitable result of economic hardships necessitating new beady-eyed marketing strategies earlier forms of Bloomsburian domestic professionalism could not accommodate. The failure of the partnership, then, represented neither John's nor Leonard's personal failure, but a failure to re-imagine modernist domestic professionalism in the wake of World War II.

Notes

1. Woolf, *Downhill* 173.
2. For Lehmann's description of the importance of *New Signatures*, see Lehmann, *Thrown* 20; for Leonard Woolf's, see Woolf, *Downhill* 174-75.
3. See Woolf, *Downhill* 173-74.
4. For a detailed account of the Press's use of its paper stock the first year of the rationing, see Willis 350-51.
5. For Woolf's description of the contract negotiations, see Woolf, *Journey* 106-07.
6. Leonard Woolf's depiction of Lehmann's role in the dissolution of the Press is contained in the final volume of his autobiography, published in 1969, the year of his death. See Woolf, *Journey* 110-14.

Works Cited

Cucullu, Lois. *Expert Modernists, Matricide and Modern Culture: Woolf, Forster, Joyce*. New York: Palgrave Macmillan, 2004.

Glendinning, Victoria. *Leonard Woolf: A Biography*. New York: Free Press, 2006.

Lehmann, John. *I Am My Brother*. Reynal, 1960.

—. *Thrown to the Woolfs: Leonard and Virginia Woolf and the Hogarth Press*. New York: Holt, Rinehart, and Winston, 1979.

Reed, Christopher. B*loomsbury Rooms: Modernism, Subculture, and Domesticity*. New Haven, CT: Yale UP, 2004.

Willis, John H. *Leonard and Virginia Woolf as Publishers: The Hogarth Press, 1917-41*. Charlottesville: UP of Virginia, 1992.

Woolf, Leonard. *Downhill All the Way: An Autobiography of the Years 1919 to 1939*. San Diego: Harcourt Brace Jovanovich, 1967.

—. T*he Journey Not the Arrival Matters: An Autobiography of the Years 1939 to 1969*. San Diego: Harcourt Brace Jovanovich, 1969.

VIRGINIA STEPHEN, BOOK REVIEWER:
OR, THE APPRENTICE AND HER EDITORS

by Beth Rigel Daugherty

In a talk to the Workers' Education Association in 1940, Virginia Woolf notes that although often ignored, a writer's education must "play a very important part in a writer's work" ("LT" 168-69). She did not have the university education the "leaning tower" generation did, writers of her generation had nothing like the apprenticeship current student writers have, and available how-to books focused more on the marketplace than on writing instruction. Virginia Stephen also had neither the individual attention nor the communal experience her sister Vanessa had at the Slade. No wonder that in "Reviewing," Woolf wished reviewers could hold hour-long conferences with writers ("R" 211-13)—Virginia *Stephen* had yearned for instruction, attention, feedback. As she writes to Madge Vaughan in June 1906, "I have had so very little criticism upon my work that I really don't know what kind of impression I make" (*L1* 227).

Virginia Stephen began her solitary apprenticeship in 1904-05.[1] At first, she sought comments from friends, but she soon "determine[d] to invite no more [criticism from them] than is absolutely necessary. I shall send things straight to the editors, whose criticism is important" (*PA* 232). Editors taught her specific "how-to's." Editors taught her the "knack of writing for newspapers" (*L1* 155) as she published almost all her apprenticeship reviews and essays in seven different papers: the *Guardian, National Review, Academy and Literature, Speaker, Cornhill, Nation,* and *Times Literary Supplement,* which had audiences ranging from narrow and clearly defined to broad and more open, and included two monthlies and five weeklies; one religious, one general, three political, and two literary; and four small, two medium, and one large in circulation. Although Leila Brosnan implies it was unfortunate that Virginia Stephen "[spoke] in the voice required and often demanded by the editorial policy of the relevant journal" (61), editors also taught Stephen to adapt her writing to multiple audiences, a skill that fueled *Woolf's* creation of a common reader.

Virginia Stephen writes to Violet Dickinson that she can't conceive how the *Guardian*, a High Anglican Church weekly newspaper, "ever got such a black little goat into their fold" (*L1* 178). Its object was to "[establish] in the public mind a clear view of the ground taken by the High Church party on matters religious and political" (*NPD* 1904: 78), and it devoted space to education, social reform, and the arts, including book reviews. Its large pages were filled with news and commentary about political events related to the church, reprints of church official lectures, and articles on social issues from a moral point of view. The majority of *Guardian* readers were members of the Church of England and many were clergy. It's "difficult to imagine," Andrew McNeillie says, "a more unlikely outlet" for the writer who would become Virginia Woolf (xii).

Yet she published 41 reviews and essays there, and it provided a fitting launching pad for Stephen's professional career because she wrote for the *women's* supplement, edited by Mrs. Arthur Lyttelton. Though religious, Mrs. Lyttelton was also "a considerable student of literature" who "devoted much of her life to fighting for the improvement of women's lives" and "for the extension of suffrage" (Kelly). The seven pages of Mrs. Lyttelton's Supplement, three of which were ads, came at the end of each week's issue and were filled with reports and commentary about women's social and political activism. The supplement gave space to girls' education, women's work, both charitable and paid, and suffrage, and included regular columns for literature, music, art, and correspondence. Virginia Stephen may have described her readers as "a Governess, and maiden Lady, and high church Parson mixed" (*L1* 178), but as S. P. Rosenbaum notes, she could assume a readership of active women (158-59).

The *National Review* might seem a more likely outlet for Stephen's early work given her father's contributions to it, but she published only once there. If the *Guardian*'s women's pages provided her with a female context and audience, the *National Review* was a male preserve, with primarily male contributors and a bellicose tone. Under Leo Maxse, the monthly 160-to-200-page journal published little on literature and much on its Conservative and Imperialist politics. It was lively: "sometimes hated and not seldom feared," no one "called it either dull or mediocre" (Dailey and Dailey). Maxse's provocative commentary on current events at home and abroad meant it was read by politicians outside the Tory Party, but most of its readership was "affluent West End," and "it made no attempt to reach a mass audience" (Hutcheson 36-37).

Virginia Stephen's "Street Music," an essay about vagrant musicians' contributions to art seems out of place between "Man-Power as a Measure of National and Imperial Strength" and "The Industrial Condition of the Country." *National Review* readers had probably demanded the regulation for London squares she starts her essay with—"'Street musicians are counted a nuisance'" (*E1* 27)—and one suspects they did not want to be bothered by art of any kind, let alone that practiced by the homeless.

If the *Guardian* provided Virginia Stephen with her first women readers, *Academy and Literature* provided her with her first literary ones. Once "the liveliest literary journal in England" (Kent 4), its editors kept changing between 1903 and 1914. Between 1905 and 1907, it was co-edited by Peter Anderson Graham and Harold H. Child, and Child tried to regain the weekly paper's former dignity (Roll-Hansen 218-19). Although Stephen had "more space and time" for the four pieces she placed there, Rosenbaum suggests that Child "typecast her as the reviewer of books about notable women of the past" (173).

The *Speaker* was a Liberal weekly, the opposite of the *National Review*. Edited by John L. Hammond, the 24- to 28-page paper was devoted to "politics, literature, science, art, and finance" (*NPD* 74). Whereas Maxse lauded imperialism, Hammond critiqued it. Whereas the *National Review* seems narrow because of Maxse's obsession with right wing politics, the *Speaker* seems broad because literature and art are not alien and more writers contribute differing opinions: it ranged freely over many topics and generated passionate correspondence about militarism in boys' schools, lynching in the U.S., suffrage, and higher education for working people, for example. "San Francisco is in flames"(45) begins the editorial commentary on the events of the day in the April 21, 1906 issue that contains Stephen's "Poets' Letters."

Arthur Clutton-Brock was the *Speaker*'s literary editor from 1904-1906, and Stephen contributed three reviews in 1906. Clutton-Brock left to become an art critic for the

TLS and *TES*, where he addressed the general topics in books, "[read] authors from their works," included "general speculation of a more personal nature," and invited the reader's participation (Blank 71-2).

The *Cornhill* had the closest associations with her father since Leslie Stephen had edited it, and it had been the "premier fiction-carrying magazine of the [19th] century" (Sutherland 150). It clung to "remembrances of past glories" (Schmidt), continuing to serialize two novels an issue long after most magazines had discontinued the practice. It advertised itself as being "full of good reading from beginning to end" (*NPD* 553), but in 1908, when Virginia Stephen and Nelly Cecil alternated to produce twelve reviews for the "Book on the Table" series, it seemed confused about its identity: inconsistent format, headings not indicating fiction or nonfiction, and few regular columns.

Reginald Smith (George Smith's son-in-law) may have confused Virginia Stephen with her father, assigning her memoirs and biographies rather than the literature she wanted (Curtis 149; *L1* 327). Known as a conscientious and considerate editor (Schmidt), he could also be rigid in his assignments, meticulous in his instructions (*L1* 327), and infuriating in his editing (*L1* 332).

The *Nation* (that became the *Nation and Athenaeum* in England) supplanted the *Speaker* as the liberal weekly in 1907, and until 1921, the more radical H. W. Massingham edited a "livelier, more comprehensive, and much more controversial" publication than "its predecessor or most of its contemporaries" (Morris). He allowed argument across the spectrum of liberal opinion and also served literature well by "open[ing] up the columns of the *Nation*" to "celebrated men of letters [. . .], those not so successful [. . .], and the young aspiring to fame" (Havighurst 174). Henry W. Nevinson "dominated the literary side of the *Nation* in its first years" (149) and may have been the literary editor (148-49). Stephen contributed one review in 1911.

When Virginia Stephen submitted her first review to the *Times Literary Supplement* in March 1905, it was still relatively new, having begun in 1902 on the cusp between the 19th century reviews and the 20th century little magazines. *TLS* gave Stephen a larger audience, exceeding the daily circulation of the *Times* for awhile (Child, *TLS* 33). The first issue set the tone: "literature was for keen general readers, not for specialists," and the role of *TLS* was to be "an educated reader" helping other readers find the "books [. . .] most worth reading" (May 11). The paper assumed its readers were interested in both new literature and the literary tradition, and its lack of editorial commentary and book trade gossip communicated respect for writers *and* readers. Too, *TLS* had a stable editor in Bruce Richmond, whose tenure lasted 35 years. As T. S. Eliot would write in 1961, Richmond "was a great editor" (17).

Mrs. Lyttelton, of the *Guardian*, taught Virginia Stephen the importance of length requirements. When her editor asked her to cut a third to a half of her review of Henry James' *The Golden Bowl*, Stephen was angry, blaming "the worthy Patronesses" who "want to read about midwives" in her diary (*PA* 237). But she neglects to mention that her assignment, also written down in her diary, was to boil 550 pages of "Henry James print" into "7 or 800 words" (*PA* 234-35), the exact length of the review we now have, the result of her "cut[ting] two sheets to pieces, [writing] a scrawl to mend them together, and . . . sen[ding] the maimed thing off" (*L1* 178). What she "forgets" in her diary, though, she learns in her professional life. As she confides about a later review, "I hadn't much difficulty [. . .]—not that I over flowed my limit. I shant waste words again!" (*PA* 251). Noting that a typewritten foolscap sheet has approximately 450 words (*PA* 277), she would be conscious of word count averages the rest of her life.

Visits from Mrs. Lyttelton in mid-December 1904 and January 1905 may also have contributed to the great strides Virginia Stephen made between her second and sixth reviews. Her review of *Son of Royal Langbrith* has all the marks of a novice: one very long paragraph, three-fourths of it plot summary; three sentences in a row with the verb "is;" a vague "this;" unclear referents; and a "needless to say" (*E1* 3-5). But in her review of *The Feminine Note in Fiction*, she evaluates from the start and confidently goes beyond the book's content to define what readers want from critics (*E1* 15-17).

From Leo Maxse at the *National Review*, Virginia Stephen learned it is fatal to misread your audience. Two years after he published "Street Music," Leo was "constantly trying to think of subjects that would be likely to appeal to you" (*L1* 309), but he never did. Perhaps equating street musicians with Beethoven had not appealed to his readers?

Under Harold Child at *Academy & Literature*, Virginia Stephen experienced severe pruning. Her "A Plague of Essays" would have arrived in the *Academy* offices just as Child was making the changes he would formalize in a manifesto three weeks later. In it, he bemoans journalism's decay, decries American "slang and colloquial expressions," and criticizes writers who are "as personal and egotistical as . . . possible" (225). He concludes by contrasting the old style with the new journalism and again uses the word "decay" (225). His desire to reform the *Academy* may be why Child changed Stephen's title to "The Decay of Essay Writing," cut it in half, and added and altered words without consulting her (*L1* 181; *PA* 243). Because the draft has not survived, we cannot know how he edited it, but what remains suggests he transformed "tongue-in-cheek" criticism of the genre into serious comments about decay. Mrs. Lyttelton became "really angelic in comparison" (*L1* 181), as Stephen learned that if cuts must be made, it's better to make them yourself.

At the *Speaker*, Virginia Stephen's reviews indicate she may have learned some of Clutton-Brock's aesthetic principles: critics should 1) be judged first as writers, 2) provoke thought, not suppress it, and 3) enrich readers' experience by "expressing [their] own" (Blank 72). His assignments also allowed Stephen to try out aesthetic ideas; all her *Speaker* essays evolved into longer, more well-thought-out pieces.

In Reginald Smith, Virginia Stephen met a controlling editor who may have seen her only as her father's daughter. However, her work for Smith (and the work he rejected) may have made her realize she must break with the past. Too, Smith gave her ample space, so she began to use reviews as an excuse to blend the subject's biography, the era's history and culture, and the work's content in essays that barely mention the work's author.

Giving Stephen a book about the post-impressionists, to review the *Nation* allowed her to formulate ideas about art a year after critics had savaged the London exhibit at the Grafton Gallery. Praising C. Lewis Hind's ability to reconcile the conventional with the new and his suggestions about point of view (*E1*: 379), she begins to define her own modernism.

Finally, in Bruce Richmond and the *TLS*, Virginia Stephen had steady work and time to improve. From Richmond, she learned what Eliot called "the discipline of anonymity" (*TLS* 3072: 1) and "a lot of my craft [. . .]: how to compress; how to enliven; & also was made to read with a pen & notebook, seriously" (*D5* 145). He pelted her with 51 popular novels between 1905 and 1907 (*PA* 252), but when she protested she did not want to do current fiction any more (*L1* 331), he began assigning her new editions of canonical authors such as Sidney or Sheridan. By the time he gave Stephen her first *TLS* "lead review" on Laurence Sterne in 1909, she was ready.

Virginia Stephen thus learned to meet length requirements, use summary sparingly, think carefully about her audience, take control of editorial changes, state her aesthetic values, move beyond the work to consider biographical and cultural issues, refuse to compromise her integrity, and work with an editor. Most important, she learned to adapt to different audiences while maintaining her own views, persona, and voice.

Writing for the *Guardian*'s women, she quarrels with W. L. Courtney's assertion that because more novels are written by women for women, the novel as a work of art is disappearing. Yes, "women [have] found their voices," but to link *that* to a decline is "more doubtful" (*E1* 16). She misjudges her *National Review* audience, but targets her *Academy* readers well when she defines the essay, refers to Montaigne, and humorously equates improved "manual dexterity with a pen" with the proliferation of essays (*E1* 26) . "Trafficks and Discoveries," a review of *The English Voyages of the Sixteenth Century* for the anti-imperialist *Speaker*, focuses on the concealed poetry in the sailors' lists and quotes Walter Raleigh's description of the age as "'a carnival of plunder'" (*E1* 121-22). Writing about Louise de La Vallière, she wonders whether *Cornhill*'s prudish readers will allow her to "call a prostitute a prostitute, or a mistress a mistress" (*L1* 343). Stephen uses *neither* word, but leaves readers in no doubt about de La Vallière's relationship to Louis the XIV *and* makes us sympathize with her. Stephen counts on the *Nation*'s debate-oriented readers to appreciate her argument about the impact of point of view on what is seen (*E1* 380). Betting that *TLS* readers cared about how Thackeray and Dickens live "in our brains," she suggests in "Literary Geography" that books that say "great men were once alive because they lived in this house or in that" have little reason for being (*E1* 35).

Admittedly, in moving from reading notes to reviews, Virginia Stephen sometimes softened harsh responses. But rather than attribute such a move *just* to her "tea table training" ("Sketch" 150), we might also credit "distrusting the critical attitude of mind" (*L1* 167) and learning professional respect. The reader never mistakes her opinion. Certainly, she occasionally reacted with justifiable anger to being "tamed" (*L1* 295), "improved" morally (*L1* 214), or cut (*L1* 332). But given the 160 pieces Stephen produced during her essay apprenticeship, if the editing changes she records in her diaries and letters are the only ones that caused her ire, we might also acknowledge that her work was rarely tampered with—she did well for a novice. Yes, she learned to shape her work for editors, for a marketplace, for readers. But some of her editors' suggestions and changes are surely part of any learning process and not an attempt to silence her. To define learning to consider one's audience as *only* repression or oppression rather than the normal course of events for a young writer overstates the case and denies what we teach in classrooms every day. Virginia Stephen's reviewing practices and her relationships with editors reveal a fairly typical arc for a young person learning to negotiate between the approval of the reader/teacher/editor and the integrity of one's self/ideas/voice. Her editors collectively taught her to imagine different readers, to shift according to publication and audience, to aim *beyond* a coterie. Thus, when Virginia Woolf later positioned herself as a common reader, an amateur writing for other amateurs, she did so both as a deeply felt response to her lack of education and the insecurity that lack engendered *and* as a strategic move designed to invite a variety of readers into the conversation. She had learned her lessons well.

Note

1. In my book manuscript, *The Education of a Woman Writer: Virginia Woolf's Apprenticeship*, I divide Virginia Stephen's struggle to educate herself into three roughly chronological learning periods: her homeschooling, which lasted from her childhood through 1904; her teaching at Morley College, from 1905 to 1907; and her nonfiction writing apprenticeship, which began in 1904 and ended in 1912 when she became Virginia Woolf. I argue that Virginia Stephen's education shaped Virginia Woolf into an essayist who taught and believed that "literature is no one's private ground; literature is common ground ("LT" 181).

Works Cited

Blank, G. K. "Arthur Clutton-Brock." *Modern British Essayists, First Series*. Ed. Robert Beum. Vol. 98. Detroit: Gale, 1990. 69-72.
Brosnan, Leila. *Reading Virginia Woolf's Essays and Journalism*. Edinburgh: Edinburgh UP, 1997.
Child, Harold. "The Literary Week." *The Academy: A Weekly Review of Literature, Science & Art* 11 March 1905: 225-226.
—. "The Times Literary Supplement: A Record of its Beginnings." *Times Literary Supplement* 18 January 1952: 33-39.
Curtis, Anthony. *Lit Ed: On Reviewing and Reviewers*. Manchester: Carcanet, 1998.
Dailey, Kazuko and Harold E. Dailey. "*The National Review*, 1883-1900." *The Wellesley Index to Victorian Periodicals, 1824-1900*. Ed. Walter E. Houghton. Vol. II. Toronto: U of Toronto P, 1972. 529-35.
Eliot, T. S. "Bruce Lyttelton Richmond." *Times Literary Supplement* (13 January 1961): 17.
Havighurst, Alfred F. *Radical Journalist: H. W. Massingham*. Cambridge: Cambridge UP, 1974.
Hutcheson, John A., Jr. *Leopold Maxse and the National Review, 1893-1914*. New York: Garland, 1989.
Huxley, Leonard. "Smith, Reginald John (1857-1916)." Rev. Barbara Quinn Schmidt. *Oxford Dictionary of National Biography*. Ed. H. C. G. Matthew and Brian Harrison. Oxford: Oxford University Press, 2004. Online ed. Ed. Lawrence Goldman. 27 Sept. 2007 <http://www.oxforddnb.com/view/article/36154>.
Kelly, Serena. "Lyttelton [*née* Clive], Mary Kathleen (1856-1907)." *Oxford Dictionary of National Biography*. Ed. H. C. G. Matthew and Brian Harrison. Oxford: Oxford UP, 2004. 22 Sept. 2007 <http://www.oxforddnb.com/view/article/50712>.
Kent, Christopher. "Introduction." *British Literary Magazines: The Victorian and Edwardian Age, 1837-1913*. Ed. Alvin Sullivan. Westport, CT: Greenwood Press, 1984. xii-xxvi.
May, Derwent. *Critical Times: The History of the Times Literary Supplement*. London: HarperCollins, 2001.
McNeillie, Andrew. "Introduction." *The Essays of Virginia Woolf*. Ed. Andrew McNeillie. Vol. 1, 1904-1912. San Diego: Harcourt, 1986. ix-xviii.
Nevinson, H. W. "Massingham, Henry William (1860-1924)." Rev. A. J. A. Morris. *Oxford Dictionary of National Biography*. Ed. H. C. G. Matthew and Brian Harrison. Oxford: Oxford University Press, 2004. Online ed. Ed. Lawrence Goldman. 19 Dec. 2007 <http://www.oxforddnb.com/view/article/34923>.
Newspaper Press Directory. London: C. Mitchell & Co., 1904-1907. *NPD*
Roll-Hansen, Diderik. *The Academy: 1869-1879, Victorian Intellectuals in Revolt*. Copenhagen: Rosenkilde and Bagger, 1957.
Rosenbaum, S. P. *Edwardian Bloomsbury: The Early Literary History of the Bloomsbury Group*, Vol. 2. New York: St. Martin's, 1994.
Sutherland, John. *The Longman Companion to Victorian Fiction*. Stanford: Stanford UP, 1989.
Woolf, Virginia. *The Diary of Virginia Woolf*. Ed. Anne Olivier Bell and Andrew McNeillie. Vol. 5. New York: Harcourt, 1984.
—. *The Essays of Virginia Woolf*. Ed. Andrew McNeillie. Vol. 1. San Diego: Harcourt, 1986.
—. "The Leaning Tower." *Collected Essays*. Ed. Leonard Woolf. Vol. 2. New York: Harcourt, 1967. 162-81. "LT"
—. *The Letters of Virginia Woolf*. Ed. Nigel Nicolson and Joanne Trautmann. Vol. 1. New York: Harcourt, 1975.

—. *A Passionate Apprentice: The Early Journals 1897-1909*. Ed. Mitchell A. Leaska. San Diego: Harcourt, 1990.
—. "Reviewing." *Collected Essays*. Ed. Leonard Woolf. Vol. 2. New York: Harcourt, 1967. 204-17. "R"
—. "A Sketch of the Past." *Moments of Being*. 2nd ed. Ed. Jeanne Schulkind. San Diego: Harcourt, 1985. 61-159.

Virginia Woolf within Italian Literary Periodicals under Fascism

by Elisa Bolchi

The years between 1930 and 1945 were difficult and yet fundamental for the Italian nation. It was in this period that Fascism gained power, becoming the dictatorship that all the world came to know. But, as often happens under dictatorships or among revolutions, these were also extremely lively years for Italian culture. One of the places where culture was not only discussed and examined, but *made*, was in periodicals. It was among cultural and literary periodicals that intellectuals were able to meet and discuss, sometimes even expressing ideas which were opposite to those of the regime. Cultural and literary periodicals became so influential in Italian culture that some critics described the twentieth century as "the Century of Periodicals" (Langella 4). In a country that was closing its barriers in search of strong nationalism, it was inside those periodicals that culture could find its place, that Italian intellectuals could exchange their knowledge and so remain in contact with foreign countries and, when the war broke out, sometimes even with enemies' countries, as was the case with the United Kingdom.

It was therefore most interesting to discover whether an Italian literary criticism existed under Fascism, not only for a writer who came from a foreign and enemy country, but for a female writer: a woman who was a critic, a writer, and also a feminist who, thanks to literary periodicals, Italians could read and discover before her novels were translated into Italian and published.

Even if the subject is of the utmost interest, and even if we are used to thinking that everything has already been written about Virginia Woolf, I could find no existing works examining the presence of the English writer within Italian literary periodicals. That is how I decided to create a kind of "Critical Heritage" of Italian literary criticism on Virginia Woolf, like the one already existing edited by Majumdar for Routledge, and so I collected the entire corpus of articles that appeared within Italian literary periodicals from 1927 (the year the first article on Virginia Woolf appeared in an Italian periodical) up to 1945, and then published them in a volume with the title *Il paese della bellezza* (*The Country of Beauty*). 1945 was in fact a crucial year in Italian history as it marked the end of the Second World War, the end of Mussolini's dictatorship, and the beginning of the Republic.

At the end of my research I found and collected 34 articles about Virginia Woolf and eight translations from her novels or essays. The periodicals where these articles appeared were among the most interesting and influential: it is enough to mention that the very first article appeared in a cultural supplement of the *Corriere della sera*, the main Italian newspaper, written by Carlo Linati, one of the main Italian literary critics, translator and also friend of James Joyce.[1] Moreover, most of the articles were written by important intellectuals such as Alberto Moravia and Sibilla Aleramo, two of the main Italian writers of the 20th century, Moravia was shortlisted for the Nobel Prize more than once, or important critics such as the already mentioned Carlo Linati or Carlo Bo.

In analyzing Virginia Woolf's works, Italian critics mainly concentrated on three aspects: her prose style, her concept of time and the psychological analysis of her characters. It was, however, her prose style that startled the critic from her "arrival" in Italy, and in fact the first words dedicated to her by an Italian critic are about her prose: Linati, in the already mentioned article, says that her prose "is a delicate, original and most effective instrument of expression" (3). And he goes on to use words such as "flexibility," "modulation," "richness of tones"—a lexicon more suitable to music than to prose—but he also uses words closer to art, speaking about "chiaroscuro" or "colours" of her writing.

This attention to her style is quite significant considering how important the form of her prose was to Virginia herself. It did not simply have to do with style or technique, but with a real quest for the perfect embodiment of the thoughts of the mind. It was probably her friend Roger Fry who taught her the importance of form, and she became obsessed by this quest, by this necessity to give a form to the experience of life through language, which was her instrument. Italian critics understood this quest very well, perceiving how her prose had characteristics quite different from the prose to which they were accustomed. Alessandra Scalero, the Italian translator of *Orlando, Flush* and *Mrs Dalloway*, wrote for example that *The Waves* cannot even be called a novel (512). And in fact it is from *The Waves* that Virginia feels to have found her own style, as she writes in her Diary: "this is the first work in my own style . . . the furthest development so far" (*AWD* 171) because she understands that with this book she finally found the form for which she had been looking.

To describe Woolf's new and complicated prose, which does not even resemble a traditional novel any longer, the adjectives specific to narrative prose and literature were no longer enough and Italian critics borrowed adjectives from other arts: music, poetry, and painting. What Italian critics mostly appreciate is the "sound" of her voice, and they understand from the very beginning the music of her prose. *Mrs Dalloway* will be described by Umberto Morra as a novel entirely dedicated to rhythm (*Il nuovo romanzo inglese* 40), Linati describes her prose as a "refined music" (*Virginia Woolf. A Room* 175) and Guglielmo Serafini, another critic, will say that her novel is a "wide symphony of the great city" (11). The word symphony will be used more than once, particularly for novels such as *To the Lighthouse* or *The Waves*. Augusto Guidi will write that in "*To the Lighthouse*, which is the most perfect of her works, the narration is arranged in three long chapters which are the three movements of a symphony" (120). And it is this rhythm that takes her closer and closer to poetry.

Poetry, in fact, is not only characterized by the verse form, but also by its rhythm, its sounds, and by rhetorical and stylistic proceedings such as those used by Virginia Woolf. Salvatore Rosati defines her prose as characterized by "rhythms, assonances, rhymes and alliterations" ("Virginia Woolf-Aldous Huxley" 638), all devices more typical of poetry than of prose. He will also understand how, "from the first novels, closer to narrative, she gets, with *To the Lighthouse*, to an intense lyricism and often to poetry. Once arrived at this stage Virginia Woolf . . . writes the poem of poetry: *Orlando*" and he will add that "those who are trying to narrate with the seriousness and the courage that we must acknowledge to Virginia Woolf, find themselves inevitably led to poetry" (638).

Italian critics finally associate the prose of Virginia Woolf with painting. We find a reference to painting from the very first article that appeared in Italy, where Carlo Linati asks himself if Woolf is an impressionist as many English critics had already called her (c.f.

Majumdar). He answers that it is true that there is a picturesque style in her writing, but this picturesque does not steal reality and life from her writing. Other critics, such as Umberto Morra, will also say that in her novels Woolf moves from the picturesque to painting.

There was also another element that interested and fascinated the critics: Woolf's representation of time. Italian critics described her novels as "governed" by time, and Morra, in an important periodical like *Solaria*, explains how she uses time as a frame inside which she places her work. Alessandra Scalero, in reviewing *The Waves*, says that time should be considered a *"leitmotiv"* of the novel (513). However, critics will soon understand how time, in Woolf's novels, is not only a frame or a *leitmotiv*, but a dominant element in her works, so important as to become, as Morra will say, "the rhythm of her prose" (*Il nuovo romanzo inglese* 35).

As we know, Woolf's time is a "relative" one, influenced by Einstein's recent theories of relativity and, even if Mrs. Woolf said she had never read Bergson, at least I would say that she is influenced by his same common feelings about time. Alberto Moravia, himself a novelist, noticed this ability of Virginia Woolf to widen and shorten time during the narration according to her necessities, a procedure noticed also by other critics, such as Ugo Dettore, who said that time is "the most elusive of Woolf's protagonists," the one she studies "more deeply and more obstinately" (7). But it is Salvatore Rosati who best understands Woolf's treatment of time. In an article that appeared in 1945 he writes:

> One of the most interesting characteristics of her best novels, and no doubt one of the greatest achievements of the novelist, is to be seen in the fact that, even though the representation of the continuous stream of consciousness acts as an atomizer of the characters' individuality and of the narrative texture, she is nonetheless able to obtain a poetic unit . . . This unit is obtained thanks to the coincidence of characters' time (its inward duration) with narration time. (8)

And speaking of characters' inward time one is led to speak of Woolf's "psychologism." I have already mentioned Bergson and his influences on Woolf's work; about these influences it is interesting to read what Carlo Bo wrote in 1933:

> Woolf's world is the kingdom of souls . . . Virginia Woolf often managed to let us feel what Bergson calls "la mélodie interrompue de notre vie interieure."
> And . . . as I was writing Bergson I was thinking about how much the writer of *To the Lighthouse* owes him indirectly. She confessed she has never read the French philosopher, but Bergsonian ideas have so impregnated our literature, and above all novels, that it must have been quite impossible for her not to be influenced by them. In fact, isn't she very close to the two novels of the *durée*, that is, to Proust and to Joyce? (14)

So, from the beginning, she is associated with Joyce and Proust, above all with what concerns the psychological aspects and the inward analysis of the characters. Both Joyce and Proust were already very popular when the name of Virginia Woolf officially appeared in Italy in 1927. But these parallels, these associations, were mostly made by Italian critics to show how her style was more accurate, how the measure of her novels surpassed that of her more popular colleagues. In his article about *Mrs Dalloway* in the *Corriere della sera* Linati writes that "it is perhaps Joyce's method that she uses in these introspective pages of visions and of interior monologue, but with so much more chastity and measure!" (3) Alberto Consiglio in *L'Italia letteraria* will even write that

> Getting a feeling of perfect balance between Proust's psychologism and Joyce's *Ulysses* desperate experiments could be, in European literature, nowadays, the best ideal . . . The novelist Virginia Woolf could claim for some of her latest works the merit to have realized this ideal of balance. (6)

Once again, it will be Salvatore Rosati, in an article which appeared in 1933 in the *Nuova Antologia*, to deny this derivation from Joyce, Proust and Bergson, saying that:

> It was enough that Woolf worried, in a first moment, about the relationships between psychology and art to mention Proust. It was enough that she conceived psychological life as a never ending series of juxtaposed moments, replacing the concept of unit with that of continuity and of relative value of time in human spirit, to mention her strict derivations from Bergson's theory of continuity in mobility and from his notion of duration of time. One cannot deny that these similarities exist, but they are fortuitous, based on spiritual and intellectual trends which are the distinctive mark of our time and that can, therefore, be easily found in any other artist that today occupies a so called eminent position. This fortuitous analogy seems to exist also in the often mentioned imitation of Joyce by Woolf, above all in her novel *Mrs Dalloway*, which is about a day in the life of the protagonist, as well as *Ulysses* tells about a day in the life of Mr. Bloom. (637)

From this passage, it is clear that Rosati understood the path Virginia Woolf had undertaken, a personal path, which had the same assumptions and the same reflections and inspirations as her colleagues, but which she developed in a very personal and original work. After 1933, in fact, no critic ever spoke again about Woolf in comparison with Joyce or Proust but simply related her to herself, to her own personal discoveries.

Italian critics also have another merit: that of having understood how the lack of an exterior picture of characters in her novels did not mean that Woolf was unable to create characters. This was, as we know, the famous accusation from Arnold Bennett, to whom Virginia Woolf answered with her essay "Mr Bennett and Mrs Brown." Italian critics, on the contrary, understood from the beginning how the picture of characters in her works is made from the inside, and not the outside. They understood how she describes the inward states of characters, and not the outward. Rosati is once again the one who best realizes it, understanding how the novelist had been working on this process of inward investigation since her very first works, improving it novel after novel. The critic says that inside Woolf's works "psychological life is made by a sequence of mental facts" and that "a character consists in the continuous passage of these sequences through a conscience" ("Virginia Woolf and Aldous Huxley" 638), showing, with his words, that he well understood what Woolf used to call in her diaries her "great discovery," her ability to "dig out beautiful caves" behind her characters (59).

Referring to great discoveries, I would like to close this paper with a reference to a nice discovery I made during my research. To find out any possible information regarding articles about Virginia Woolf, I searched many different archives. One of these, and by far the most interesting one, was at the Mondadori Foundation, where there are some letters between the Italian editor Arnoldo Mondadori—still today the greatest Italian publishing house—and Leonard Woolf. What is most interesting is that among these letters I found probably the first contract signed by Virginia Woolf with an Italian publisher, F.lli Treves, which then became Garzanti, still one of the greatest Italian publishers.

This document is not only interesting and fascinating in itself, but also because through the letters between Mondadori and Leonard Woolf it appears that this contract was never fulfilled. It is a contract for the Italian translation and publication of *To the Lighthouse*, which, according to the contract, should have been published before the end of March 1931. If the publisher had published the novel in time, *To the Lighthouse* would have been the first novel by Virginia Woolf published in Italy, but he did not, and so *Orlando* was the first novel to be translated into Italian—by Alessandra Scalero—and then published by Mondadori. Of course, this also influenced the reception of the writer, who was introduced to the Italian reading public through *Orlando*, first, and then through *Flush*, her two funniest works, both indeed *divertissements* compared with her more serious works. Interestingly enough, however, this "incident" did not influence Woolf's reception among Italian Literary critics, who were able to understand her art deeply and had the strength to introduce her to a country that was becoming more and more totalitarian. As a matter of fact, even on a cultural ground such as that of literary periodicals, some journals were actually under the control of the Fascist regime, or aligned with it. Those were the journals of the so-called *Strapaese*, a literary movement which wished to defend national traditions against the tendencies of a new culture open to foreign influences, and in those journals, predictably, there are no traces of Virginia Woolf. But in response to the *Strapaese*, in 1926 the review *900* was created to represent *Stracittà*, a cultural movement opposed to *Strapaese*, that wished to spread a culture open to modernity and to the influences of the industrial civilization. In 1929, *900* published a good and uncensored translation of a passage from *Mrs. Dalloway* where Mrs. Woolf is described as the "spokeswoman of the young English literature" (154).

We can only speculate about if and how the Fascist regime tempered the critical response to Virginia Woolf within Italian literary periodicals. What is certain is that from 1938 to 1945—during the years of World War II—no article about Mrs. Woolf appeared in Italian periodicals, not even to mention the writer's death. It is true that those were difficult years, during which people concentrated on subjects that had little to do with literature, but it is also true that, nonetheless, articles about other authors such as James Joyce or T.S. Eliot were published. Italian critics, however, had not forgotten about Virginia Woolf, as the article published by Salvatore Rosati in the *Nuova Europa* a few months before the end of the conflict proves. The article is a review of *A Haunted House* (that Leonard Woolf had just published with the Hogarth Press) showing a renewed interest in the writer and in her works, confirmed by the agreement signed by Mr. Woolf with Arnoldo Mondadori's publishing house on February 9, 1945 to assign him the rights of translation of all his wife's works. Even during those difficult years, Italian critics proved able to follow the writer's work and to read her, I think, as Mrs. Woolf would have liked to be read.

Note

1. It is thanks to Linati if readers and critics now have the Linati Schema of *Ulysses*, as Joyce wrote it in a letter to the Italian critic to help him understand the novel.

Works Cited

Bo, Carlo. "Nota su Virginia Woolf." *Il Frontespizio* 12 Dec. 1933: 14.
Bolchi, Elisa. *Il paese della bellezza. Virginia Woolf nelle riviste italiane tra le due guerre*. Milano: I.S.U. Università Cattolica, 2007.
Consiglio, Alberto. "Virginia Woolf." *L'Italia letteraria* 19 May 1929: 6.
Dettore, Ugo. "Virginia Woolf e il tempo." *Meridiano di Roma* 20 June 1937: 7.
Guidi, Augusto. "Appunti da una lettura di Virginia Woolf." *Mercurio* 9 May 1945: 119-123.
Langella, Giuseppe. *Il secolo delle riviste*. Milano: Vita e Pensiero, 1982.
Linati, Carlo. "Virginia Woolf." *Corriere della Sera* 24 Jan. 1927: 3.
—. "Virginia Woolf. A Room of One's Own." *Leonardo* March 1930: 175-176.
Majumdar, Robin and Allen McLaurin. *Virginia Woolf: the Critical Heritage*. London: Routledge, 1975.
Morra, Umberto. "Virginia Woolf – Orlando – A Biography." *Solaria* May 1929: 55-56.
—. "Il nuovo romanzo inglese. Virginia Woolf." *La Cultura* Jan. 1931: 34-51.
Rosati, Salvatore. "Virginia Woolf e Aldous Huxley." *La Nuova Antologia* 16 Dec. 1933: 636-643.
—. "Virginia Woolf postuma." *La Nuova Europa* 11 Feb. 1945: 8.
Scalero, Alessandra. "The Waves." *Leonardo* Nov. 1932: 512-514.
Serafini, Guglielmo. "Nota su Virginia Woolf." *Il Saggiatore* Jan. 1933: 10-14
Woolf, Virginia. *A Writer's Diary*. London: The Hogarth Press, 1953; San Diego: Harcourt, 1982.
—. "Passaggio di un'automobile per il Mall." *900* Apr. 1929: 149-154.

Reading over Her Shoulder: Virginia Woolf Reads *Anna Karenina*

by Roberta Rubenstein

Virginia Woolf first read *Anna Karenina* sometime between 1909 and 1911[1]—before her own literary career began—and re-read it in 1926. On both occasions, she recorded her impressions on the novel. Evidence suggests that she read it for a third time in 1929. What remains constant in Woolf's comments about the novel over time is her admiration of Tolstoy's skillful transformation of the quotidian into literary art—as she phrases it, "the normal raised to its . . . highest power" (Smith H 4). Her unpublished holograph notes on two of her readings of *Anna Karenina*,[2] along with references to the novel in her correspondence and elsewhere, illuminate her sustained fascination with this masterpiece of Russian literature and its author. It is instructive to read over Woolf's shoulder (figuratively speaking) to discover which elements of Tolstoy's novel captured her attention and stimulated her thinking about narrative practices at different points in her own writing career. As evidenced by her observations in literary essays, letters, and diary entries, she was indelibly impressed by Tolstoy's narrative skill, which, in her view, was more than sufficient to override the neutralizing effects of translation.

Woolf's initial notes on reading *Anna Karenina* demonstrate her early critical acuity and also indicate the elements of Tolstoy's masterpiece that most engaged her at the outset of her literary career. The comments comprise a single page that resembles a condensed, informal book review.[3] Woolf begins by observing, "There seems to me, at first sight, a remarkable cleanness about his [Tolstoy's] work. Things are seen with just so much atmosphere as is necessary to enclose them; never a hair's breadth more of space. Look at the way that the train is [seen?] as it comes into the station. Tolstoy himself makes no reflections. They seem contained in the action" (HRN 3). On the basis of her first encounter with the novel, she was prepared to "put Tolstoy among the highest" (HRN 3), adding that he has the "power of insight into character in such a degree that he seems to anticipate emotions: not to see them after they have happened; from their effects upon external things. Some scenes & passages thus seem to me indelible, like scenes one has witnessed for a second, among live people oneself" (HRN 3). More than decade later, she refashioned and amplified several of her initial reflections for her extended discussion of the major Russian writers, "The Russian Point of View" (1925). In the essay, she remarks of Tolstoy's work that, "even in a translation, we feel that we have been set on a mountain-top and had a telescope put into our hands. Everything is astonishingly clear and absolutely sharp" (*E4* 188).

Though Woolf's initial impressions of *Anna Karenina* were primarily appreciative and descriptive, she also expressed some critical reservations, specifically concerning the author's tendency toward polemic and an occasional excess of "social tract." Not only does Levin's "moral about agriculture threaten to be dull," she wrote, but "the answers to social questions are not important enough to decide the questions of so many lives" (HRN 3).

She also found "an occasional lack of depth & beauty, the result of the fact that many of the actions are not very remarkable; but they are all observed with the same precision & solidity, & often subtlety, as tho' [Tolstoy] overheard & and reported, but made no comment" (3). Reservations aside, Woolf's initial notes on *Anna Karenina* conclude with the judgment that the novel is "a work of genius" (3).

Re-reading the novel in 1926, Woolf expanded on judgments she had established during her initial reading. Her six pages of impressionistic and less concentrated observations[4] follow a format more typical of her other holograph reading notes: references to passages that struck her as noteworthy for one reason or another (usually accompanied by the corresponding page numbers in the text), along with impressionistic comments and questions jotted down *en passant*. Her impromptu notes thus offer unique opportunities to observe her reading—or re-reading—practice in the rough. Though of course we can't read Woolf's mind, we can figuratively follow some of its processes by observing her notations and discovering which thematic and structural elements stimulated her thinking.

Thus, for example, Woolf notes a moment early in *Anna Karenina*, when Stiva Oblonsky and his valet silently acknowledge their mutual understanding through glances exchanged through a mirror. The scene prompts Woolf's broader question: "Why should one assume that the object of the novelist is to get as much into his character's mind or soul as possible? Psychoan[alysis] is not fiction; not specially valuable for novelists" (Smith H 1). Another noted passage underscores Tolstoy's psychological perspicacity. In the cited scene, Vronsky is irritated by a conversation between Anna and her brother Stiva that he knows has nothing to do with him. Woolf remarks, "this is the kind of psychology in wh[ich] T. is so good—" and adds with bemusement, "but what kind is it?" (Smith H 1) Elsewhere, she admires Tolstoy's skill in bringing major and minor characters together in group scenes, conveyed both through closely observed external details and through his exceptional comprehension of his characters' inner dynamics. Of a party scene, she notes, "This party is all very masterly—[Tolstoy] moves people about. Knows what they say" (Smith H 2).

Of even greater consequence for Woolf scholars, Tolstoy uniquely rendered his characters' interiority. Leon Edel credits him as an early pioneer in the narrative representation of the "inner condition" of characters in fiction, a method that ultimately evolved into the signature techniques of literary modernism—interior monologue and stream of consciousness (*The Modern Psychological Novel* 147). The Russian critic Nikolai Chernyshevsky, a contemporary of Tolstoy, was the first to discern the writer's adroit evocation of his characters' inner lives—not simply their interiority but the "dialectic of the mind" (qtd. in Edel 148). Edel refers to several passages from *War and Peace* and *Anna Karenina* for illustration of Tolstoy's pioneering representations of reverie, associative processes, and the "'scrambled data' of stream-of-consciousness writing" (147-53).[5] More recently, George R. Clay has underscored Tolstoy's "daring attempts," for his time, to render "the psychic process itself: the spontaneous, chaotic, rapidly spinning or uncannily sloweddown interchange of feelings and thoughts as they unfold into surprising new feelings, or perhaps into fleeting memories which double back on themselves, blending the real with dreamlike fusions of past, present, and future" ("Tolstoy in the Twentieth Century" 207). Surprisingly, Woolf makes few comments about this dimension of Tolstoy's narrative technique. However, she does remark that he often accomplishes "the Proust trick of anticipating emotion: *what is passing in the mind*; but tends always to make things show . . . the surface visible" (Smith H 5, my emphasis).

Several passages in *Anna Karenina* apparently interested Woolf because they hint at Tolstoy's ideas about artistic method. She comments on a scene in which the portrait artist Mihaylov imaginatively "saves" certain striking visual impressions and draws on them later, removing only "the coverings which partially [obscure] the figure. . ." (*Anna Karenina* 427). When the artist observes Anna Karenina as she waits in the shadow of a porch for her scheduled portrait sitting with him (427), he "seize[s] this impression, just as he had retained the tobacconist's chin and hidden it away where he could find it when it was wanted" (428). Woolf notes the equivalence in creative processes that guide different aesthetic forms: the artist "seized & absorbed this impression wh[ich] he had hid till wanted – true of T.[olstoy]. What strikes me is the encyclopedic nature of his knowledge. This all written down. He has only to turn up the page he wants" (Smith H 3).

During the same portrait-sitting scene, several characters debate ideas about artistic technique itself. Vronsky, who has recently taken up painting and bemoans his lack of technical skill, praises one of Mihaylov's canvases for its masterful "technique." The artist is initially pleased and then troubled by Vronsky's terminology: "He had often noticed—as now when his picture was being praised—that technique was contrasted with inner quality, as if it were possible to paint well something that was bad. He knew that much attention and care were needed not to injure one's work when removing the wrappings that obscure the idea, and that all wrappings must be removed, but as to the art of painting, the technique, it did not exist. (*Anna Karenina*" (431). Woolf underscores the key point that the artist uncovers and reveals, rather than invents, the most fitting expression of his or her subject. As she reiterates in her notes, "T[olstoy]'s view of technique—removing the wrapper from the idea" (Smith H 3).

Woolf consistently expressed admiration for the depth and comprehensiveness of Tolstoy's vision, the "sensation that every side of life is being turned round & exhibited. . . . Seems able to see all round his people" (Smith H 3-4). One of many successful elements of his art, she observes, is his technique of individualizing characters through small but noticeable idiosyncrasies, such as Alexey Karenin's annoying habit of cracking his knuckles. (One may recall Peter Walsh's equally irritating habit of fidgeting with his pocket knife. *Mrs. Dalloway* was published a year before Woolf noted this detail in *Anna Karenina*.) According to Woolf, such minutely observed details "bring reality home" or have "suggestive power" (Smith H 4). Yet she occasionally questions the underlying principle of selection, wondering, "What are the laws that govern realistic art? That one sh[ould] follow life exactly? Give all thrills & ups & downs, even if they don't show character or philosophy, but only life[?]" (Smith H 3).

The saturation of detail prompts Woolf to generalize about the larger implications of "the physical side" of the story itself—the adulterous passion that ultimately destroys Anna Karenina. She remarks, "All this is sensual love, so far. About the copulation, A[nna] feels that this act gives her forever to V[ronsky]. Yet she was not in love with Karenin" (Smith H 2). She concludes that the matter of sexual infidelity upon which the story pivots so centrally is "founded upon a convention which no longer holds" (2). In a letter to Vita Sackville-West during the same time period, she amplifies her observation concerning the modern shift in moral assumptions: "I will tell you about Anna Karenina, and the predominance of sexual love in 19th Century fiction, and its growing unreality to us who have no real condemnation in our hearts any longer for adultery as such. But Tolstoy hoists all his book on that support. Take it away, say, no it doesn't offend me that AK. should copulate with Vronsky, and what remains?"(*L3* 254-5).

Exchanges such as this epistolary one between Virginia and Vita make their way into actual conversations in several of Woolf's novels, during which characters discuss and disagree about books and writers. In *To the Lighthouse*, drafted in part during the same year that Woolf re-read *Anna Karenina*, Mrs. Ramsay and her dinner guests discuss Tolstoy and Sir Walter Scott over *bouef en daube*. Mrs. Ramsay, more interested in people than in their reading tastes, prefers Paul Rayley's diffidence to Charles Tansley's smugness. Paul, trying to remember the "books one had read as a boy," ultimately recalls the name of Vronsky because "he always thought it such a good name for a villain" (*To the Lighthouse* 108). From the dinner conversation, the subject migrates into Mrs. Ramsay's private thoughts, coloring her impressions of the two very different young men at her dinner table:

> "Vronsky," said Mrs. Ramsay; "O, *Anna Karenina*," but that did not take them very far; books were not in their line. No, Charles Tansley would put them both right in a second about books, but it was all so mixed up with, Am I saying the right thing? . . . That, after all, one knew more about him than about Tolstoi. . . . Now [Paul]was thinking, not about himself or about Tolstoi, but whether she was cold, whether she felt a draught, whether she would like a pear. (108)[6]

While composing *To the Lighthouse*, Woolf was attentive to certain formal and stylistic matters in *Anna Karenina*. An aspect that significantly separates her from Tolstoy is the virtual absence of lyrical or figurative language in his writing. She finds "no metaphor in T[olstoy]. Rather surprised if one finds a hint of one. Compare Proust in this matter" (Smith H 3). She also questions whether Tolstoy has a sense of humor and concludes that he does, but that it is very subtly expressed—"implicit" but "never insisted on" (Smith H 4). She notes an amusing detail concerning Princess Scherbatsky, who counts heads before meals; "if there chanced to be thirteen, she would make a grandchild sit at the side-table" (*Anna Karenina* 500; Smith H 4). On the whole, however, Woolf concludes that Tolstoy has "too grave a mind" and that he is "not lenient in his attitude" (Smith H 4), qualities that explain what she regards as his "lack of 'charm'" (4).

One of Woolf's few critical reservations about *Anna Karenina*, articulated in her 1926 reading notes, concerns its formal design, specifically the double narrative structure of parallel marriage plots. The rising trajectory of Levin and Kitty's pursuit of "family happiness" intersects with the falling course of Anna's adulterous and ultimately destructive relationship with Vronsky. What she finds "disturbing" is "the constant change from place to place—one story to another—the emotional continuity is broken up—unavoidable, but there seems to be a . . . diversion of power" (2). Later in the notes, she returns to this formal deficiency, concluding that that "the construction is a good deal hindered by the double story"(4).[7] She speculates that the "awkwardness of having to tell the same story twice from different points of view[,] c[oul]d be removed in a film" (4). Perhaps that insight prompted her further discussion of the strengths and limitations of an untraced film adaptation of Tolstoy's novel.[8] In her essay, "On Cinema," published during the same year,[9] she approached the celluloid adaptation of Tolstoy's novel primarily from the position of a reader—in this case, a reader dissatisfied with the novel's film transformation.[10] What was not successfully captured in the silent film medium was the characters' inner lives and their emotional essence. At least in one regard, however, Woolf saw that film might be the superior medium for solving certain kinds of narrative problems. Although she does not work out her theory in detail, she imagines that a celluloid technique could bridge "by some device of scenery" the "terrible dislocations which are inevitable when Tolstoy has to pass from the story of Anna to the story of Levin. . ." (*E4* 352).

In her 1926 reading notes, Woolf mulls further on the structure of *Anna Karenina*, remarking, "It offends me that the book ends without any allusion to Anna. She's allowed to drop out; never comes into Levin or Kitty's mind again. All the stress finally upon his [Levin's] religious feelings . . . but this is unsatisfactory in a work of art where the other feelings have been around for so long" (Smith H 4-5). She was impatient with Tolstoy's concentration on Levin's extended spiritual struggle at the expense of further attention to the novel's doomed female protagonist. She could not have been aware that a Russian audience reading *Anna Karenina* as it originally appeared in serial form concluded that the novel ended with Anna's suicide at the end of Part VII.[11] Moreover, according to Morson, the continuation of the story beyond what seemed like a conventional tragic *denouement*— Anna's suicide at the train station—produces an absence of closure that more accurately typifies "lived experience" (*Narrative and Freedom* 171).[12] Had Woolf known these details of the novel's serial publication history, she certainly would have been interested in their implications. By 1926, she had already moved away from traditional narrative closure to a greater focus on "lived experience," beginning with *Jacob's Room* (1922).

Despite her reservations about the novel's double plot structure, Woolf found far more to admire than to criticize in Tolstoy. Among other things, she found "his physical eye amazing. And the loveliness of the emotion. For instance the scene between Kitty & Anna at the end." (She means the end of Part VII, not the end of the novel.) The scene to which she refers occurs shortly before Anna's suicide. Visiting Kitty soon after she has given birth to her first child, Anna learns that Levin has already left for the country and begs Kitty to "remember" her to her husband. The younger woman feels both awkward and sympathetic because she knows of Anna's disgrace. "'I will be sure to,' Kitty repeats naïvely, looking compassionately into her eyes" (*Anna Karenina* 687). Woolf remarks that the younger woman's innocent assent "gives Kitty's pity to Anna." Yet she queries, "why tell one this? Sometimes of course it happened so, but there is no point in things happening except for a reason" (Smith H 5). As she discerned, such details may indeed be extraneous in that they do not lead to significant consequences. Rather, they function as part of the thick texture that supports character and event and expresses more authentically the randomness of ordinary experience.

In 1929, Woolf returned to Tolstoy again, either re-reading *Anna Karenina* for a third time or reflecting back on her previous readings of the novel, and offered a dramatic revision concerning own her literary development. In a letter to Vita, she declared that Tolstoy—and *Anna Karenina* in particular—was more directly responsible than were the more-frequently cited Edwardian "materialists" for catalyzing the Modernist break—and, implicitly, her own—from outworn literary conventions. As she phrased it,

I've been reading Balzac, and Tolstoy. Practically every scene in Anna Karenina is branded on me, though I've not read it for 15 years. *That* is the origin of all our discontent. After that of course we had to break away. It wasn't Wells, or Galsworthy or any of our mediocre wishy washy realists; it was Tolstoy. How could we go on with sex and realism after that? (8 January 1929; *L4* 4, emphasis in original).[13]

During the last years of her life, with rumors of war rumbling in the background, Woolf recorded her intention to re-read both of Tolstoy's masterpieces once again. She unhesitatingly declared *War and Peace* "the greatest novel in the world," adding, "and if I'm not bombed I shall read that and Anna Karenina this winter" (*L6* 361). There is no evidence that she did so, though, in 1940, in preparation for a projected essay on the author, she did re-read Goldenveiser's *Talks with Tolstoy*, which she had co-translated with S. S. Koteliansky for the Hogarth Press publication in 1923 (*D5* 273). Thirty years after her first exposure to Tolstoy's fiction, she still recalled her first reactions: "Always the same reality—like touching an exposed electric wire. Even so imperfectly conveyed—his rugged short cut mind—to me the most, not sympathetic, but inspiring, rousing; genius in the raw. Thus more disturbing, more 'shocking'[,] more of a thunderclap, even on art, even on lit.[eratu]re than any other writer. I remember that was my feeling about W. & Peace, read in bed at Twickenham [in 1910]" (273).

Though one can only regret that Woolf's projected essay did not materialize, it is no exaggeration to say that Tolstoy remained indelible in her literary imagination from the earliest to the final years of her writing life. She admired so many aspects of his fiction—from characters so fully realized that they appear to live outside the pages of fiction to the writer's profound comprehension of human experience—that it is impossible to single out one that Woolf regarded as most important. Indeed, what Tolstoy represented for her was the great novelist who "feels, sees, believes, with such intensity of conviction that he hurls his belief outside himself and it flies off and lives an independent life of its own, becomes Natasha, Pierre, Levin, and is no longer Tolstoy" ("George Moore" *DM* 101). Her 1926 reading notes on *Anna Karenina* fittingly conclude with her lyrical tribute to the writer who represented for her that pinnacle of narrative achievement. In Tolstoy's fiction, things happen as if "his mind were as old as the rocks & had taken the impression of all forms of life so that there they exist in him, layer upon layer" (Smith H 6).

Notes

1. Brenda Silver dates Woolf's first reading of Tolstoy's novel—in French—in 1909-11, based on its listing as *Anna Karenine* among novels entered in the table of contents of her 1909-1911 reading notes (*Virginia Woolf's Reading Notebooks* 148, 149). Emily Dalgarno concludes from Woolf's 1929 letter to Vita Sackville-West, in which she comments that she "had not read [*Anna Karenina*] in fifteen years" (*L* 4: 4), that the date was probably closer to 1914. "A British *War and Peace*? Virginia Woolf Reads Tolstoy." However, one can speculate that in 1929 she may have forgotten precisely in which year she first read the novel. Page numbers in Woolf's notes refer to an unidentified edition of *Anna Karenina* translated by Louise and Aylmer Maude; where located, the passages she cites directly or by paraphrase refer to the Maudes' translation published in 1918.
2. I have transcribed and edited thirty-five pages of Woolf's holograph reading notes on Tolstoy, Dostoevsky, Chekhov, and Turgenev, including two sets of her reading notes on *Anna Karenina*. The full transcrip-

tions will appear in *Virginia Woolf and the Russian Point of View*, to be published by Palgrave/Macmillan in 2009.
3. Reading Notebook 29. Page 3 of Reading Notes (reverse side of page) of Holograph of *Night and Day* (Chapters 11-17). Citations are abbreviated in the text as "HRN" with page number. Excerpts from the holograph are quoted with permission of the Estate of Virginia Woolf and The Henry W. and Albert A. Berg Collection of English and American Literature, The New York Public Library Astor, Lenox and Tilden Foundations. **Passages from these manuscript materials may not be quoted or reprinted without new permissions.**
4. Holograph, 1926. 22 pages, including 6 on *Anna Karenina*. Virginia Woolf Papers (Box 4, folder 180), Mortimer Rare Book Room, Smith College. References in the text are abbreviated as "Smith H" with page numbers from 1 through 6. Excerpts from the holograph notes are quoted with the permission of the Estate of Virginia Woolf and Smith College. **They may not be quoted or reprinted without new permissions.**
5. See also Gleb Struve, "Monologue Intérieur," 1101-1111.
6. When she revised this scene, Woolf substituted *Anna Karenina* for *War and Peace* as the subject of dinner table discussion (Briggs, *Virginia Woolf* 446 n102) and replaced Charles Tansley with Paul Rayley as the character who recalls his youthful reading of Tolstoy (*To the Lighthouse* holograph draft 177, 179).
7. The double structural organization of *War and Peace* similarly troubled Woolf. I disagree with Emily Dalgarno's conclusion that Tolstoy's narrative structure was a model for the parallel plot structure of *Mrs. Dalloway*. Dalgarno argues that Woolf the critic found herself in conflict with Woolf the writer and that, "as a novelist, [she] made creative use of precisely those features that as a reader she had questioned. . ." ("A British War and Peace?" 132). In *Virginia Woolf and the Russian Point of View*, I argue that it was Dostoevsky, not Tolstoy, who influenced the technique of doubled characters in *Mrs. Dalloway*. Woolf mentions reading Dostoevsky while writing the novel (*D* 2: 248); she later explains that "in the first version [of *Mrs. Dalloway*] Septimus, who later is intended to be [Clarissa's] double, had no existence; and . . . Mrs. Dalloway was originally to kill herself, or perhaps merely to die at the end of the party" (*E* 4: 549).
8. Maggie Humm speculates that Woolf saw the 1915 American Fox Film Company production of *Anna Karenina*. *Modernist Women and Visual Cultures* 188.
9. The essay appeared in slightly different form in different publications in June, July, and August, 1926. McNeillie, *E* 4: 353 n 1.
10. For fuller discussions of "The Cinema," see Maggie Humm, "Virginia Woolf and 'The Cinema,'" *Modernist Women and Visual Cultures* 185-91; Laura Marcus, "Virginia Woolf and the Cinema," *The Tenth Muse* 99-178, esp. 107-16; and Leslie Hankins, "'Across the Screen of My Brain,'" in *The Multiple Muses of Virginia Woolf*, ed. Diane Gillespie, 148-79 .
11. According to Tolstoy scholar Gary Saul Morson, later readers of the novel invariably miss "what must have been obvious to Tolstoy's contemporaries: the events in part VIII [the final section of the novel] *could not* have been part of Tolstoy's original plan because the Eastern War [discussed in that section] had not yet begun when the novel began to be published." *Narrative and Freedom* 171, emphasis in original.
12. "Tolstoy's events take place in a universe like the one in which we live, where things happen by contingency." Morson, *Narrative and Freedom* 159-60.
13. From this statement, Brenda Silver concludes that Woolf was reading *Anna Karenina* in January 1929. *Virginia Woolf's Reading Notebooks* 78.

Works Cited

Briggs, Julia. *Virginia Woolf: An Inner Life*. New York: Harcourt, 2005.
Clay, George R. "Tolstoy in the Twentieth Century." In *The Cambridge Companion to Tolstoy*. Ed. Donna Tussing Orwin. Cambridge: Cambridge UP, 2002, 206-221.
Dalgarno, Emily. "A British *War and Peace*? Virginia Woolf Reads Tolstoy." *Modern Fiction Studies* 50.1 (2004): 129-150.
Edel, Leon. *The Modern Psychological Novel*. 1955. New York: Grosset and Dunlap, 1964.
Hankins, Leslie Kathleen. "'Across the Screen of My Brain': Woolf's 'The Cinema' and Film Forums of the Twenties." *The Multiple Muses of Virginia Woolf*, ed. Diane Filby Gillespie. Columbia, MO: U of Missouri P, 1993, 148-79.

Humm, Maggie. *Modernist Women and Visual Cultures: Virginia Woolf, Vanessa Bell, Photography and Cinema.* Rutgers: Rutgers UP, 2003.
Marcus, Laura. *The Tenth Muse: Writing about Cinema in the Modernist Period.* Oxford: Oxford UP, 2007.
Morson, Gary Saul. *Narrative and Freedom: The Shadows of Time.* New Haven, CT: Yale UP, 1994.
Silver, Brenda. *Virginia Woolf's Reading Notebooks.* Princeton: Princeton UP, 1983.
Struve, Gleb. "Monologue Intérieur: The Origins of the Formula and the First Statement of Its Possibilities." *PMLA* 69: 5 (Dec. 1954), 1101-1111.
Tolstoy, Leo. *War and Peace.* Trans. Aylmer and Louis Maude. 1918. Ed. George Gibian. New York: Norton, 1970.
Woolf, Virginia. "The Cinema." *The Essays of Virginia Woolf.* Vol. 4. Ed. Andrew McNeillie. London: The Hogarth Press, 1994.
—. *The Death of the Moth and Other Essays.* 1942. New York: Harcourt, 1970.
—. *The Letters of Virginia Woolf.* Vol. 3. Ed. Nigel Nicholson and Joanne Trautmann. New York: Harcourt Brace Jovanovich, 1978.
—. Reading Notebook XXIX. Holograph reading notes, January 1909-March 1911 [one page on Tolstoy's *Anna Karenina*]. Page 3 of Reading Notes (reverse side of page) of Holograph of *Night and Day* (Chapters 11-17). The Henry W. and Alfred A. Berg Collection, The New York Public Library, Astor, Lenox and Tilden Foundations.
—. Reading notes on "Anna Karenina." 6 pages included in *Holograph 1926.* Virginia Woolf Papers (Box 4, Folder 180). Mortimer Rare Book Room, Smith College, Northampton, MA.
—. *To the Lighthouse.* 1928. San Diego: Harvest/Harcourt Brace Jovanovich, 1981.

Straightening the Scraps & Scratches: Editing the Diaries of Virginia Woolf, Vera Brittain, and Katherine Mansfield

by Joanne Campbell Tidwell

In March 1926, Woolf wonders what Leonard might do with her diaries: "He would be disinclined to burn them; he could not publish them. Well, he should make up a book from them, I think; & then burn the body. I daresay there is a little book in them: if the scraps & scratches were straightened up a little" (*D2* 67). Editing Woolf's *Diary* down to a "little book" was a feat of editing indeed, and her observation leads one to consider the influence an editor has on a diary. What did she think a reader would gain from reading a "little book" made of excerpts from her diary, and would an editor keep to her vision? Of course, Leonard did "make up a book," titled *A Writer's Diary* and published in 1953. Readers were not satisfied by this volume, however, and the full diary was published from 1977 to 1984, followed by *A Moment's Liberty*, an abridged version, in 1990. How do these various incarnations of Woolf's diary differ? What different understandings of Woolf are gained from these diaries? And what, exactly, is the role of the editor in determining that understanding? This paper analyzes the effect of editing on diaries and will consider the diaries of Virginia Woolf, Katherine Mansfield, and Vera Brittain.

Woolf writes in *A Passionate Apprentice* on 31 May 1905, "All but six months find some sort of mirror of themselves here; the sight is one that profits or pleases" (273). She recognizes that she is unable to give a full portrait of her life in the pages of her diary; to do so would require constant writing that would prevent actually living. Instead, she must omit some information and present what is important at the time, considering perhaps what she thinks she will find most interesting to reread in years to come or what is most appropriate to the form. Regardless, she edits what she writes; she gives some thought to what is significant and what is not in the context of her diary. The editor continues this practice by choosing what entries to include, what to omit, and by interpreting Woolf's handwriting[1]. In his preface to *A Writer's Diary*, Leonard Woolf writes that omissions made by an editor in deference to the living "almost always distort or conceal the true character of the diarist or letter-writer and produce spiritually what an Academy picture does materially, smoothing out the wrinkles, warts, frowns, and asperities" (vii). A similar argument might be made for most editing of a diary. Indeed, Leonard continues:

> At the best and even unexpurgated, diaries give a distorted or one-sided portrait of the writer, because, as Virginia Woolf herself remarks somewhere in these diaries, one gets into the habit of recording one particular kind of mood—irritation or misery, say—and of not writing one's diary when one is feeling the opposite. The portrait is therefore from the start unbalanced, and, if someone then deliberately removes another characteristic, it may well become a mere caricature. (vii-viii)

Why then do we read diaries? If the best we as readers can hope for is an unbalanced portrait, what do we hope to gain from reading someone's private writings?

Much has been written about why we, especially women, write diaries, what we hope to gain from that experience, and what some of the positive effects of keeping a diary are, but less research has been done into why we read the diaries of other people, both famous and everyday. In the case of Woolf, do we hope to gain admittance to the mind of an author we adore so much, somehow to learn something from the diary that we cannot learn from her fiction? Do readers hope to find validation in Woolf's diary, some personal connection with her unavailable from her fiction, essays, and letters? Rita Felski discusses confessional writing in her book, *Beyond Feminist Aesthetics* (1989), and asserts that women read the private writings of other women to find someone with whom to identify, to see some sort of reflection of themselves in the experiences of others. Readers appreciate the authenticity of confessional writing, especially those forms that are less literary in style. But does the editing of a diary damage that authenticity?

Woolf once famously remarked that she had no inner life; critics have supposed that whatever inner life she did have, she put into her fiction, which would imply that Woolf's fiction is a more direct line to her soul than her diary is. Recall that Woolf once banished her soul from her diary: "How it would interest me if this diary were ever to become a real diary: something in which I could see changes, trace moods developing; but then I should have to speak of the soul, & did I not banish the soul when I began?" (*D2* 234). Later she writes that the soul sneaks into her writing when she comments on people or when she least expects it, and readers suspect that she is being somewhat disingenuous when she claims not to allow it in, as we see moods and changes throughout the diary. Does her soul live and breathe in her fiction, whereas it only slips into the margins of her diary, a marginal genre itself? If she does not recognize her soul in the diary, is the portrait of her in its pages incomplete?

Complicating the question of why we read diaries and what we hope to learn from them is the role of the editor of the published diary. If we hope to commune with a diarist, what happens if an editor purposefully or accidentally creates a persona for the diarist? How much creation does an editor do when she or he decides what to leave out and what to put in? Is the diary at best "some sort of mirror" of the life of the diarist, altered as it is by the diarist's choice of what to write about and further shaped by the aims of the editor? Is the diary a "mere caricature," a funhouse mirror that emphasizes some aspects of the diarist and diminishes others, giving us only a distorted vision?

Barbara Lounsberry's presentation at the 1994 Woolf conference, titled "The Art of Virginia Woolf's Diaries," discusses the omission of several entries by Anne Olivier Bell in her editing of the complete diaries. She indicates that Woolf kept two volumes of diary at the same time, one at Asheham and one at Hogarth House, in 1917 and 1918. At times, Woolf wrote twice in one day, making entries in each volume. Bell chose between the two entries instead of including both. Lounsberry argues that "such omissions—acknowledged though they are—tend to create a slightly misleading sense of Woolf as a diarist" (267). Lounsberry asserts that the manuscripts leave an impression of a "steadier diarist than the published editions do" (268). Other omissions include corrections that Woolf made to her wording or her facts; if Woolf went back and corrected an entry, Bell chose the corrected version and did not indicate the original. Unimportant, perhaps, except when one is arguing that diaries are not literature because they are not revised or reconsidered. If one is arguing for a more deliberate sort of writing, those corrections take on greater importance. Some critics have also used the diary to trace Woolf's mental health, and a "steadier diarist" might leave a different impression.

Woolf's diary has been edited by Leonard Woolf, Anne Olivier Bell and Andrew McNeillie, and Anne Olivier Bell on her own. Each editor had different goals, largely acknowledged in prefaces and introductions. Leonard writes, "The book throws light upon Virginia Woolf's intentions, objects, and methods as a writer. It gives an unusual psychological picture of artistic production from within. Its value and interest naturally depend to a great extent upon the value and interest of the product of Virginia Woolf's art" (ix). He seems to define the purpose of this set of diary excerpts more as illuminating Woolf's methods as a writer and less as a portrait of her as a person, and consequently he sees the audience as readers already familiar with her fiction and most likely her critical essays. He warns the reader to "constantly [bear] in mind" that this collection is only a small portion of the full diary and that otherwise "the book will give a very distorted view of her life and her character" (ix). Leonard is quite right. In an effort to consider the different effects—affects?—of the versions of the diary, I reread sections that covered similar time periods. *A Writer's Diary* makes Woolf seem to live only in what she reads and contains very little self-reflection. She seems almost one-dimensional. Few living people figure in her life, and she seems to live an entirely cerebral or intellectual life.

Anne Olivier Bell edited *A Moment's Liberty* intending to "preserve the overall character of the original, to follow the autobiographical thread, and to present a comprehensible and readable distillation of the 2,000 or so pages of Virginia's manuscript diaries" (xi). Her audience is the general reader, whose only characteristics seem to be those who perhaps do not have the money, time, or inclination to read the full five-volume diary. Quentin Bell wrote an introduction in which he seems to see the shorter diary as an introduction to the personage of Virginia Woolf. I choose the word *personage* over *person* deliberately, as he thinks it likely that the reader has heard of Woolf and may indeed have heard negative things said about her and about Bloomsbury in general. He describes the writing of the diary as "plain sailing" compared to her fiction and delights in the everyday subjects Woolf treats in the diary. Upon rereading entries from this version, I found Woolf to be almost completely bound up in the people she saw and the relationships she both took part in and gossiped about. There is very little about her writing, which Bell said she purposely reduced because of the full treatment in *A Writer's Diary*, and there is surprisingly little self-reflection. Ironically, Bell was forced to limit the number of people mentioned in the diary in order to eliminate the footnotes, which would seem to limit the amount of time spent discussing people.

Thus we are brought to the full five-volume diary. Reading entries of the same time period, I see familiar phrases and descriptions but also passages that appear in neither of the other two volumes. Despite the concentration on people and relationships in the shorter diary, missing are some of Woolf's more cutting or judgmental remarks found in the full published diary. Did Bell wish to make Woolf seem more likeable or kinder than she truly was in the pages of her diary? Although Bell did not include each and every word that Woolf wrote in the manuscripts of her diary, the full diary still presents a more balanced portrait than available elsewhere. But is it still a distorted view of Woolf? Is it still the funhouse mirror?

The diary of Katherine Mansfield casts some of these issues in clear relief. John Middleton Murry edited and published two editions of her diary, the first in 1927 and the definitive edition in 1954. In 1997, Margaret Scott published the complete edition of *The Katherine Mansfield Notebooks*. Attempting to compare these diaries proved to be more difficult than I expected. Murry's edition looks more like a typical diary than does Scott's; entries are dated, and Murry provides brief notes periodically to explain what is going on in Mansfield's life at the time, aided by two biographies of her that had been published. Scott also provides biographical data, but she does not provide explanations of the same sort that Murry does. She clearly attempts to be more transparent in her transcription of Mansfield's writing, and Mansfield can be quite obscure at times. Scott's purpose, according to her introduction, "is to reproduce what KM wrote" (xvi). She praises Murry's "courage and honesty" in publishing portions of the notebooks that were heavily critical of him as a husband but clearly disapproved of his efforts to punctuate and neaten Mansfield's writing (xvii).

While Woolf used different notebooks for different purposes—the Asheham diary mostly for notes about gardening, food, and groceries, her reading notebooks for notes on texts she thought she might write about critically, the diary for more personal writing, and still other notebooks dedicated to writing her books—Mansfield was not so organized. She wrote everything in a single notebook, and she did not always write in one notebook until it was full or pick up the same notebook two days in a row. Her dating is also inconsistent; when she appears to be writing stories or vignettes she does not always date them, and some of these writings merge into diary entries with little demarcation. When she does date entries, she does not always give the year, which is complicated by the fact that sometimes when she fills a notebook, she simply picks up another that has empty leaves but which may have been begun two years earlier. To compound these difficulties, Mansfield also had a fair number of loose papers that include all sorts of writing. Murry and Scott are faced with the task of putting the pages into chronological order, and they differ in their decisions. Murry also left out some passages, often claiming that they were illegible, but Scott transcribes many of these passages with little difficulty, according to her footnotes. Murry may also have left out passages to spare the feelings of people still alive at the time, including his own. In fact, Scott asserts that "Almost his only deliberate suppressions were names of people still alive at the time of publication" (xvii).

The difficulties in comparing the two versions of Mansfield's diary highlight the role of the editor. While Murry makes the diary more readable for the audience, he constructs a persona for Mansfield that seems somewhat regular in her writing habits. On the other hand, Scott's goal of transparency leaves much to the judgment of the reader but also creates an image of Mansfield that is quite fragmented and confusing, which can, perhaps, interfere with the reader's ability to connect with Mansfield. Which is the more valid view? Which is the more genuine or authentic portrait of Mansfield? Or have we returned to the question of why we read diaries in the first place?

Vera Brittain and her editor speak directly to the issue of why one publishes a diary. Brittain's diary is edited by Alan Bishop with Terry Smart, and Bishop does not publish the diary in its entirety. Brittain herself had prepared two editions of the diary for publication, and she composed two forwards to volumes she edited; however, these volumes were never published. In her 1922 forward she writes, "I belong to the few who believe in all sincerity that their own lives provide the answers to some of the main problems which puzzle humanity" (13). She also hopes that her youthful record will remind older readers of how it feels to be young and especially will warn people of the cost of war. She did not write a full forward to her revision, but the notes she wrote in 1939 are illuminating. In particular, she finds the "day-by-day suspense & anguish" (15) present in the diary to have merit. This quality is specific to diaries, as is her claim that the diary allows one to see the trees individually while the memoir allows one to see the forest at the cost of the trees.

Bishop found great value in the diary independent from and in addition to *Testament of Youth*, the memoir Brittain wrote based on the diary. He saw it as representative of the experiences of young women of World War I, as a record of a young woman's psychological development in a time of great stress, and as a highly readable and literary work (17-18). He argues that "the diary has a compelling immediacy which her 'autobiographical study' lacks" (18). While he obviously greatly valued the diary for the qualities unique to the genre, he did find a need for considerable editing, although he "attempts to represent the nature and concerns of the diary as closely as possible" (19). He cut the diary by about half in order to avoid repetition and omits sections that appeared at length in *Testament of Youth*. Despite these omissions, the diary reads very much like a novel, with a clear climax and denouement. Indeed, Bishop comments that in Brittain's editions, her editing stressed the qualities that make it a tragic love story (xv).

In his introduction to the 2000 reprint of Brittain's diary, Bishop discusses the relationship between reader and diarist and the issue of whether editing a diary damages its authenticity. He writes, "The question of integrity must always be under some scrutiny by the reader of a diary, and cannot be disentangled from the trust a reader gives to—or withholds from—its writer, on the basis of evidence in the text. Indeed, the tense, ever-unfolding relationship between writer and reader imposed by a diary is one of the genre's sharpest delights" (xvii). He further argues that many of the changes Brittain made did weaken the authenticity of the diary, as she felt it necessary to change the names, cut the diary by almost half, and make other substantial changes. Consequently, Bishop decided to make his selections independently from hers, keeping in mind the value she felt the diary would have to readers. In the 2000 introduction, Bishop wishes that he might have had time to re-edit the diary, leading the reader to wonder how he would change the diary again. And to what purpose? What effect did his editing have on the 1981 edition that he would like to change or remove for the 2000 edition? Bishop would like to see the diary published in full, but he does not indicate that he had hoped for that in his 2000 reprint. He clearly disagreed with the choices Brittain made in the two editions she put together and thought he might convey a more accurate version of the diary with his own choices, and perhaps he thought he could do an even better job with a second attempt.

Considering the diary as a funhouse mirror proves to be an accurate metaphor. If the reader is the diarist herself, she is well aware of how the mirror distorts her; was she standing before the fat mirror or the tall mirror as she wrote that day? The rest of us, however, have no memory to reference. We can only look at the image—not the thing itself—and try to figure out the distortion. Was she overly gloomy that day? Overly optimistic? What did the editor remove? What crossings out, what doodles are missing? Then again, do we ever see ourselves or those around us clearly? We always see through the lens of our own perceptions, coloring even those images most immediate to us. We never see the whole person, only the fragment presented to us at the moment, much like the final image of the play in *Between the Acts*. Is the image of Woolf we see through the pages of her diary any less complete or distorted than the picture we might have formed of her ourselves had we met her in person? Woolf's diary offers us the most options, existing as it does in three separate incarnations. Mansfield's notebooks, transparent as Scott attempted to make them, baffle as much as they reveal, and Murry's attempts to neaten and straighten perhaps only conceal the true Mansfield. Brittain's diary brings us the question of whether a diarist should edit her own work for publication or whether a truer picture is in fact given by a more objective editor, one with a less personal stake in the image conveyed to the reader. A diary provides a unique opportunity to see both how the author saw herself in what she chose to write and how others saw her in how they edited her writing, colored, as always, by many layers of perception.

Note

1. Woolf's handwriting is notoriously difficult to read, and editors occasionally differ on how they read her writing.

Works Cited

Bell, Anne Olivier. Editorial Note. *A Moment's Liberty: The Shorter Diary of Virginia Woolf*. New York: Harcourt Brace Jovanovich, 1977. xi-xii.
Bell, Quentin. Introduction. *The Diary of Virgina Woolf*. 5 vols. New York: Harcourt, 1983. xiii-xxviii.
Bishop, Alan. Introduction. *Chronicle of Youth, War Diary, 1913-1917*. London: Victor Gollancz, 1981. 13-20.
—. Introduction. *Chronicle of Youth, War Diary, 1913-1917*. London: Phoenix Press, 2000. xiii-xx.
Felski, Rita. *Beyond Feminist Aesthetics: Feminist Literature and Social Change*. Cambridge, MA: Harvard UP, 1989.
Lounsberry, Barbara. "The Art of Virginia Woolf's Diaries." *Virginia Woolf: Emerging Perspectives*. Eds. Mark Hussey, Vara Neverow, and Jane Lilienfield. New York: Pace UP, 1994. 266-71.
Murry, John Middleton. Preface. *Journal of Katherine Mansfield*. Definitive ed. London: Constable & Co., 1954. ix-x.
Scott, Margaret. Introduction. *The Katherine Mansfield Notebooks*. Complete ed. Minneapolis: U of Minnesota P, 1997. xiii-xxv.
Woolf, Leonard. Preface. *A Writer's Diary*. By Virginia Woolf. New York, Harcourt Brace, 1953. vii-x.
Woolf, Virginia. *The Diary of Virginia Woolf*. Ed. Anne Olivier Bell. 5 vols. New York: Harcourt Brace, 1983.
—. *A Passionate Apprentice: The Early Journals, 1897-1909*. Ed. Mitchell A. Leaska. New York: Harcourt Brace Jovanovich, 1990.

ADJACENCIES: VIRGINIA WOOLF, CORA SANDEL, AND THE KÜNSTLERROMAN

by Erica L. Johnson

Readers of Virginia Woolf turn to Lily Briscoe's painting, Miss La Trobe's drama, Clarissa Dalloway's domestic artistry, and Orlando's fanciful poem in order to explore one of the most intimate themes in Woolf's own life: her experience and identity as a writer. Such examinations of Woolf's artistic persona are necessarily routed through these surrogate figures due to the conspicuous absence among Woolf's novels of a more autobiographical "portrait of the artist." Autobiographical novels are central to the oeuvres of many modernists from James Joyce and Dorothy Richardson to H. D. and Gertrude Stein, although few flesh out the genre as fully as Woolf's Norwegian contemporary, Cora Sandel. Born just two years before Woolf, Sandel presents her authorial identity in a trilogy of autobiographical novels written in the 1920s and '30s. In these novels, known as the "Alberta trilogy," Sandel recounts her journey from an isolated port town near the Arctic Circle to bohemian Paris and finally back to Scandinavia in pursuit of a writing career thwarted by poverty, domestic responsibilities, and a contemptuous husband. The trilogy conveys with sublime eloquence a narrative of "coming to writing," as Hélène Cixous terms the process, and is structured by what can only be called moments of being. My goal in reading these two authors together is two-fold: by drawing on Woolf as a writer-critic whose reflections on writing form a critical framework for reading Sandel, I reveal the ways in which Sandel carefully edits her self-portrait as an artist.[1] And, by reading for the figure of not just the "artist" but more specifically the "novelist" in Woolf's and Sandel's novels, I explore the ways in which both authors edit their autobiographical subjectivity.

My means of comparing these two women modernists cannot be that of describing one writer's influence over another since Sandel did not read Woolf until after she had written her trilogy, and Sandel's work became available in English translation only after Woolf's death. Sandel's direct literary influences were primarily Scandinavian and French (she adored Colette) yet the regrettably few critical studies of Sandel regularly invoke Woolf on a variety of shared feminist topics that span the two writers' works. I therefore propose to read the works of Sandel and Woolf through a series of *adjacencies*. The term "adjacencies" can refer to texts or bodies of work that literally stand beside one another in time or within a particular context (such as a national literature or a shared contextual condition like postcolonialism), but more importantly adjacencies can be characterized as a uniquely productive relationship between literary texts in that the shared representational systems of the *texts* become evident against the receding backdrop of context. I build on Wai Chee Dimock's theory of resonances, which Anne Fernald has so fruitfully applied to Woolf in her recent book, *Virginia Woolf: Feminism and the Reader*, because Dimock's notion of diachronic historicism lends itself to my analysis of adjacent texts. Essentially, Dimock argues that one hears a text not in its "pastness," but as kinetic object moving continuously through time and thus "yield[ing] its words differently across time, authorizing contrary readings across the ages and encouraging a kind of semantic democracy" (Dimock 1067). Seen thus—as an inexhaustible, spatially and temporally mobile, and democratic entity—the literary text produces different hearings among its readers who might therefore "want to dislocate it, relocate it, and line it up against competing voices... to see how it sounds and resounds" (Dimock 1065). My goal in reading Woolf's and Sandel's texts as adjacent to one another draws on the idea that texts produce resonances that exceed their original contexts yet I emphasize as well the function of a structured comparative reading. That is, Woolf's and Sandel's writing is diachronic not only because the resonances of their respective texts change over time, but because they travel together from a shared historical moment in which they are also linked by a common aesthetic theory as well as a preponderance for auto-critique.

In reading these adjacencies, I found answers to pressing questions raised by Sandel's trilogy. Like Ruth Essex and Linda Hunt, two of a handful of critics to write about Sandel in English, I initially approached the trilogy as a *Künstlerroman*—as a feminist claim to writing—yet found this reading to be deeply dissatisfying for reasons that I could not explain until I read Sandel with Woolf. The trilogy clearly sets forth to chronicle Alberta's development as a writer, from her adolescent attempts at poetry in the first book, *Alberta and Jacob* (1926), onward. The second volume, *Alberta and Freedom* (1931), opens with the poverty-stricken Alberta posing as a nude model for a painter in Paris, a point of departure quite clearly designed to set up Alberta's trajectory from object to subject status in the narrative of artistic production. But it is not until the third volume, *Alberta Alone* (1939), that Alberta does any significant amount of what her awful husband persistently refers to as "scribbling." In the second book, in which Alberta is understood to be a struggling writer, the only evidence of her vocation is a series of exercise books she carries around in her trunk.[2] The *absence* of her writing is palpable and frustrating but it is understandable when read in tandem with Woolf's fiction, in which women novelists are edited out altogether—again with the playful poetic caveat that is Orlando—and in light of Woolf's observations in her diary that writing about one's own writing poses a dire risk and must be withheld from her fiction and reserved for her diary. For Woolf, a diary is "a kindly blankfaced old confidante. Well, you see, I'm a failure as a writer..." (*AWD* 31) she confesses, only shortly after observing that "Melancholy diminishes as I write. Why then don't I write it down oftener? Well, one's vanity forbids. I want to appear a success even to myself" (*AWD* 29). This last comment alludes to the fact that her "writer's diary" has two clear foci: first, it records Woolf's experience of writing, but equally importantly it catalogs the critical response her writing receives.[3] The tension between her use of the diary as an unfettered means of "sweep[ing] up accidentally several stray matters which I should exclude if I hesitated, but which are diamonds in the dustheap" (*AWD* 7) and, simultaneously, as an inventory of the laudatory or censuring voices of her critics makes the diary a fraught, intersubjective document. Many diaries are intersubjective in the sense that the author envisions that his or her writing will one day be read by an audience, but Woolf incorporates her critics' voices into her own, thus inscribing an intersubjective, interactive identity into what is supposed to be a deeply private writing space. Evidently, the subject of Woolf's diary struggles unsuccessfully to separate her self image from the image that others hold of her, and she senses both the vitality and frailty of this division. Woolf's anxiety about her authorial identity, which rests on a painful axis of the protected self who can express herself freely in her diary and the self utterly defenseless against her readers, results in a careful sorting of artistic personae in her work: the novelist is expressed in diary entries and letters while characters engaged in *other* artistic and aesthetic endeavors populate her novels.

Sandel makes a similar move in the second of her autobiographical novels by tucking Alberta's writing away in her text so that its absence in her heroine's daily life makes silence a central theme of the novel (achieving, in a sense, Terence Hewet's unrealized goal in *The Voyage Out* of writing a novel about "silence").[4] Whether Alberta hides her writing due to an intrapsychic sense of shame and anxiety about exposing herself to the public gaze—as Woolf indicates one does—or due to the very real limitations of poverty and social prohibitions, *Alberta and Freedom* depicts Alberta *not* writing. Surrounded by artists, Alberta asserts at one point, "If I were a painter, I would paint life" (*AF* 198), but as a writer she produces just enough text to earn a few kroner from the Norwegian newspapers (and she shares Woolf's ambivalence toward the bread-and-butter writing of journalism). As a novelist, though, she lives in an agonizing state of suspended animation. Her awareness of her situation makes it all the more poignant; at one point she experiences "a rent in my ignorance, a membrane split before my eyes... other forms of writing were possible besides putting together casual articles... New, bold ideas stirred in Alberta. Supposing she were to try! To find form for a little reality ..." (*AF* 227).

One point to be taken from this is that, in speaking of the figure of the artist in Sandel's and Woolf's work, it becomes crucial to distinguish carefully between the different arts. Woolf tries to maintain a private vs. public line by sequestering her representation of a woman novelist in her diary whereas Sandel blurs this line, as both Shari Benstock and Graziella Parati argue that women's autobiographical work necessarily does. Beyond the generic distinctions between the two writers' self-representation, though, there is a parallel between the absence of a portrait-of-the-writer among Woolf's novels and Sandel's portrayal of Alberta's novel as an absence. I therefore offer another perspective on the critical trend of collapsing the differences between Woolf's painter, dramatist, aesthetes, and scholarly characters with an underlying novelist persona, and suggest that we examine the distinctions between them. Read in this light, Lily Briscoe and Miss La Trobe, to cite the most prominent examples, are demonstrably stand-ins for Woolf as an artist in many respects, but they are also markers of an absent self-portrait of the novelist. And the present absence of the novelist in Sandel's second novel resonates with Woolf's distinction between the writer and other artists: Alberta is surrounded by painters and sculptors in Paris but despite Sandel's frequent ekphrastic passages designed to convey Alberta's aesthetic sensibility through her regard of other artists' works, her own artistry is largely unrepresented in the text. The painful tension between Alberta's writerly identity and her persistent failure even to put pen to paper arguably defines the book as an anti-*Künstlerroman* in the sense that artistic expression on the part of the protagonist is markedly absent.

It comes as a joy and a relief to the reader when, in the third book, Alberta moves back to Norway and finds a little room of her own in the farmhouse of a sympathetic neighbor: there she retreats from the domestic duties at which she is a dismal failure and finally brings her manuscript to light. In working through her manuscript, Alberta reflects upon aesthetics and comes to articulate a writing process and an aesthetic vision similar to that of Woolf. Facing the sheaf of papers:

a few of them brought clarity, others nausea and fear, all of them bother and rewriting. She would be seized with hatred of this old manuscript, and a desire to destroy it. Life passes, we alter, we change position in relation to things, seeing them from different points of view... Half in delirium she struck out and cut down, took sections out and put them back in again... Together they would perhaps turn into something one day, but wall after wall of doubt had to be broken down, doubt that this irrelevant story could possibly interest anyone. (*AA* 266)

Certainly, Stephen Dedalus never referred to his as an "irrelevant story," but this passage does evoke Woolf's regular references in her diary to "the futility of it all" (*AWD* 123) or the conviction that "I have trained myself to silence" (letter to Ethel Smyth, in Moran 51). In her expression of self-doubt, Sandel evinces a self that contains within it a critical public regard just as Woolf does in her diary. She formulates her aesthetic project in response to this condition, for the endeavor of delving beneath the surface of a social order that defines artists as men goes hand in hand with that of breaking down walls of self-doubt. Alberta is regularly subject to such sexist pronouncements: for example, a male artist in Paris informs a newly-arrived aspiring woman painter that she should cut her losses by marrying and having a baby, and her mother-in-law offers the baffled suggestion, "Wouldn't dress-making or something like that be better [than writing novels]" (*AA* 278). If this is surface reality, then it follows that she must break it down and push beneath its surface, and in so doing she must reformulate the subject of autobiography as one that externalizes and thus gains leverage from the censure of others.

Similarly, Woolf accompanies notes of self-doubt with expressions of being "plunged in the richest strata of my mind. I can write and write and write now: the happiest feeling in the world" (*AWD* 69). And, as Sandel battles chronic moments of "weariness and despondency [with] a stubborn will to continue, a hungering uneasiness, that could only be quieted by life itself; that could intoxicate itself with small, fluttering verses on a clear evening in spring..." (*AA* 266), Woolf shores up her anxieties about "superficial, glittery writing" with the conviction that she does, in fact, reach "life" through a deeper layer of representation (*AWD* 69). The play of surfaces and depths, of dispersal and condensation, in the discourses of both Woolf and Sandel underlies their ambivalent/absent self-portraiture as novelists. Their shared aesthetic theory confers upon language the power to manifest the depths of mind, life, and experience which they plumb while maintaining skepticism about the writer's ability to wield language in such a way. As Woolf explains in *A Room of One's Own*, the writer is more attuned to "reality" than others, but she goes on to define reality as "something erratic, very undependable," with the consequence that "it makes the silent world more real than the world of speech" (*AROO* 110). Thus the tension between what can be expressed in language and what *cannot* defines both authors' works and results in particular silences. As Patricia Lawrence argues in her reading of different forms of silence in Woolf's work, the "unsaid," the "unspoken," and the "unsayable" all form integral elements of her novels. Similarly, Julia Briggs writes that Woolf's "concern with the as-yet-unsaid, or even the not-to-be-said remained a feature of Woolf's fiction from first to last" (Briggs 2006, 162). One result of this aesthetic of silence, Lawrence concludes, is that "Woolf displaces the 'speaking subject'... in the novel" (Lawrence

11)—including, I would add, herself. As Woolf critics have noted, her fiction is full of gaps and lacunae, one of which is occupied by the present absence of her autobiographical subjectivity.[5] The absence in Woolf's fiction of her self-portraiture as a novelist can thus be read as a function of her aesthetic; as she explains in *A Room of One's Own* she eschews the "arid" shadow cast by the pronoun "I," preferring instead the anonymity of the disembodied, androgynous mind (*AROO* 100).

Sandel corroborates Woolf's aesthetic vision in both lamenting the limitations of language and celebrating its transcendent properties, and this plays into her deferred portrayal of the woman novelist in the first two novels of her trilogy. However, she proceeds through the fraught process that Evy Varsamopoulou stipulates in her study of the *Künstlerinroman*.[6] Drawing on Cixous, Varsamopoulou expands on the idea that "I" is the arid, overshadowing pronoun rejected by Woolf. Varsamopoulou writes, "In order to write, the subject must let go of the socio-cultural 'I' of daily exchange in the world of real time and fall into the 'abyss' where she may discover the 'limitless' and the 'infinite'" (Varsamopoulou). Sandel's chronology—which moves from *Alberta and Freedom* to *Alberta Alone*—articulates a process of "coming to writing" that amounts to a tearing away from others and thus from a socio-cultural pronoun. While *Alberta and Freedom* culminates in marriage and motherhood, *Alberta Alone* depicts her reasoned abandonment of her family in order to pursue her writing. This rupture is not an easy one, and it involves the "sudden overthrow of the guardian element in herself, which hurt for a second, then was good" (*AA* 276) as well as the certainty that "she had finished groping in a fog for warmth and security... No arms around her any more, not even those of a child: [only] naked life, as far ahead as she could see" (*AA* 283). The peril and pain of separating from an anterior self is crystallized in a scene uncannily adjacent to Charlotte Perkins Gilman's "The Yellow Wallpaper" in which Alberta is commanded to "break through" by her own voice screaming at her from the other side of a wall: "Stumbling, she reached a wall. In a corner there was a black hole, just big enough for her arm to pass through. She put it in, groped in the empty air inside, understood nothing, called again, heard her own voice in a cracked howl. Then an answer came from the other side of the wall: You must break through!" (*AA* 252). The trilogy essentially closes with Alberta going forth to forge in the smithy of her soul the uncreated consciousness of herself but, read in adjacency with Woolf, Sandel's deferral of the novelist persona in the first two volumes of the trilogy emerges as a reflection of an underlying aesthetic theory she shares with Woolf—of wanting to reach behind the cotton wool, find the elusive thread, tap the hidden vein, exceed the limits of the social body. If Woolf edits her writerly shadow out of her novels altogether, Sandel demonstrates the strategy of self-editing in the case where her identity as a writer is her primary subject matter. Her self-portrait ultimately stands on the culmination of transitory moments seized in language—a language about which Sandel marvels: "What a language! What a concise and descriptive and direct language, full of clarity, clothing thought compactly. My language." [And lest we forget, this perfect language reads: "For et sprog. For et knapt og malende og omsvøpsløst sprog, rett på og klart, sluttende tett om tanken. Mitt sprog" (*Bare Alberte* 343)]. Yet she quite clearly regards herself as does Woolf: as "sealed vessels afloat upon what it is convenient to call reality; at some moments, without a reason, without an effort, the sealing matter cracks; in floods reality" (*MOB* 142) that can be grasped in language. By editing out the vessel itself, the socio-cultural "I" who casts a shadow "shapeless as mist" (*AROO* 100), Woolf and Sandel strive to immerse their writing in what they refer to as life or reality, and in the cases where this life or reality is their own, their strategy of self-editing results in artfully deferred and rerouted self-portraiture.

Notes

1. I refer to Barbara Christian's concept of the writer-critic. Christian, whose purpose is to design a theoretical tool for reading African American literature, explains how literary texts are both subjects of study and critical tools that can be used to theorize other literary texts addressing shared topics, themes, aesthetics, and bodies of human experience.
2. This also puts one in mind of another contemporary, Jean Rhys, who carted her black exercise notebooks around London and Paris.
3. Brenda Silver makes the important point that Leonard Woolf was the architect of *A Writer's Diary* and that he organized and published this collection of diary entries in the interest of establishing his wife's legacy as a great writer.
4. It is noteworthy that Woolf includes male novelists among her artist figures in contrast to female figures who do not write. For example, in *The Voyage Out*, Rachel eventually loses her ability to read, much less write, when she abandons her Gibbon tome on a hillside, and Katherine Hilbery is emphatic when, surrounded by literary figures in *Night and Day*, she insists, "I don't write myself."
5. Such readings include that of Briggs, who concludes, "loss and absence lie at the heart of Woolf's art" (Briggs 2005, 3) as well as analyses of the ways in which Woolf routes her fiction around unrepresentable scenes of trauma.
6. Varsamopoulou pointedly uses the feminine form of the masculine German word, Künstlerroman to analyze women writers' self-portraiture.

Works Cited

Benstock, Shari. *The Private Self: Theory and Practice of Women's Autobiographical Writings*. Chapel Hill, NC: U of North Carolina P, 1988.
Briggs, Julia. *Virginia Woolf: An Inner Life*. New York: Penguin, 2005.
—. *Reading Virginia Woolf*. Edinburgh: Edinburgh UP, 2006.
Christian, Barbara. "The Race for Theory." *Making Face, Making Soul: Haciendo Caras: Creative and Critical Perspecties by Feminists of Color*. Ed. Gloria Anzaldua. St. Paul: Aunt Lute Books, 1995. 335-345.
Dimock, Wai Chee. "A Theory of Resonance." *PMLA* 12.5 (1997): 1060-71.
Essex, Ruth. *Cora Sandel: Seeker of Truth*. New York: Peter Lang, 1995.
Fernald, Anne. *Virginia Woolf: Feminism and the Reader*. New York: Palgrave Macmillan, 2006.
Hunt, Linda."*The Alberta Trilogy:* Cora Sandel's Norwegian Künstlerroman and American Feminist Literary Discourse." *Writing the Woman Artist: Essays on Poetics, Politics and Portraiture*. Ed. Suzanne Jones. Philadelphia: U of Pennsylvania P, 1991.
Lawrence, Patricia Ondek. *The Reading of Silence: Virginia Woolf in the English Tradition*. Stanford: Stanford UP, 1991.
Moran, Patricia. *Virginia Woolf, Jean Rhys, and the Aesthetics of Trauma*. New York: Palgrave Macmillan, 2007.
Parati, Graziella. *Public History, Private Stories: Italian Women's Autobiography*. Minneapolis, MN: U of Minnesota P, 1996.
Sandel, Cora. *Alberta Alone*. Trans. Elizabeth Rokkan. Athens, OH: Ohio UP, 1984.
—. *Alberta and Freedom*. Trans. Elizabeth Rokkan. Athens, OH: Ohio UP, 1984.
—. *Bare Alberte*. Oslo: Gyldendal, 1939.
Silver, Brenda. *Virginia Woolf Icon*. Chicago: U of Chicago P, 1999.
Varsamopoulou, Evy. *The Poetics of the Künstlerinroman and the Aesthetics of the Sublime*. Hants, UK and Burlington, VT: Ashgate, 2002.
Woolf, Virginia. *A Room of One's Own*. San Diego, New York, and London: Harcourt Brace and Co., 1981.
—. *A Writer's Diary*. London: The Hogarth Press, 1954.
—. *Moments of Being*. San Diego, New York, and London: Harcourt Brace and Co., 1985.

Reading the Other, Editing the Self: Mentoring in Woolf and Welty

by Cheryl Hindrichs

In April and May of 2008, there was a fascinating discussion on the Virginia Woolf list-serve regarding the complicated effects of Woolf's lines "There she was" and "There she sat." Like the many Woolfians who responded, I've been beguiled by these epiphanic bombs or blossoms of three words that serve central structural and thematic functions in Woolf's fiction. Their appearances have a basic structure: through free indirect discourse, a narrator conveys the point of view of a character who is engaged in reading the signs of another character, editing, interpreting, and projecting those signs in a series of readings that re-imagine the other. This process culminates in a suspended moment when the character, transfixed, paradoxically finally "sees" the other. It is in this moment that the narrator, through the character's vision, conveys the duality of the reading process—these statements of three words ("There she was" or "There she sat") point simultaneously to a fixing of meaning or pinning of personality and the impossibility of intimately knowing the other or of formulating the self neatly sprawling on a pin. And it is this tension—between the lure of knowing and capturing the other and the endless play that the indeterminacy of the self and the signifier entails—that Woolf captures in her three words, words that in turn transfix us, her readers.

The reader's gaze is directed here, like the character who reads the other in the story, in a double movement. We are invited by the other (the author) to participate in the creative pleasures of imagining and projecting the other, and further, to become aware of our own imaginative capacity. The author-reader-text dynamics in these epiphanic moments of "seeing" the other in Woolf's fiction lead us to examine the role of the reading process in perceiving the other as a creative process, one that, moreover, plays a central role in formulating the self.

The particular three-word moment that I had in mind in following this thread appears in one of Woolf's short stories, "Moments of Being: Slater's Pins Have No Points." The story opens with Miss Julia Craye, a piano teacher, asking the question, "Slater's pins have no points—don't you always find that?" of her student, Fanny Wilmot, who stoops to find the pin for the rose that had been fastened to her dress (103). The question, accompanied by the final chords of the Bach fugue Miss Craye has just played as a special treat for her "favorite pupil," gives Fanny "an extraordinary shock" (103) and indeed sets up the thematic and synthetic dynamics of the story.[1] The rest of the story follows Fanny's exploration of this question and other snatches of dialogue she recalls spoken by or about Miss Craye, as she engages in an elaborate back and forth of reading and interpreting her and then re-editing and projecting a vision of Miss Craye ultimately in order to come to some kind of intimate knowledge of her mentor. The story ends when, having tried out a number of different narratives, Fanny rejects the conventional narrative of the lonely spinster and affirms the complexity and beauty of the life she imagines Miss Craye lives, and, quoting the story, "She saw Julia—" (111).

The dynamics of Woolf's three-word epiphany are echoed in another short story that seems to use this scene of the piano teacher mentor and her protégé to comment on the role of the reading process in formulating the self: Eudora Welty's "June Recital." The story begins with the point of view of the young Loch Morrison, who is sick in bed, watching the activities in the vacant house next door: upstairs he has seen the young Virgie Rainey engaged in a tryst with a sailor; meanwhile, downstairs a mysterious old woman whom we learn is Miss Eckhart arrives and decorates with newspapers and other flammable materials the rooms where she once gave piano lessons to Virgie as well as to Loch's sister Cassie Morrison. The story's point of view shifts to Cassie in her room where she has heard Miss Eckhart playing *Für Elise*, a song she had always played for the favorite pupil Virgie. The scene playing out next door is ultimately an occasion for Cassie to explore half-remembered, half-imagined scenes of her mentor and peer and, finally, to come to a critical awareness of her self. As *Für Elise* plays, Cassie's "uncritical self of the crucial present [...] slowly came forward—as if called on" and, as Welty writes, "Cassie saw herself" (33).

But, here I pause to ask: is my linking of these stories of piano teachers and their students only a very personal quirk and not appropriate for a scholarly audience? I came to two deductions. First, I hypothesized, we think back through our teachers if we are academics. And, second, if we are raised in a family for whom the very idea of the extravagance of piano lessons is unimaginable, then we are likely to develop as an adult a virulent case of pianist envy. The former, an opportunity to examine mentorship in Woolf studies, certainly might be of interest to an audience of Woolf scholars and common readers. Indeed, Suzan Harrison's *Eudora Welty and Virginia Woolf: Gender, Genre, and Influence* reveals the richness of examining "Welty's keen, perceptive, and lifelong interest in Woolf's writing" by tracking the relationship of Woolf's and Welty's novels (1).[2] The latter hypothesis, pianist envy, may indeed be a personal quirk; nonetheless, that Woolf and Welty choose a teacher of music for scenes exploring the relationship of mentor and protégé is significant given that both authors function as mentors for readers in these works of fiction, guiding us to discover the polyphonic potential of prose. In both stories, music functions as a structural device that serves thematic purposes. In Woolf a Bach fugue and in Welty a metronome's ticking are mimetic content that set up, in the opening pages, a synthetic device by which the stories unfold and which serve the thematic purpose of exploring the knowability of the other: how we come to know the other, and thus, ourselves.

In comparing these short stories, then, I focus on how the reader is asked to place his or herself in the role of one of the characters (Fanny or Cassie) reading, interpreting, and projecting another character's narrative (Julia Craye's or Miss Eckhart's). More than nicely done psychological portraits, these stories enable readers to become aware of their own reading and editing processes in literature and life. In portraying the dynamic process of interpreting and re-imagining the other, Woolf and Welty lead us to examine how internalized narratives shape our perceptions and how the other—in this case the mentor and protégé—can open a space for creative action and critical self-reflection, not only for the character but also for the flesh-and-blood reader. Part of the seduction of these texts, captured in their affirmative yet mournful three-word variations of "There she was," ultimately is in the mirroring they offer, the element of narcissism in all our interpretive work which is, after all, rudimentary to the formation of identity.

Although those readers who have had flesh-and-blood piano teachers may object, I want to emphasize that to a great extent *we choose* our own mentors. In examining how Woolf and her protégé Welty portray these character-centered scenes about reading and interpreting, it is useful to note what Woolf chose from *her* mentors, particularly those consummate portrait painters and lovers of music Laurence Sterne and Walter Pater. In "Phases of Fiction," Woolf praises Sterne for his narrator's ability to build up "an extraordinary portrait of a character" while ultimately giving "his characters that little extra push which frees them from [the author's] tutelage so that they are something more than the whims and fancies of a brilliant brain," and indeed it is a push that activates the reader: "In no other book are the writer and reader so involved together" (92-3). In subverting all the usual conventions, Sterne takes us "beyond the range of personality into a world which is not altogether the world of fiction" (93). Indeed, it is our world, where, in the best author-reader-text dynamics, as in the best mentor-protégé dynamics, we are kindled by the author's gem-like flame and led to burn creatively and self-critically, are invited to experience, as "'the children of this world' in art and song" the "fruit of a quickened, multiplied consciousness" (Pater 153) .

It is not a coincidence, then, that I should take as a mentor and theoretical frame for this comparative analysis Wolfgang Iser, who, in "The Reading Process: A Phenomenological Approach," marshals Pater, Sterne, and Woolf to show that the pleasures of the literary text are its inspiration in the reader to active and creative participation (1002-03). Iser also models a means of mapping the "playground between author and reader" that is helpful in approaching the questions raised by these two stories, in which playing and learning to play figure so largely not only within the story but between author and reader. In "The Play of the Text," Iser proposes this play "can be described on three different levels: (1) structural, (2) functional, and (3) interpretive" (253). The structural and functional dimensions of Woolf's and Welty's works compound the polyphonic potential of our interpretations and privilege dynamic models of reading/writing. My claim is that these stories playfully employ structures that function to invite readers to reflect on how our minds use structures. In inviting such self-reflexivity, Woolf and Welty act as mentors, calling us to reflect on and make use of the modernist forms they model, thus performing for us—their favorite pupils—what Paul Armstrong has described as the social use of modernist form. According to Armstrong, modernist forms that "explore the vicissitudes of consciousness and the constitution of the self are not self-referential aesthetic exercises" (Armstrong 172). Rather, the "play" they undertake with the reader creates a stage for fostering "the ability to communicate *about* differences *across* differences in order to test and explore opposing, incompatible visions of freedom and fulfillment" (Armstrong 174).

The structural devices employed as vehicles for a meditation on perception and subject formation are one of the great pleasures of these texts. As I have mentioned, Woolf's "Slater's Pins" unfolds in a kind of literary transposition of the form of a musical fugue: Julia Craye's opening question, "Slater's pins have no points—don't you always find that?" serves as a theme that Fanny takes up, repeats, and tries out in a series of variations that play out short narrative scenes of her teacher's life which are fabricated out of heard or remembered discourse and Fanny's own imagination. Welty's "June Recital" also prominently features a musical device—a metronome: its relentless marking of time provides a device for Welty to portray her characters' attempts to live within or outside of conventional narratives.[3] Both stories also prominently incorporate visual technologies as structural devices in their narrative progression—specifically the telescope and cinema.[4]

In Welty's "June Recital," the telescope that Cassie's brother Loch uses, the "keyhole" viewpoints the text models, and Cassie's montage of memories underscore the paradox of such technologies—they seem to bring the subject into intimate proximity but ultimately disclose an unbridgeable gap, which is the central thematic dimension Welty explores through Cassie's point of view. We learn from Cassie's reconstruction of the relationship of Virgie and Miss Eckhart that Virgie's great musical talent has culminated not in her moving on from Morgana to further studies (as Miss Eckhart desired), but in her playing accompaniment at the local picture show. Moreover, the climax of the plot progression, when Miss Eckhart has set fire to the piano and parlor, is depicted from Cassie's point of view as a kind of Keystone Cops vignette when "Old Man Moody, the marshal, and Mr. Fatty Bowles" arrive (69). Through the dissonance of the Wagnerian tragedy of Miss Eckhart's immolation playing out in a Chaplinesque ragtime, Welty eschews sentiment and conveys the bitter, complicated tragedy threading the lives of Cassie, Virgie, and Miss Eckhart.

Such structural devices which play out at each level of the texts' dimensions—mimetic, thematic, and synthetic—enable readers to reflect on the role of schemata in our perceptual processes. As Iser notes, we utilize schemata "to pattern things which are otherwise ungraspable or that we want to bring within reach on our own conditions" ("Play" 254). Both social conventions and conventions of art function then to manage and edit our perceptions. Schemata, however, not only enable us to adapt to the world, but also allow us to adapt the world to our own dispositions (Iser 154). In each story, we see a character utilizing a schemata her mentor has modeled and then utilizing those forms, first, to grasp "things which are otherwise ungraspable," and, second, to subvert social conventions and open an imaginative space outside of them.

Given the very conventional narratives about unmarried, mature women who teach piano, what is the "ungraspable" that both Fanny and Cassie reach for in their imaginative questioning, narrating, editing, and projecting of their piano teachers? A primary interest is their mentors' choices to live alone. In both stories, Fanny and Cassie imagine a series of possible scenes, first trying out their society's conventional narratives for their teachers' lives—Fanny considers the view of pitying Miss Craye "for always doing everything alone" (104, 109), and Cassie reflects on Morgana's small-town views which pin Miss Eckhart as an outsider—a foreigner, a lover of art, and a single woman (38). Having suspended these conventional views, both Fanny and Cassie then take up the thread of a conventional scene of courtship in examining their teachers' singleness. Cassie imagines the tentative relationship of Miss Eckhart and the shoe salesman Mr. Sissum, creating a fuller and more complex picture of that relationship than Morgana's ultimate conclusion that "[Miss Eckhart] didn't know how to do about Mr. Sissum at all" (44). Fanny similarly imagines an old friend, the painter Mr. Sherman, calling on Miss Craye and taking her rowing on the Serpentine. Fanny reflects that the scene could be edited in any number of variations, "but one thing was constant—her refusal" and ultimately Miss Craye's "immense relief" for having not "sacrificed her independence" (108). In both stories, these protégés each begin with the conventional form, a familiar frame and ground, but both ultimately use the figure of their teacher to break from the conventional narrative. Realizing the editor they've internalized from social conventions, both use their mentors to imagine, in Cassie's case, alternative perceptual frames, and in Fanny's, altogether alternative narratives.

The "ungraspable" of these teachers has also suggested to critics a homosexual subtext. For example, Susan Clements offers a useful discussion of misrecognition and sexual identity in narrative choice in Woolf's story, and Janet Winston examines homoeroticism and mentoring in Woolf's story and Katherine Mansfield's "Carnation." However, both interpret Fanny's reading as obscuring or avoiding "an awareness of Julia's lesbianism" (Winston 69); in contrast, I argue that Fanny's reediting of Julia's life illustrates, on the one hand, the difficulty of the creative subject in realizing the "design that has been traced upon our minds which reading brings to light" (Woolf "Phases" 56) and, on the other, the potential of using art to break from that design. Critics' views of the homosexual subtext of Welty's story tend to reiterate the "design that has been traced upon our minds" by the dominant discourse; for example, Heather Cam's and Carey Wall's essays on "June Recital" read Miss Eckhart's possible lesbianism as a canker festering in Morgana that must be contained. In *One Writer's Beginnings*, however, Welty reflected that her character Miss Eckhart, while fashioned from some details of her own piano teacher, ultimately "derived from what I already knew for myself," a "passion" and vision of art very similar to Woolf's: "Exposing yourself to risk is a truth Miss Eckhart and I had in common. What animates and possesses me is what drives Miss Eckhart, the love of her art and the love of giving it, the desire to give it until there is no more left" (101). Julia's and Miss Eckhart's passion for their art coupled with the desire for an intimate knowledge evidenced in Fanny's and Cassie's imaginative explorations, suggests, if not the love that dare not speak its name, at the very least a kind of love that is not adequately formulated by existing narratives. Indeed, these are stories about using the inadequate, existing forms to reveal what is excluded and delimited, and, in so doing, they open a space for free-play. The figure of the piano teacher is thus the ground that Fanny and Cassie use to open up possibilities for their own life narratives. Whether the desire that circulates between these characters can be pinned as homosexual or not, we are drawn into an important reciprocal romance between the mentors and protégés. Moreover, in doing so through such dexterous narrative forms, Woolf and Welty draw attention to our relationship as readers to the texts and their authors.

As Iser writes, "herein lies the uniqueness of play: it produces, and at the same time allows the process of production to be observed" ("Play"259). The stories' play, then, draws us to consider how and why we use narratives—to ask why we "play the text." According to Iser, we may play the text to come to a particular meaning, a defensive "means of warding off the unfamiliar" (259); alternately, we may play the text to "open ourselves up to the unfamiliar" and thus obtain experience (259). In addition to these regulative and aleatory functions, Iser lists "that of pleasure" (259)—which in Woolf's and Welty's texts lies in the intimacy they create with readers through their modernist innovations of form which draw us to examine the tensions we negotiate in the reading and editing process—the familiar and the unfamiliar, the graspable and the ungraspable. Further, these characters' interest in reading these particular others elucidates how Woolf and Welty make their readers so interested in reading these stories—they call upon the narcissistic desire implicated in the reading process by inviting our creative expansion.

That is, the open-endedness of key moments in these texts (signified most tellingly in the three-word epiphanic moments such as "She saw Julia—" (Woolf 111) and "Cassie saw herself" (Welty 33) flatter readers' powers of interpretation, thus opening up a subject-position for us as "favorite pupil[s]" who can rightly "read" or appreciate the complexity of their mentors and thus take up the creative work they model. Readers thus are invited to "see" themselves in these texts. According to Iser, we read both to formulate ourselves and to expand the field of play in which we formulate ourselves.

The significance of these stories is not simply that they ask us to extend our imagination sympathetically into the subjectivity of a spinster piano teacher. Rather it is that these stories ask us to examine, if not interrogate, our very act of imagining such an other's subject position. In Woolf's case, the examination leads to an expansion, the opening up of a field of play which had been closed to conventional perceptual frames of consciousness. In Welty's case, the interrogation leads to an indictment, a warning to consider the power dynamics in any act of imagining the other and the need to examine our own investment in certain blindnesses. The final scenes of each story reflect this aspect of doubleness in the reading process; the stories diverge in the tenor of their final gestures—the tenor of their three-word epiphanic moments of "There she was." In Fanny's case, the phrase opens out, ascends expansively and opens doors, whereas Cassie's phrase illuminates a closing in, descends sorrowfully and delineates chosen boundaries, closed windows.

Notes

1. At the end of "Slater's Pins," Fanny finds the pin on the floor and picks it up, simultaneously formulating an affirmative vision of her teacher: "Was Miss Craye so lonely? No, Miss Craye was steadily, blissfully, if only for that moment, a happy woman" (110). In this "transparent" moment, Fanny has a vision "as if looking through Miss Craye," followed by a telescoping series of narrative scenes which she has conjured up to signify her independent, singular, rich life, and concludes, "She saw Julia— / Julia blazed. Julia kindled. Out of the night she burnt like a dead white star. Julia opened her arms. Julia kissed her on the lips. Julia possessed it" (111).⁵ And here Woolf's three-word epiphanic moment spins us out into manifold interpretive possibilities. The phrase "dead white star," for example, might lead us to binary stars, discovered as a result of the eclipse Woolf had traveled with Vita Sackville-West to witness, and an apt metaphor for these characters. "Julia blazed. Julia kindled," might bring us back to Walter Pater, Woolf's relationship to her mentor Clara Pater, and the gem-like flame of art Miss Craye models for her student. A flame that might also lead us to Woolf's protégé Welty and her piano teacher who is literally set ablaze, and her student who is led to recall a line from Yeats's "The Song of Wandering Aengus," "*Because a fire was in my head*" (85). Woolf's story gives us, her readers, as Miss Craye has given her student Fanny, "that little extra push which frees them from [her] tutelage," as Woolf wrote of Sterne (92), and we are propelled into the pleasure of the text—of formulating and reformulating our field of meaning.

    In contrast to the opening out of Woolf's story, which is figured in the image of Julia seeming to fling the night of the uncurtained window "like a cloak behind her" (110), at the end of Welty's "June Recital," we are made intensely aware of the closed window of Cassie's room. Loch, who has climbed onto a tree branch and hangs there like "the morning star" (67), reflects to Cassie her own isolation. While she has imaginatively seen more than any of the other characters in the story, she ultimately sees herself as shut out:

    > She could never go for herself, never creep out on the shimmering bridge of the tree, or reach the dark magnet there that drew you inside, kept drawing you in. She could not see herself do an unknown thing. She was not Loch, she was not Virgie Rainey; she was not her mother. *She was Cassie* in her room, seeing the knowledge and torment beyond her reach, standing at her window. (68, emphasis added).

After Miss Eckhart has been taken away by the law, Cassie reflects that she and Loch "were spies too," who like the others in the town had, in seeing such events, "only hoped to place them […]. Then Morgana could hold them, and at last they were this and they were that" (79). Although Cassie has pinned her own complicity to want to pin Miss Eckhart and Virgie, such awareness proves a false comfort. In bed that night, she sees Miss Eckhart and Virgie as past gratitude and rescue, as "human beings terribly at large, roaming on the face of the earth. And there were others of them—human beings, roaming, like lost beasts" (85). The resonance of that line, echoing "She was Cassie," brings us as readers round to ourselves as "others of them." We are the "face [that] look[s] in" on Cassie's dreaming, Welty having drawn the curtain round us as well in this contemplation of "human beings terribly at large" (85).[6] Welty, for whom Woolf "was the one who opened the door" ("Art" 3), makes us aware of our presence in the room, our potential as favorite pupils and our responsibilities as compelling teachers. Having looked in on Fanny and Cassie—on how these characters read, reinterpret, edit, and narrate their mentors' lives—Woolf and Welty gently give us that little extra push, asking that we consider how we too participate in this process of reading and narrating the lives of our mentors and so formulate, reformulate, and edit our own.

The "shock" as an impetus to the creative process, a recurrent motif in Woolf's fiction, is analyzed by Woolf in "A Sketch of the Past," in which she posits her "shock-receiving capacity" as that which "makes [her] a writer" (72). The "shock" is "followed by the desire to explain it," and Woolf describes the "great delight" and "pleasure" of constructing a "whole" of "severed parts," of "making a scene come right; making a character come together" (72); this is the pleasure that I will argue that Woolf's Fanny experiences in imagining Miss Craye's character, and that Woolf invites us, too, to participate in through her depiction of Fanny's initial "shock" and subsequent efforts to "explain" Miss Craye.

2. Like Harrison, I follow Bakhtin's "concepts of dialogism and heteroglossia," rather than Bloom's concept of influence, in considering Woolf as a mentor for Welty, as well as her assertion that their works' resemblance lies not merely in surface motifs but in a "shared epistemology" (3).

3. Marilyn Arnold sees "the metronome [as] Welty's particular device for sounding the voice of time," both time's relentless "regularity" and its threatening reminder of mortality (107).

4. Holly Henry's analysis of the "powerful shaping effect" the telescope had "on Woolf's aesthetic imagination" (1) provides a useful frame for analyzing the "scoping" narrative strategies in Welty's story, as does Leslie Hankins's extensive work on Woolf's incorporation of cinematic techniques, particularly, "'Across the Screen of My Brain': Virginia Woolf's 'The Cinema' and Film Forums of the Twenties."

5. In the Januray 1928 version of the story, the paragraph that follows "She saw Julia—"appears: "She saw Julia open her arms; saw her blaze; saw her kindle. Out of the night she burnt like a dead white star. Julia kissed her. Julia possessed her" (63). The double voicing of the Haunted House revision creates a more powerful simultaneity of vision of implied author and implied reader.

6. In "The Modern Essay," Woolf notes the mentor-student relationship that "good" writing exercises: "it must draw its curtain round us, but it must be a curtain that shuts us in, not out" (50).

Works Cited

Armstrong, Paul B. *Play and the Politics of Reading: The Social Uses of Modernist Form.* Ithaca: Cornell UP, 2005.

Arnold, Marilyn. "'The Magical Percussion': Eudora Welty's Human Recital on Art and Time." *Southern Humanities Review* 23.2 (1989): 101-18.

Cam, Heather. "Learning from the Teacher: Alice Munro's Reworking of Eudora Welty's 'June Recital'." *South Pacific Association for Commonwealth Literature and Language Studies* 25 (1987): 16-30.

Clements, Susan. "The Point of 'Slater's Pins': Misrecognition and the Narrative Closet." *Tulsa Studies in Women's Literature* 13.1 (1994): 15-26.

Hankins, Leslie Kathleen. "'Across the Screen of My Brain': Virginia Woolf's 'The Cinema' and Film Forums of the Twenties." Gillespie, *The Multiple Muses of Virginia Woolf.* 148-79.

Harrison, Suzan. *Eudora Welty and Virginia Woolf: Gender, Genre, and Influence*. Baton Rouge, Louisiana State UP, 1997.
Henry, Holly. *Virginia Woolf and the Discourse of Science: The Aesthetics of Astronomy*. Cambridge: Cambridge UP, 2003.
Iser, Wolfgang. "The Play of the Text."*Prospecting: From Reader Response to Literary Anthropology*. Baltimore: Johns Hopkins UP, 1989. 249-61.
—. "The Reading Process: A Phenomenological Approach." *The Critical Tradition: Classic Texts and Contemporary Trends*. Ed. David H. Richter. Boston: Bedford/St. Martin's, 2006. 1002-14.
Pater, Walter. *The Renaissance: Studies in Art and Poetry*. 1873. Ed. Adam Phillips. Oxford: Oxford UP, 1985.
Wall, Carey. "'June Recital': Virgie Rainey Saved." *Eudora Welty: Eye of the Storyteller*. Kent, OH: Kent State UP, 1989. 14-31.
Welty, Eudora. "The Art of Fiction No. 47: Eudora Welty." Interview with Linda Kuehl. *The Paris Review* 55 (Fall 1972): 1-26.
—. "June Recital." *The Golden Apples*. New York: Harcourt, 1947.
—. *One Writer's Beginnings*. Cambridge: Harvard UP, 1984.
Winston, Janet. "Reading Influences: Homoeroticism and Mentoring in Katherine Mansfield's 'Carnation' and Virginia Woolf's 'Moments of Being: Slater's Pins Have No Points'." *Virginia Woolf: Lesbian Readings*. Ed. Eileen Barrett and Patricia Cramer. New York: New York UP, 1997. 57-77.
Woolf, Virginia. "The Modern Essay." 1922. *Collected Essays: Virginia Woolf*. Vol. 2. New York: Harcourt Brace and World, 1967. 41-50.
—. "Moments of Being: Slater's Pins Have No Points." *A Haunted House and Other Short Stories*. New York: Harvest, 1972. 101-11.
—. "Phases of Fiction." 1929. *Collected Essays: Virginia Woolf*. Vol. 2. New York: Harcourt, Brace and World, 1967. 56-102.
—. "A Sketch of the Past." *Moments of Being*. Ed. Jeanne Schulkind. 2nd ed. New York: Harvest, 1985.

ON NOT BEING ABLE TO PAINT: WRITING INHIBITIONS AND SELF-EDITING IN VIRGINIA WOOLF AND SYLVIA PLATH

by Nephie Christodoulides

Talking about a stasis in her writing, Plath notes in a 1959 Journal entry, "Feel oddly barren. My sickness is when words draw in their horns and the physical world refuses to be ordered, recreated, arranged and selected. I am a victim of it then, not a master" (*Journals* 516). Referring to Virginia Woolf's writing frustrations, Plath observes: "And she works off her depression over rejections [....] by cleaning out the kitchen. And cooks haddock & sausage. Bless her. I feel my life linked to her, somehow" (269).

In this paper I look into the two authors' link, casting into sharper relief their writing inhibitions and the way this discussion summons a consideration of borders and orality. Further, I examine briefly the way in which Woolf and Plath overcome their writing inhibitions by textual revision (self-editing) as part of their efforts to resolve their predicament with subjectivity. Marion Milner's book *On Not Being Able to Paint* provides me with a preliminary hypothesis for my analysis along with Julia Kristeva's theory of abjection.

Milner posits that when the painter, whom she equates with the writer, paints, she experiences fusion, a sort of transcendence of the separateness of self and objects (68). Talking about her own experience, Milner observes:

> [w]hen painting [...] there occurred [...] a fusion into a never-before-known wholeness; not only were the object and oneself no longer felt to be separate, but neither were thought and sensation and feeling and action. All one's visual perceptions of colour, shape, texture, weight, as well as thought and memory, ideas about the object and action towards it, the movement of one's hand together with the feeling of delight in the "thusness" of the thing, they all seemed fused in to a wholeness of being .... (142)

Milner sees the inhibition to create as closely associated with the fear of regression to this undifferentiated state in which the boundaries between self and object become blurred (xv).

As a springboard, Milner's theory informs my discussion of the writing inhibitions experienced by Plath and Woolf. Both related painting intrinsically to writing. Plath often saw her poems as visual representations of words, she reproduced many of her paintings in language; she was inspired by artists (De Chirico) and wrote "art poems." Woolf was fascinated with visual art, and as Roger Fry very wisely observed, she used "language as a medium of art" and made "the very texture of the words have a meaning and quality" (Roger Fry to Virginia Woolf, 18 Oct. 1918).[1]

☙

Preoccupation with boundaries is manifested in different parts of Woolf's work; occasionally, her characters seem to vacillate between states of complete worldly fusion, manifested as maternal or oceanic and the attainment of a well and tightly composed self whose borders are rigidly demarcated. Lily Briscoe desires to be reunited with the mother whom she re-finds in Mrs. Ramsay: "Could loving, as people called it, make her and Mrs. Ramsay one?" She seeks the "device for becoming, like waters poured into one jar, inextricably the same, one with the object one adored" (*TTL* 274). Further in *Between the Acts*, Mrs. Swithin, the intuitive visionary, claims: "But we have other lives, I think, I hope ... we live in others ... we live in things" (296). What she suggests here is an oceanic feeling, what much later Plath would term as "fusion with the things of this world" (JP 120). At the same time, Woolf periodically experiences a euphoric, maternal-uterine union with nature: "If you lie on the earth somewhere you hear a sound like a vast breath, as though it were the very inspiration of earth herself & all the living things in her" (qtd. in Lee 171).

It is my contention that the oscillation between borders and infinity, as Milner would read it, reflects Woolf's preoccupation with notions of productivity and inhibition. Since writing was important as a means of ordering reality by "putting it into words," writing inhibition was the loss of "all power over words" (qtd. in Lee 753). Very often, Woolf felt blocked when she toiled with ideas that seemed to elude her; they would then "travel on, over the horizon, like clouds, & I want peacefully for another to form or nothing" (qtd. in Lee 246). She felt that "there [was] something there," but its elusiveness puzzled her and she ended up writing "arrant nonsense" (246). Very often, especially with the "blank space in front of her," she resorted to domesticity: "planning meals and beating carpets and scrubbing the kitchen floor" (qtd. In Lee 755). What demands attention, however, is her preoccupation with orality manifested as cooking: "And now with some pleasure I find that its [sic] seven; & must cook dinner. Haddock & sausage meat. I think it is true that one gains a certain hold on sausage & haddock by writing them down" (*D5* 358). In 1929 she wrote to Vita, "I have only one passion in life – cooking. I have just bought a superb oil stove. I can cook anything [....] I cooked veal cutlets and cake today. I assure you it is better than writing these more than idiotic books (*L4* 93)."

Critics have occasionally noted a conspicuous absence of references to food in Woolf's *oeuvre*, which however, pays little justice to the topic, since a more profound consideration of the issue reveals subtle, albeit powerful allusions to food. A representative example includes a letter to Leonard about a dinner she had with Vita, "We began with pâté of duck, went on to trout. Gnocchi, stuffed chicken and spinach made with cream and then sour cream and a delicious cake and then pears a lib (*L3* 534)."

Further, Mrs. Ramsay's exquisite *boeuf en daube* in *To the Lighthouse* constitutes another food allusion that reinforces Woolf's preoccupation with food. This is a recipe which quite interestingly has been handed down to Mrs. Ramsay from her grandmother (330), thus establishing a maternal lineage, a relationship based on orality, which apart from the maternal nourishing quality, presupposes fusion in incorporation. For Kristeva nourishment constitutes the most "archaic relationship" between the mother and the child (*Powers of Horror* 75). Thus, by resorting to descriptions of food, Woolf enters the maternal realm, assumes the mother's nourishing role and is thus fused with her.

References to food are closely associated with borders and fusion: Mrs. Ramsay reflects on *boeuf en daube*: "And she peered into the dish with its shiny <u>walls</u> [my emphasis] and its <u>confusion</u> [borderless state – my emphasis] of savoury brown and yellow meats and its bay leaves and its wine" (330). Further, Mrs. Ramsay laments cookery in England, an "abomination" which wants the "delicious skins" of vegetables cut (330), as if depriving them of their right to possess a bordered, unified and stable entity.

Woolf's problem with creativity is often resolved in "madness," or what I would call "revelatory disease," a "reversion to a state anterior to language, to the sounds and cries a human being makes before language is learned" (Scarry 4). During this state, she attains depths of insight and emotional intensity: "Once or twice [while in the process of writing *The Waves*] I have felt that odd whirr of wings in the head which comes when I am ill so often" (*D* 3, 286). Further, she notes: "In health meaning has encroached upon sound. But in illness, with the police off duty [....] the words give out their scent and distill their flavour, and then, if at last we grasp the meaning, it is all the richer for having come to us sensually first" ("On Being Ill" 108).

Whereas writing inhibitions are associated with orality, manifested as cooking, madness, which induces the flow of writing upon the blank page, triggers refusal to eat. Quentin Bell, her nephew, observes: "She became convinced that her body was in some way monstrous, the sordid mouth and sordid belly demanding food — repulsive matter which must be excreted in a disgusting fashion; the only course was to refuse to eat" (qtd. in Caramagno 56). During attacks of *illness,* she would either refuse to eat, or she would "flip meat from her plate onto the tablecloth" and occasionally had to be spoon-fed (Southworth 148). In his memoir of the years 1911-1918, Leonard notes, "It might have been said that she had a (quite unnecessary) fear of becoming fat; but there was something deeper than that, at the back of her mind or in the pit of her stomach a taboo against eating" (163).

Far from being an illustration of the anorexic's determination to abstain from food, the above shows a close affinity between Woolf's preoccupation with food and the Kristevian notion of the abject.[2] Oral disgust is the most archaic form of abjection and has to do with the realization and ensuing repulsion of one's borders. The skin of the milk which causes retching and disgust reminds the self of its corporeality and the "walls of the skin" which divide it from the world; thus, food becomes abject as it signifies a border "between two distinct entities or territories" (75). Kristeva observes that the food which is proffered to her by her father and mother, is a sign of "their desire": "since food is not an 'other' for 'me,' who am only in their desire, I expel *myself,* I spit *myself* out. I abject myself within the same motion through which I claim to establish myself" (*Powers of Horror* 3). Refusal of food is a refusal of maternal and paternal love, the child's determination not to reciprocate their love, to reject the borders the paternal and maternal law would impose. Thus, Woolf's eating inhibitions manifest her determination not to resort to orality, which would remind the self of the maternal dependence. Conversely, since she rejects both paternal and maternal borders, she can attain a state of primary narcissism, experience the lost oceanic feeling and use this experience as the starting point for the redrawing of boundaries and reformulation of the self. That the self is trying violently to do away with the childlike dependence on food is well manifested in Woolf's violent behavior towards the female nurses who try to feed her. Most importantly it is milk, which was recommended --- imposed might be an more apt term --- by "rest cure" specialists such as Dr. Silas Weir Mitchell that disgusts her.[3]

Far from merely being a disgusting beverage, it becomes abject since it is *par excellence* the maternal food.[4]

※

Until 1942 Plath felt elated at being part of the universe; however, with the birth of her brother she felt her oceanic feeling deserting her; she wasn't completely fused with the world but constituted a mere prosthesis, much like the addition of her baby brother to the world: "As from a star I saw, coldly and soberly, the *separateness* of everything. I felt the wall of my skin: I am I. That stone is a stone. My beautiful fusion with the things of this world was over" (*JP* 120). The move away from the Atlantic when the family left Winthrop to go to Wellesley after her father's death cut Plath off from her physical bond with the sea, thus contributing further to the loss of her oceanic feeling: "My father died, we moved inland. Whereon those nine first years of my life sealed themselves off like a ship in a bottle — beautiful, inaccessible, obsolete, a fine, white flying myth" (124).

Plath's preoccupation with borders resulting from the grim realization of the loss of her oceanic feeling was reflected much later in the resurfacing of her writing inhibition as fear of maternal attack. Writing for Plath was a means of "forg[ing] a selfhood," a recreation of "the flux and smash of the world through the small ordered word patterns [she] ma[d]e" (*J* 232). Conversely, not being able to write, being "stymied, stuck at a stasis" (232) and experiencing "some paralysis of the head" that got her "frozen" (272), was equated to effacement. Her 1953 breakdown and ensuing suicide attempt are seen as the collapse of her linguistic self: she was not accepted into Frank O' Connor's creative writing class at the Harvard Summer School; she could not concentrate, she could not read or write (Hayman 5). Wilbury Crockett's (her high school teacher) *pharmakon* was miraculous. He, according to Edward Butscher, "had sufficient sensitivity and experience with students to realize that language, above all could rescue Sylvia from the chaos of fragmented identity" (120). Crockett brought back and put together the shattered linguistic self by engaging her in linguistic games and thus restoring language.

The linguistic self that Plath longed to don was created by her mother Aurelia. From the very beginning, communication between mother and daughter was achieved through poetry, witty letters, and drawings: "I have made up some poems, here they are. I would like to give all these things to you" (*Coming to Light* 190).[5] When it came to creative writing and the agonizing months of linguistic sterility, Plath knew that her inhibition was the result of the suffocating presence of her mother: "To spite your mother, you don't write because you feel you have to give the stories to her or that she will appropriate them" (*J* 448). What Aurelia perceived as an "osmotic" relationship Plath saw as a maternal attack against her, threatening to turn her into "an extension of herself" (448). Thus, the writing inhibition freed her from Medusa's suffocating tentacles. "MY WRITING IS MY WRITING. Whatever elements there were in it of getting her approval I must no longer use it for that" (*J* 449).

Plath refused to write to avoid fusion which in this case is manifested as a maternal attack on her "encroachable self" (*J* 445). Since nourishment as already seen constitutes a primary characteristic of maternality, it is my conviction that Plath's writing inhibition was both maternal and oral. Plath was obsessed with food. Her *oeu-*

vre is interspersed with food references from *The Bell Jar's* succulent meals to detailed and meticulous food descriptions, especially after 1956, as well as food images in the poems, her children's books (*The Bed Book*, *The It-Doesn't Matter Suit*) and letters home. Images of defiled and abject food also feature prominently in her works and most significantly in the *Journals*. In her discussion of the abject, Kristeva endorses Mary Douglas' analysis of purity and defilement. For both Douglas and Kristeva, anything not characterized by strict classification into clear-cut categories, i.e. anything that does not respect borders is abject, hence polluting and forbidden. Plath is preoccupied with this pollution: in *The Bell Jar*, Esther is food poisoned during the Ladies' Day gala dinner. Also in the *Journals*, she hints at food poisoning, reflecting on the way the rancid and defiling food is ejected as the body boundaries are not strong enough to contain it (*J* 301-302).

Excrement permeating the walls of the skin also shows the malleability of the self and Plath was fascinated with other excrement as well: urine, menstrual blood, mucus (*J* 103, 165, 168, 602). According to Kristeva when "guts [sprawl] I am in the process of becoming another at the expense of my own death. During that course in which 'I' become, I give birth to myself amid the violence of sobs, of vomit" (*Powers of Horror* 3). The self expels itself, to be reborn. Thus, for Plath vomiting becomes a means of solving her predicament with subjectivity; the self is expelled only to be regenerated. With vomiting, the borders of the skin are loosened, the self enjoys a momentary release into worldly fusion, and although Plath may opt for that, she chooses to go back into the skin to be formed anew, thus being fortified this time against maternal attack.

ଔ

Once both Woolf and Plath overcome their inhibitions, whether in madness or near madness, the flow of words pours unstaunched onto the blank page, and the self engages in a process of revising, or self-editing the new material. As already noted, if for both writing is a means of establishing a selfhood, it can be said that by revising drafts, they revise the self and engage in reformulating the subject. A visit to Plath's archive at the Lilly Library (Bloomington) and Smith College (Northampton) highlights her elaboration and struggle over the written words: there are more than 100 drafts for the 40 poems of the *Ariel* collection. Plath ponders the choice of words, deleting and rewriting, considering several titles for poems.

Woolf also manipulates her fictionalized predicaments, exerting a hitherto unknown power over them, one that she is not able to exert over reality; doing so, she acquires further insight into things and is in a position to solve predicaments which would otherwise remain unsolved: "There is no Shakespeare; there is no Beethoven; certainly and emphatically there is no God; we are the words; we are the music; we are the thing itself" ("Sketch of the Past" 81). Manipulating words, she manipulates life and usurps God's creative power, thus endowing the self with divine creativity, much like Plath who wished to call herself "the girl who wanted to be God" (*Letters Home* 40)

ଔ

In 1962, a few months before her suicide, in a *nachtraglich* manner, Plath reminisces about her blissful oceanic feeling and deplores the erection of the "walls of her skin" which put an end to her primary narcissism. Under the stewing air of the bell jar, writing blocks vanish and writing is done in a creative rush; her "blue dawn" semiotic poems are free from any inhibition; nothing can staunch the flow of her creative energy. Now she longs for the worldly fusion which she finally achieves, answering, as Kristeva sees it "the call of the mother" (*About Chinese Women* 39), that emerges from the semiotic maternal *chora* and not from the suffocating tentacles of the Aurella-Medusa. Since the "motherly pulse" (*JP* 117) of the Atlantic was far away, there was only one way to partake in the cosmos: gas, which filled the self with the Ariel spirit and let her dance in a "beautiful fusion with the things of this world" (*JP* 120).

During her own "stymied" writing moments, Woolf resorts to domesticity, food preparation and orality. Her inhibition is healed in creative, "revelatory disease," when the mind "shuts itself up [and] becomes a chrysalis." Paradoxically, it is inside this enclosed space that "suddenly something springs ... & all doors opening ... I then begin to make up my story ... before I can control my mind or pen." The opening of all doors, however, beckoned in another call, the archaic voice of the maternal, semiotic sea with the "eternal renewal, the incessant rise and fall and fall and rise again" (*The Waves* 211), '[t]he song ... the call to our primitive instincts/Rhythm – Sound. Sight" (Fletcher 176), the semiotic call of the mother, which led to death.

Notes

1. The letter is housed in the University of Sussex Library and is cited by Frances Spalding in *Roger Fry: Art and Life*, Norwich: Black Dog Books, 1999.
2. For Julia Kristeva, the abject is manifested as the impossibility of clear-cut borders, lines of demarcation, and divisions between the clean and the unclean. It entails both revulsion and fascination with what existed in "the archaism of pre-objectal relationships," i.e. the chaos out of which the self was formed (*Powers of Horror* 9-10).
3. For a detailed discussion of the rest cure treatment see Achille Proust and Gilbert Ballet, *The Treatment of Neurasthenia*, translated by Peter Campbell Smith, London: Henry Kimpton, 1902.
4. References to Woolf's refusal to eat and especially her aversion of the milk diet prescribed by her physician Octavia Wilberforce are cited in *Word of Mouth: Body Language in Katherine Mansfield and Virginia Woolf*, UP of Virginia, 1996.
5. Writes Aurelia Plath: "Between Sylvia and me there existed – as between my own mother and me – a sort of psychic osmosis [....] Sylvia read almost all the books I collected while I was in college, used them as her own, underlining passages that held particular importance for her" (*Letters Home* 32). For Aurelia, who always encouraged Plath to be meticulous (see *Coming to Light*, Barbara Antonina Clarke Mossberg's article "Sylvia Plath's Baby Book" 189), the word "osmosis" was carefully chosen to indicate the kind of bond she would have liked to see formed between her and Plath, A denotative meaning of the term is "the tendency of a fluid to pass through a semi-permeable membrane into a solution where the concentration is lower, thus equalizing the conditions on either side of the membrane" (*Webster's Unabridged Encyclopaedic Dictionary* 1018). The attribute of the fluid to pass through and the ensuing condition where equalization is achieved is what Aurelia would have liked to have. Most importantly, since she knew that absolute fusion with the daughter was impossible, she wanted the border to be "semi-permeable" so that the flow of communication, what Plath resented in "Medusa" would be open. Further, she is proud to have observed Plath's underlining, as if this initiates an entrance to the maternal realm. By writing on her books she is writing on the maternal body, thus actually contributing to the formation of a bond between them.

Works Cited

Bishop, Edward. *Virginia Woolf (Modern Novelists)*. London: Palgrave Macmillan, 1991.
Briggs, Julia. *Virginia Woolf: An Inner Life*. London: Penguin Books, 2006.
Butscher, Edward. *Sylvia Plath: Method and Madness*. New York: Pocket Books, 1976.
Caramagno, Thomas. *The Flight of the Mind: Virginia Woolf's Art and Manic Depressive Illness*. Berkeley: U of California P, 1996.
Douglas, Mary. *Purity and Danger. An Analysis of Concepts of Pollution and Taboo*. London and New York: Routledge, 2000.
Fletcher, John and Andrew Benjamin, eds. *Abjection, Melancholia and Love*. London and New York: Routledge, 1990.
Hayman, Roland. *The Death and Life of Sylvia Plath*. Gloucestershire: Sutton Publishing Ltd, 2003.
Kristeva, Julia. *About Chinese Women*. Trans. Anita Barrows. New York: Marion Boyars Publishers Ltd, 1986.
—. *Powers of Horror: An Essay on Abjection*. Trans. Leon S. Roudiez. New York: Columbia UP, 1992.
Lee, Hermione. *Virginia Woolf*. London: Vintage Books, 1997.
Middlebrook Diane, and Marilyn Yalom. *Coming to Light: American Women Poets in the Twentieth Century*. Ann Arbor: Michigan UP, 1985.
Milner, Marion (Joanna Field). *On Not Being Able to Paint*. Los Angeles: J. P. Tarcher, Inc., 1957.
Plath, Sylvia. *The Bell Jar*. 1963. London: Faber & Faber, 1990.
—. *Collected Poems*. Ed. Ted Hughes. London Faber & Faber, 1981.
—. *Johnny Panic and the Bible of Dreams*. London: Faber & Faber, 1979. *JP*.
—. *The Journals of Sylvia Plath*. Ed. Karen V. Kukil. London: Faber & Faber, 2000. *J*.
—. *Letters Home*. Ed. Aurelia Plath. London: Faber & Faber, 1978.
Scarry, Elaine. *The Body in Pain: The Making and Unmaking of the World*. New York and Oxford: Oxford UP, 1985.
Southworth, Helen. *The Intersecting Realities and Fictions of Virginia Woolf and Colette*. Athens, Ohio: Ohio State UP, 2004.
Showalter, Elaine. *A Literature of Their Own: British Women Novelists from Bronte to Lessing*. London: Virago, 1982.
Woolf, Leonard. *Beginning Again: An Autobiography of the Years 1911-1918*. London: Hogarth Press, 1964.
Woolf, Virginia. *Between the Acts*. 1941. London: Penguin Books, 2000.
—. *The Diary of Virginia Woolf*. Ed.Andrew Mc Neillie. Vol. 3. 1925-1930. Eds. Anne Olivier Bell and Andrew Mc Neillie. London : Hogarth Press, 1980.
—. *The Essays of Virginia Woolf*. Ed. Andrew McNeillie. Vol. 4. London: Hogarth Press, 1985.
—. *The Letters of Virginia Woolf*. Eds. Nigel Nicolson and Joanne Trautmann Bankes. 6 vols. Vol. 3, 4. London: Hogarth Press, 1975-1980.
—. "On Being Ill" in *Selected Essays*. Ed. David Bradshaw. Oxford: Oxford UP 2008. 101-110.
—. *To the Lighthouse*. 1927. In *Three Great Novels*. London: Penguin Books, 1992. *TLL*.
—. *A Passionate Apprentice. The Early Journals.1897-1909*. Mitchell A. Leaska. London: Harcourt Brace Jovanovich, 1990.
—. *The Waves*.1931. In *Three Great Novels*. London: Penguin Books, 1992.

"THE INFLUENCE OF SOMEBODY UPON SOMETHING": *TO THE LIGHTHOUSE* IN SYLVIA PLATH'S WORK

by Luke Ferretter

Sylvia Plath's relationship to Virginia Woolf is most frequently discussed with reference to Plath's poetry. Even when critics such as Steven Axelrod and Tracy Brain discuss Woolf's influence upon Plath's fiction, the emphasis tends to be upon *Mrs. Dalloway*, which, it is argued, is a precursor of *The Bell Jar* (Axelrod 113-25; Brain 142-50). It is true that *Mrs. Dalloway* provides Plath with a model of writing about women's lives. What has been overlooked, however, in critical discussion of Plath's relationship to Virginia Woolf is the central role that *To the Lighthouse* plays in that relationship. In this essay, I will discuss the place of *To the Lighthouse* in Sylvia Plath's work. Plath learns from this novel in a complex series of ways, and its influence pervades her work. In particular, I will argue, it provides her with a model of feminist fiction. If *Mrs. Dalloway* enables Plath to write about the details of women's lives, it is *To the Lighthouse* that enables her to write about the gender politics that govern those lives.

Woolf's novel is the kind of semi-autobiographical narrative which Plath herself was most interested in writing. Almost all of Plath's fictions are closely based on incidents and events in her own life. Plath was able to identify especially closely with *To the Lighthouse*, since it is based on Woolf's childhood by the sea, tragically interrupted by the death of a parent. Plath herself had spent her own childhood by the sea, also to have it tragically interrupted by the death of a parent. These events were fundamental in the formation of Plath's sensibility, as they were of Woolf's:

> In the spring of 1895 mother died. Father instantly decided that he never wished to see St Ives again. And perhaps a month later Gerald went down alone; settled the sale of our lease to some people called Millie Dow, and St Ives vanished for ever. (Woolf, *MOB* 136)

> My father died, we moved inland. Whereon those nine first years of my life sealed themselves off like a ship in a bottle – beautiful, inaccessible, obsolete, a fine, white, flying myth. (Plath, *Johnny Panic* 116)

Plath knew from *A Writer's Diary* that writing *To the Lighthouse* was a cathartic work for Woolf: "I used to think of [father] and mother daily; but writing the *Lighthouse* laid them in my mind…I was obsessed by them both, unhealthily, and writing of them was a necessary act" (Woolf, *AWD* 129). Some of Plath's best writing also results from working through her memories of her relationship with her mother and father. Her first volume of poetry, *The Colossus*, takes its title from a poem in which the speaker attempts to work out her relationship to her dead father. "I shall never get you put together entirely," she tells him (*Collected Poems* 129). Indeed, Plath's key symbolic term for her father, "colossus," can be found in Woolf's portrayal of her own father-figure in *To the Lighthouse*, as Mr.

Ramsay's "remarkable boots" are described, in Lily Briscoe's view, as "sculptured; colossal" (167). His children watch him as "he rose and stood in the bow of the boat, very straight and tall, for all the world, James thought, as if he were saying, 'There is no God'" (224). In the same way, many of Plath's father-figures stand in the place of God. In "Daddy," the speaker's father is a "bag full of God" (*Collected Poems* 222), and in the world he creates for her, there is "No God, but a swastika / So black no sky could squeak through" (223). In Plath's story "The Shadow," the disappearance of the narrator's father to a detention camp for German Americans during World War II is also the disappearance of God from her life. "I don't think there is any God, then," she tells her mother, "Not if such things can happen." Plath ends the story with her mother's reply: "'Some people think that,' my mother said quietly" (*Johnny Panic* 344).

In March 1957, Plath reads *A Writer's Diary*, as she is working on the draft of her first, unpublished novel. She writes, "I get courage by reading" Woolf's recently published diaries, adding, "I feel very kin to her" (*Letters* 305). That summer, on vacation in Cape Cod, Plath reads three of Woolf's novels, describing them as "excellent stimulation for my own writing" (*Letters* 324). In her journal, she reflects, "Virginia Woolf helps. Her novels make mine possible" (*Journals* 289). One of the most important ways in which Woolf's novels make Plath's possible is that they provide her with a model of feminist fiction. This is true most of all of *To the Lighthouse*. Woolf's portrayal of Mr. Ramsay, the great philosopher with a "splendid mind," is a precursor of the many male experts of Plath's fiction, highly regarded by society but of whose relationships to women she is deeply critical, from Henry Minton in "Sunday at the Mintons," through Dr. Gordon in *The Bell Jar*, to President Eisenhower in her collage of Cold War images. Perhaps the clearest debt is over the question of spatial thinking in men and women. Mr. Ramsay can scarcely believe his daughter cannot locate points on a map:

> He wished she would try to be more accurate, he said: "Tell me – which is East, which is West?" he said, half laughing at her, half scolding her, for he could not understand the state of mind of anyone, not absolutely imbecile, who did not know the points of the compass…He thought, women are always like that; the vagueness of their minds is hopeless. (*TTL* 182)

In Plath's "Sunday at the Mintons," Henry is scandalized in precisely the same way by his sister Elizabeth's different, feminine mode of thinking to his own: "'Really, I don't think direction matters so much. It's the place you're going to that's important,' she announced petulantly. 'I mean, do you truly think about the direction you're going in all the time?' (*Johnny Panic* 145)" The entire room seems to take offence at this "open insolence," and Henry declares "staunchly," "Of course I think where I'm going on the map…I always trace out my route beforehand, and then I take a map with me to follow as I travel" (146). Elizabeth's response to Henry's lifelong assumption of superiority to her is her fantasy of his death with which the story ends. This fantasy begins with Elizabeth losing her mother's brooch by the sea. As Karen Kukil has pointed out, this incident echoes the episode in *To the Lighthouse* in which Minta Doyle loses her grandmother's brooch by the sea. Plath wrote "Sunday at the Mintons" in April 1952, shortly after she had first encountered *To the Lighthouse* in her sophomore course at Smith College, Literature of the 19th and 20th

Centuries. This borrowing is no doubt unconscious, but it indicates the extent to which Woolf's novel had permeated Plath's sensibility as a writer. With the device of the lost brooch, Plath situates her story within the tradition of feminist fiction that she found in *To the Lighthouse*.

In *A Writer's Diary*, Woolf worried that *A Room of One's Own* had a "shrill feminine tone" that her friends would dislike (145). Plath underlined this phrase in her copy of the text. What Plath learns above all from *To the Lighthouse* is a model of feminist writing that could not be criticized in these terms. She found in Woolf's novel a kind of fiction that clearly and firmly articulates feminist criticism of the patriarchal society in which it is set, but which remains feminine in a socially acceptable sense. In *To the Lighthouse*, as in much of *A Room of One's Own*, Woolf does this with humor. She portrays gender relations with a dry, understated, ironic wit that Plath found extremely attractive and that she looked to imitate in her own work. Indeed, Woolf's feminist irony is one of the most fundamental precursors of Plath's humorous voices, more so than the irreverent wit of Salinger's alienated adolescents, which is more frequently cited. This irony is at work throughout *To the Lighthouse*. We see it in Lily Briscoe's vision of the kitchen table in a tree, subverting with its quotidian feminine nature and ridiculous position the importance of Mr. Ramsay's philosophy, of which the kitchen table is all she can understand. Mrs. Ramsay subverts the self-importance of her husband's academic disciple Mr. Tansley in the same way, able to remember only that he is writing a dissertation about "the influence of somebody upon something" (*TLL* 73). Lily Briscoe represents the technique directly. Mr. Tansley tells her "Women can't write, women can't paint," and as she struggles with her response to this, she decides to focus on her painting and all it means to her, "Could she not hold fast to that, she asked herself, and not lose her temper, and not argue; and if she wanted a little revenge take it by laughing at him?" (*TLL* 94). Lily's response to Mr. Tansley's patriarchal attitude is also the narrator's own, throughout the novel: she does not lose her temper, and when she wants revenge on the men who denigrate women in the society she describes, she takes it by laughing at them. This is how Plath's humor works, and she learns it directly from Woolf. A frequent example in Plath's work is the understated juxtaposition of an expert male view with a feminist subversion of this view. This is how Plath portrays Dr. Gordon, the psychiatrist who botches Esther's electric shock treatment in *The Bell Jar*. During the treatment, Esther remains conscious and in agony – "with each flash a great jolt drubbed me till I thought my bones would break and the sap fly out of me like split plant" (*Bell Jar* 138). Nevertheless, Dr. Gordon's only response is his self-absorbed reminiscence about the "pretty bunch of girls" (126) he treated in the WAC station at Esther's college during the war:

> "Which college did you say you went to?"
> I said what college it was.
> "Ah!" Doctor Gordon's face lighted up with a slow, almost tropical smile. "They had a WAC station up there, didn't they, during the war?" (139)

Plath subverts Buddy Willard's sense of his own manhood in the same way, as Esther comments, when Buddy exposes himself to her in preparation for marriage, "The only thing I could think of was turkey neck and turkey gizzards and I felt very depressed" (*Bell Jar* 64).

In a way she learned directly from *To the Lighthouse*, Plath does not lose her temper, but takes her revenge on the society she portrays by laughing at the men who run it.

I have argued thus far that Plath learns a model of feminist fiction from *To the Lighthouse*. An examination of her copy of the novel, now held at Emory University, however, complicates this case. Plath's markings and marginalia in this copy of the book do not reflect a conscious choice to attend to or emphasize the novel's feminism. When Woolf portrays Mr. Ramsay's emotional demands upon his family, his authoritarianism, his children's violent responses to him, and even the sexism of characters like Mr. Tansley, Plath tends not to underline or mark these passages. In the fourth paragraph of the novel, for example, we hear about the suppressed violence James Ramsay bears towards his father, "Had there been an axe handy, a poker, or any weapon that would have gashed a hole in his father's breast and killed him, there and then, James would have seized it" (*TLL* 8). This kind of suppressed violence is a dominant theme of Plath's work, and her portrayals of such emotion characterize some of her finest short fiction. In "Sunday at the Mintons," the outwardly meek and obedient Elizabeth fantasizes the murder of her overbearing brother, imagining him drowning in the sea beneath the pier, "With a growing peace Elizabeth watched the flailing arms rise, sink and rise again. Finally the dark form quieted, sinking slowly down through level after level of obscurity into the sea" (*Johnny Panic* 151). In "The Fifty-Ninth Bear," the heroine Sadie fantasizes the death of her husband, for some marital wrong he has done her, and this murderous desire is so strong that it becomes reality in the story. As Norton, her husband, goes out of their tent to chase a bear away from their car, Plath writes, "There was another will working, a will stronger, even, than his" (*Johnny Panic* 95). The end of the story makes clear that this will is Sadie's. She has called up the bear that kills her husband. As he dies, Norton hears, "as from a far and rapidly receding planet," a shrill cry, "whether of terror or triumph, he could not tell." As Plath ends the story, "It was...her bear" (*Johnny Panic* 96). Despite this interest in portraying the violence of suppressed emotions, however, Plath does not mark Woolf's account of precisely such emotions in James Ramsay at the beginning of *To the Lighthouse*. In the entire paragraph which describes James and his father, rich with the kind of feminist concerns Plath shared, she underlines only the words, "lean as a knife, narrow as the blade of one," with which Woolf described Mr. Ramsay's stance, noting in the margin, "sterile male."

Plath's work clearly shows that she owes a considerable debt as a feminist writer to *To the Lighthouse*. Nevertheless, she makes no conscious acknowledgement of this debt in the pages of her copy of the novel. The reason for this can be seen in the markings and marginalia that Plath actually does make. These are almost entirely products of the interpretation of *To the Lighthouse* that she learned from her Smith College professor Elizabeth Drew. In 1957, Plath recalled, "I can still hear Elizabeth Drew's voice sending a shiver down my back in the huge Smith class-room, reading from *To The Lighthouse*" (*Journals* 269). Drew published several pieces of criticism of *To the Lighthouse*, both before and after she was lecturing on it to Plath. Her position is made clearest in her early book *The Modern Novel*. There, one year before Woolf wrote *A Room of One's Own*, Drew takes a view diametrically opposed to Woolf's of the conditions in which women are able to write: "Under modern codes of social ethics woman is free. She has complete liberty of action to develop her personality as she will...and complete liberty of speech to show the truth of existence as it appears to her, without blinking any facts or upholding any hypocrisies" (110). As a result of this position, Drew takes a consciously anti-feminist stance in her criticism of women's writing. She concludes her chapter on women's fiction, "There is distinction in all these [women's] books and brilliance in some, but when all is said, and in spite of the feminists with the queen bee in their bonnets, the fact remains that the creative genius of woman remains narrower than that of man, even in the novel" (116). For Drew, feminist criticism is simply misguided, a distortion of the facts of women's writing. As a result, her criticism of *To the Lighthouse* never mentions questions of gender politics. Rather, she describes Woolf's "metaphysical" vision in the novel, according to which Woolf is interested in portraying the nature of reality, the "central theme" of the book, and does so through a system of "complex and subtle symbolism," in which four main symbols (the sea, the lighthouse, Mrs. Ramsay, and Lily Briscoe's picture) are "woven together into a central meaning, a revelation of what Virginia Woolf sees as the nature of life" (*Novel* 265-6). Drew lectured to Plath's class on these symbols, and Plath remembered the lectures, annotating her copy of the text accordingly, emphasizing the same passages Drew does, and making notes on the themes and symbols to which Drew points in the margins of her text. Plath's annotation, "sterile male," by the passage on James Ramsay and his father, derives from these lectures, reflecting Drew's argument that "Mr. Ramsay stands as the symbol of the sterile, destructive barriers to relationship" (*Novel* 277).

At the same time as she makes use of the feminism of *To the Lighthouse* in her own writing, Plath consciously interiorizes Drew's anti-feminist interpretation of the novel. This was possible because of the conflicted relationship in which Plath herself stood towards feminism. Plath did not want to identify herself as a feminist, despite the fact that her thinking and writing is, from a second-wave perspective, almost nothing else. As she writes to her mother from Smith about whether or not to plan for a "career," she comments, "Ugh – I hate the word" (*Letters* 68). She repeatedly denigrates her unmarried female professors at Cambridge, "Our women supervisors at Newnham are…bluestocking grotesques, who know about life second-hand…It seems the Victorian age of emancipation is yet dominant here: there isn't a woman professor I have that I admire personally!" (*Letters* 219). In her college journals, she thinks of women's rights activism like that of Lucretia Mott as a form of escape from the moral responsibility of creating for oneself the life one wants, a form of losing oneself comparable to serving one's husband, "I think that is why there are so many women's clubs and organizations. They've got to feel emancipated and self important somehow…God forbid that I become…a second Lucretia Mott" (*Journals* 100). As Isobel Armstrong and Alan Sinfield write, "Like other women in the 1950s, Plath puts down old-style feminists as 'blue-stockings'" (76).

Plath's relationship to *To the Lighthouse* is a complex one. She learns from the novel an array of fictional techniques, which she puts to work in her own writing. She finds in Woolf's novel a model of semi-autobiographical fiction, in which complex family relationships can be worked out. Above all, she finds in it a model of feminist fiction which, whilst critical of the patriarchal society it portrays, remains acceptably feminine. If Plath does not consciously acknowledge these debts as she reads and reflects upon the novel, they are nevertheless clearly discernible in the pages of her own fiction. Although Plath chose not to identify herself as a feminist, her fiction is almost nothing else, and one reason she was able to write such fiction was that she had read *To the Lighthouse*. Plath's debt to this novel is as great as her debt to *Mrs. Dalloway*, on which critics have thus far focused. If *Mrs. Dalloway* provided Plath with a model of writing about women's lives, *To the Lighthouse* provided her with a model of doing so politically.

Works Cited

Armstrong, Isobel, and Alan Sinfield. "'This Drastic Spilt in the Functions of a Whole Woman': An Uncollected Article by Sylvia Plath." *Literature and History* 1 (1990): 75-9.
Axelrod, Steven Gould. *Sylvia Plath: The Wound and the Cure of Words*. Baltimore: Johns Hopkins UP, 1990.
Brain, Tracy. *The Other Sylvia Plath*. Harlow: Longman, 2001.
Drew, Elizabeth. *The Modern Novel: Some Aspects of Contemporary Fiction*. New York: Harcourt Brace, 1926.
—. *The Novel: A Modern Guide to Fifteen English Masterpieces*. New York: Norton, 1963.
Kukil, Karen. "Discovering Sylvia Plath and Virginia Woolf in the Archives." 18th Annual Conference on Virginia Woolf. University of Denver. 21 June 2008.
Plath, Sylvia. *The Bell Jar*. London: Faber, 1963.
—. Collage of Cold War Images. Mortimer Rare Book Room, Smith College. *Eye Rhymes: Sylvia Plath's Art of the Visual*. Ed. Kathleen Connors and Sally Bayley. Oxford: Oxford UP, 2007. Plate 37.
—. *Collected Poems*. London: Faber, 1981.
—. *Johnny Panic and the Bible of Dreams, and Other Prose Writings*. 2nd ed. London: Faber, 1979.
—. *The Journals of Sylvia Plath 1950-1962*. Ed. Karen Kukil. London: Faber, 2000.
—. *Letters Home*. London: Faber, 1975.
Woolf, Virginia. *Moments of Being*. Ed. Jeanne Schuldkind. 2nd ed. San Diego: Harcourt, 1985.
—. *To the Lighthouse*. 1927. Ed. Stella McNichol and Hermione Lee. London: Penguin, 1992.
—. *A Writer's Diary*. Ed. Leonard Woolf. San Diego: Harcourt, 1953.

Editions in the Classroom: Does It Matter?

by Beth Rigel Daugherty

Several years ago, I participated in a scholarship of teaching and learning project about reading in a general education classroom. (In SOTL, teachers ask research questions about student learning, gather data, and then use it to modify practice. "How do you know that?" often lies behind such a project, and the idea is to go beyond self-reporting, observations, and assumptions and ask *students* about what and how they learn.) So when Karen Levenback approached me about presenting on Woolf and editing in the classroom, I said I would construct a SOTL project on editions for an upcoming Woolf seminar. At Otterbein, getting students to purchase books can be difficult, and even English majors may not understand why I'm so passionate about their buying the correct edition. But why *am* I so passionate about it? Perhaps it doesn't matter? It's nice to have everyone on the same page when we're looking at a passage in class, but does the edition matter to the students' reading experience? What helps students make sense of difficult texts?

With the IRB's approval, I created a project that used three kinds of editions – no editorial apparatus: the Dover Thrift edition of *Jacob's Room* and the then-unannotated Harcourt *Between the Acts*; some editorial apparatus: the *Virginia Woolf Reader*; and extensive editorial apparatus: Harcourt annotated editions of *Mrs. Dalloway*, *To the Lighthouse*, *Orlando*, and *Three Guineas*— and two surveys. Because I collected only a small amount of data and of only two kinds, my conclusions are unreliable. I haven't answered my original question yet, either. But I did learn something—students always teach—so that's what I report here.[1]

Context and Demographics

I last taught a Woolf class in 1999, the culminating senior literary seminar. There were eight students (and one auditor). Curricular changes since then meant this time, the class was a 300-level major authors course, one of several advanced courses meant to prepare literary studies majors for sustaining a year-long research project in their 400-level senior literature capstone. In addition, creative writing majors, required to take an introductory, intermediate, and advanced literature course, could enroll. Again, there were eight students (but three auditors).

Of the eight, one was a continuing studies student completing her degree one or two courses at a time and seven were traditional-age. One Hispanic and seven Caucasian. Two sophomores (jumping over pre-reqs?), one junior, and five seniors (though the continuing studies student was not graduating). Of those seniors, three were simultaneously *in* the 400-level senior lit course and working on their research projects. Three of the eight were creative writing majors (two of whom were the sophomores). One was a double literature and creative writing major getting his license to teach in high school—he had student taught, and this was his last quarter. So "four" creative writing and "five" lit studies. Four on their way out and four continuing. Four men and four women. All came in with a desire to read Woolf; they had read her before and loved her.

Findings

Eight students and one auditor completed the first survey,[2] and since they could mark more than one answer, the numbers don't always add up. At the beginning of the class, six said they respond to a difficult reading assignment (#1) by just going ahead and reading it ("e"), though two of them also indicated they do *some* kind of preparatory work. One looks up the author on the internet, one looks up the book on the internet, and one looks up both author and book on the internet. None go to the library.

When reading a book they know is difficult (#2), three students want to know all the background, historical, cultural, and literary ("a," "b," and "c"). Three answered "a" & "b," one answered with just "a," one with just "b," and one with just "c."

Answering #3 about reading a book with no supplemental material, two said they like it, and five said they sometimes want such material and sometimes don't (two added they want the information available). Only one said he/she wants the additional material ("c"). Another circled none of the answers and wrote "expect to get it in class."

Three students reported they always read dedications and acknowledgements (#4), three sometimes do, and three rarely do. None said they never read them.

For # 5, one student ignores the bibliography, seven use it if they need to, (with one understanding some work has been done for him/her ["c"]), and one circled just "c."

For the question about footnotes (#6), one student circled "a" (ignores them), but also circled "would use them depending on where they are" ("c"). Three others use them depending on where they are. Three use footnotes occasionally (one in combination with "c"), and two use them frequently.

In response to #7, five students said they read the introduction before they read the book, with one of them also circling "c" (during). One student reads the introduction while reading the book, and three said, "only if assigned." None said "after" ("d").

Reporting on their approach to an edition (#8), three find the actual book and start reading. One checks the table of contents, reads covers, browses, and locates footnotes; one uses the table of contents, covers, and browsing; two check the table of contents and covers; one consults the table of contents and locates footnotes. One explores and browses.

Four students circled all four definitions of an edition introduction (#9) (description of book, description of author's process, critical essay, and discussion of reception), and two of them also added it can be something entirely different. Two think the introduction is a description of the author's writing process, with one also thinking it is a critical essay. For two students, the introduction is a critical essay, and for one, it discusses the book's reception.

Seven students said, given a choice (#10), they'd rather have the editorial apparatus— they want to know something about the author's life, they want it there for reference even if they don't always use it, and they appreciate having the context. Two said they prefer books with no editorial apparatus because "all that other stuff overwhelms me [. . .]; when I do read intros, footnotes, etc., I rush through them and forget them," and because "I would rather locate the information at my leisure instead of feeling interrupted constantly."

Since the class met on Tuesdays and Thursdays, I assigned the primary reading for Tuesdays and the secondary reading for Thursdays (a contemporary review, the intro, if present, and a critical essay). The idea was to encourage primary, then secondary reading. They had some assignments in Mark Hussey's *A to Z* book, a book they universally loved. They did research activities to keep them on track with their final research essays, they each facilitated a half-hour discussion, and they wrote reflective essays at mid-term and for the final exam. We began the quarter with Woolf's diaries and letters and then moved to the essays, a portion of *Room*, and all of *Three Guineas*. Next came some short stories. Only then did we move to the novels, and we read *Jacob's Room*, *Mrs. Dalloway*, *To the Lighthouse*, *Orlando*, and *Between the Acts*. (Several had already read *The Waves* in another class.) We ended the class with some of Woolf's biographical essays and portions of "A Sketch of the Past." That sequence worked well, but the rhythm of a weekly book (or set of primary readings) for Tuesday followed by criticism on Thursday never kicked in.

At quarter's end, of the eight students (a different auditor and seven enrolled) who completed the more open-ended survey,[3] three students preferred the book with *some* editorial apparatus (Leaksa). One commented, "It's nice to have some assistance with the texts I'm reading, but if a book has too much editorial apparatus, I get overwhelmed and ignore them," another said "I really liked the short introductions and brief head notes in the *Virginia Woolf Reader* because I was not coming into the reading cold, but it allowed me to get down to business," and the third noted that for the class, he/she preferred the minimal approach, but also commented, "For research purposes, though, I appreciated the extra resources. As a general rule I like to have more information to choose from and work with when I want to, but I don't always take advantage of it." Two preferred the books with no extra information—"if it's good, it'll speak to me, be timeless, and I don't need or have the desire to know what is included in footnotes or a chronology," claimed one, and another, "I prefer reading a book with no prior information or explanation, in order to perceive it as a whole, as a complete work of art (or not)." However, the latter also said he/she appreciated having the suggestions for further reading. Three preferred the annotated editions, finding them convenient (as a place to start research), but of those three, one said the *favorite* was the *Virginia Woolf Reader*, and one said that he/she preferred having nothing to hinder the reading, but thought the annotated editions "more worthwhile in the long run."

When I asked them to distinguish between preference and use, two said they did not use the editorial apparatus at all, but one (clearly the auditor) said if she'd been taking the course for credit and writing a research essay, she would have. Two used the editorial apparatus sparingly. And four used it more thoroughly – mainly the footnotes, said one, helpful for my research, said another, absolutely, and used the introductions the most, said yet another, and mainly the introductions, said the fourth.

When I asked what they would prefer in all their English major courses, one said "books should be read for the words in them, not for those about them" and felt footnotes and criticism ruin both the perception and reception of the text. One said a mix, as in our class, and six reported they'd rather have all the apparatus, even if they don't use it. Of those six, one said a happy medium would be nice ("too much information sometimes deters a reader altogether; too little can frustrate") and also mentioned the economics of book choice. One thought the apparatus should be an "optional study tool." Another admitted preferring books with little editorial apparatus, but thought "English major courses should expose you to everything."

Lessons and Implications

Lesson #1: You can't please all the people all the time. I laughed out loud at these two answers to # 3 on my last survey: "I would definitely rather read a novel 'unvarnished'," said the first, who then referred to the universality and the timeless of texts; the second said, "We're not original readers, & as such, should not pretend to be. McEwan is really of this millennium. Woolf is not. We owe her the respect of history, the weight of time, & should read accordingly, notes, footnotes, essays & all."

Lesson # 2: Teach the students you have. I've been at this for 25 years, so you'd think I'd know this by now! The course design that worked well with capstone seniors did not work so well with a multi-level and mixed group (lit studies and creative writing), and my "DUH" moment came too late for me to adjust.

Lesson # 3: Students are complex both/and people. The answers they gave were not straightforward or simple, and they scribbled all kinds of exceptions on their surveys.

Lesson # 4: Knowledge of research and criticism vocabulary cannot be assumed. I noticed confusion on the surveys, for example, with some students associating "editorial apparatus" with just the intros or just the footnotes.

Lesson # 5: Use level was not as low and attitudes not as negative as I expected. One student was close to hostile at times about the annotated editions, but was struggling to complete the primary reading and did not even try to use them. Others, though not understanding my enjoyment of research, did not resist my efforts to introduce them to it. And a couple may have caught the fever . . .

Does it matter what editions instructors use? In some ways, no – author's words *are* the most important (the complex issue of author's words differing according to edition was not taken up in this class!). But in some ways, yes, depending on the course's learning goals. If, as in my case, one course goal is to prepare students to do research, then using annotated editions makes sense—they are, as one student pointed out, convenient. They allow students to learn some research skills before tackling the library or the internet.

I will continue to use annotated editions. But I need to teach students *how* to use them and create more support for that use. So I will think more about how to ease young and creative writing majors into literary studies behaviors and strategies, including how effectively to manage the Tuesday/Thursday pattern. Complaints about having to read criticism before reading the book told me some hadn't read the primary material when they should, that they didn't know to divide a book up into Thursday to Tuesday reading. I will start with basics. What does "annotation" mean? What are the components of an annotated edition? What are some options for what you use when? I will ask students to share their own strategies with others. I will create hands-on classroom activities to help them get more comfortable with what at first seems unwieldy. For example, to teach them about footnotes, I might ask them to circle everything they don't "get" as they're reading, to write their own footnotes, and produce a class set. I might suggest one of the strategies mentioned on a survey—read the footnotes, as a whole, *first*. I will teach them some tricks—a post-it note marking where footnotes begin, and so forth. To help them with introductions, we might do several in-class exercises *after* reading and discussing the book. Again, back to basics—skim for headings first. Look for sections *you're* interested in. I might give them a worksheet with 3 or 4 guiding questions (questions that have become automatic for us, such as what is the main argument?). I might ask them to do a works cited entry for the introduction and write a brief summary of it (as for an annotated bibliography). We might do an exercise in which we read bibliographies, follow up on particular articles, and then read *their* bibliographies (a paper trail assignment).

Most important, I will think more intentionally about how to design research assignments that creative writing students can invest in (such as consulting Danell Jones' book) and that literary studies students can learn from while involved in larger projects. I will try once again to learn from Woolf, who as a reader, touted the joys of reading without encumbrances; who as a learner, used a crib sheet when the subject was difficult; and who as a critic, enjoyed the footnotes in W. S. Lewis's edition of the Walpole/Cole correspondence. Surely there's a way to reassure students that all three attitudes can co-exist in them as well.

Notes

1. I would like to thank Leslie Ortquist-Ahrens, the Director of Otterbein's Center for Teaching and Learning for her help with this project, Otterbein's IRB, and most especially my students, who so cheerfully answered my questions: Alice Click, Bonita Fee, Lisa Hartley, Jessica Hilts, Wes Jamison, Laura Joseph, Daniel Koppel, Max Lantz, Manny Melendez, Kaye Roberts, and Meredith Turanchik.
2. 1. When I am assigned a book I know is difficult, I
    a. look up information about the author on the internet
    b. look up information about the book on the internet
    c. look up information about the author in the library (print sources)
    d. look up information about the book in the library (print sources)
    e. just go ahead and read it
   2. When I am reading a book I know is difficult, I
    a. want to know about the author and/or book's historical era
    b. want to know about the author and/or book's cultural and/or social context
    c. want to know about the author and/or book's literary era and context
   3. When an edition of a book has no introduction, footnotes, or accompanying materials (chronology, bibliography, and so forth), I
    a. like it – who needs all that stuff?
    b. sometimes want such material, other times don't miss it
    c. want the additional information
   4. When a book has a dedication and/or acknowledgments, I
    a. always read them – I like seeing whom the author thanks
    b. sometimes read them
    c. rarely read them
    d. never read them
   5. When an edition of a book has a bibliography, I
    a. ignore it – who cares?
    b. use it if I need it for some other purpose (such as research)
    c. pay attention – someone has done a search for me!
   6. When an edition of a book has footnotes, I
    a. ignore them – footnotes break my flow of reading and annoy me
    b. often overlook or forget them
    c. use them depending on where they are in the book
    d. use them occasionally, when I really need to
    e. use them frequently and appreciate them

        f.   always use them
   7. When an edition of a book has an introduction, I read it
        a.   never
        b.   before I read the book
        c.   during the time I'm reading the book
        d.   after I read the book
        e.   only if assigned
   8. When I pick up an edition of a book, I
        a.   find out where the actual book begins and start reading
        b.   find the table of contents and see what's in the edition before I read
        c.   read the covers before I read
        d.   explore and browse through the accompanying materials before I read
        e.   check out the bibliography before I read
        f.   find out where the footnotes are and bookmark them before I read
   9. The introduction to a book in an edition is
        a.   a description by the editor of the characters, plot, and setting of the book
        b.   a description by the editor of the author's writing and publishing process
        c.   a critical essay by the editor that interprets or analyzes the book
        d.   a discussion by the editor of the book's reception by readers and critics
 10. If I had a choice, I'd rather have a book that has
        a.   no introduction, footnotes, and other materials
        b.   an editorial apparatus (introduction, footnotes, and other materials provided by an editor)

3. 1. This quarter, you read books with various levels of editorial apparatus: (1) *Jacob's Room* and *Between the Acts* with no editorial apparatus at all; (2) excerpts from Woolf's works in *The Virginia Woolf Reader* with a short preface, brief headnotes, and some footnotes; and (3) annotated editions that included a general introduction, a chronology, a long critical introduction, extensive footnotes, and bibliographies on Woolf and the work featured in the edition. Which type of books did you prefer, and why?

2. Whether or not you liked the editorial apparatus in the annotated editions, did you use it? What did you use the most? The least? Why? How would you describe your use of the apparatus? What did you learn from what you used?

3. On the one hand, it's nice to read Woolf as the common readers of her day read her—the works themselves and nothing else (just like picking up a novel by Ian McEwan today!). On the other hand, her common readers would have understood her allusions to current political figures and events. (It's hard to believe now, but someday, readers will need a footnote to explain "9/11.") Would you rather read a novel "unvarnished" and not "get" the topical allusions? (And maybe look them up later or ask for explanations in class?) Or would you rather have allusions explained in footnotes and not have the experience of earlier readers? (And have to imagine their experience?) Why? The answer may have something to do with you as a reader – dig into that as much as you can.

4. If you could sit down across from Mark Hussey, the general editor of the annotated editions, a person very interested in the student point of view and students' use of books, what would you tell him you liked about the annotated editions? What didn't you like? What improvements might you suggest? Why?

5. What did you learn about reading difficult books this quarter? What did you learn about yourself as a reader?

6. What would you prefer in your English major courses: all the books with extensive editorial apparatus; all the books with no or little editorial apparatus; or some books with and some books without? Why?

Wielding One's Own Pen: Virginia Woolf's Holographs in the Classroom

by Karen L. Levenback

Approaches to teaching Woolf seem to have undergone revisions, most dramatically, I should think, in matters relating to accessibility and availability. When I first began my study of Woolf as a doctoral student at Cornell, the only editions available were those published by Harcourt Brace; the number of critical works available could be counted on your fingers; and access to holographs was monitored by Lola Szladits at the Berg Collection, New York Public Library. Today, only a couple of decades later, availability and accessibility have eased and are no longer limited, as suggested in the works cited following this paper (see bulleted works). However, not unlike Robert Darnton, in a recent article in the *New York Review of Books*, I would argue that if we look at *la longue durée*—the big picture can be aligned so as to emphasize continuity instead of change (Darnton 2). Call it versioning or genetic criticism, or the problematics of the physical status of texts (Bornstein 3), our interest in using holographs may today aim at appreciating the instability of the text, and in tracing textual variation, as well as or instead of seeing through the eyes of the writer. Whatever the ultimate aim in using holographs, the methodology needs to be seen in practical, hands-on terms. Whatever the aim, I hope this paper will suggest practical methodologies and tools for integrating textual variants into consideration of Woolfian works.

My interest here is in holographs or, as Edward Bishop rightly points out, citing an important text in library studies--John Carter's *ABC for Book Collectors*--holograph drafts (Carter insists that "holograph" be used as an adjective), a term that clarifies the distinction between it and manuscripts and autographs, which, I must say, as a practicing reference librarian, and archivist, and as a former academic, is an important distinction to teach students. This is true in general and becomes especially clear in the context of genetic criticism and the *avant-texte*, that is (to use Bishop's simplified definition), "the whole range of prepublication documents" ("Alfa" 155, n.1)--what we, in the library world, might call "metadata":

> **Holograph** : Is "NOT a NOUN," according to Carter. A term from the Greek, meaning entirely by hand—or wholly written—and refers to a document written in the hand of the author and is, in this context, used for literary texts.
> **Manuscript** : Is a NOUN or an ADJECTIVE, and refers to documents written by hand—but, and this is a key distinction, not necessarily in the hand of the author.
> **Autograph**: Is a NOUN or an ADJECTIVE, and represents writing in the author's hand, but usually refers to letters, inscriptions, notes, and the like. As Bishop explains it, "in editing Woolf we might encounter her manuscript notes on other authors for her essays, her autograph letters, and her holograph drafts" ("Alfa" 155, n.1).

In addition, one can't forget the

> **Typescript** : Is a trickier term than the font might suggest—in part because the term involves "typewriters" and has not undergone serious alteration since the advent of the computer (note the serious impediment to Woolf Studies) and the need for an adequate vocabulary to represent the activity on it as distinct from that accomplished on a typewriter. Hence, the terminology is not yet settled and, rather clumsily, gives way to variations such as auto-typescript, used to distinguish an author's typewritten manuscript from that done by a copyist. Even Carter describes this as "philologically barbarous" and says that it "must be resisted" (Carter 223).

Published versions of holograph manuscripts seem, more or less, to have followed the practice established by J. W. Graham in 1979, with the format reproducing the manuscript page line for line rather than offering a facsimile transcription. Bishop does so because "it conveys more closely than any other method the process of the author's writing" (*JR* xxiii) and he, like Rosenbaum, offers some kind of "summary of signs in the transcription" (xiv), as do Helen Wussow and the others, all acknowledging Graham as having set the standard. The approach to incorporating the valuable and (as far as I know) rarely used tool herein described is one that has had a place in my classrooms, albeit, usually in upper-level classes. However, I will suggest that, with a little tweaking, it can be applied to writing classes. Duplicating one or two pages, for example, falls under "fair use" in copyright laws (though these have not caught up to technology—and is thankfully the topic of another panel) and/or you might put the entire volume(s) on reserve in your libraries and let the students do the duplication.

To continue, I hope utility will be served by illustrating how one may integrate the actual holographs, followed by autograph typescripts (or the ingenious transcription of them by the meticulous editors), and finally the published text. My preference is to use actual holographs rather than transcriptions of them—after the students have already read published works by Virginia Woolf—though not necessarily the holograph work. Writing on representing modern texts, George Bornstein believes that using a holograph version—or even a typescript sans manuscript notes—alone might well give students the illusion that they are reading a "base text" or the "real" one ("Once and Future" 176 and "Introduction" 3-5). But, my sense and practice suggest that students understand the writing process for themselves—the process of brainstorming and outlining or organization of thoughts—and drafts and revision, or can be educated in the writing ritual of Woolf herself—and this will not become a major issue. By the time one introduces holograph versions, the teaching lays the foundation and, whatever the direction taken (multiple versions, self-editing, or self-censorship, for example, or all three [see Silver]), there is the "WOW-factor" and the sense of accomplishment that comes with the process of discovery and transcription.

My own first look at holographs didn't begin with Woolf—but with Wordsworth, and my first introduction to generic research came with Paul Betz, at Georgetown University, who used holographs in both his graduate and upper-level Romantics class—to suggest versioning. In so doing, he introduced me to the challenges and rewards of using holograph versions as a learning and a teaching tool, for the act of unraveling the conundrums imposed by calligraphy added another step to the process of understanding how another's mind works. When Katie Marts, a student in my course on Woolf and war, speaks of analyzing the "manuscript pages from *Women and Fiction*, Woolf's earlier version of *A Room of One's Own*," she refers to "selected passages where war was mentioned" and how the students "compared the word choices and omissions that Woolf made in self-censorship." Marts continues, "This exercise also helped in understanding Woolf's use of indirection," the "use of many conditional words in her text demonstrating the difficulty in defining and explaining the true effects of war" (178-179).

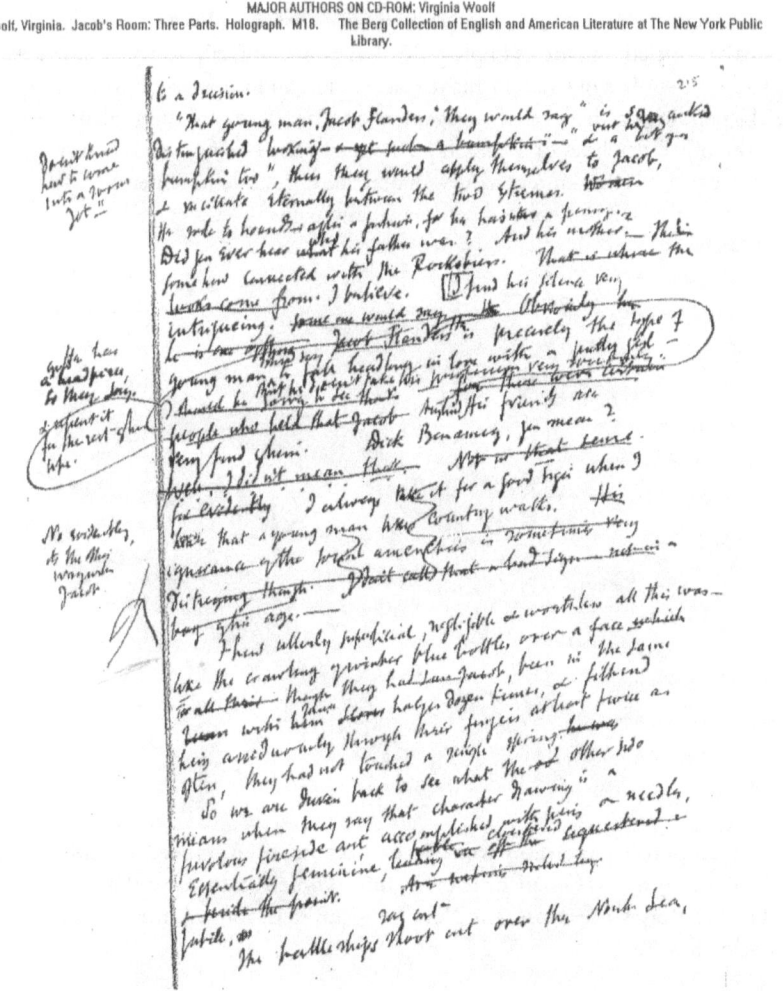

Fig. 1. Holograph page from *Jacob's Room*. Major Authors on CD ROM: Virginia Woolf: M18. Reproduced by consent of the Society of Authors, on behalf of the Virginia Woolf Estate, as well as the Henry W. and Albert A. Berg Collection, The New York Public Library, Astor, Lenox and Tilden Foundations.

Of course, selected holograph pages offer their own direction (selection, like editing, is a matter of interpretation) and some holograph pages are more welcoming—others more of a challenge (sometimes, as we've all found, choice is not possible). For a writing class, exhibiting a holograph version of *Jacob's Room* (a practice eased by Mark Hussey's CD-ROM), offers possibilities. The facsimile holograph here is also used by Bishop in "The Alfa and the Avant-text," but where Bishop likes the energy in the facsimile, what I find most to recommend it as a class illustration is its obvious reworking—and its mirror of student revision (see Fig. 1, above).

It serves as a challenge to distribute a page of holograph manuscript *before* beginning a published text and, as a homework assignment, to ask the class to transcribe it (noting insertions and deletions, for example—this last relates directly to the student example offered above)—unless one has an entire class session and wants to do this as a group exercise. Depending on the level of engagement and/or tenacity of the students, one might even to do only a few lines or a paragraph as an exercise (see figure 2). In any case, what I've found is that it is this kind of hands-on practice that students remember—particularly if the laptop *seems* to have replaced pen/pencil and paper.

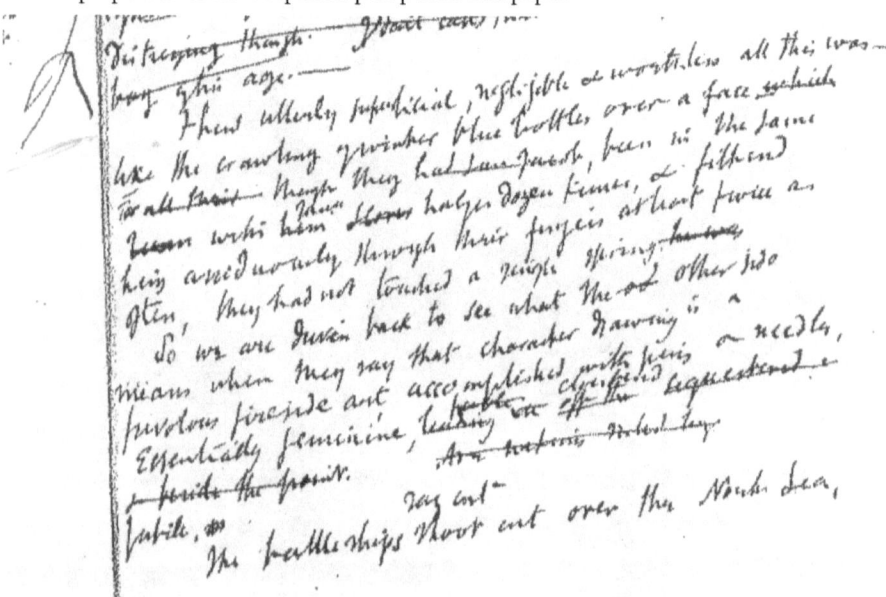

Fig. 2. **Holograph paragraph from Jacob's Room. Reproduced by consent of the Society of Authors, on behalf of the Virginia Woolf Estate, as well as the Henry W. and Albert A. Berg Collection, The New York Public Library, Astor, Lenox and Tilden Foundations.**

Whatever the aim or orientation of the class, incorporation of holograph versions serves several purposes:

(1) to demonstrate to students that calligraphy [may/or once did] precede[s] transcription/publication;

(2) to show that Virginia Woolf actually went through drafts and followed a "writing process": to show how she worked with a text, including interlineations and deletions;

(3) to build awareness of text and *avant-texte*, base text and versioning;

(4) to illustrate that it's hard work not only to be an editor, but to be a self-editor.

By the time one introduces holograph versions, the teaching can follow several orientations and lead in whichever direction suits the aim of the course and/or the interests of the students.

My own sense is that this holographic exercise might be examined in the next class, to good effect, with distributed copies of the same page from the transcribed version (see Fig. 3).

240   *Jacob's Room*   [2.215]

      to a decision.
    "That young man, Jacob Flanders," they would say, "is so very awkward
 doesn't know   but he
 how to come distinguished looking - ~~& yet such a bumpkin~~ - "& a bit of a
 into a room
 yet" — bumpkin too", thus they would apply themselves to Jacob,
   & vacillate eternally between the two extremes. ~~Women~~
   He rode to hounds –; after a fashion, for he hasn't ~~a~~ a penny.
        who
   Did you ever hear ~~what~~ his father was? And his mother? - ~~She's~~
   somehow connected with the Rocksbiers. ~~That is where~~ the
   ~~looks come from.~~ I believe. [I find his silence very
   intrigueing. ~~some one would say~~ ~~He Obviously he~~
           He
 He has ~~he is one of those Jacob Flanders~~ is precisely the type of
 good   they say
 a head piece, young ~~man~~ / to fall headlong in love with a pretty girl -
 so they say.   But he doesn't take his profession very seriously:
 & repent it ~~I should be sorry to see that. — for there were certain~~
 for the rest of his ~~people who held that Jacob~~ Anyhow His friends are
 life very fond of him. Dick Bonamy, you mean?
   ~~Well, I didn't mean that~~ Not in that sense.
 No evidently,
 its the other ~~for evidently~~ I always take it for a good sign when I
 way with
 Jacob hear that a young man likes country walks. ~~His
   ignorance of the social amenities is sometimes very
   distressing though. I don't call that a bad sign - not in a
   boy of his age.~~ -
    How utterly superficial, negligible & worthless all this was -
   like the crawling of winter blue bottles over a face, ~~which~~
   ~~For all their~~ though they ~~had seen Jacob~~, been in the same
       Jacob
   room with him [~~severa?~~] half a dozen times, & filtered
   him assiduously through their fingers at least twice as
   often, they had not touched a single spring. ~~he was~~
    So we are driven back to see what the ~~od~~ other side
   means when they say that character drawing is a
   frivolous fireside art, accomplished with pins and needles
       feeble cloistered
   essentially feminine, ~~leading all off the~~ ~~sequestered &~~
   ~~& beside the point.~~ Are nations ruled by
   futile, a
       ray out
    The battleships shoot out over the North Sea,

Fig. 3. Transcription of holograph page. Edward Bishop. Virginia Woolf's "Jacob's Room": The Holograph Draft: 240.

During this second stage—an auto-typescript and the holograph notes and corrections thereto applied might also be distributed and compared with the transcriptions made by the students and a page of published text (see, for example, the three versions of published editions of *Jacob's Room* listed in Works Cited) though clearly, this is not the final stage either, for there is no final stage or ultimate text, but one stage in understanding that the writing of Woolf can be seen to be in a state of perpetual becoming—like all writing. And these editions of *Jacob's Room* are only a sampling of those from which we may teach and learn.

Works Cited

Bishop, Edward. "The Alfa and the *Avant-texte*: Transcribing Virginia Woolf's Manuscripts." *Editing Virginia Woolf: Interpreting the Modernist Text*. Ed. James M. Haule and J. H. Stape. New York: Palgrave, 2002. 139-157.

—, ed. *Virginia Woolf's "Jacob's Room": The Holograph Draft*. New York: Pace UP, 1998.

Bornstein, George. "The Once and Future Texts of Modernist Poetry." *The Future of Modernism*. Ed. Hugh Witemeyer. Ann Arbor: U of Michigan P, 1998. 161-180.

—. "Why Editing Matters." Introduction. *Representing Modernist Texts*. 1-17.

—, ed. *Representing Modernist Texts: Editing and Interpretation*. Ann Arbor: U of Michigan P, 1991.

Carter, John. *ABC for Book Collectors*. 8th edition. Nicolas Baker, ed. New Castle DE: Oak Knoll Press, 2004.

Clarke, Stuart Nelson, ed. *"Orlando": The Original Holograph Draft*. London: S.N. Clarke, 1993.

Darnton, Robert. "The Library in the New Age." *New York Review of Books*. 55.10 (12 June 2008): 72-80. 31 May 2008 http://www.nybooks.com/articles/21514.

DeSalvo, Louise A., ed. *Virginia Woolf's Melymbrosia: An Earlier Version of "The Voyage Out."* New York: New York Public Library and Redex Books, 1981.

Dick, Susan, ed. *"To the Lighthouse": The Original Holograph Draft*. Toronto and Buffalo: U of Toronto P, 1982.

Graham, J.W., ed. *Virginia Woolf, "The Waves": The Two Holograph Drafts*. Toronto: U of Toronto P, 1976.

Hussey, Mark, ed. *Virginia Woolf: Works*. Major Authors on CD-ROM. Woodbridge CT: Primary Sources Media, 1997.

Leaska, Mitchell A., ed. *"Pointz Hall": The Earlier and Later Transcripts of "Between the Acts."* New York: University Publications, 1983.

Marts, Katie. "Opening Doors to *A Room of One's Own*." Jessica Berman and Jane Goldman, eds. *Virginia Woolf Out of Bounds: Selected Papers from the Tenth Annual Conference on Virginia Woolf*. New York: Pace UP, 2001. 176-180.

Rosenbaum, S.P., ed. *Virginia Woolf, Women and Fiction: The Manuscript Versions of "A Room of One's Own."* Oxford: Shakespeare Head Press, 1992.

Silver, Brenda R. "Textual Criticism as Feminist Practice: Or, Who's Afraid of Virginia Woolf Part II." Bornstein, ed. *Representing Modernist Texts*. 193-222.

Woolf, Virginia. *Jacob's Room*. 1922. Ed. Susan Roe. London and New York: Penguin, 1992.

—. Dover Thrift Edition. Mineola NY: Dover, 1998.

—. Harvest Book. San Diego: Harcourt Brace Jovanovich, n.d. Rpt. 1960 ed.

Wussow, Helen, ed. *"The Hours: The British Museum Manuscript of "Mrs. Dalloway."* New York: Pace UP, 1997.

Complicating Adaptation: Virginia Woolf's 1925 novel, *Mrs. Dalloway*, and Abel Gance's 1918-1919 film, *J'accuse*

by Leslie Kathleen Hankins

> ... a case of shell shock—very sad—who hears behind the chorus the voices of the dead singing, and sees his own apotheosis or damnation in the sky. That dreadful war!
> E.M. Forster *New Criterion*
>
> A young poet and visionary has gone mad through the horrible sights he has seen in the trenches, and continually imagines that he sees this procession of the heroic dead.
> —C. R. from *The Daily Mail*

Readers of Virginia Woolf may be startled to learn that one of these epigraphs refers, not to her novel, *Mrs. Dalloway*, but to Abel Gance's 1918-1919 French film, *J'accuse*. As the epigraphs indicate, the film and the novel overlap in profound ways; putting the two together can be an eye-opening experience. For that reason, the 2008 restoration and release of Abel Gance's *J'accuse* is a breakthrough for Woolf studies as well as for film studies. Just as early 20th century readers also screened films, we, as early 21st century readers, can bring film back into the cultural equation. Gance's epic film exposé of the destruction and waste of war provides a stunning intertext for Virginia Woolf's anti-war novels, *Jacob's Room* (1922) and *Mrs. Dalloway* (1925).

It is both tricky and fascinating to relate literary texts to cinematic ones, and not the least part of the fascination is the conceptual tangle such relating invites. Film adaptations of literary works are notoriously vexing; Woolf herself complained about them in her 1926 essay, "The Cinema." But, in the cultural free-for-all of the 1920s, the relationship between literature and cinema strikes me as being more than one-directional. It isn't simply about adapting novels. Dare I suggest that writers sometimes adapted film? I would argue that writers were eager to engage with cinema in the 1920s, attempting to capture its speed and immediacy, not to mention its viewers. And, I've argued before, we can read familiar texts—such as Woolf's *Jacob's Room* and *Mrs. Dalloway*—in refreshingly new ways if we read them by the light of the silver screen. Though we cannot know for certain whether Virginia Woolf screened *J'accuse* when it reached London in 1920, evidence from the London *Times* asserts that the film was a much discussed cultural event. When films were cultural phenomena—as was Abel Gance's *J'accuse*—we may ask if writers such as Virginia Woolf rewrote them, paid homage to them, or adapted them, in novels. If that is too daring, too audacious without more of a paper trail of proof, we may at least imagine how a reader/viewer of that cultural moment might have encountered a film and a novel together.

It is fascinating to explore ways readers and spectators of that day might have linked *J'accuse* and *Mrs Dalloway*, as well as to posit ways readers and spectators of our day may find delights and insights in the interplay between the two texts. Imagine someone in

London in 1920 reading the blitz of advertisements for *J'accuse* in April, perhaps screening the film at the trade show in London on Friday April 23rd at 2:30 p.m. ("with a vocal soloist, choir and Augmented orchestra") and perusing reviews in the *Times, Bioscope, Kinematograph Weekly, Daily Mail, Daily Telegraph* and others. In one review of April 29, 1920, *Kinematograph Weekly* predicted, "*J'accuse* has created a furore in its native France; it will do the same wherever it is shown in Britain" (94).

The "furore" of the film quite likely reached Virginia Woolf and other intellectuals. Woolf was an avid anti-war activist and her writing responds deeply to World War I, as scholars such as Karen Levenback and Mark Hussey document. She wrote several essays and essay/reviews about the war, including "The War from the Street" (1919); "Heard on the Downs: The Genesis of Myth" (1916); "Mr Sassoon's Poems" (31 May 1917) and "Two Soldier Poets" (11 July 1918). Her diary as early as January 25, 1915 shows her keen interest in seeing the war on film: "The Picture Palace was a little disappointing—as we never got to the War pictures, after waiting 1 hour & a half" (*D1* 28). In her essay on Sassoon in the *Times Literary Supplement* of May 31, 1917 Woolf ponders the complicated mixed feelings she had about the spectator position in relation to war:

> What Mr Sassoon has felt to be the most sordid and horrible experiences in the world he makes us feel to be so in a measure which no other poet of the war has achieved. As these jaunty matter-of-fact statements succeed each other such loathing, such hatred accumulates behind them that we say to ourselves, 'Yes, this is going on; and we are sitting here watching it,' with a new shock of surprise, with an uneasy desire to leave our place in the audience, which is a tribute to Mr Sassoon's power as a realist. It is realism of the right, of the poetic kind. ("Mr Sassoon's Poems" 120)

With her mixed fascination with the role of the spectator of cinema and her avid anti-war activism, it is tempting to wonder what Woolf might have made of the rousing descriptions of *J'accuse* in widely-circulated journals such as *Kinematograph Weekly*. On April 8, 1920, a two-page advertisement spread in *Kinematograph Weekly* tinted blood red, scrawls the title as if it is handwritten in dripping blood over a two-page collage of stills from the film. This issue also includes an article, "*J'accuse*: a Big Pathé Film," which begins, "Claimed to be one of the biggest Continental successes of modern times" and describes the film as an anti-war tragedy: "The idea of accusation conveyed in the title is insistent throughout. The horrors of the shell-stricken trenches turns the poet's mind, and he accuses the war for all the disasters which follow, he typifies his lover as the sun and denounces it for the catastrophes which have steadfastly and remorselessly accumulated" (94). A week later, on April 15, 1920, *Kinematograph Weekly* presents a two page with color advertisement spread with the background black and white still of Jean Diaz standing over the graveyard/battlefield full of bodies and crosses, and the blood-red dripping scrawl of the title across the entire two pages (see fig. 1). It is worth noting that the next day, on April 16, 1920, Woolf began writing *Jacob's Room*, her elegiac novel that inscribes the waste of Jacob Flanders. On April 22, 1920, in addition to a new colorful advertisement, *Kinematograph Weekly* includes a preview article, "The Spirit of France: A Big French Film to be Shown This Week," stating:

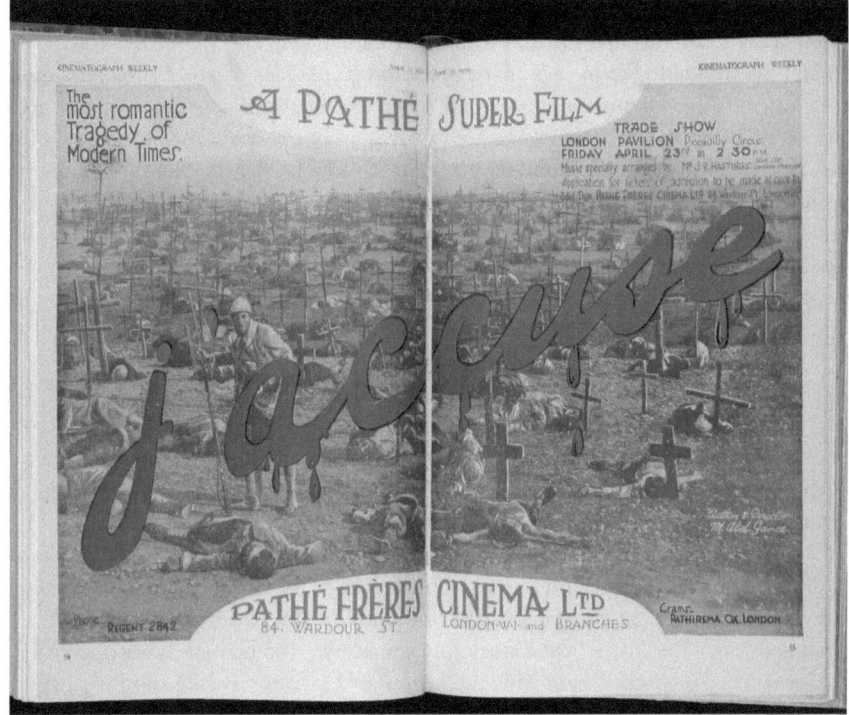

Fig. 1 April 15. 1920 *Kinematograph Weekly* advertisement for *J'accuse* © British Library Board. All Rights Reserved LD94.

the picture created an enormous sensation in France at the time of its exhibition not very long ago, and even making full allowance for the temperamental difference of the two peoples, it is safe to assert that it will cause an almost equally great sensation in this country. Taken as a whole it forms one of the most terrible indictments against war which it is possible to imagine. Every Imperialist, Junker, *jusqu'autoritist* and militarist should be forcibly made to see this picture. But the effect is not produced by insistent horrors or by sheer frightfulness. It is obtained by the emphasis of simple, natural humanity. (95)

April 23, 1920 featured the Trade Show of *J'accuse* at the London Pavilion, and was followed by reviews by C. R. in the *Daily Mail* and Alder Anderson in the *Daily Telegraph*, and by the *Bioscope* review on April 27, 1920 which notes, "The central character in the story—a poet who has been driven mad by the mental anguish of his war experiences—dreams that, while keeping watch among the graves of his comrades, he beheld the spirits of the dead rising and marching through the country [. . .] Then, railing in a frenzy of rage and despair against all humanity, cursing the sun itself, he dies." Two days later, the April 29, 1920 issue of *Kinematograph Weekly* includes a review of "*J'accuse*" which finds the film "a sermon against war," praising the "realistic" scenes in the front lines and finding the performance of Marise Dauvray as Edith "one as near approaching genius as we have ever seen upon the screen" (94). According to the London *Times*, the film was shown publicly starting May 24, 1920 and "has already caused a good deal of discussion" (86). All of this demonstrates that the film was highly anticipated, and well-reviewed.

And no wonder! *J'accuse* is a marvel to view; it includes dazzling cinematic experimentation, intelligent, moving drama and fierce anti-war critique. The epic film tells a complex, nuanced and moving drama across the span of the war years; it includes bittersweet, intense romance, male-bonding beyond the usual battlefield clichés, sublime tragedy, in-depth psychological development of characters, social critique, and breathtaking cinematic poetry. At the Virginia Woolf conference, we screened 35 minutes of the film; the entire film, at just under three hours, is stunning.[1] For those readers who have not yet screened the film, perhaps the best introduction to *J'accuse* (for Woolf readers) is to quote in full the London *Times* review, because Woolf did read the *Times*:

"J'ACCUSE." A WAR ALLEGORY ON THE FILM

J'accuse, the French war film which has already caused a good deal of discussion, was exhibited publicly for the first time yesterday. It is being shown at the Philharmonic Hall twice a day, and—apart from a topical gazette—is the sole item of the programme.

The film, which is a Pathé production, is a trifle uneven. For three-quarters of its length it is nothing but a conventional story of the Great War. It tells of the loves and hates of private people and how they are affected by the great public convulsion. The males in the story join the army. The heroine is outraged by Germans. The pacifist hero wins the Legion of Honour. There is nothing new in all this. We have already witnessed these incidents too often, and it is very probable that they will reappear countless times more. But in *J'accuse* they are set forth with more conviction, and at the same time with more bitterness than they have ever been before.

For two hours the conventional runs riot, and then there is shown an allegory of war that is nothing less than inspired. There is no real reason why this allegory should be inserted in the film or why the film should surround the allegory. The one has very little connexion with the other, but no one can fail to be impressed with the allegory when it does appear. One of the protagonists is wounded in the head and loses his reason. He is inspired by a vision, returns to his native village, summons all the inhabitants, and tells them how he was on sentry duty over a graveyard filled with French dead. As he stood there they rose from their graves and wildly demanded whether those they had left behind were worthy of the dead. One multitude made its way towards his own village, and he had run in front to warn the inhabitants that they were on the way. His audience is terror-stricken, and he goes on to catechize them to see if they are really worthy of their dead. He first of all speaks to a young widow. Her husband had died at the front. Already she was married again. A landlord had driven into the street a mother. Example after example of unfaithfulness, unworthiness, and greed are shown. One and all promise to amend.

All this sounds crude when reduced to words, but the effect of the incidents on the film is almost overwhelming. For a quarter of an hour the audience is lifted out of itself and held above its usual rut. At the end of that quarter of an

COMPLICATING ADAPTATION   133

hour it is carefully placed back in that rut, but that does not matter. The miracle has been achieved. A film has caused an audience to think. (86)

J'ACCUSE AND VIRGINIA WOOLF: COMPELLING CONNECTIONS

Abel Gance and Virginia Woolf were both experimental artists; Gance worked with the new medium of cinema, using visual poetry, superimposition, cross-cutting and other innovations in film, as Woolf invented comparable literary innovations to map consciousness in new ways in writing. Both crafted scathing indictments of war. One of the film's pointed accusations is that the war kills mothers as well as soldiers; Woolf's novel, *Jacob's Room*, published in 1922, may contain traces of *J'accuse* in the foregrounding of the mother/son relationship on the home front and the attention to the mother's loss. We might imagine a hypothetical reader/viewer reading Virginia Woolf's *Jacob's Room* in 1922, along with Abel Gance's *J'accuse: D'Après le Film,* the book version with dozens of stills, also published in 1922 (see Fi. 2). Perhaps our hypothetical reader would read the reviews of those, and then, a few years later, read Virginia Woolf's *Mrs. Dalloway* with *J'accuse* in mind.

The film, *J'accuse*, dazzles with cinepoetics, and with fierce anti-war critique in its powerful depiction of the shell-shocked poet/soldier as social critic. *Mrs. Dalloway*, published six years later, contains enough parallels to *J'accuse* that one cannot but wonder if she intended parts of her novel to pay homage to that film. The sections of *Mrs Dalloway* about the doomed war veteran, Septimus Warren Smith, resonate most richly with *J'accuse*. Septimus, like Jean Diaz, is a poet who became a soldier, is marked by an intense relationship with another soldier, is shell-shocked and goes mad. Septimus indicts Human Nature and authority figures, converses with the dead (especially his close friend, Evans), and has vivid hallucinations about the returning dead. He alternately feels he has been condemned to death by Human Nature and that he is a prophet bringing poetic revelations to save the world. For Septimus, as for Jean Diaz, the madness is fierce and almost super-sane in its prophetic power; both initiate anti-war performance art that takes the form of communicating with the dead and serving as their spokesperson to the living. One can easily imagine a reader of *Mrs. Dalloway* familiar with *J'accuse* mentally casting Romuald Joubé (Diaz) as Septimus Warren Smith (see Fig. 3).

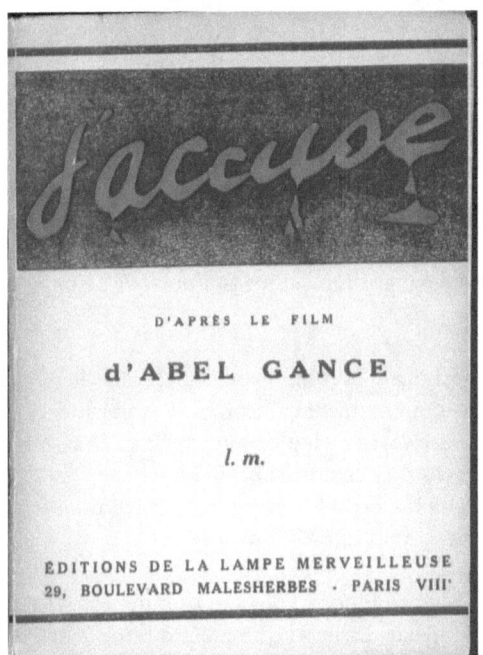

Fig. 2 Cover of the 1922 *J'accuse: D'Après le Film*

Woolf's use of visionary moments and the Shakespearean "Fear No More" passages recall the way Gance uses experimental hallucinatory cinematic elements such as repeated superimposed dancing skeletons and the phrase "J'accuse!" Diaz' poetic opus, *Les Pacifiques*, includes an ode to the sun visualized as a montage of images repeated with signifi-

Fig. 3 Jean Diaz from *J'accuse*, cinematic poet precursor of Septimus Warren Smith?

cant changes. In Woolf's novel, Septimus's deranged revelations and poetry also mingle around an ode:

> The word "time" split its husk; poured its riches over him; and from his lips fell like shells, like shavings from a plane, without his making them, hard, white, imperishable words, and flew to attach themselves to their places in an ode to Time; an immortal ode to Time. He sang. Evans answered from behind the tree. The dead were in Thessaly, Evans sang, among the orchids. There they waited until the War was over, and now the dead, now Evans himself – (69-70)

In *J'accuse*, the director Gance makes the revolutionary leap to capture Jean Diaz's poetry in purely visual form. No title cards intrude; there is no attempt to bring in actual words until the final poem. Instead, the visuals, at first lovely and pastoral, then haunting and bittersweet, then scathing images of no man's land—produce poetic cinema. In the film's final scene, the poet reflects upon his earlier poetry and finds that the soldier has killed the poet; however, he pauses as he rips up the poetry and grasps the window sill to declaim a new poem accusing the sun for having been a passive spectator of the horrors, before he collapses and dies. In Woolf's novel, Septimus acts as a director, projecting his hallucinations like avant-garde and war films onto the screen in his Bloomsbury sitting room or in the open air of the park. Echoing Jean Diaz's final scene in *J'accuse*, Septimus' final scene in *Mrs. Dalloway* comes as the authoritarian doctors (linked with the warmongers) have used their power to entrap, rather than to help him, and he is driven to suicide:

"(He sat on the sill.) But he would wait till the very last moment. He did not want to die. Life was good. The sun hot" (149). In imagery and intensity, Septimus' death scene, at the window sill in the hot sun, recalls the close of *J'accuse*. The funeral lament, Shakespeare's Song from *Cymbeline* which moves through the text of *Mrs. Dalloway* and Jean Diaz's final *Ode to the Sun* resonate with one another:

JEAN DIAZ' FINAL *ODE TO THE SUN*

Wait a moment, Sun, before disappearing,
To the land of the dead, tonight, I go,
And if my hand grips my windowsill,
It is because, bitter whim! . . . to die, I want to be
At the place where I sang to you.

A poet was there, festoons and astragals,
Genius laughed in my face!
I return to you a soldier, a drunken, spectral statue,
From my tomb, I shout while pushing back the gravestone,
As if the Earth were shrieking!...

Listen, in the name of those that your splendor deceived!
Are you afraid? You're turning red!
I called myself Jean Diaz, but I changed my muse,
My sweet name of the past has become: *I accuse*!
And I accuse you, you, Sun . . .

To have illuminated the gruesome saga,
Mute, calm, without disgust,
Like a horrible face with the tongue cut out,
At your blue balcony, sadistically contorted,
To have watched almost to the end!
                    (translation by Clarissa Rappoport-Hankins)

"FEAR NO MORE" SONG FROM SHAKESPEARE'S *CYMBELINE*

Fear no more the heat o' the sun,
   Nor the furious winter's rages;
Thou thy worldly task hast done,
   Home art gone, and ta'en thy wages:
Golden lads and girls all must,
   As chimney-sweepers, come to dust.

Fear no more the frown o' the great,
   Thou art past the tyrant's stroke;
Care no more to clothe and eat;

> To thee the reed is as the oak:
> The scepter, learning, physic, must
> All follow this, and come to dust.
>
> Fear no more the lightning-flash,
>   Nor th'all-dreaded thunder-stone;
> Fear not slander, censure rash;
>   Thou hast finished joy and moan:
> All lovers young, all lovers must,
>   Consign to thee, and come to dust.
>
> No exorciser harm thee!
>   Nor no witchcraft charm thee!
> Ghost unlaid forbear thee!
> Nothing ill come near thee!
> Quiet consummation have;
> And renowned be thy grave!

Embedded between the lines of *Mrs. Dalloway*, "Fear no More" may be read as a response to the tortured farewell poem of Jean Diaz in *J'accuse*.

The parallels between *J'accuse* and *Mrs. Dalloway* are rich and provocative. Yet, the changes and contrasts may be equally fascinating. For example, Woolf incorporates the death of the poet/soldier into Clarissa's narrative that celebrates life. Though one could argue that Edith and Angel live on in *J'accuse*, the denouement is hardly a celebratory one. If *Mrs. Dalloway* ends with the party, *J'accuse* ends with death and the image of a crucifixion. Did Woolf adapt and re-frame the film *J'accuse* as part of her novel? We can only surmise. But there is no doubt that bringing the two works of art together invites enriched viewings and readings, shedding light on the complex inter-arts relationship between literature and film in the early 20th century.[2]

Notes

1. To order the DVD, which includes both French and English versions of subtitles and a booklet with essays by Kevin Brownlow and Leslie K. Hankins and restoration notes by Annike Kross contact Flicker Alley at http://www.flickeralley.com.
2. I would like to thank Jeffrey Masino from Flicker Alley for his assistance throughout this project, the British Library for permission to publish the advertisement, and my daughter, Clarissa Rappoport-Hankins, for her help with translation.

Works Cited

"Criticism of the Films: 'J'accuse.'" *Bioscope*. April 29, 1920: 48-49.
Forster, E. M. "The Novels of Virginia Woolf." *New Criterion* (Apr.1926): 277-86.
Gance, Abel. *J'accuse: D'Après le Film*. Paris, Éditions de la Lampe Merveilleuse, 1922.
Hankins, Leslie Kathleen. "Abel Gance's *J'accuse* and Virginia Woolf's *Mrs. Dalloway*: Re-reading a Modernist Novel by the Light of the Silver Screen. *J'accuse*: the Newly Restored 1919 Version. The Flicker Alley Collection. DVD and booklet. September, 2008: 14-17.

Hussey, Mark. Ed. *Virginia Woolf and War: Fiction, Reality, and Myth*. New York: Syracuse UP, 1991.
"J'accuse" advertisement. *Kinematograph Weekly*. April 1, 1920: 46-47.
"J'accuse" advertisement. *Kinematograph Weekly*. April 8, 1920: 50-51.
"J'accuse" advertisement. *Kinematograph Weekly*. April 15, 1920: 54-55.
"J'accuse" advertisement. *Kinematograph Weekly*. April 22, 1920: 42-3.
"'J'accuse'—A Big Pathé Film." *Kinematograph Weekly*. April 8, 1920.
"J'accuse: A War Allegory on the Film." London *Times*. May 25, 1920: 86.
"J'accuse." Rev. *Kinematograph Weekly*. April 29, 1920.
Levenback, Karen. *Virginia Woolf and the Great War*. New York: Syracuse UP, 1999.
Marcus, Laura. "The Great War in twentieth-century cinema." *The Cambridge Companion to the Literature of the First World War*. Cambridge: Cambridge UP. 280-301.
"The Spirit of France: A Big French Film To Be Shown This Week." *Kinematograph Weekly*. April 22, 1920: 95.
Woolf, Virginia. *Mrs Dalloway*. [1925] San Diego: Harcourt Brace, & Co. San Diego, 1983.
—. *The Diary of Virginia Woolf*. Vol. 1, Ed., Anne Olivier Bell. London: Penguin. 1979.
—. "Mr Sassoon's Poems." *The Essays of Virginia Woolf*. Vol 2 Ed., Andrew McNeillie. San Diego: Harcourt Brace Jovanovich, 1987. 119-122.

CINEMATIC EDITING OF VIRGINIA WOOLF: *MRS. DALLOWAY* AND STEPHEN DALDRY'S *THE HOURS* AS REFLECTIVE ECOSYSTEMS

by Justyna Kostkowska

This paper is an ecocritical examination of the movie *The Hours* as a cinematic edition of *Mrs. Dalloway*. Ecofeminist criticism insists that the world remains an integrated system devoid of the traditional, patriarchally generated divisions between the external and the internal, the human and the non-human, nature and culture, and art and life. Consequently, as a practice of reading, ecocriticism is "a study of how the activities of reading and writing mediate human experiences of the environment as well as how the environment shapes the way these processes of cultural mediation contribute to making meaning out of texts" (Long 6). Ecocriticism promotes "a move toward a more biocentric world view, an extension of ethics, a broadening of human conception of global community to include nonhuman life forms and the physical environment" (Long 3). Theoretical work of ecofeminist philosophers Anthony Weston and Karen J. Warren poses a concept that "we are all connected" as "A moral community based on loving perception of oneself in relationship with a rock, or with the natural environment as a whole. . . which acknowledges and respects differences, whatever 'sameness' also exists" (Warren 138). Weston quotes Margaret Walker's definition of ethics as "a collection of perceptive, imaginative, appreciative, and expressive skills which put us and keep us in contact with the realities of ourselves and specific others" (32). Moving beyond the anthropocentric world, multicentric ethics encourages relationship and dialogue—which perceives, appreciates, and relates with the non-human others in the universe—"a move from the familiar one –species monologue to a truly multi-polar dialogue" (38).

Virginia Woolf practiced ecocritical thinking in persistently seeking to "capture Mrs. Brown," pursuing connections between art and life, and refusing to concede to the dichotomy between the two. I would like to suggest that Woolf's narrative experiment anticipates the multicentric, dialogic configuration proposed by today's ecofeminists. Woolf's close awareness of and relatedness with nature warrants a conclusion that she was one of the first practicing ecofeminists. Her experiments in *Kew Gardens*, featuring the point of view of a snail in a flower bed, and later in *Jacob's Room*, with its multiple points of view from different observers of Jacob, form a logical progression towards her method in *Mrs. Dalloway*. There, and later in *The Waves*, she develops a non-linear, multicentered stream of consciousness that approximates the real-life, associative thought process. Woolf resolves fragmentation, the main challenge of her project, by placing Clarissa, Septimus, and other characters in the shared environment of the city, weaving them together through their interactions with the outside environment, especially with nature. Because of her consistent thinking of the world as an integrated system, evidenced in her *Diary* as well as in the novel, I present her method in *Mrs. Dalloway* as an ecological gesture, whose spirit was successfully recaptured by Stephen Daldry and David Hare in their film, *The Hours*.

I want to argue that the film re-creates Woolf's novel in mirroring her structural concept of interconnectedness, and the larger spirit of unity of the human and the non-human, and of art and life, as expressed by the recurring thought of Clarrissa's that "the unseen part of us, which spreads wide, the unseen might survive, be recovered somehow attached to this person or that, or even haunting certain places after death" (*MD* 153). It is my, as well as several other critics' contention, that the essence of Woolf's novel reverberates through the film much more pervasively than it does through its novelistic namesake (Alley 417, Low 10). Just as Woolf's novel uses nature and the outside environment to fuse the parts of the novel, the makers of the movie turn the natural and physical elements of its setting into a connecting glue, creating a closely integrated artistic whole.

Writing *Mrs. Dalloway* between October 1922 and January 1925, Virginia Woolf makes numerous records of her intention for the book to be the most integrated artistically of her books so far. From the beginning of her process, Woolf configures the novel in terms of unity and interconnectedness: she wants to "press it together" (*D3* 189), "foresee this book better than the others..."(209), "Wrench my substance to fit it (249); "knit... together everything and end...on three notes" (312). She wants poetry, "concentration... all the words glued together, fused, glowing" (310). She emphasizes the "design" multiple times, as "more remarkable than in any of my books" (272). All during the writing, she remarks that she wants to integrate the worlds of the two main characters: "the caves shall connect" (263). She describes her final revisions: "one works with a wet brush over the whole, & joins parts separately composed & gone dry" (323). In a letter to Gerald Brennan, she writes: "I certainly did mean that Septimus and Clarissa should be entirely dependent upon each other" (*L3* 189). To Eliot, she says "the novel is getting too interwoven for a chapter broken off to be intelligible" (178).

Interestingly, over the timeframe in which she creates the book, Woolf records thinking of herself and her process in terms of physical nature: she says "Mrs. Dalloway has branched into a book" (207); she describes "her greatest discovery" as digging caves [in the earth], and connecting them to come "to daylight at the present moment" (263), as "touch[ing] the hidden spring" (263). She wants to "pour everything in" (302). Water and earth imagery is prominent here—she also describes her soul, so far restrained by prose as a "plant in a pot, it begins to crack the earthenware" (304). She says she imagines her mind as "lighted rooms" and her walks in the fields as "corridors" (*D2* 311). The consistent parallels she draws between her creative world and nature show that Woolf perceives them as intertwined, if not inseparable. This idea of interconnectedness is rooted in Woolf's ecological imagination: she sees herself and the writing process as a part of a larger natural ecosystem. "Does human identity exist outside nature—ever?" (Waller 148).

The finished novel is a masterpiece of integrity which is achieved through repetition of themes and motifs but made possible through creating one shared environment with which the characters, who often do not know each other, interact. Lawrence Buell notes that Woolf's "London is a concatenation of human pulsations thrusting in and around each other through a common environment of buildings, streets, walks, parks, traffic.... The novel is exceptionally sensitive to the vibrations of environmental unconscious" (107). Woolf's characters share a sensitivity to the "minutest stimuli" of external environment (Buell 107). This physical environment, and especially its natural component such as parks, the sky, and plants constitute an ecosystem that unites all the characters. Clarissa, Septimus, Rezia, Peter, and numerous others move around the same city streets and park alleys, looking at the same sky, and breathing the same air. Clarissa's positioning in the open window ties her to Septimus, just as her foreshadowing image of standing at the top of the stairs reoccurs several times to unify the book. Flowers and trees connect Clarissa to Peter and to all characters in the central reference to her being spread "like a mist" on trees, "being a part of the trees at home" (9). The park setting unites Peter to Septimus and Rezia; Clarissa and Peter share the memory of the lake, while flowers connect Sally and Clarissa, floating in vases as well as handled during their memorable kiss; roses, particularly, bring Richard and Clarissa together, and tie in Septimus and Rezia when she buys them in the street (93). The old crone woman, whose eternal love hymn evokes Peter's, Clarissa's, and Sally's love, reminisces about asters and heather (81). Lady Bruton is very awkward with the carnations that Hugh brings her (110), and Sally and Peter reconnect when she writes to Peter about blue hydrangeas (72). Clarissa and the flowers she buys make possible her artistic creation of the party, connecting Septimus and her within one environment.

Nature in Woolf is never objectified, but often takes the role of a character, and is an important semantic element that brings out the meaning of the text and its subtle connections. As Charlotte Walker notes, "Just as Woolf's characters, and through them her readers, relate sensuously to nature, often receiving through it the shocks… that bring them into the state of creativity that leads to transformation and to art, Woolf also hints . . . at a merging of writing, reading, and nature" (149). Apart from physical nature, Woolf uses nature elements such as birds and flowers figuratively in descriptive similes and metaphors, to construct and connect the characters' identities. Clarissa, Rezia, and Peter are described as birds; Elizabeth is compared to a hyacinth (123), Clarissa to a lily (193). She shivers as a "plant on a river-bed feels the shock of a passing oar and shivers" (30). This last image figures in the diary description of Woolf's own experience she records on May 5, 1924: "the beauty brimmed over me & steeped my nerves till they quivered, as I have seen a water plant quiver when the water overflowed it" (*D3* 301). Her mind reaches out to the natural world for the closest description of her personal aesthetic experience. Woolf transposes that description into the novel, configuring the world of the book and the world of the author as part of one reality: a larger ecosystem where art and life overlap. Interestingly, Woolf again describes her experience of being interrupted while writing the last chapter of the novel in natural terms: "my house down, my wings broken, & I left on the bare ground" (*D2* 314). Her vision does not discriminate between the natural and the human, between her world and the world of the book. The Woolfian conceptualization of the reality of the writer and the written as one finds its equivalent in the film in the rich relationship between Woolf's life, Woolf's book, and the lives of Laura Brown and Clarissa Brown. Woolf is featured as author as well as character, as is, more briefly, Michael Cunningham in his cameo appearance. Writer, character, reader, book and movie all coexist in the same universe, seemingly separate yet centrally entwined with each other.

The movie makes the relationship of art to life and their influence on each other its central theme. Just as Woolf's challenge was to connect the characters' separate stories, the screenplay and the director's design is to make the tripartite film one whole. It is my contention that this effort succeeds mainly due to what I call the movie's ecological spirit: the precise and masterful networking of connections among the characters through their relationship with their physical environment. The setting rises to the importance of a character. The way the characters are framed in the shots, e.g. how they interact with their physical surroundings, is, as in Woolf's novel, the mortar that connects the three stories. In this respect, the movie is a creative cinematic reimagining of Woolf's method.

As Stephen Daldry comments, an effort was made from the very beginning to reassure the viewer that the three stories would be connected (*Director's Commentary*). The movie is truly an ecosystem, providing consistent parallels between each plot's settings. We follow the main characters' partners as they come home and find the women, from Laura to Virginia to Clarissa, each shown in the same context and from the same angle, each in the mirror, each washing her face. Clarissa's action of picking up a vase of flowers is seamlessly continued by Dan into his and Laura's "universe," despite a cut between the scenes. The camera catches all women at the same tasks, from Virginia flipping the pages of the manuscript, to Laura thumbing through the published novels, to Clarissa writing in her notepad. The sentence about the flowers is first written, then read by Laura, and then spoken by Clarissa. We, as the audience, witness all three in a succession.

The natural elements are a large part of the setting, and among them flowers are the one overwhelming presence. At the florist's, Clarissa wants "hydrangeas and buckets of roses," echoing Woolf's two most featured species of flowers, the movie's hydrangeas blue like Woolf's Sally's, and featured in many vital scenes such as the crucial coming together of Clarissa and Julia on the bed in the conversation about happiness. Vases upon vases of flowers line Clarissa's apartment, and are often in the foreground or on the same plane with the character. As she prepares for the party, the flowers in vivid reds and blues are a vibrant symbol of bringing people together. Clarissa brings flowers to Richard, connecting her world physically to his, and making his apartment look like hers. Importantly, when she reenters it in his death scene, no flowers are in view, and the apartment is desolate, emphasizing Richard's separation from her. In her conversation with the aged Laura, the flowers are muted whites and greys, only in the background, because of Clarissa's antagonism, later melting, with the colorful calla lilies featured again in the hallway. Yellow roses are brought by Dan to Laura, and by Virginia to the dying bird, connecting Woolf's death theme to Laura's metaphorical state of death, and ultimately to Richard's real one. Woolf's character continues to lay roses and giving the bird the deserved respect despite the fact that Vanessa and the children depart from the scene. Potted plants figure in kitchen window sills behind both Clarissa and Laura, particularly when Clarissa talks about "holding herself together all these years," pointing to their shared containment, and the "smallness" of their lives.

Place is literally emphasized as the unifying factor when Woolf's character says in death "we all return to the place where we came from." Nicole Kidman brings her face down and stares into the dead bird's eyes. The movie carries the concept of shared space further by cutting straight to Laura's face in bed, at the same angle as Virginia's and the bird's. Woolf's ecological imagination is directly echoed here. "We" truly includes everyone, human and non-human, sharing one world. The concept is further carried out by camera angles and frames. Leonard and Dan appear identically in their respective door frames urging their partners to go to bed. Window frames, of Richie looking out at his mother and Richard looking out from behind the curtain, all emphasize the shared world. Shared objects, such as flower vases being moved across plot settings, tea and coffee cups held, food, especially symbolically fraught eggs, being handled, fabric worn, pictures looked at, are all elements of the physical world that bind the three plots together as the characters interact with them. A notable example is the fabric of Richie's childhood sheets returning in adult Richard's dressing gown. The same fabric is the first sign that Richard is Laura's son, coming long before we see her wedding picture in his apartment. But the most spectacular natural unifying element is certainly the water from Woolf's river Ouse flowing under Laura's hotel bed and submerging her, only to subside as Woolf decides to give her character a reprieve from death.

Like Woolf's novel set on one June day, the movie presents three one-day plots from diverse time periods, only to obliterate that difference through the commonality of their shared conflicts. The purposeful editing consistently shuffles the stories together, reducing temporal linearity to the minimum and creating an integrated effect. The pieces of the stories form a mosaic and eventually seep through each other, with Laura's reappearance, and Woolf's words bleeding into the other stories. Space is equally flexible and accommodating. The settings' elements overflow from one plot to another, much like the river's water, in one shared ecosystem of the physical and the artistic. The plots are framed together on the outside through the unifying, period-neutral piano music and the sound of Woolf's/Nicole Kidman's voice, and ultimately, the audience's act of watching the movie in the scope of two hours. Our emotions are also an internal unifying factor, overflowing the boundaries of the three plots as in the rapid transition from Richard's suicide to Dan's birthday party, when we continue to process our horror as we watch the birthday celebration. In the outmost "stratum" of this ecosystem, the audience co-creates the movie as an art object through their reactions. Just as in Woolf's vision, art and life participate in one system.

Woolf's spirit pervades the film from the first to last scene. Like contemporary ecofeminists, both she and the creators of the film see their work and the world as an ecosystem where nothing exists in isolation. The movie's meaning is built on an internal structure of interconnected themes, characters, parallel images and unifying manipulation of the setting nearly as intricate as Woolf's novel. The way the characters interact with the setting, and are presented in relationship to it, creates parallels that make the film an integrated whole. What is more, this ecosystem includes the audience ourselves, our responses cementing the scenes further. This is the system Woolf imagined in her pursuit of integrating art with life: writer, book, reader, film, audience, all reach out beyond themselves and invite a view of the world as larger and more connected than we often imagine.

Works Cited

Alley, Henry. "*Mrs.Dalloway* and Three of Its Contemporary Children." *Papers on Language and Literature: A Journal for Scholars and Critics of Language and Literature* 42.4 (Fall 2006): 401-19.

Buell, Lawrence. *Writing for an Endangered World: Literature, Culture, and Environment in the U.S. and Beyond.* Cambridge, MA: Harvard UP, 2001.

Hughes, Mary Joe. "Michael Cunningham's *The Hours* and Postmodern Artistic Re-Presentation." *Critique* 45.4 (Summer 2004): 349-361.

Long, Mark C. "Ecocriticism as a Practice of Reading." *Reader* 53 (Fall 2005): 4-20.

Low, Lisa. "A Fit Audience Though Few." *Virginia Woolf Miscellany* 62 (March 1, 2003): 10.

The Hours. Director's Commentary. Dir. Stephen Daldry. Prod. Scott Rudin and Robert Fox. With Nicole Kidman, Julianne Moore, Meryl Streep. Paramount Pictures and Miramax films, 2002.

Walker, Charlotte Z. "'The Book Laid Upon the Landscape': Virginia Woolf and Nature." *Beyond Nature Writings: Expanding the Boundaries of Ecocriticism.* Eds. Karla Armbruster and Kathleen Wallace. Charlottesville, VA: UP of Virginia, 2001.

Waller, L. Elizabeth. "Writing the Real: Virginia Woolf and an Ecology of Language." *The Bucknell Review* 44.1 (2000): 137-156.
Warren, Karen J. "The Power and the Promise of Ecological Feminism." *Environmental Ethics* 12.2 (1990): 125-146.
Weston, Anthony. "Multicentrism: A Manifesto." *Environmental Ethics* 26 (1990): 25-40.
Woolf, Virginia. *The Diary of Virginia Woolf.* Ed. Ann Olivier Bell. Vols. 2 and 3. London: The Hogarth Press, 1978.
—. *The Letters of Virginia Woolf.* Eds. Nigel Nicolson and Joanne Trautmann. Vol.3. New York: Harcourt Brace, 1977.
—. *Mrs. Dalloway*. 1925 Rpt. New York: Harcourt Brace, 1981.

AFTER TEA: ADAPTING VIRGINIA WOOLF'S *A WRITER'S DIARY* FOR STAGE PERFORMANCE

by Carol Samson

In a recent *Independent* article entitled "My Book Of A Lifetime: *A Writer's Diary* by Virginia Woolf," novelist Susan Hill writes of chancing upon Woolf's diary in the Coventry Public Library in 1958 when she was 16 and of keeping it as a companion for the last 50 years:

> The diary introduced me to the woman, and led me to her books, which came as a revelation. . . . I pick up *A Writer's Diary* every day, at random. It opens on her description of visiting Thomas Hardy, on her ecstatic race across the final pages of *The Waves*, on how hurt she is by a bad review in *The Times*, on Leonard's opinion of *To the Lighthouse*, or how she cares that Lytton Strachey is getting more attention that she is. It has so many moods, contains so much intelligence, opinon, feeling—gossip. . . .I have never exhausted *A Writer's Diary*, never will. (Hill)

I understand Hill's response to the work; for in adapting *A Writer's Diary* for stage production at the 18th International Virginia Woolf Conference, I learned to read Woolf's strange and lyrical genius. Even as she described her ordinary moments at dinner or buying a blouse or watching Leonard try to resuscitate a hedgehog, I found that, in her hands, the diary genre became its own reward, not merely on the level of Woolf's ability to supply character portrait and scene study, but—more deeply—as an enactment of the forming of images. In her observations of Thomas Hardy's dog Wessex or of a French woman embroidering a cloth, Woolf's flat description is philosophical introspection. Admitting that making images is a regenerative process, Woolf measured out her moments after tea, as she said many times, trying to find a reality beyond the physical world, attempting to construct a bridge across the abyss, to hold her mind together in language. In keeping her diary she was honing her writing skills, practicing scenes and portraiture, alleviating her own anger, and, as she liked to put it, doing the scales. While the diary partakes of rambling and disjunctions, Woolf's hand is a steady recreation of her relationship to art. She is watching her writing-self write, finding a meta-cognitive stance. Regardless of the prompt, there is no observation without introspection, no introspection without expanding circles of more introspection. Everything must be dissolved into the mind and, then, the mind must make more images because the manufacture of images restores her to good health. In designing my adaptation of her diaries, I had to distill that argument and to set it on stage, in relief, much as Jenny, on the beach in Woolf's *The Waves*, places a flower on the waters.

The diaries were first edited by her husband Leonard Woolf in 1953. Since then a five-volume publication of the diaries has expanded and opened the text. For my purposes, though, I allowed Leonard his vision, the primary cut. I read the last years of his edited version and compared it to the complete version, and I found that Leonard in his thoughtfulness kept an eye on her poetry and her honesty, on the moments of despair and on the images that carried psychological weight. He has, as Virginia Woolf said of E.M. Forster, the eye of an artist, not just the eye of a clever reader. He allows Virginia her own crabbings and her own experiments in modernist prose poems. He allows for moments wherein he is himself a character. In his introduction to his edition of the diary, a 350 page version taken from the 26 handwritten volumes, Leonard Woolf states his editorial purpose simply:

> This book throws light upon Virginia Woolf's intentions, objects, and methods as a writer. It gives an unusual psychological picture of artistic production from within. . . . She was, I think, a serious artist and all her books are serious works of art. The diaries at least show the extraordinary energy, persistence, and concentration with which she devoted herself to the art of writing and the undeviating conscientiousness with which she wrote and rewrote and again rewrote her books. (ix)

Leonard was, of course, her ideal reader.

As a road into the making of a play out of a diary, I appropriated Woolf's own sense of situating a diary in aesthetic terms. In the diary of April 1919, where the play begins, she wrote:

> I should like this diary to resemble some deep old desk, or capacious hold all, in which one flings a mass of odds and ends without looking them through. I should like to come back, after a year or two, and find that the collection had sorted itself and refined itself and coalesced, as such deposits so mysteriously do, into a mould, transparent enough to reflect the light of our life, and yet steady, tranquil compounds with the aloofness of a work of art. (13)

In this passage she also explains her method of reading the diaries: "The main requisite, I think on re-reading my old volumes is not to play the part of censor, but to write as the mood comes or of anything whatever, since I was curious to find how I went for things put in haphazard, and found the significance to lie where I never saw it at the time" (13-14).

Herein Woolf sets my course: I must make the clutter of the odds and ends coalesce mysteriously into a tranquil mould with the aloofness of a work of art. The word "mysteriously" attached to the idea of coalescence concerned me; and, yet, I found the genre of the diary form allowed for an interesting and serendipitous collage texture. It called for a post-modern exploration of disjunctions, meditations, fragments and orts and notes and play. It allowed for the sublime to co-exist with the ordinary: Leonard gathering apples, cows feeding, set against Woolf's thoughts on what it must feel like to be killed by a bomb--all in the same few sentences. In editing the diary, I wanted to keep the flavor of the chronology of her careful system of noting the day and the date. I wanted the diary juxtapositions of matters ordered by Time to maintain their immediate quality, to keep the simple authenticities of a mind at work. I wanted a sensation of flux and of oddities wherein serious matters sit side-by-side with the mundane: Woolf's deep pain over criticism of her work by Wyndham Lewis and her note that she will buy a blouse to get over it; her comments on Henry James' prose style embedded with a note that, just as she was writing, Leonard was bitten by a flee. The diary is, as Woolf says, where she notices things. Leonard Woolf chose to call it *A Writer's Diary* and gave much attention to her thoughts on her individual works and on editing and on the "voice" of a writer talking her self. In my adaptation, I think we see her with many eyes in the selected cuttings. We view her as what she calls a "fanlike membrane of her species," as a woman of culture, a feminist, a barren wife, a sister, a portrait painter, and a philosopher of metaphysical spaces.

Almost immediately as I began my editing, Woolf showed me what she wanted. In January 1919, the young Virginia, about to turn 37, considers her own being as it will exist at age 50:

> If Virginia Woolf at age of 50, when she sits down to build her memoirs out of these books, is unable to make a phrase as it should be made, I can only remind her of the existence of the fireplace, where she has my leave to burn these pages to so many black films with red eyes in them. But how I envy her the task I am preparing for her! Already my 37th birthday next Saturday is robbed of some of its terrors by the thought. Partly for the benefit of this elderly lady (no subterfuge will then be possible: 50 is elderly. . .though I anticipate her protest and agree that it is not old), partly to give the year a solid foundation I intend to spend the evening in making out an account of my friendships. . .with some account of my friends' characters. . .and a forecast of future works. The lady of 50 will be able to say how near the truth I come. (7-8)

In this passage Woolf offered me a significant form, a design for the production. I understood that I must have two Virginias on stage: the energetic, competitive writer, age 37, about to make her claim and the older, famous, war-weary Virginia, age 58, about to take her own life. In a theatre space, the two Virginias would have conversation. One's hope would confront the other's fatalism. The waves of the manic self would co-exist with the depressive. One self could present questions the other could mediate or answer. And, ironically, the young woman, caught in the beauties of the world, could remind the older woman to "look her last on all things lovely" (348).

I read the diary twice, marking the workable sections in green, finding new moments and re-considering old choices as I went along. I then typed out all of the viable segments, allowing, amidst the lyrical rhythms, occasional bits of flatness, the necessary "diary" tone: "Car mended. Leonard changed the oil. Won at bowls." I broke the diary into four parts, worked each section separately based on the rhythms of her life: the apprenticeship, the fame, the ripening, the depression. I looked for the visual moments, the dialogues, the introspection into her character and into her friends. I noticed that Woolf often refers to the comfortable moments after tea when she could write; and, noting that we would be having tea at the conference, I titled the piece *After Tea*. I worked each of the four sections again and again, finding the dramatic arc before compiling them, keeping Time, so to speak, by working the journal dates into the dialogue thereby requiring the actors to read the date as part of the line and, once again, allowing diary genre its due. The two actors,

I decided, would carry diary books and read parts from them. At first I imagined many volumes on stage, the actresses drawing up book after book; but I was forced to conclude that simplicity must rule, that the retrieval of too many books meant cumbersome stage movement. I knew that, in the end, I wanted a language piece, a fluent run of poetry in 90 minutes.

In preparation for a first reading I had the actresses listen to Woolf's voice from a BBC program done in 1939. We agreed that she sounded like Queen Elizabeth, but we chose not to do any sort of imitation, preferring instead a slight English accent. At the first reading, I explained the wave-like rush in the adaptation, the rhythm of youth, the build, the decline, the epiphany, the break. I told them how the piece works to explain ageing and obsolescence, societal issues of gender, experiences of warfare and illness. I wanted them to see, though, that the significant form of the piece, the underlying design, was a segmenting of the debate about capturing "reality" in words and exploring phantom realities, about concepts of death as a passing into mist, about her own theories that she "insubstantizes." Clearly, Woolf feels that reality itself is "cheap" but that the reality within and beyond the "thing in itself" with all of its sensory possibilities and its "hauntings" is intriguing. Perception of the "thing in itself," followed by the act of recording, the act of writing things down, stabilizes Virginia Woolf. The essence of the play, then, is really how, given the world with its pressures and deaths, given what she called her "squirrel cage mind," Woolf creates a dialogue with self where two voices try to help each other. The creative part attempts to restore the health of it all, forming and re-visioning images. This young self is conscious of the nursing role; but sometimes she, too, must be reined in and held in abeyance as she comes to wish to lie down in the snow and stay there. The critical self keeps measuring, falling into slumps, finding herself unable to exist, despising the people who judge her, gnawing at old bones, yet determining that the only recourse to inner peace is looking at things, dahlias instead of war rubble, mist instead of solid mass.

As the rehearsals progressed, I told the actresses that we were not going to present a styled reproduction of Woolf as per the Nicole Kidman version of Woolf in the film version of *The Hours*. Rather, working with the diary genre as a "self writing to self" or as a mind envisioning moments with "self" as percipient and as participant, I directed them to gossip and chat and laugh and confess to one another. I wanted them to take on characters, one becoming Lytton Strachey and having tea with the other as Virginia, one actress creating Woolf and Thomas Hardy and Mrs. Hardy in a single memory scene, one taking Leonard's part and the other Virginia's as they wait for bombs to drop near Rodmell. I watched as the actresses worked to subdue the thicket of what Woolf herself, speaking of *The Waves*, called the "grinding" stuff of the words and of sentences that issue out in silk tangles. With the language foremost in my mind, I blocked the scenes with continual movement reminiscent of the lyricism of the Woolf's lines. I avoided straight "crosses" from place to place. I worked for serpentine loops and moments of arrest where the actresses faced each other and explained matters of health and reputation and despair. I also tried to find the humor, the "mischief" in her. As one conference delegate from Yorkshire told me, "I'm so glad you played the mischief. Few people see it. And I think that a diary reading could have been deadly dull without it."

In terms of the set, I kept the "self talking to self "of the diary genre in mind. I wanted a simple image: two chairs, a tea table, a carpet. The script, as I adapted it, dictated two geographical spaces: London Bloomsbury and rural Rodmell. I wanted an Arts and Crafts chair for London and a tall, wicker-backed chair for Rodmell. I studied the pictures from Monk's House, noting the lamps and the oddments. I looked at catalogues of Virginia Woolf's sister's farmhouse at Lewes, considering the screens and the teapots. The philosophy of the play may call for things "insubstantial," but the set had to suggest Woolf's world, her taste. I found the chairs. I found a Brown Betty teapot like one that appeared in one of Vanessa Bell's paintings. And, while I considered the use of demi-lune tables to hold the tea-cups, half tables that could be placed together to form one table, an echo of my vision of the younger and older Virginia having tea, I ultimately opted for the tea-cart and two chairs and two blue diary notebooks. I concluded that the diary notebooks the actresses carried were more important than the tables. The notebooks were, in fact, characters. The physical presence of the diary gave substance to the words. Better, I thought, that the actresses open the books and read or, at times, clutch the diary to their chests, thereby bringing the diary genre to the forefront, than to shift demi-lune tables into circles.

Cutting some of the parts of the text that I thought I could not do without was difficult; but in the fifth draft, the "sweating it down" as Woolf would say, I began to see the poetry take over from the academic diatribes or the random moments I had to eliminate--the moment, for example, when, having had to miss the ballet, she turns the flight of zeppelin in the sky into a ballet dancer and feels better. The script, as I edited it, relies not so much on plot as on repetition of image, on themes that reoccur, on sketches of old women, pale and ill and obsolete, and women, beautiful--a French woman in a green dress, and on interpretations of her women friends like Mary Sheepshanks and Ethel Smyth. Woolf "takes the fences," as she says, recording issues of mortality, the death of friends, the mental struggle to make the later works, *Flush* and *The Years* take shape. She feels the stings of "being despised" by the young male writers of the 1930's, senses the loss of "reputation," but she continues to talk herself into observing and writing. With the coming of World War II, the threat to Leonard Woolf who was Jewish, the destruction of London, the nightly flights of German air-raids over the house at Rodmell, we see a breaking:

> Wednesday, January 15, 1941 London: I wandered in the desolate ruins of my old squares, gashed, dismantled, the old red bricks all white powder . . .Sunday, January 26: Rodmell. The solitude is great. The house is damp. The house is untidy. I begin to dislike introspection: Sunday, February 16: . . . No country to look at. No butter, no jam. Old couples hoarding marmalade and grape nuts on their tables. (349-351)
> Sunday, March 8th: Suppose I bought a ticket at the Museum; biked in daily and read history. Suppose I selected one dominant figure in every age and wrote round and about. Occupation is essential. And now with some pleasure I find that it's seven; and must cook dinner. Haddock and sausage meat. I think it is true that one gains a certain hold on sausage and haddock by writing them down. (351)

I pondered the line about haddock and sausage meat. At first, I thought that it would serve me well as an ending. I thought: Here is the objective correlative for my piece—that is, to name is to gain hold of the thing, to record is to control. But, again, "mysteriously"

Woolf showed me otherwise. She had, I discovered, trained me well. I considered the endings of her novels. I knew that the artist must redeem the last moment, in art if not in life. I remembered *To the Lighthouse* and Lily Briscoe's triumphant gesture in finishing her painting in one purple stroke. I considered Peter Walsh's feelings of terror and ecstasy at the end of *Mrs. Dalloway*, his lines: "What is it that fills me with extraordinary excitement? It is Clarissa, he said. For there she was." I re-read Bernard's verbal assault on Death in *The Waves*. I thought of the young protagonist of Woolf's early novel, *The Voyage Out*, who—in her dying—chooses to return to a world of images, and of the short story "Kew Gardens" where in the final moments Woolf moves the visual camera eye through space, lifting us off the ground into a higher life of color and shape, into forms within forms like Chinese boxes. Woolf showed me, "mysteriously," that I must do what she says she does: I must see beyond the real. I must "insubstantise." Perhaps, in the end, this was her personal gift as I worked with her diary. She did not tell me, as Ezra Pound would, to "Make it Strange." She seemed to say, "Make it Metaphysical." She asked me to read the soul in concrete matter, to look hard to find the eternal in the garden, in the steeple, in the game of bowls, in the "purple" color in the sky over Asheham, in the thing itself.

I found the ending for my adaptation early on in my editing when I read her entry for October 4, 1934. I read it seeing it in the light of her final diary entries, the entry in March of 1941 in particular, when she reminds herself to mark Henry James's dictum "Observe perpetually" and when she extends his thought: "Observe the oncome of age. Observe greed. Observe my own despondency. By that means it becomes serviceable" (351). I read the October 1934 entry, remembering that she spoke often about the fact that the look of things had a great power over her, that she watched the rooks beat in the wind and searched for a phrase for that, that she wanted to get down into her pen what was vivid to her eyes. It seemed appropriate, then, to end the play in this single diary moment as Woolf uses rapid brushstrokes of images to record her view over the river toward one house she loved, the large white house at Asheham. I hoped that the audience would understand the way this passage was, in its lyrical impressionism, a statement of the wave-like rhythms of her psychology and of the restorative nature of the process of language-making, of the way one gains control of haddock and sausage by writing them down. I divided the speech into the short bits, into a moulded collage of single images that the actresses spoke, alternating turns, two voices creating one picture, the speech thus becoming a final chorus containing the light and the dark and the metaphysical:

> Thursday, October 4th, 1934: A violent rain storm on the pond. The pond is covered with little white thorns; springing up and down; the pond is bristling with leaping white thorns like the thorns on a small porcupine; bristles; then black waves; cross it; black shudders; and the little water thorns are white: a helter skelter rain and the elms tossing it up and down; the pond overflowing on one side; lily leaves tugging; the red flower swimming about; one leaf flapping; then completely smooth for a moment; then prickled; thorns like glass; but leaping up and down incessantly; a rapid smirch of shadow. Now light from the sun; green and red; shiny; the pond a sage green; the grass brilliant green; red berries on the hedges; the cows very white; purple over Asheham. (220)

In the last moments of the production, as the actresses performed this chorus and came to the end, I used the final movement of Beethoven's *Piano Sonata Number 21*, called "The Waldstein," as background. It is a delicate piece of music that skips and sweeps, plunges into darkness and holds light for a moment. Virginia Woolf's diary words and that piece of music seemed, to me, to give a "certain hold" on what we wanted to say of her.

Works Cited

Hill, Susan. "My Book Of a Lifetime: *A Writer's Diary*, by Virginia Woolf." *Independent.* 26 Oct.2008 <http://www.independent.co.uk/arts-entertainment/books/reviews/my-book-of-a-lifetime-a-writers-diary-by-virginia-woolf970632.html>.

Woolf, Virginia. *A Writer's Diary*. Ed. Leonard Woolf. New York: Harcourt, 1982.

WAVE TO THE DEPTHS: A PERFORMANCE OF
THE WAVES' HIDDEN MUSIC

by Danaë Killian-O'Callaghan

And when the sense of rhythm was thoroughly alive in every mind we should if I mistake not, notice a great improvement ... in the art of writing, which is nearly allied to the art of music, and is chiefly degenerate because it has forgotten its allegiance. We should invent—or rather remember—the innumerable metres which we have so long outraged, and which would restore both prose and poetry to the harmonies the ancients heard and observed. (Woolf "Street Music" 31)

Such a reunion of music with the writer's art Woolf prophetically achieves in *The Waves*, is in a way not limited to the play-poem's extraordinary features of sonority, rhythm and form. A fundamentally musical element permeates *The Waves*' whole exploration of psychological constitution to inform Woolf's narrative technique. Jinny, for example, when she kisses Louis in the garden (9), is related to him as the musical interval of the *seventh*—dissonantly enlivening, unwelcomely awakening, mobile and vibrant like quicksilver—is related to the musical *prime* in its leaden stasis, gravity. Susan's anguished response to the event reverberates with the quality of the musical *third*, expressive in its within-one's-own-skin intimacy of most personally soul-felt sympathies and antipathies ("I love and I hate" [*W* 11]), and the natural differentiator, therefore, of the polar moods of major and minor harmonies. Thus a narrative sequence of immense symbolic and psychological import for the whole of *The Waves* can be experienced as the verbal inscription of a hidden melody yet with definite tones and distinct harmonic colour.

The infusion of musical essence into the literary medium manifests itself on or above the surface of *The Waves* in its glowing aura of sound repetitions and relations, but not only there. Each of *The Waves*' words is articulated to shine like a "bead of water," a "drop of ... light," against a pulsing "web" of sonorities (*W* 6), which develops out of the echoes of words past, echoes which seem to become, as they are woven into a new textual moment, premonitions of future words. As sequences and constellations of sounds recur, vary and develop, as they merge or metamorphose, crystallize or unravel, they become rhythmically formative motives, finer but also stronger, as the spider's light silk stretched out is stronger than steel, and more elastic, than the plot-drive of any conventional narrative. "I am writing," stated Woolf to her composer friend, Ethel Smyth, "to a rhythm and not to a plot" (*L* 204). Like a great composer, Woolf sculpts her form with a virtuoso rhythmic technique that seems to make time move in multiple directions, transcending limited uni-linear conceptions of plottable connections between events. To experience *The Waves* whole in all the intricacy of its form and meaning, the reader must listen for its "rhythmic harmony," for the "vast pulsation," which is only "partially ... transcri[bed]" ("Street Music" 31). Whereas the sounds of language are sense-perceptible, transcribable phenomena, the powerful rhythmic dimension of Woolf's sound-weaving manifests itself *beneath* the sensory surface of the words, moves in the partial hiddenness that belongs to rhythm's being-in-becoming, being-in-passing, to its perpetual rise and fall. The sound is borne into appearance on waves of rhythm; we do not perceive *whence* the evanescent sound that we physically hear "cometh, nor whither it goeth" (John 3: 8). The being of rhythm is half-silent, always mysterious, like the virtually silent "said Bernard, ... said Susan, ... said Rhoda," which can be felt as *The Waves*' heartbeat, always present, yet always beneath the surface.

So Woolf's reunion of music with language transpires suprasensorily *through* the audible and sheer sensual beauty of *The Waves*' voices' pellucid cantilena, *by* eurhythmic movement unfolding beneath the surface, and—deeper still—by individual consciousnesses resonating within, even when dissonantly against, each other, as if the voices' bodies' skins were made of permeable musical interval-substance, of the ethereal, inaudible 'space' that lives between tones. The transpiration is at once silent and resonant, the moving of a threshold-crossing music, like waves of water, against the shores and into the crevices of the English language.

The Waves' hidden yet palpably sonorous music is so complete that any attempt at translation into 'actual' music will be in a certain sense as redundant as the call to do so, for me, has been irresistible. Of less importance to me, in following that call, was the production of a new text to place alongside Woolf's—of another transcription onto paper of *The Waves*' music, this time in musical notation—than the *performative* uncovering of the music Woolf has already ("partially") transcribed. Only the life-in-movement of a musical performance, as distinct from a setting-down on paper, can answer the particular call to make a hidden music boldly manifest, while retaining its mystery of phenomenal evanescence. A new *text*, therefore, I have not woven.

Indeed, the musical composition through which I have chosen to perform *The Waves* on the piano is not only or even necessarily or for all contexts inspired by Woolf's *The Waves*, although my performance is. Its composer is my fellow Melburnian Eve Duncan in whose ear I whispered of *The Waves* from the moment she told me of the piece's conception, when I dared to suggest that it shared with *The Waves* a common spiritual source. Duncan has written in connection with this piece:

> Behind the material world one senses a deeper world of inspiration, mathematics, spiritual beings, living physical and psychological archetypes; a living, breathing reality of invisibility. Composition is the means by which I swim through this sea of complex activity, trying to understand what influences human, animal and mineral evolution. (2006)

To my insistent invocation of Woolf's presence Eve Duncan has responded with interest and enthusiasm, willingly allowing Woolf a dwelling-place in her composition *Wave to the Depths* (2003) when I perform it. This openness to the interpretative will of the performer is consistent with Duncan's philosophy of composing for individuals, "My music is architecturally conceived; however I allow the individuality of specific musicians to strongly influence the compositional elements such as rhythm, harmony, texture and melody: they are a rich resource for the unfolding of the music. (2006)"

Wave to the Depths is articulated in two parts. The first explores those unfocussed yet translucent, horizonal moments of consciousness between waking and sleeping that are often structurally pivotal in *The Waves,* and which seem to be attuned always to the characters' (if we can call the voices "characters") mode of perception and reflection—not quite solidly embodied, yet, paradoxically, acutely aware of sense impressions. The second part engages with the tension between the immense ground or *Abgrund* of the death-containing, death-resistant natural world; and the mortal-immortal human being, fragile, who yet rises "unvanquished and unyielding" saying "Fight! Fight!" (*W* 211, 191).

Works Cited

Duncan, Eve. *Australian Music Centre Composer Biography.* 2006. Accessed 13/6/2008. <http://www.amcoz.com.au/composers/composer.asp>

Woolf, Virginia. *Letters.* Vol. 4. Ed. Nigel Nicolson and Joanne Trautmann. New York: Harcourt Brace Jovanovich, 1975.

——. "Street Music." 1905. *The Essays of Virginia Woolf.* Vol. 1. Ed. Andrew McNeillie. London: Hogarth, 1986. 27–32.

——. *The Waves.* 1931. 3rd ed. London: Hogarth: 1963.

Editing Virginia Woolf and the Arts: Virginia Woolf and the Royal Academy

by Maggie Humm

By the turn of the twentieth century there were over thirty women art critics writing for London journals with some, for example, Alice Meynell, earning over £400 a year. Press Day at the Royal Academy, for the annual summer exhibition, accommodated women critics by changing viewing times to safer daylight hours. Also by 1914, government ministries organizing World War One, began to appoint women war artists. It is surprising, therefore, that in Virginia Woolf's review of the Royal Academy 1919 summer exhibition, "The Royal Academy," she should obscure the contribution of women artists as well as the significant date of the exhibition which was the first since the end of the war (*E3*). Since 2008 is the 90th anniversary of the armistice, it is an appropriate moment to look at Woolf's response to that "war" exhibition. Woolf's "The Royal Academy," together with the 1919 exhibition itself, raise gender and political issues in a crucial case study of ambiguities in Woolf's writings as well as in our contemporary critical difficulties with "modernism" itself.

In 1919, Roger Fry was also emphatically attacking "subject pictures" (Fry 71). As prolific as Woolf, Fry's several reviews in that year for the *Athenaeum* included "Art and Science" in which Fry specifically denigrated "the ordinary historical pictures of our annual shows" (Fry 71). But Fry had exhibited non-abstract, figurative war images in his solo exhibition at the Alpine Club Gallery in 1915. *German General Staff*, a large-scale 6 x 5 feet work, was seen as "patriotic," and Fry submitted the painting to the Ministry of Information in a failed attempt to be appointed as a World War One official artist (Collins 293).

Woolf's dislike of the Royal Academy precedes the 1919 exhibition. In 1903, Woolf attacked the Academy's Annual Soiree, by associating its art with those of the rich attendees, men with "a surprising number of decorations" (*PA* 176). Importantly for my argument, she associates the Academy with death and mausoleums. The building is "a kind of catacomb, damp" (*PA* 177). In Woolf's later short story "A Society," Helen is deputed, by the other women of the society, to assess men's achievements at the Royal Academy. On her return, Helen's account engenders hostile taunts of "sentimental" and "gibberish" (*CSF* 127). In "Genius: R. B. Haydon," her affectionate tribute to the painter, Woolf suggests that Haydon's attempt to meet the Academy's commercial priorities by learning "to toss off pictures of Napoleon musing, at the rate of one in two hours and a half" directly led to his decline (*M* 192). In "The Private View of the Royal Academy," she similarly deplores historical and mimetic paintings (*E3* 405). Woolf's satirical subversion of establishment values is a consistent theme throughout her life, from the Dreadnought Hoax of 1910, to refusing the award of a Companion of Honour in 1935.

However, in 1924, she happily made commercial use of the Royal Academy's mailing lists to publicize a Hogarth Press book *Living Painters - Duncan Grant*. By 1930 Woolf was delighted to be asked "to lecture on Art at the Royal Academy" on Zoffany's paintings (*L4* 142). Although there was no exhibition of Zoffany by the Academy that year, Woolf may have admired Zoffany's famed conversational pieces, particularly *Sondes Children* with its depiction of children's cricket - the favourite game at Talland House, St. Ives[1]. And 'Walter Sickert', as Diane Gillespie acutely notes, is "a culminating piece of formal art criticism" (Gillespie 8). Yet the 1919 review betrays artistic uncertainty.

In her 1919 manuscript and letters to Vanessa, Woolf is less condemnatory. The manuscript[2] has full notes of the title, date and painter of *Landing of the 1ˢᵗ Canadian Division at St. Nazaire, February 1915* suggesting she may have wished to analyse the painting in more detail; and she wrote to Vanessa that the Academy "is a very amusing and spirited place. I get an immense deal of pleasure from working out the pictures" (*L2* 377). The disparity between the published attack and Woolf's private pleasure is instructive. Her refusal to publish anything other than a somewhat reductive construction of the Academy as an outmoded art institution, may stem from Woolf's need to commit to Bloomsbury's avant-gardism[3].

Again in the manuscript notes on *Cocaine* by Alfred Priest, Woolf describes the painting as "very good"[4] and wrote to Vanessa "I think Cocaine is one of the best" (*L2* 378). *Cocaine* was a "problem picture," always a very popular feature of the Royal Academy summer exhibition, and widely reproduced. Pamela Fletcher, in *Narrating Modernity*, presents a convincing case for revising art history's conventional dismissal of such works. Fletcher argues that, although "problem pictures" involved figurative narratives, they did focus questions of gender, sexuality and identity in modernity (Fletcher 7). Rather than characterizing the representational quality of "problem pictures" as "non modernist," instead pictures like *Cocaine* "initiated wide-ranging cultural conversations" about gender representation (Fletcher 7).

In the 'Private View of the Royal Academy," Woolf presents *Cocaine* as a moral story in which a woman gazes at two photographs, the first of a presumed baby and another of the man she "might have married...unless it is her father" (*E3* 91). Woolf matches her fictional character with risqué fictional spectators. "The little group of gazers begin to boast that they have known sadder cases themselves. Friends of theirs took cocaine. 'I myself as a boy for a joke'" (*ibid*). Woolf's use of dramatized quotation creates an air of reality, yet the narrator's alienation, from spectators and subject, is a constructed fiction. *Cocaine* does not depict photographs but two indecipherable wall paintings. What Woolf downplays is a more serious treatment of the exhibition's aims and historical moment, coming the year after the armistice, as well as the exhibition's inclusion of significant and well-known women artists.

Woolf does mention the war in conclusion, in her account of spectator reaction to John Singer Sargent's *Gassed*, a painting depicting soldiers blinded by mustard gas. Woolf describes spectators over-reacting to the painting "the great rooms rang like a parrot-house with the intolerable vociferations of gaudy and brainless birds" (*E* 3 93). Sargent *was* patriotic about his adopted home and returned his German honors. It was Lloyd George the Prime Minister who had invited Sargent to be a war artist, "if you will undertake this task you will be doing a work of great and lasting service to the nation" (Mount 291). Also in 1925, in a letter to *The Nation*, Sargent publicly disassociated himself from Fry's 1910 Post-Impressionist Exhibition (Mount 258).

Yet Woolf's exaggerated satire is misplaced and inaccurate. Sargent's desire to focus on the suffering of soldiers, not on their heroism, rather than deterring spectators, earned Sargent public respect and *Gassed* was praised as "Picture of the Year." To seek experimental and avant-garde painting scarcely a year after the war is disingenuous. Richard Cork points out that "advanced modernist abstraction soon proved an inadequate starting-point for developing a viable approach to the conflict" (Cork 8). While the hanging of *Gassed* was certainly inappropriate, placed, according to the archive catalogue, between No. 118 *Chrysanthemums* and No. 121 *The Smithy*, nevertheless *Gassed* was not painted for the summer exhibition but rather requested by the Academy, from the Imperial War Museum, in order to display war horrors.

Sargent painted *Gassed* from his first-hand experiences and sketches made while travelling in France with fellow artist Henry Tonks in July 1918, and witnessing gassed soldiers on the Arras-Doullens Road when "wheeling his barrow of canvases and sketches about behind the lines" (Mount 293). Sargent, a close friend of Woolf's friend Ethel Smyth, chose his title *Gassed* precisely because it was un-heroic, "very prosaic and matter of fact" (Mount 299). The canvas emphasizes the loss and suffering of soldiers contrasted with a background football match depicting physically well-bodied young men. By creating a spatial relation between gassed and active men, Sargent recuperates the abject. The entire foreground is filled with severely wounded men forcing spectator engagement with the horrors of war. The liminal space between the active and inactive men problematizes the self/other relation. It is also a very legible painting drawing on traditional painting codes from classical friezes. But the overwhelming physicality of the painting (Sargent was the only World War One painter to paint a twenty-foot canvas) reclaims the un-representability of the abject and posits mourning in a public space as an alternative to war's aggression.

Although the Royal Academy displayed Edward Burne-Jones's massive 24 foot *Arthur in Avalon* in 1916 to glorify the war dead, it also welcomed anti-heroic works depicting the horrors of war. For example, also in 1916, the Academy accepted Charles Sims's *Clio and the Children* although the painting portrayed a blood-stained parchment representing the death of Sims's eldest son at the Front. And, in 1923, the Academy's display of William Orpen's disturbing picture *To the Unknown British Soldier in France*, depicting the futility of war, was voted "Picture of the Year." The summer exhibition was a "war" exhibition in other ways. Woolf omits to mention the customary display, in each summer exhibition, of architectural drawings. In 1919, many drawings were of reconstructions planned for a more optimistic Britain. To obscure, as Woolf does, this post-war witnessing of traumatic events, and attempted reconstruction, devalues the exhibition in favor of an inappropriate elitist response.

A more unexpected lacuna is Woolf's lack of attention to women artists, who were major contributors to the 1919 summer exhibition, including the vivid painting No. 157 *Women's Canteen at a Munitions Factory* by Flora Lion. In 1914 Lion turned from the society portraiture for which she was renowned, to paint a war-time scene with details of worker's tools, akin to Woolf's use of objects in her fiction. Lion creates a mediated image, not a romanticization of war, a large oil painting dramatically portraying war work, accurate technology and women's very active roles. Lion's war paintings share that wide-ranging European artistic enthusiasm for technological endeavours. For example, the Vorticists entitled *Blast* in 1914 to celebrate blast furnaces in Britain's industrial north. Unlike the Vorticists, Lion never breaks the art frame, but nor does she over-idealize industrial products to erase the human figure and therefore gender. To me, Lion makes a critical representation of women's new, major, modern experience that is, the factory. By 1918 there were over one million women working in munitions factories. The painting also draws in the viewer into modernity by refusing spectator distance.

Lion painted this particular factory, the Phoenix Works, Leeds, because she already knew its Head and, in her commitment to depicting women workers, travelled north in advance of the necessary permits. The Imperial War Museum Archive contains many moving letters revealing her battles with bureaucracy, particularly with the Ministry of Munitions, housed at one time, rather splendidly, in the Grand Hotel, Northumberland Avenue, London. Although by this date a noted portrait painter, and 37 when war broke out, Lion was forced to state that she "considered herself very fortunate" in being permitted to paint the works and even offered her painting to the Ministry for "one hundred and fifty guineas," almost half the price of £300 routinely paid to male war artists.[5]

The Ministry refused to purchase her paintings and, by 1927, Flora had to donate *Women's Canteen at a Munitions Factory* to the Imperial War Museum. Even then, the letters record, the Museum "could not promise to exhibit [the painting] at once and that in common with other paintings it would have to take its turn" and remain in Lion's frame "until we can afford to buy another one."[6] The Museum's final misogynist gesture, in response to Lion's husband's request for permission to send photographs of the painting to the press, was to request that Flora's copyright be transferred to the Crown. Sadly Flora agreed. What this protracted archival correspondence reveals is the Imperial War Museum's misogyny; how, in opposition, the Royal Academy welcomes both women artists and art critical of the war; and therefore how odd that Woolf overlooks this enthusiasm.

It is surprising hat Woolf ignores women artists and anti-war art, given her pacifism and support for women workers throughout her life. A year later, in "Pictures and Portraits," she was castigating the National Portrait Gallery for lacking a portrait of Harriet Taylor Mill, and in *Three Guineas* she describes women's war-time actions, praising the Mayoress of Woolwich for refusing "to darn a sock to help a war," a brave act given that Woolwich at that time contained over 12, 000 electors employed in armament factories (*E3* 163; *TG* 177). In World War One Woolf, of course, experienced personal trauma. In her diary she noted the alarming possibility of food riots and strikes at Woolwich, "& the guards have notice to march there at any moment, & fire on the people," and German air raids, "16 German aeroplanes have just passed over Richmond [...] we went and sat in the cellar" (*L2* 185).

Woolf was writing letters of exemption on behalf of Duncan Grant and suffered the anxiety of Leonard's two conscription call-ups. In addition, she experienced a nervous breakdown, the death of Cecil, and the injury and post-war trauma of Philip, Leonard's brothers; as well as the deaths of Rupert Brooke and other friends.

Karen Levenback, in *Virginia Woolf and the Great War*, argues convincingly that to assess Woolf's writings or her life without a sense of her experience of the Great War would be totally incomplete, and Mark Hussey points out that "*all* Woolf's work is deeply concerned with war" (Hussey 3). Woolf's careful mapping of the gendered dimensions of war in her non-fiction and fiction is powerful. So Woolf's inability, in her 1919 review, to acknowledge *artistic* representations of gender and politics is therefore all the more surprising. Lion's painting does detail, with sophisticated technical expertise, a new space of modernity and one consciously depicting gender and work that carries inevitable political import. Rather than promoting establishment values, it could be argued that the Royal Academy's Summer Exhibition of 1919 offered a therapeutic aesthetic, for an audience still traumatized by modernity's aggression, - a war which had killed 950,000 of the eight million mobilized (Levenback 67). Rather than glorifying war, the exhibition included memorable art, contributing to a general feeling that there might be a national artistic renaissance, stimulated by the Academy itself with another exhibition in 1919 *The Nation's War Paintings*, of younger, radical artists which received much critical praise.

Woolf's unconscious prohibition against celebrating the 1919 exhibition suggests un-integrated experience in a deeper sense. War deaths, including World War One deaths, are often narrated indirectly in her fiction, for example, in *To the Lighthouse*. Nigel Nicolson notes that World War One rarely registers in her letters because "she thought the war an inevitable outcome of male chauvinism" (*L2* xvii), And Woolf wondered "how this preposterous masculine fiction [the war] keeps going a day longer" (*L2* 76). In "The War From the Street," she argued that historians' versions of war "never will be written from our point of view," and felt disconnected, in a more psychic sense, having a "profound" conviction "that nothing is ever to touch you" (*E3* 4). I have no space here to examine what I see as Woolf's sense of the abject. But it is important to note that other writers, for example, Vera Brittain, unlike Woolf, *celebrated* 1919: "1919...it appeared to an exhausted world as divine mortality, the spring of life after the winter of death" (Brittain 46). Brittain experienced the death of her lover, her brother and the horrors of nursing but resolved, very positively, "to read History at Oxford instead of English…in a desire to understand how the whole calamity had happened," although, post-war, she "could not even recollect the trivial procedure for getting books out of the library" (Brittain 471 and 477).

Conclusion

Rather than devaluing the Academy, as Woolf does, we need to acknowledge a wider aesthetic continuum, coming at that historic moment. Flora Lion's *Women's Canteen at a Munitions Works* has disappeared from art history (although I intend to recuperate Flora). But Lion's work, and, indeed, the Royal Academy, should not be dismissed solely as establishment. Perhaps as Sir Kenneth Clarke, Bloomsbury patron, said about Tolstoy's *What is Art?* a book in the Woolfs' library, the counter question should be what isn't?

Notes

1. See *The Changing Face of Childhood: British Children's Portraits and Their Influence in Europe*. London: Dulwich Picture Gallery. 2007, 105; and Humm 2006.
2. Monk's House Papers B2. University of Sussex.
3. In addition, of course, as Diane Gillespie suggests, from Virginia's attachment to Vanessa (personal email).
4. Monk's House Papers B2.
5. Flora Lion File 255/6, Imperial War Museum Archive, London.
6. Flora Lion File 255/6, Imperial War Museum Archive, London.

Works Cited

Brittain, Vera. *Testament of Youth*. London: Virago, 1978.
Collins, Judith. *The Omega Workshops*. London: Secker & Warburg, 1984.
Cork, Richard. *A Bitter Truth: Avant-garde Art and the Great War*. New Haven: Yale UP, 1994.
Fletcher, Pamela. M. *Narrating Modernity: the British Problem Picture, 1895-1914*. Aldershot: Ashgate, 2003.
Fry, Roger. "Art and Science." *Vision and Design* (1920). Harmondsworth: Penguin, 1961.
Gillespie, Diane F. *The Sisters' Arts: the Writings and Painting of Virginia Woolf and Vanessa Bell*. Syracuse, NY: Syracuse UP, 1988.
Humm, Maggie. *Snapshots of Bloomsbury*. New Brunswick, NJ: Rutgers UP, 2006.
Hussey, Mark. "Living in a War Zone: an Introduction to VirginiaWoolf as a War Novelist." *Virginia Woolf and War: Fiction, Reality, and Myth*. Ed.Mark Hussey. Syracuse, NY: Syracuse UP, 1991.
Levenback, Karen. *Virginia Woolf and the Great War*. Syracuse, NY: Syracuse UP, 1991.
Mount, Charles Merrill. *John Singer Sargent*. London: Cresset Press, 1957.
Woolf, Virginia. "Genius: R. B. Haydon." *The Moment and Other Essays*. Orlando: Harcourt Brace Jovanovich, 1947. 186-192.
—. *The Letters of Virginia Woolf*. 6 vols. Eds. Nigel Nicolson and Joanne Trautmann. London: Hogarth Press, 1976-1980.
—. *A Passionate Apprentice*. Ed. Mitchell A. Leaska. London: Hogarth Press, 1990.
—. "The Private View of the Royal Academy." *The Essays of Virginia Woolf*. Vol. 3. Ed. Andrew McNeillie. London: Hogarth Press, 1988. 405-406.
—. "The Royal Academy." *The Essays of Virginia Woolf*. Vol. 3. 89-95.
—. "A Society." *The Complete Shorter Fiction of Virginia Woolf 2/E*. Ed. Susan Dick. Orlando: Harcourt, Brace Jovanovich, 1989. 124-136.
—. *Three Guineas*. London: Hogarth Press, 1991.
—. "The War from the Streets." *The Essays of Virginia Woolf*. Vol. 3. 3-4.

BLOOMSBURY WEST: LONDON BOHEMIANS FIND A NEW WORLD IN THE AMERICAN SOUTHWEST

by Elisa Kay Sparks

Perhaps I should have titled this talk, Garsington West, because it is about the connections among a group of writers and painters, most of whom had been guests of the society doyen, Ottoline Morrell, at her country estate, Garsington, outside of Oxford, who found a new patroness on the other side of the Atlantic Ocean and the American continent in the personage of Mable Dodge Luhan. Luhan was an American counterpart to Ottoline who was less aristocratic, wealthier, married many more times, and more entrepreneurial in her cultural mission. The impact of this Bloomsbury migration on the cultural life of the New Mexican art community is of course far too vast a topic to explore in a single paper. However, a review of the contents of Georgia O'Keeffe's library (a complete data base of which is housed at the Georgia O'Keeffe Research Center in Santa Fe) provides a significant sampling. By looking at the books in O'Keeffe's library we can get something of a core sample of the impact of British Modernism upon American Modernism, a kind of test case in defining the trans-Atlantic currents of Modernism, and the next step in my continuing exploration of the relationship and parallels between the two women artists, Virginia Woolf and Georgia O'Keeffe.

There are a surprising number of connections between the apparently disparate worlds of Modernist London and the burgeoning art community of the American West, especially the colonies centered around Santa Fe and Taos, New Mexico. The way west was first forged by that unusual pair of pied pipers D.H. and Frieda Lawrence, who were invited by Mable Dodge Luhan to visit her ranch in Taos, New Mexico in the autumn of 1922. Although put off by the gossip-driven chaos of life with the Luhan set, Lawrence fell deeply in love with the landscape, and he and Frieda stayed on through the winter and spring. Back in London, he tried to enlist John Middleton Murray and friends in a scheme to return to New Mexico and found a utopian community, but only one person joined up, the Honorable Dorothy Brett. One of the "cropheads," a painter trained at the Slade with Dora Carrington, Brett had met Lawrence at Garsington. In March of 1924 she set sail with Lorenzo and Frieda. The Lawrences returned to Europe in September of 1925; Brett followed them briefly, but returned to Taos, where she remained for 53 years, until her death in 1977. A few years after Lawrence's death in 1930, Frieda also returned to New Mexico where she lived until her death in 1962. Another, later, recruit was Aldous Huxley, who had learned about Lawrence's love of the high desert Southwest during his stay with Lawrence in Italy in 1926, incorporating a mythologized version of the landscape and the native people into his 1932 dystopian classic, *Brave New World*. Huxley came out to visit "Mableland" in 1937, staying with his wife at the Lawrence ranch from June to September and eventually settling permanently in Los Angeles (Rudnick, *Utopian Vistas* 151). All these émigrés from Bloomsbury and Garsington are represented in O'Keeffe's library, as well as many central figures of expatriate and European Modernism such as Joseph Conrad, Sigmund Freud, Henrik Ibsen, James, Joyce, Ezra Pound, Marcel

Proust, Gertrude and Leo Stein, as well as notable British Modernists such as Wyndham Lewis, John Middleton Murray, Bertrand Russell, Bernard Shaw, the Sitwells, Lytton Strachey, and . . . Virginia Woolf.

O'KEEFFE AND WOOLF

At the time of her death, Georgia O'Keeffe owned five books by Virginia Woolf (we don't know for sure if she ever owned any others; she gave away quantities of books to a Methodist school in Espanola, for example, and no one apparently kept any kind of record [Fine 11]). The first three of these volumes have her property stamp, but are not listed in the personal catalogue of books she kept in the Book Room at her home in Abiquiu. She had a 1931 hardbound, American edition of *The Waves*, a 1940 Hogarth Press edition of *Roger Fry*, and a 1946 paperback Penguin edition of *Orlando*. A paperback, 1976 edition of volume II of the *Letters*, the selection dealing with the years 1912-22, was also found; it is neither property-stamped nor catalogued.

While we might quite fertilely and enjoyably speculate on what this choice of titles suggests about O'Keffee's knowledge of and interest in Virginia Woolf, there is some concrete evidence offered by the circumstances surrounding her reception of the fifth Woolf book in her library, *To the Lighthouse,* that can help focus and contain our speculations. This Hogarth Press reprint, a 1977 hardbound edition, was sent to O'Keeffe by Angelica Garnett on February 27, 1981 as a thank you for O'Keeffe's (rather uncharacteristic) hospitality in receiving an unannounced visit from Angelica. The enclosed note reads:

> This is simply to say thankyou [*sic*] for a lovely afternoon, and to apologize for the intrusion on your privacywhich [*sic*], though it may have surprised you, you were kind enough to overlook.
>
> I am sending you the novel of my aunt's which I thought you might enjoy, and hope that you have someone to read it to you. It is to a large degree autobiographical as well as being one of her best books, and one of the most accessible. I sincerely hope it will please you;
> Yours sincerely and with best wishes,
> Angelica Garnett. (GOKRC, Bookroom Date Base, item#5431)

In 1981, O'Keeffe would have been 94 years old. (She died five years later at the age of 99.) She had lost her central vision to macular degeneration at least ten years earlier. Angelica's note suggests that O'Keeffe certainly knew of Virginia Woolf, that perhaps part of the reason why she welcomed Angelica in and spent time talking to her was her interest in her famous aunt. Angelica's comments about *To the Lighthouse* further suggest that what interested O'Keeffe the most was Woolf's life (hence the purchase of the *Letters*?), and that she had tried reading some other Woolf books and found them rather inaccessible (I am not sure any of us would recommend starting out with *The Waves* and *Orlando*).

So where and how would O'Keeffe have learned of Virginia Woolf? The two women, of course, never met as Woolf never travelled to America and O'Keeffe, being rather determined not to admit any influence from or interest in European culture, didn't travel to Europe until 1953, when she visited France, Spain, and Tangiers (Robinson 490). In

May 1925, Woolf and O'Keeffe's ***works***, at least, met in the transatlantic magazine of the modern arts, *The Dial*, where two of O'Keeffe's paintings of a small house with a flagpole were placed immediately before Woolf's "Lives of the Obscure." But as I explained in my article about O'Keeffe and Woolf's appearances in *The Dial*,

> It is a sad probability that these two women modernists, with so much in common in their vision and method, would have been led by the culturally gendered presentations in *The Dial* to discount each other as stereotypes of the kind of femininity they most feared or despised: Woolf the fussy, repressed aristocrat; O'Keeffe the brazen, oversexed American. (Sparks 257)

So why would O'Keeffe wind up with five of Woolf's books in her library? Where would she have heard enough about Woolf to counter the portrayal of her as a charming, tea-drinking, British lady? The answer is to be found in the intricate tangle of cultural, political, and social relationships fostered by the hospitality available at Mable Dodge Luhan's ranch in Taos, New Mexico.

Mable

Mable Ganson Evans Dodge Sterne Luhan, like her British counterpart Ottoline Morrell, grew gradually into her career as a social lionizer. Born in 1879 (six years after Ottoline, three years before Virginia Woolf and eight years before Georgia O'Keeffe) into a wealthy Buffalo family, she made a quick escape from her repressive childhood into an unhappy early marriage which produced her only child and ended after only two years with the tragic death of her husband in a hunting accident. Determined to break loose from the expectations of a staid widowhood, she sailed for France, met and married an American architect, Edwin Dodge, and settled into the Villa Curonia in Florence, at about the same time that Ottoline was beginning to hold her salons in Bedford Sq. For the next seven years Mable collected not only Florentine art but also a growing circle of cosmopolitan artists, appreciators, and critics, including Leo and Gertrude Stein, who changed her life by introducing her to post-impressionist art.

Mable left Florence for Greenwich Village in 1912, and for the next five years, her apartment on Fifth Avenue was at the center of the American avant-garde, hosting political and social radicals such as Emma Goldman, Max Eastman, Margaret Sanger, and John Reed (with whom Mable had a protracted affair), and artistic innovators such as Carl Van-Vechten, Alfred Stieglitz, Marsden Hartley, Isadora Duncan, and the stage designer Robert Edmund Jones, and helping to put on the Armory Show—the American version of Roger Fry's Post-Impressionism Exhibition. In August 1917, Mable married again, this time to the painter Maurice Sterne, whom she promptly sent out West for a vacation. Responding enthusiastically to Santa Fe and its native American culture, in November he sent Mable the following challenge: "Dearest Girl—Do you want an object in life? Save the Indians, their art—culture—reveal it to the world" (qtd. in Rudnick, *Utopian Visions* 71). She arrived in December, tired of her political world in New York City, disillusioned by her country's entrance into WWI, and looking for change. Planning to stay a fortnight; after a few days, she and Maurice went north to Taos to get away from the crush of people (and tea parties!)

in Santa Fe, and, as she wrote in the last volume of her autobiography: "My life broke in two right then, and I entered into the second half, a new world . . . more strange and terrible and sweet than any I had been able to imagine" (Luhan, *Taos Desert* 6).

Within a few days of arriving in Taos, Mable began to go out to the pueblo to observe the native dances and ceremonies and absorb the lessons of their calm, nature-oriented, generous, non-materialistic life-style. Here she met Antonio Luhan, her fourth and final husband. Within a few months, he had found a property on the edge of the Tiwa reservation for her to buy, and for the next several years they cemented their relationship by renovating and expanding "Los Gallos" together.

Mable did indeed take on the challenge that Maurice Sterne had sent her and began an active campaign to preserve and publicize the purity of the Indian lifestyle and culture as a transformative return to long-forgotten American values, recruiting the finest modern artists in every field to photograph, paint, and write about the culture, climate, and geography of the American Southwest. When she read D.H. Lawrence's travelogue *Sea and Sardinia* excerpted in *The Dial* magazine in October and November 1921—she had already read *Sons and Lovers* and his mystical semi-Freudian treatise *Psychoanalysis and the Unconscious* (Rudnick, *Mable* 193)—she became convinced that he was the artist who was destined to discover the magical secrets of Pueblo life and transmit them to the world.

BRETT

Although she knew Lawrence's work and its author fairly intimately, there is no evidence that Mable Dodge Luhan knew the work of Virginia Woolf, who is not mentioned anywhere in her four-volume autobiography. But people around Mable and around O'Keeffe were reading Woolf, especially after Lawrence's death in Italy in March of 1930, and the spate of memoirs and reminiscences appearing about Lawrence brought news of Mable to Woolf. When Lawrence and Frieda arrived back in Taos in 1924, they were accompanied by the painter Dorothy Brett, an old acquaintance of Woolf's who is the most likely conduit through which information about Virginia Woolf might have reached Mable Dodge Luhan and Georgia O'Keeffe and *vice versa*. Woolf's reply to two letters from Dorothy Brett, on March 8, 1929 and May 10, 1930, acknowledge Brett's praise of *To the Lighthouse* and *A Room of One's Own* (*L4* 31-2; 166-7) and show that Brett was keeping up with Virginia's writing. These letters were written at the exact time when Brett was also getting to know Georgia O'Keeffe with whom she remained only friendly terms for the rest of her life. Brett had met Georgia in the winter of 1928 (just before Woolf's first reply) when she and Mable had visited New York City in an effort to get Stieglitz to mount a show of Brett's paintings of Indian ceremonies. Mable inevitably invited O'Keeffe to visit Taos, and O'Keeffe accepted, staying from April through August, 1929. Brett sent her letter praising *A Room of One's Own* to Woolf early in 1930. It is fascinating to note that in March 1930, in a public debate over art's political responsibilities, O'Keeffe stated: "I have had to go to men as sources in my painting, because the past has left us so small an inheritance of women's painting that has widened life" (qtd. in Peters, 317).

Am I the only one who hears an echo here of Woolf's claim that women novelists "when they came to set their thoughts on paper. . .had no tradition behind them, or one so short and partial it was of little help"? (*AROO* 75)

Vita & the Jefferses

An additional set of connections among Woolf and Mable Luhan and Dorothy Brett, if not between Woolf and O'Keeffe, was provided by Una and Robinson Jeffers by way of Vita Sackville-West. Robinson Jeffers was known to Leonard and Virginia. The Hogarth Press published three volumes of his poetry in 1928, 1929, and 1930, the years of his greatest popularity, and on October 4, 1929, Virginia complained of a social engagement to have tea with Jeffers: "Mr. Jeffers is a genius so one must see him" (*L4* 96). We also know that when Mable published her memoir of D.H. Lawrence, *Lorenzo in Taos*, in 1932, Una Jeffers sent a copy of the book to Woolf (Rudnick, *Mable* 292). When Vita Sackville-West traveled to America in 1933, she visited Robinson and Una in Carmel, California, where they were living next door to Mable and Brett. Mable had decided that Jeffers was the poet to replace Lawrence in singing the praises of the Pueblo and was courting him assiduously. On March 28, 1933, Vita wrote Virginia about her encounter:

> I met your friend Brett and gave her your love. She blushed all over. I met her in a crazy household at a place called Carmel where she is living with Mable Dodge Luhan. . . . the woman who gave the ranch in New Mexico to D.H. Lawrence. She wrote a book about it all. (Sackville-West, *Letters* 390)

Vita's account of this visit in her travel journal reveals that Una Jeffers was a knowledgeable fan of Woolf's work, for when she was introduced to Vita, she exclaimed "Orlando!" (Sackville-West, *Selected Writings* 166).

Despite Una Jeffers and Dorothy Brett's knowledge of Virginia Woolf's work, and Vita's knowledge of Una, Brett, and Mable, it is not clear how much information Woolf actually processed about the Taos ménage. The copy of Luhan's book on Lawrence sent by Una remains in the collection at WSU, along with a second copy, not inscribed. Woolf's reaction to the plethora of books that came out following Lawrence's death was largely negative. A letter to Ethyl Smyth of April 15, 1931, speaks disparagingly of Murray's book on Lawrence (*L4* 312). Writing to Vita Sackville-West in America (in February of 1933) Woolf said "I don't think I can ever look at Lawrence again—they've cheapened him so" (*L5* 157). In a letter to Ottoline on the same day, she again referred to "Murray's last spurt of oil and venom and other filth" (*L5* 159). And a few months later in July, when she had received Brett's book on Lawrence, she wrote her old friend to confess "I looked into your book and shut it," claiming she could not read anything by or about Lawrence while there was "so much coloured dust about his horizon" (*L5* 202).

So, Virginia Woolf had several opportunities to learn about Brett and Mable, and perhaps even O'Keeffe, but was too put off by the sad politics of the growing Lawrence legend to bother. And Georgia O'Keeffe had five books in her library by Woolf, but we have no real evidence that she read any of them. So, the two women artists remain—ships passing closer and closer in the night—still obscured from each other by a literal ocean and a metaphorical continent of "coloured dust" that edits them out of each others' stories.

Works Cited

Fine, Ruth E., Elizabeth Glassman, and Juan Hamilton, curators. *The Book Room: Georgia O'Keeffes' Library in Abiquiu.* Catalogue entries by Sarah L. Burt. O'Keeffe Foundation/ Grolier Club. 1997.

Luhan, Mable Dodge. *Edge of Taos Desert: An Escape to Reality.* Vol. 4 of *Intimate Memories.* New York: Harcourt Brace, 1937.

Peters, Sarah W. *Becoming O'Keeffe: The Early Years.* New York: Abbeville, 1991.

Robinson, Roxana. *Georgia O'Keeffe: A Life.* New York: Harper Collins, 1989.

Rudnick, Lois Palken. *Mable Dodge Luhan: New Woman, New World.* Albuquerque: U of New Mexico P, 1984.

—. *Utopian Vistas: The Mable Dodge Luhan House and the American Counterculture.* Albuquerque: U of New Mexico P, 1996.

Sackville-West, Vita. *The Letters of Vita Sackville-West to Virginia Woolf.* Ed. Louise DeSalvo and Mitchell A. Leaska. 1984; rpt. London: Virago, 1992.

—. *Selected Writings.* Ed. Mary Ann Caws. New York: Palgrave, 2002.

Sparks, Elisa Kay. "*The Dial* as Matrix: Periodical Community between Virginia Woolf and Georgia O'Keeffe." *Virginia Woolf & Communities: Selected Papers from the Eighth Annual Conference on Virginia Woolf,* ed. Jeanette McVicker and Laura Davis. New York: Pace UP, 2000, pp. 251-8.

Woolf, Virginia. *A Room of One's Own.* 1929; rpt. Mark Hussey, ed. Intro and Annotations by Susan Gubar. New York: Harcourt, 2005.

—. *The Letters of Virginia Woolf.* Ed. Nigel Nicholson and Joanne Trautmann. Vols. 4 and 5. New York: Harcourt, 1975-80.

BIOGRAPHY, PORTRAITS AND THE FINE SPIRIT: DOROTHY BRETT, ARTIST

by *Pamela Hall Evans*

Every biographer is a portraitist, and to a large degree, every portraitist is a biographer. Each researches the subject: the writer uses tangible documents, interviews and personal impressions relating to the subject; the painter studies every curve, wrinkle, and shadow, every expression and glance, every observed action. For a painter this probing may even extend to inanimate objects, both natural and man-made, but the questions asked by both writer and painter are the same: how do I reveal the subject's essence? What point of view will bring me closest to the truth of the subject? How can I know whether I am correct in my understanding and conclusions? The goal of each is to reveal, to the greatest depth possible, the true character, or spirit, of the subject. It took me several years to realize that I, as an historian, am becoming a portraitist of the painter/portraitist, Dorothy Eugenie Brett.

The question may be asked why she would be a topic of discussion at a Virginia Woolf conference, but in the context of editing as biography, Brett's life, connected only tangentially to Woolf and Bloomsbury, is a model of how a person creates his or her own story and thus becomes the subject of a portrait in words. One of my primary jobs as Brett's biographer is to sort information about her and do my best to arrive at some compilation of ordinary facts, colorful stories, her own memories of her life, as well as her friends' and family's recollections—to try to come to some semblance of truth about who she was and what her life was about. Complicating matters, Brett firmly believed that we each make the stories of our own lives through how we choose to live, to work and to love, as well as how we interpret and communicate our memories. She was aware that she was creating her life as an artist, almost as willfully as she created her art, so the larger puzzle, the one with the elusive title, "The Truth," on it, will probably always have unexplainable holes in it. This paper will provide an edited biographical portrait of Brett, constrained by conference requirements and my desire to show you what she believed best expressed her own essence, her life as an artist.

Some conference attendees will make a trip to Taos and Santa Fe after the conference closes. It's likely they will hear about Brett, the English painter who came to the U.S. in 1924 with D.H. and Frieda Lawrence when they made their second trip to New Mexico. Brett's intention was to spend six months in a kind of self-imposed exile from her unconventional but painfully-muddled London life which Lawrence assured her could be simplified with a break, an absence from all things English and familiar.

Taos abounds with stories about her, Lawrence, Frieda and Mabel Dodge Luhan, the woman who inveigled the Lawrences into coming to New Mexico in 1923. Brett, who had resolved to be a painter when she was just a teenager, was often more fascinating to Taos for what she had shed, her Englishness. For instance, she was the daughter of a viscount who had vast influence with both Crown and Parliament; while she is often referred to as "Lady Brett," she was actually an Honorable, the only title allowed to children of a viscount, and a title she preferred not to use; as a small child she took dance lessons with Queen Victoria's grandchildren; she came from well-off aristocracy, though she had only a small inheritance which, at its highest value, was worth only $200 per month.

While Brett knew members of Bloomsbury, she was in no way a Bloomsberrie herself. However, at Garsington, the country home-cum-salon of Ottoline and Philip Morrell, she painted Ottoline's larger-than-life-sized portrait and met her friends, many of whom were at home in the realms of politics, philosophy, government, and the arts. But she never could have been part of Bloomsbury, that group of writers, thinkers and painters whose connections rested squarely in the one art denied to Brett: conversation. Brett was deaf by the time she came to Garsington, the result of an acute infection at age seventeen. Even with the help of a hearing device, comprehension was always two or three steps behind the flow of conversation. Thus the spontaneous rhythm and sparkle of talk among Garsington's Bloomsbury guests was impossible for her. Add to this her natural shyness and a lamentably late emotional maturity, and Bloomsbury's quick-witted, quick-silver intellectual company had no use for her. There was no patience in that milieu.

There were, however, others willing to be patient, to slow down in order to know Brett. During the ten years between her Slade School art studies and her departure for America, Brett and Ottoline were intimate friends, and Brett both lived and kept a studio at Garsington off and on for several years. She was also close friends with fellow painters, Dora Carrington and Mark Gertler. Katherine Mansfield, a woman of such intellectual and literary prowess that Virginia Woolf envied her, was her best friend until Mansfield's death in 1923. With Bertrand Russell, Britain's premier philosopher for many years, Brett maintained correspondence throughout his incarceration as a conscientious objector during WWI. She formed friendships with writers Aldous Huxley and J. Middleton Murry that lasted all their lives. D.H. Lawrence enjoyed her company, her quiet, intuitive way of interacting with the world around her, her sense of fun. But each of these was willing to exercise patience with her deafness.

Even so, by 1924, Brett's life had lurched into an uncomfortable state; she thought to change everything with a "Mexican" interlude. By 1926 New Mexico was Brett's permanent home, but much has been made of the prior year and a half that Brett, Lawrence and Frieda spent together in Taos in and out of company with Mabel Dodge Luhan, including tales of fights and jealousies. Less often referred to are the twenty-five years of friendship among the three women after Lawrence died. Mabel, for instance, was Brett's first patron, helping her to meet Alfred Stieglitz, Georgia O'Keeffe, and Leopold Stokowski. Frieda, who returned to New Mexico in 1931, gave her land for a house. These women talked, fought, shared gossip and family troubles, engaged in passionate crusades on behalf of New Mexico's Indians, and reaffirmed their long connections in letters, some sent across town, some across the world. Writing allowed Brett to display her vibrancy, sense of humor, interest in all things artistic, and delight in Taos gossip in ways that she could not through conventional conversation.

With the support of these friendships, Brett's fascination with the Pueblo Indians became the impetus for change in her life as a painter. Her English work had been generally uneven. Most of the work was academic, tight—in a word, self-conscious. Early still life studies, such as *Yellow Calla Lilies, (1915)*, and portraits like *Maurice's Children*, painted in

Fig. 1. Sun Dance Song (Kiowa), by Dorothy Brett, 1926. Oil on board. Private collection. Photograph. Dorothy Brett Pictorial Collection (PICT 000-494), Center for Southwest Research, University Libraries, University of New Mexico. Courtesy, Dorothy Brett Estate.

Scotland in 1921, are examples of this lack of confidence. Occasionally there were gems; for instance: *War Widows*, painted in 1916, at a time when all bravado about a rapid end to the war was gone, and *Umbrellas*, an idyllic, garden party group portrait which included Ottoline Morrell, Katherine Mansfield, Middleton Murry, Aldous Huxley and Lytton Strachey, completed in 1917 in the security of Garsington. But Brett's painting life was reinvented with her arrival in Taos. From 1926 to 1930, she enthusiastically represented on canvas what she believed portrayed the dynamic strength and liveliness of the Indians as she observed, then grew to know and become friends with them. *Sun Dance Song* is an early example of her efforts to paint them from what she believed was their own point of view (see fig. 1). During these years Brett's goal was to attain some semblance of skill and vision that could be compared with that of her friend, Georgia O'Keeffe, to whom she always referred as a "pure painter."

With the deaths in 1930 of the two men she counted most influential in her life, her father, Reginald, Viscount Esher and D.H. Lawrence, her focus shifted more fully towards the challenges and satisfactions of the dedicated artist. Freedom from these two larger-than-life personalities brought bitter grief, but also the realization that she was finally free to do exactly as she pleased, and at age 47 was perfectly capable of thinking for herself, an acknowledgment that allowed her and her painting to mature.

In the 1930s and 1940s Brett set out to "try things," not to, as she said, "be stuck," and to become a painter with something to say. While continuing to paint Pueblo Indian life, she also experimented with other subject matter and media. In search of her own voice, three forms of expression preoccupied her: writing, painting portraits, and painting Indian ceremonials. The first of these, the book *Lawrence and Brett: A Friendship*, which she published in 1932, was a memoir, poignantly written through the eyes of a friend, as well as an artist, about Lawrence, Frieda and Brett together in New Mexico. Using language rather than paint, Brett drew images with the same care and attention to meaning, atmosphere and unspoken feeling that she gave to her Indian paintings. She described it to her friend, Alfred Stieglitz, as a "series of pictures" (November 5, 1932). Though often disregarded by Lawrence scholars, the book's portrayal of Lawrence was felt by many in New Mexico who knew him intimately to be the most accurate portrait of him.

Fig. 2. Leopold Stokowski Portrait: Hands, by Dorothy Brett, 1934. Oil on canvas. Private collection. Photograph. Dorothy Brett Pictorial Collection (PICT 000-494), Center for Southwest Research, University Libraries, University of New Mexico. Courtesy, Dorothy Brett Estate.

While Brett had long found inspiration for life and work in literature, one influence was Virginia Woolf's work. In the autumn of 1931 while planning her memoir of Lawrence, she was also reading *The Waves*. Writing to Stieglitz, she asked whether he had read it, commenting that it "fascinated her," but more, that she longed to write like Woolf, to make of her memoir what Woolf had accomplished in her book (November 16, 1931). Its stream-of-consciousness writing style could well have been a model for the "series of pictures" Brett envisioned for her memoir of Lawrence. The success of Woolf's book rested on that method of thinking and working Woolf knew so well: the blending of intuitive understanding of character and narrative within a carefully planned and executed framework. Brett applied this to both writing and painting: logical and intuitive thinking had to be joined so that her imaginings could be brought to the page or canvas with focused, willful effort, thus making her pictures, whether written or painted, products of the whole mind.

During this same period, through Mabel Dodge Luhan, Brett met Leopold Stokowski, at that time principal conductor of the Philadelphia Symphony Orchestra. Completely charmed by his personality, looks, manners and intelligence, she convinced him to allow her to paint his portrait, despite his refusal to sit for her. Watching him from house

Fig. 3. Indian Spring, by Dorothy Brett, 1935. Oil on Canvas. Panhandle-Plains Historical Museum, Canyon, Texas, James D. Hamlin Collection. Courtesy, Dorothy Brett Estate.

seats or through the slit of a door opened only a crack at the back of the stage, she was determined to part from tradition, to depict "the life behind the life" of Stokowski (see fig. 2). The result was a series of portraits which proved to be a turning point in her career. Over three winter symphony seasons, she sketched, absorbed the music and decided that she had seen Stokowski's true self. In all she produced sixteen pieces which evolved from her first traditional sketches to the final two abstract pieces.

In the process, Brett began uncovering her own psychological, spiritual and artistic strengths. She wrote to Mabel Dodge Luhan that she felt her paintings had something "Blake-like" about them, but she feared Stokowski would be "tearing mad" when he saw them because they were so unconventional (January 4, 1934). Further, she said they "must have a certain amount of likeness....not merely...a man waving his arms about.... [They've] got to have all the subtle feeling and emotion of MUSIC" (Luhan June 16, 1934). To Alfred Stieglitz she explained: "[My goal] is to become more abstract, to have the essentials of form and then the rest a poem of color and line...," something she felt she had achieved with the *Parsifal* portrait, which she based on Stokowski's orchestrations and performance of *Parsifal* from Wagner's *Die Walkurie* (March 20, 1933). She believed for the rest of her life that these paintings, which had come "from a different stream, from the Inner Core of Myself" marked a maturation in herself and her art, while serving as the launching pad for the distinctive work that marked her later years (Stieglitz September 20, 1934).

It's possible to believe that during this period Brett had time for nothing else, but the reverse is true. Her creative juices were running like a river and would continue to do so for another nearly forty years. She continued to depict the Indians and their lives in such paintings as *Indian Boy on a Horse* (1930), *Summer in the Pueblo* (1931), *Spring* (1932), *Robed Indians Ahorse* (1934), *Boy on the Buckskin Horse* (1935), and *Indian Spring* (1935) (see fig. 3). These years also embraced experimentation with "moving paintings," prompted by her fascination with full-length animated films, forays into stage design for several operas, and work in completely abstract forms, such as *Golden Images and the Moons of Troy* (1939), painted while she was studying Dynamic Symmetry.

Brett also returned to portraiture. Whether working on self-portraits or portraits of others she was further convinced of "the importance of the impersonal in art, the supreme beauty drawn out of the object itself, the emotion rarefied until the impersonal slips into the universal..." (Stieglitz March 20, 1933). Her desire was "to paint the spirit of a man or woman [as]...more than merely making a portrait....I try and draw through the fine spirit....Ye gods HOW DIFFICULT but HOW FASCINATING" (Stieglitz June 28, 1936). She had done several portraits of Lawrence over the years, but when she painted him in 1937 she felt newly justified in her belief that "without the heart the object....neither stirs the pulse nor moves the soul" (Stieglitz February 1, 1937) (see fig. 4). This portrait was done from the memory of him, fifteen years earlier, "a moment when he stood outside the barn on the Ranch and watched me ride away; I have never forgotten the look in his eyes, the blueness of them, or the power radiating from him" (*Journey* N. pag*).*

Fig. 4. Self-Portrait with Toby, by Dorothy Brett, c. 1933? Graphite on paper. Private collection photograph. Dorothy Brett Pictorial Collection (PICT 000-494), Center for Southwest Research, University Libraries, University of New Mexico. Courtesy, Dorothy Brett Estate.

By the 1940s, Brett was dedicating her efforts to work that would be her crowning achievement: understanding and painting the spirit of a people. During the war years she worried about a local problem: New Mexico saw many young Indian men "torn out of their blankets, their pigtails cut off, and in the army....they come back in khaki unrecognizable" (Stieglitz December 12, 1942). She feared the effects of war on Indian communities and communal life, that "the young American...Indian will give up his tribal dances and ways...[and] they will die out" (Stieglitz December 12, 1942). So, relying on skills of observation learned from the Stokowski paintings, and using a meditative method learned for portrait painting, she began to memorize and paint these sacred tribal dances. Because certain aspects of the dances were forbidden from being portrayed through photography, paint, or written word, she painted ceremonial dances such as *The Antelope Dance* with the advice and "help of Indian friends who understand what I am doing and are not shocked" (Stieglitz July 23, 1947).

Summoning up her own life experience, a strengthening personal philosophy, a sharply-honed intuition, polished painting skills, a carefully refined style designed for her purpose, and a firm belief in the spirit or essential self of both individuals and a people, she painted the religious, ceremonial dances of the Indians of New Mexico.

As she rendered what she was convinced was a vanishing world with ever-increasing passion, she wrote to her friend, Dorothy Norman that she believed she had become "an Evangelist...in paint..." (March 24, 1956). "The world around us is a peg on which to hang...WHAT? I have hung on the peg...the Indian, [his] WAY OF LIFE, [his] pattern of living, the Indian as he sees himself, feels himself, thinks of himself and [the] UNIVERSE around him. That may not be art. I have only limited talent....but I have a vision..." (Norman March 2, 1958). It was a vision that led her, from her early days of painting young Indian mothers with their babies, through the experimentation and stretching of her talent that produced the Stokowski series, to the recording of the ceremonial dances, to develop a vision based on the search for the finest attributes of life in general, but finally concentrated in the search for the essence of the life of the Indians among whom she lived for over fifty years. Among her most vivid and remarkable works are: *The Turtle Dance* (1947), *Walpi Snake Dance* (1965), *San Geronimo Foot Races* (1965), *Blessing of the Mares* (1965), *The Women's Dance* (1967), and *Jemez Corn Dance* (1967) (see fig. 5). Through this vision Brett spent the last thirty years of her life as the portraitist of Pueblo Indian culture in New Mexico, producing a body of work that became the hallmark of her reputation, proving that even though deaf, she had a voice that allowed her to preserve on canvas the "life behind the life" of the Indians.

Fig. 5. Jemez Corn Dance, by Dorothy Brett, c. 1967. Oil on board. Courtesy, Eugene B. Adkins, 1997. Courtesy, Dorothy Brett Estate.

Works Cited

Brett, Dorothy. Letters to Mabel Dodge Luhan. MS. Yale Collection of American Literature, Beinecke Rare Book and Manuscript Library, New Haven, CT.
---. Letters to Dorothy Norman. MS. Yale Collection of American Literature, Beinecke Rare Book and Manuscript Library, New Haven, CT.
---. Letters to Alfred Stieglitz. MS. Yale Collection of American Literature, Beinecke Rare Book and Manuscript Library, New Haven, CT.
---. *My Long and Beautiful Journey.* Unpublished MS. Dorothy Brett Papers, Center for Southwest Research, General Library, University of New Mexico, Albuquerque, NM.

Images Cited

Fig. 1. *Sun Dance Song (Kiowa)*, by Dorothy Brett, 1926. Oil on board. Private collection. Photograph. Dorothy Brett Pictorial Collection (PICT 000-494), Center for Southwest Research, University Libraries, University of New Mexico, Albuquerque, NM. Courtesy, Dorothy Brett Estate.
Fig. 2. *Leopold Stokowski Portrait: Hands*, by Dorothy Brett, 1934. Oil on canvas. Private collection. Photograph. Dorothy Brett Pictorial Collection (PICT 000-494), Center for Southwest Research, University Libraries, University of New Mexico, Albuquerque, NM. Courtesy, Dorothy Brett Estate.
Fig. 3. *Indian Spring*, by Dorothy Brett, 1935. Oil on Canvas. Panhandle-Plains Historical Museum, Canyon, Texas, James D. Hamlin Collection, Albuquerque, NM. Courtesy, Dorothy Brett Estate.
Fig. 4. *Self-Portrait with Toby*, by Dorothy Brett, c. 1933? Graphite on paper. Private collection. Photograph. Dorothy Brett Pictorial Collection (PICT 000-494), Center for Southwest Research, University Libraries, University of New Mexico, Albuquerque, NM. Courtesy, Dorothy Brett Estate.
Fig. 5. *Jemez Corn Dance*, by Dorothy Brett, c. 1967. Oil on board. Courtesy, Eugene B. Adkins, 1997. Courtesy, Dorothy Brett Estate.

THE BOTANICAL WORKS OF MARIANNE NORTH (PAINTER, WRITER, AND TRAVELER) EDITED BY ABSORPTION INTO VIRGINIA WOOLF'S WRITING

by Evelyn Haller

Readers of Virginia Woolf ideally encounter "Kew Gardens," her botanically evocative short story, in its first edition with twenty-one Post-Impressionist frames of scrolloping, cross-hatched, and architecturally-inspired forms designed by her artist-sister Vanessa Bell. These do not, however, exhaust the elements of Kew as Woolf would have known it. Another Chinese box within "the vast nest" is the Marianne North Gallery. I propose that the paintings and writings of Marianne North, who was Madge Symonds Vaughan's aunt, influenced Woolf's writings by absorption. When Virginia was seven Madge spent the winter of 1889-90 with the Leslie Stephen family at 22 Hyde Park Gate, "so that she might meet more people and also have drawing lessons" (Symonds 3:403). Madge made her mark on the children of the Stephen family because she was thereafter known as "The Chief." She also became a probable model for Sally Seton in *Mrs. Dalloway*.[1] Madge's mother, Catherine North Symonds, was the sister of Marianne North and edited her sister's letters and diaries which were published in 1892 and 1893. Before Marianne North's death in 1890 her eponymous Gallery was opened at Kew Gardens in 1882, the year of Woolf's birth, with 627 botanical paintings. The following year an extension added to the Gallery brought the total to 848 paintings whose arrangement was determined by North herself. Marianne North was known to Woolf, for she quotes her description of posing for Julia Margaret Cameron in Ceylon (*JMC* 14, 18, 19). Evidence of the probable absorption of Marianne North's botanical art into Woolf's work occurs in passages of jungle description in *The Voyage Out* and the characterization of Mr. Cobbet of Cobbs Corner standing under the Monkey Puzzle Tree in *Between the Acts*. I also discuss a curious passage in Woolf's essay on Sickert in which she conjures insects "in whom the eye is so developed that they are all eye" (*CDB* 173), and I examine incidents that led to the composition of her essay particularly as they related to the work of Vanessa Bell.

Fifteen years before the publication of Woolf's essay on Sickert in 1934, she attended an exhibition of his work for which her brother-in-law, Clive Bell, had written the preface to the catalogue, and declared it "the pleasantest, solidest most painter-like show in England" (*D1* 240). Woolf had been acquainted with Sickert (1860-1942) for many years. At a Twelfth Night party in 1923 she enjoyed his acting Hamlet in a charade, sat by him, "liked him, talking in his very workmanlike . . . manner, of painting" (*D2* 223). Her admiration for his work was probably influenced by his insistence that he was "a literary painter" (*D4* 194) "Do you think one could treat his paintings like novels?" she asked her nephew, Quentin Bell (*L5* 253). As a novelist of independent means whom Sickert admired: "You are the only person who understands me—kissing my hand" (*D4* 194), Woolf was not dependent on the Sickert summed up by Germaine Greer as "The archetypal teacher-lover, who exploited his female students to the limit" (46-49).

Consider how Woolf's essay about Walter Sickert (originally titled "A Conversation about Art" and first published in the *Yale Review*, Sept. 1934) came to be written. Not only had Sickert asked Woolf to write about him aided by the good offices of both Vanessa and Clive Bell, but Vanessa also urged her to be kind to the impoverished old man. Vanessa's support of Sickert was indeed an act of kindness because he had shown impatience if not contempt for the serene art Woolf's sister practiced. As Christopher Reed delineates Sickert's focus on "the subject matter of the urban working class" and quotes from Sickert's *The Study of Drawing* wherein he "exhorted painters to explore modern life by following their models as they 'leave the studio and climb the first dirty little staircase in the first shabby little house . . . . Follow her into the kitchen, or better still . . . into her bedroom,'" the contrast is strong (Reed 28ff. and 281n54). Sickert invoked "the artist's right to 'treat pictorially the ways of men and women, and their resultant babies'; otherwise, he says, 'we must affect to be . . . seduced by oranges'" (Reed 28 and 281n55). Reed suggests that Bell's still life, *Apples: 46 Gordon Square*, 1908 is "a riposte" to Sickert. Moreover, Sickert excluded women from his Camden Town Group. As he wrote two women whose work he knew, Nan Hudson and Ethel Sands: "The Camden Town Group is a male club, and women are not eligible. There are lots of 2 sex clubs, and several one sex clubs, and this is one of them" (Reed 28 and 281n59). Reed comments: "Bell, therefore, found little in Sickert's example of the modern artist as *flâneur* to support her creation of domestic modernism" (Reed 28). The "institutionalized" masculine bias of Walter Sickert's practice in the formation of the Camden Town Group, especially in its *flânerie* can be contrasted with Vanessa Bell's domestic modernism as shown in her interior scenes often of women or of women with children. Still, Vanessa Bell delighted in the intense colors of seductive fruit and flowers such as *Red-Hot Pokers* (1921).

An earlier alternative to Sickert's bias toward urban sensationalism is Marianne North's botanical art encompassing ancillary specimens of fauna and insects enabled by her enterprise in taking the natural world as her theater of operations. Indeed Woolf's essay contains a hidden allusion to Marianne North's art with its genesis in travel not to "the boarding houses, brothels, and pubs of Camden town" (Reed 28 ff.) but to exotic places within the British Empire and beyond. How, then, did Woolf come to conjure insects "in whom the eye is so developed that they are all eye" in her essay on Walter Sickert?

I argue that the likely exposure Woolf had to the intensely concentrated paintings of Marianne North at Kew contributed to her perceptions of and associations with color. Thus, it was not only Walter Sickert's groundbreaking use of color through underpainting and attention to tonal color values that is sub-textually present in her essay about him, but also Woolf's own perhaps unconscious editing of the splendid colors and extraordinary shapes of plants and insects in North's botanical paintings that enliven the text. By casting the Sickert essay in the form of a conversation descended from the Greek symposium, Woolf could accommodate a range of ideas less available in a stricter form:

> In the course of time the talk turned . . .to color; how different people see color differently; how color blazes, unrelated to any object in the eyes of children; how politicians and business men are blind, days spent in an office leading to atrophy of the eye; and so, by contrast, to those insects, said to be still found in the primeval forests of South America, in whom the eye is so developed that they are all eye, the body a tuft of leather, serving merely to connect the two great chambers of vision. . . . these insects who are born with the flowers and die when

the flowers fade. . . . these little creatures drinking crimson until they became crimson . . . and becoming for the moment the thing they saw . . . . when the flowers died, the life went out of them, and you might mistake them as they lay on the grass for shriveled air-balls. Were we once insects like that, too . . . all eye? (*CDB* 173-74)

If Woolf's evolutionary flight is aesthetically true, all is not lost: "Do we still preserve the capacity for drinking, eating, indeed becoming color furled up on us, waiting proper conditions to develop?" (*CDB* 174) Might we recreate an Edenic phase of human existence through art? "On first entering a picture gallery, whose stillness, warmth and seclusion from the perils of the street reproduce the conditions of the primitive forest, it often seems as if we reverted to the insect stage of our long life" (*CDB* 188-89).

It was after North had amassed a sufficient number of paintings for an exhibition in Conduit Street in 1879 that she responded to the suggestion of a critic at the *Pall Mall Gazette* that her work have a more public and permanent display. Not only did she offer her paintings to the Royal Botanic Gardens at Kew, but she also offered to build a gallery to house them. As she had responded to the suggestion that her flower paintings be permanently available to the British public, North also responded to Charles Darwin's suggestion in 1882 that she "should not attempt any representation of the world's flora without seeing the peculiar vegetation of Australia" (Ponsonby 77).

After North painted in Australia, Tasmania, and New Zealand at Darwin's suggestion, one continent remained by her own reckoning: Africa. Still, that was not the end of her intensive 13 year pilgrimage. Despite failing health in the autumn of 1884, North's goal on her last trip, one to Chile (she spells the word "Chili") was to paint the Monkey Puzzle Tree. Indeed she painted and described the Chili Pines (*Araucaria araucana*) as if they were companionable people: "I saw none of the trees over one hundred feet in height or twenty feet in circumference, and, strange to say, they seemed all very old or very young. I saw none of those noble specimens of middle age we have in some English parks, with their lower branches resting on the ground" (*Eden* 228). She continues to describe their ecology: "The smaller cones of the male trees were shaking off clouds of golden pollen, and were full of small grubs; these attracted flights of bronzy green parakeets, which were very busy over them" (*Eden* 228-29). North follows with an explanation for the popular name of the tree: "The most remarkable thing is its bark, which is a perfect child's puzzle of slabs of different sizes, with five or six distinct sides to each, all fitted together with the neatness of a honeycomb. I tried in vain to find some system on which it was arranged" (*Eden* 229). North's painting demonstrates the great height of the Monkey Puzzle Tree by placing it in the middle distance with guanacos for scale of which she observes that they "looked strange enough to be in character with" the Monkey Puzzle Trees "having the body of a sheep and the head of a camel." By foregrounding a partial view of the trunk of the tree we see the puzzling pattern of its bark (*Eden* 229).

In *Between the Acts*, consider a local man's perplexity about Miss La Trobe's pageant: "Here Cobbet of Cobbs Corner, alone under the monkey puzzle tree, rose and muttered: 'What was in her mind, eh? What made her indue the antique with this glamour—this sham lure, and set 'em climbing, climbing, climbing up the monkey puzzle tree?'"(*BTA* 97) The triply repeated gerund suggests evolutionary movement through a hierarchy of species. Later "Cobbet of Cobbs Corner who had stooped—there was a flower—was pressed on by people pushing from behind" (*BTA* 120) His botanical impulse is an obstacle to progress. He returns "there, under the Monkey Puzzle Tree" and is dismissed as reclusive: "One don't see him often" (*BTA* 160). When he observes Mrs. Manresa following Giles, he takes the long view of creation and favors plants:

> Cobbet in his corner saw through her little game. He had known human nature in the East. It was the same in the East. It was the same in the West. Plants remained—the carnation, the zinnia, and the geranium. Automatically he consulted his watch; noted time to water at seven; and observed the little game of the woman following the man to the table in the West as in the East. (*BTA* 110)

A further shading of Darwinism occurs in the pageant at a Picnic Party set about 1860 with repeated references to a fossil held by the paterfamilias. Mr. Hardcastle "fumbles with his fossil" as he prays "for the understanding with which Thou hast enlightened us" (*BTA* 171).

Although Charles Darwin's lifespan (1809-1882) was longer than Marianne North's (1830-1890), they were essentially coevals. Darwin's voyage on *The Beagle* early in his life provided him with his epoch-making life's work. Although North's autobiography is significantly titled *Recollections of a happy life,* her comfortably upper class status in England placed her within limited and limiting expectations. Many women of her time learned to paint flowers–then considered a lady-like pastime–but few discovered within their developing talent the means to order and transfigure their lives. Although Vanessa Bell also painted flowers, unlike Marianne North her choice of subjects was not constrained, for she also photographed and painted nudes.

North's contribution to botanical cultural history was significant, for she provided images of plants in their environments–many of which were remote–when such information was not readily available. As Anthony Huxley explains, "[B]otanical explorers . . . had to set down their experiences in writing, with the help only of engravings made from sketches" (*Eden* 9). North's paintings, however, are not the only way her name has survived in natural history. As Leslie Stephen wrote in North's entry for the *Dictionary of National Biography*: "Five species, four of which she first made known in Europe, have been named after her." Although Leslie Stephen does not name them, the four species are as she painted them: "Foliage, flowers, and fruit, of the Capucin Tree of the Seychelles" (*Northea seychellana*); "A pitcher plant from the limestone mountains of Sarawak, Borneo" (*Nepenthes northiana*); "A giant Kniphofia (*Kniphofia northiae*) near Grahamstown, South Africa; *Crinum northianum* from Borneo (*Eden* 6). We find a disturbing contemporaneity in James Hooker's Preface to the First Edition of the *Catalogue of the North Gallery*: "very many of the views here brought together represent . . . objects that are amongst the wonders of the vegetable kingdom . . . these . . . are already disappearing or are doomed shortly to disappear before the axe and the forest fires, the plough and the flock, of the ever advancing settler or colonist. Such scenes can never be renewed by nature, nor when once effaced can they be pictures to the mind's eye, except by means of such records as this lady has presented to us" (Hooker iii-iv).

Needless to say, contemporary access to color images of encyclopedic variety from computers on desks and laps does not correspond to the experience of people living in Marianne North's time. Nonetheless, even today, an image-glutted public is rewarded by her paintings in the building that North provided the funds to have erected at Kew Gardens. Although the format of 832 closely packed pictures resembling a sheet of postage stamps requires an adjustment for the eyes of contemporary art museum-goers who expect placement governed by a "less is more" aesthetic, one can make the transition and be rewarded for the effort.

To design her gallery North chose her friend the architectural historian James Fergusson who designed few other buildings. Her choice was sound, for he was inspired by his conception of a Greek temple with light entering from windows set in the high gallery with Greek-derived ironwork railings. The visitor does indeed see North's monument by looking up and down as well as around. A downward glance takes in the dado made of various woods she collected on her global travels.

The January 2008 issue of the British shelter magazine *The World of Interiors* has an article by Frances Spaulding about the North Gallery at Kew Gardens entitled "Female of the Species." The photographs taken by Tobias Harvey benefit from a wide angle lens which brings in light from windows set in a high gallery. As a practical matter, Harvey's inclusion of benches in a photograph reassures the magazine reader that one can take in the profuse display at a meditative and easeful pace which is what Marianne North had in mind when she told the Director Sir Joseph Hooker that she wanted coffee, tea, and biscuits available to the public at a neighboring guest house. She did not get her wish, however, because of Hooker's policy of not allowing refreshments to be served in Kew Gardens. In a satirical reference to her thwarted desire she painted one of two internal doors with the white flowers of *Camellia sinensis*, the tea plant; the other with a coffee plant. By 1919 the matter had been resolved, for in "Kew Gardens" after Woolf describes "little white tables, and waitresses" the very young man says, "'Come along, Trissie; it's time we had our tea'" (*CSF* 94).

How, then, was Marianne North able to break with Victorian expectations for women by making art the controlling factor of a life she described as happy? Moreover, how was she able to serve her art through travel often undertaken by herself? And, finally, how was she able to arrange permanent housing for the preservation and maintenance of her gift to the nation?

Although North found emotional contentment in her family, her experience was not limited to a domestic setting; for she was introduced to travel at an early age and turned to it throughout her life until declining health dictated otherwise. Her father, when he was not sitting in Parliament for Hastings, took his family to the Continent and beyond. These were not the frenetic time-pressed trips of today; rather, the Norths would, for example, stay eight months in Heidelberg before two years of European travel in 1848 and 1849 despite the disturbances and dangers posed by revolutions.

Secondly, Marianne North had no inclination to marry. An observation she made on the married state encapsulates her view:

> It is a terrible experiment . . . for a man especially, as a woman is something like your cat and gets to love the person who feeds her and the house she lives in, but men, if they have brains, have a romantic idea of companionship in their wife

and then discover they have no two ideas in common I pity the poor wife too when she finds herself snubbed, and a sort of upper servant to be scolded if the pickles are not right and then she will have to amuse herself by flirting with the most brainless of the Croquet-Badmintons. (Ponsonby 15)

It is, therefore, safe to assume that Marianne was not that sad and perhaps mythic stereotype: an embittered Victorian spinster. Her sister, Catherine--also a painter who took flora as her subject--did marry, but her paintings are not recognized and celebrated as are Marianne's. It was she, Catherine North Symonds known as Mrs. John Addington Symonds, who edited Marianne's *Recollections of a happy life* and *Some further recollections of a happy life* drawn from her letters and diaries.

Thirdly, at the death of her beloved father in 1869 when Marianne North was nearly forty, she received an inheritance sufficient to allow her to pursue her interests in painting flora and in travel once she had reclaimed those pursuits after a period of disabling grief. Of him Marianne North wrote "My first recollections relate to my father. He was from first to last the one idol and friend of my life, and apart from him I had little pleasure and no secrets" *(Eden* 18). But in fact she had another pleasure: oil painting which she compared to "a vice like dram-drinking almost impossible to leave off once it gets possession of one" (Ponsonby 15). The fact that she was unmarried in 19th century England meant that she retained control of her assets.

What of her command of her art itself? North wrote: "In London during 1850 I had some lessons in flower-painting from a Dutch lady, Miss von Fowinkel, from whom I got the few ideas I possess of arrangement of colour and grouping" (*Eden* 18). Magdalen von Fowinkel is likely to have continued the tradition of Dutch masterpieces of botanically precise flower painting. Valentine Bartholomew (1799-1879), a flower painter to Queen Victoria, gave her "a few lessons in water-colour flower painting" (*Eden* 18). North had worked in watercolor until she was introduced to oil painting by a Christmas house guest at Hastings: Robert Dowling (1827-1886), an Australian artist. Then she made a rapid transition. All her experiences as an art student were relatively brief with the possible exception of her having observed Edward Lear, a landscape painter as well as a composer of nonsense verses, when he lodged in the Norths' gardener's cottage.

Did Marianne North have other instances of metaphorical "dram-drinking"? In her youth, she had been intensely focused on music. She devoted eight hours a day to the piano and developing her contralto voice despite her beloved father's thinking music "a horrid noise which must be submitted to for the sake of others who like it" (Ponsonby 12). Severe attacks of nerves impeded her public performances, however, and "the beautiful voice deserted her just when its cultivation reached its highest peak" (Ponsonby 12). Although obsession has a bad name, it can lead to accomplishment. It appears that Marianne North was never less alone than when she was in her own company. During her travels she repeatedly sought the joys of solitude. She could set up her easel outside a hut or a tent in the tropics, for example, and escape the inconsequential chatter of colonial sociability.

What was Marianne like as a person? Her brother-in-law, John Addington Symonds, described her as "blond, stout, tall, good humored and a little satirical" (Ponsonby 17). His description only partially prepares us for the photographs Julia Margaret Cameron took of Marianne North in Ceylon. "Her oddities," Marianne wrote of Julia Margaret, "were most refreshing, after the 'don't care' people I usually meet in tropical countries" (*Eden* 119). As Virginia Woolf observed in her Introduction to the 1926 edition of her great-aunt's work, *Victorian Photographs of Famous Men & Fair Women*: "Certainly Julia Margaret Cameron had grown up an imperious woman" (*JMC* 14). One of the ways Woolf would have known about Mrs. Cameron was through the entry her mother, Julia Stephen, had written on her in the *DNB*. Citing her son's gift of a camera to his fifty-year-old mother in 1865, Woolf recognized a prism-focused obsession in a fellow artist: "[A]t last an outlet for the energies which she had dissipated in poetry and fiction and doing up houses and concocting curries and entertaining her friends. Now she became a photographer. All her sensibility was expressed, and, what was more to the purpose, controlled in the new born art" (*JMC* 18). Although Mrs. Cameron's photographs of Marianne North do not appear in the 1926 collection, Woolf quotes from the account by "the traveller" of the three days and twelve plates taken while she was a house guest in Ceylon: "She made me stand with spiky coconut branches running into my head . . .and told me to look perfectly natural" (*JMC* 19). Marianne North's surrounding text demonstrates both her aforementioned humor and satirical bent:

> She dressed me up in flowing draperies of cashmere wool, let down my hair . . . the noonday sun's rays dodging my eyes between the leaves as the slight breeze moved them, and told me to look perfectly natural (with a thermometer standing at 96 degrees)! Then she tried me with a background of breadfruit leaves and fruit, nailed flat against a window shutter, and told *them* to look natural, but both failed. (*Eden* 119)

Bearing in mind the many minutes required for the exposure of the plates, Marianne's appraisal of the results of her ordeal is self-deprecating: "It was all in vain, she could only get a perfectly uninteresting and commonplace person on her glasses, which refused to flatter" (*Eden* 119). On the contrary, the Marianne of one photograph is somehow improbably captured mid-eye roll; she of the second has a stateliness and elegance missed by the sweetly painted portraits of her youth; she of the third is the weary and ailing traveler obliging a generous hostess and fellow spirit whom she respects. The fourth photograph despite the sun flare is an iconic moment of Empire: Marianne not in her usual knee-exposing but practical garb that irritated the British-born Ranee of Sarawak, but Marianne in a dark Victorian dress at her easel under the exposed rafters of a Tuscan columned arcade. Her subject: a male child holding a jar (*Getty Cat*. Nos. 1197-1200). But this was not a picture Marianne actually painted as far as I can tell; it was Julia Margaret Cameron's conception of what would make an aesthetically satisfying photograph. Julia Margaret had her own standards and demons as Marianne had hers.

Not only did Marianne North contribute to the science of botany, but her art and writings might well have provided an entomological/botanical dimension to Woolf's convivial conversation about art in response to Sickert's masculinist views. North also inspired Woolf to sketch a minor character who gave his allegiance to plants as he observed human nature and suggested to her the visual spectacle of a journey on the Orinoco for her first published novel, *The Voyage Out*.

Note

1   Stephen Barkway has kindly provided an extract from his talk given at the International Woolf Conference in Birmingham, U.K.:

> For me, in Sally Seton, Virginia created her younger self's ideal female companion who comprises many elements of Madge Symonds. The link between the two started, I think, when Virginia, traveling in France with Vita Sackville-West, told of her—and I quote from Vita's journal—'early loves—Madge Symonds, who is Sally in *Mrs. Dalloway.*' However, the famous passage linking the fact with the fiction was written in June 1921 when Madge came to Hogarth House and Woolf noted all her faults and changes from the adored Madge of her youth. In her diary it is as if we catch the 'tunnelling process' she would perfect in the writing of *Mrs. Dalloway*. She concluded: "And this was the woman I adored! I see myself now standing in the night nursery at Hyde Park Gate, washing my hands, & saying to myself 'At this moment she is actually under this roof.'"
>
> Three years later and drawing towards the end of writing *Mrs. Dalloway*, she makes it abundantly clear that Clarissa is feeling that self-same remembered emotion, the excitement of the close proximity for a person once adored:
>
> "Sally Seton! Sally Seton! She loomed through the mist. For she hadn't looked like *that*. Sally Seton, when Clarissa grasped the hot water can, to think of her, under this roof, under this roof! Not like that!"
>
> For the citation from Vita's journal, see "Diary of a Journey to France with Virginia Woolf in 1928" in Mary Ann Caws, *Vita Sackville-West: Selected Writings* (New York: Palgrave, 2002), p. 145: "V. told me the history of her early loves—Madge Symons [sic], who is Sally in *Mrs. Dalloway*."

Works Cited

Cox, Julian and Colin Ford, eds. *Julia Margaret Cameron: The Complete Photographs*. Los Angeles: Getty Publications, 2003.

Greer, Germaine. *The Obstacle Race: The Fortunes of Women Painters and Their Work*. New York: Farrar Straus Giroux, 1979.

Hooker, J. D. "Preface." *Catalogue of the North Gallery*. Royal Botanical Gardens, Kew, 1882.

North, Marianne. *A Vision of Eden: The Life and Work of Marianne North*. Royal Botanic Gardens, Kew; Exeter: Webb & Bower Ltd; New York: Holt, Rinehart and Winston: Winter, 1980.

—. *Recollections of a happy life: Being the autobiography of Marianne North*. Ed. Mrs. John Addington Symonds. 2 vols. London: Macmillan, 1892.

—. *Some further recollections of a happy life: Selected from the journals of Marianne North chiefly between the years 1859 and 1869*. Ed. Mrs. John Addington Symonds. London: Macmillan, 1893.

Ponsonby, Laura. *Marianne North at Kew Gardens*. 2nd ed. Royal Botanic Gardens Kew; Exeter: Webb and Bower, 1996.

Reed, Christopher. *Bloomsbury Rooms: Modernism, Subculture, and Domesticity*. Bard Graduate Center; New Haven: Yale UP, 2004.

Spaulding, Frances. "Female of the Species." *The World of Interiors* Jan. 2008: 154-59.

Symonds, John Addington. *Letters of John Addington Symonds*, 1885-1893. 3 vols. Eds. Schnoller and Peters

Woolf, Virginia. *Between the Acts*. 1941. London: Hogarth Press, 1960.

—. *Mrs. Dalloway*. *The Mrs. Dalloway Reader*. Ed. Francine Prose et al. Orlando: Harvest-Harcourt, 2004.

—." Kew Gardens." 1919. Ed. Susan Dick. *The Complete Shorter Fiction of Virginia Woolf*. 2nd ed. New York: Harcourt Brace, 1989. 90-95.

—. "Introduction." *Victorian Photographs of Famous Men & Fair Women by Julia Margaret Cameron*. With Introductions by Virginia Woolf & Roger Fry. 1926. Expanded and Revised Edition. Ed. Tristram Powell. Boston: David R. Godine and Hogarth Press, 1973. 13-19.

—. "Walter Sickert." Rpt. Slightly revised "A Conversation about Art." *Yale Review* Sept. 1934.

—. *The Captain's Death Bed and Other Essays*. London: Hogarth Press, 1950. 172-185.

"A Few Cigarettes in Lilian's Ash Tray": Woolf's Revisions to her Essays

by Stuart N. Clarke

Virginia Woolf was a compulsive reviser, as her husband Leonard pointed out in his "Editorial Note" to *The Death of the Moth*: "I do not think that Virginia Woolf ever contributed any article to any paper which she did not write and rewrite several times." As an example, he mentioned an unnamed article written "[s]hortly before her death." This was "Mrs Thrale" (*L6* 467, n. 1). He found among her "papers the original draft of the article in her handwriting and no fewer than eight or nine complete revisions of it which she had herself typed out." Nevertheless, he stated: "If she had lived, there is no doubt that she would have made large alterations and revisions in nearly all these essays before allowing them to appear in volume form" (*DM* 7).

In November 1929 Woolf broadcast a slightly bowdlerized version of her essay "Beau Brummell" on the wireless, in the series Miniature Biographies. The BBC appears to have lost Woolf's script, but, as often happened, the talk was printed in the *Listener*, on 27 November, in which the first part of her story reaches this climax:

> there came a day, May 16, 1816, to be precise, and it was a day upon which everything was precise, when he dined alone off a cold fowl and a bottle of claret at the club, attended the opera, and then took coach for Dover. He drove rapidly all through the night and reached Calais the day after. He never set foot in England again. (721)

The *Listener*, however, appended a note at the end:

> Among the correspondence which has been received since Mrs. Virginia Woolf broadcast the above talk on November 20, is the following from Messrs. Berry Bros. and Co., Wine Merchants of 3 St. James's Street, S.W.1, which adds an interesting historical detail to her account. ¶ "With reference to the talk on the life of Beau Brummell given by Virginia Woolf during last evening's broadcasting, it was mentioned that Beau Brummell left this country in May, 1816, never to return again. We think it might be of interest to you to know that we have, at the above address, records showing that Beau Brummell DID return to this country after that date and was weighed upon the scales in these premises on the 26th of July, 1822."

Woolf did not correct her facts in the limited edition of *Beau Brummell* published by Rimington & Hooper of New York in 1930, which was sold at the princely sum of $10 in the US and two guineas in the UK. When she came to include "Beau Brummell" in *The Common Reader: Second Series* in 1932, once again she did not modify her essay, but appended a note with more details from Berry Bros.: "Mr. Berry of St. James's Street has courteously drawn my attention to the fact that Beau Brummell certainly visited England in 1822. He came to the famous wine-shop on 26th July 1822 and was weighed as usual. His weight was then 10 stones 13 pounds. On the previous occasion, 6th July 1815, his weight was 12 stones 10 pounds. Mr. Berry adds that there is no record of his coming after 1822" (*CR2* 156).

Not all new facts were worth Woolf's taking on board. Following the publication of "Geraldine and Jane" in the *Times Literary Supplement* of February 28, 1929, five letters to the Editor were published, praising the essay—"entertaining," "brilliant and amusing," "entirely delightful and illuminative"—but attempting to supply additional information about Geraldine Jewsbury. Here is the relevant sentence from Woolf: "Until she was twenty-nine we know nothing of her except that she was born in the year 1812, was the daughter of a merchant, and lived in Manchester, or near it" (149). One of the letters was from O. H. T. Dudley who had been Inspector of European Schools in the Bombay Presidency:

> some years ago I discovered hidden away behind the main street of Poona cantonment a large cholera cemetery.... In the middle of it was a large stone obelisk with a marble slab recording in Latin the virtues and achievements of Maria Jane Jewsbury, Geraldine's elder sister.... As for Geraldine, your readers may like to be reminded of.... Prosper Merimée's "Lettres à une inconnue." There he tells his fair correspondent that he has met the author of a romance called "Zoe"....

In her essay Woolf referred several times to the touchy subject of women smoking cigars. Although Jewsbury was enthusiastic about smoking (*Selections* 140, 220-1), Ella Hepworth Dixon (1857–1932), the daughter of William Hepworth Dixon (1821–79), editor of the *Athenæum*, wrote to the *TLS* to say that she remembered Jewsbury "when I was a small child[,] as a person of infinite charm. She never smoked a cigar in our house—that must have been one of the audacious gestures of her youth—on the contrary, when she was reading the proofs of one of my father's new books she would ask my mother to give her 'something to darn.'"

Of course, what Woolf was interested in was the relationship between Geraldine Jewsbury and Jane Carlyle. When John Hayward wrote to congratulate her on her essay in the *TLS*, she replied: "I daresay one could have found out more about Miss Jewsbury; I had only one volume of her letters to go upon. I could not read more than one of the novels, and I expect that some old gentleman who has read all mid-Victorian memoirs will blast my theories completely. Her relation with Mrs Carlyle was interesting, and I had to be discreet" (*L4* 30).

And when the essay was revised for *The Common Reader: Second Series*, the sentence remained unchanged: "Until she was twenty-nine we know nothing of her except that she was born in the year 1812, was the daughter of a merchant, and lived in Manchester, or near it" (*CR2* 186).

Most egregious of all were the minor errors in "George Gissing," the subject of a kind of one-sided running battle with Gissing's son. This was one of Woolf's most frequently revised essays, yet the factual errors were never corrected. Woolf wrote to Jonathan Cape on 18 October 1932 about her introduction to Gissing's *By the Ionian Sea*: "I would suggest that you should print from the version just issued in the second series of my Common Reader. I have altered it to a certain extent. I do not think that I could alter it any further" (*L5* 112). Nonetheless, when she returned the proofs to Cape's office on November 25, 1932, she had made a few more revisions.

However, when he received his copies of the book, Gissing's son, Alfred (1896–1975), complained to Cape. On March 2, 1933, Cape wrote to Woolf, but, as Pierre Coustillas puts it, he "reported Alfred Gissing's objections, minus his indignation, so that the echo of the latter's angry protest was made hardly perceptible" (15). Gissing wrote to the *TLS*, and here is the key part of the exchange:

> I am glad to have this opportunity of replying to the question of Mrs. Virginia Woolf regarding the errors to be found in her introduction to "By the Ionian Sea," more particularly because there are readers of the book who are quite naturally blaming me for the appearance of the introduction. I cannot guarantee that the following list of mistakes and inaccuracies is exhaustive, but at any rate it includes the most obvious of them. (*TLS* Apr. 27, 1933: 295)

He listed seven and concluded: "May I ask Mrs. Woolf to be good enough not to make further use of her introduction? It would be a kindness to myself and others." Here is Woolf's response:

> I am sorry to find that in my introduction to George Gissing's "By the Ionian Sea" I have left out three dots to indicate that the words "with a cart" are omitted. Otherwise the quotation is accurate. I also regret that I may have led the reader to suppose that Gissing dined off lentils a year after he had given up eating them: still got up at five when he had stopped getting up at five; took six journeys to a bookseller when in fact he took only two: referred to a fog and a landlady when there was not a fog or a landlady: and used the phrase "as he died" instead of "two days before he died." Such mistakes do not seem to me, I admit, of a serious nature. (*TLS* May 4, 1933: 312

She then concluded with a seeming concession that was subtly offensive: "But I apologize for having stated that the Gissings had 'to scrape together what education they could get' when it appears that there was no shortage of money for educational purposes." As a pedant my sympathies should be with Gissing, but, having looked at the book Woolf was initially reviewing—*Letters of George Gissing to Members of his Family*—I can only agree with her: "when we take up Gissing's letters...there are gaps in plenty, and many dark places left unlit. Much information has been kept back, many facts necessarily omitted" (*CR2* 220).

With "Memories of a Working Women's Guild," Woolf was later forced to make changes, and she did not like it. In 1929 Margaret Llewelyn Davies had invited Woolf to introduce the book of autobiographies she was then editing. At some point during the following year Woolf agreed to undertake the project (*D3* 304). She wrote to Davies on Friday, July 25, 1930:

> I have not yet gone through your suggestions about my Guild paper.... Meanwhile an American editor [Helen McAfee of the *Yale Review*], to whom I had promised an article, has read it; and wants to publish it in September as an article—or rather as fiction. What I want to know is whether you would object to my doing this, if I suppressed all real names, did not mention you or Lilian [Harris], and made it my personal view of congresses in general?... It has to be sent off on Tuesday, and thus I have no time to make the alterations in detail which you suggest. Can you trust me to make the thing blameless? I dont suppose any Guildswoman is likely to read the Yale Review. (*L4* 191)

Although Davies's letters to Woolf are not held in the Leonard Woolf or the Monks House Papers at the University of Sussex, it is clear from Woolf's side of the correspondence that Davies wanted a number of changes to the introduction before publication. On September 14 Woolf wrote to Davies, with a threat:

> I have at last gone through the Letter and your suggestions, and enclose it for your inspection. I have made some alterations, but I'm afraid by no means all. We both feel, for Leonard agrees, that if I made all the alterations you suggest, the point of view would be so much altered that it would no longer give my own meaning. And as the only merit of the letter is that it gives a particular persons impression we feel that it would be foolish to publish a modified version. One would simply fall between two stools. ¶ On the other hand we both think that you are very likely in the right, and that to publish my version would give pain and be misunderstood—and that of course is the last thing we want. Of this we think you and Lilian are the only judges, and therefore we suggest that you should look through the paper again and decide whether you think it can be printed with the alterations I have made. Honestly, I shall not mind in the very least (in fact in some ways I shall be rather relieved) if you say no. I have had my doubts from the first. Then, if you feel that it wont do, we suggest that we should send the papers to Barbara Stephen, unless you can think of anyone better, and ask her to write an introduction. (*L4* 212-3)

On 10 October she updated Davies:

> What rather appals me (I'm writing in a hurry, and cant spell, and dont please take my words altogether literally) is the terrific conventionality of the workers. Thats why—if you want explanations—I dont think they will be poets or novelists for another hundred years or so. If they cant face the fact that Lilian smokes a pipe and reads detective novels, and cant be told that they weigh on an average 12 stone—which is largely because they scrub so hard and have so many children—and are shocked by the word "impure" how can you say that they face "reality"?, (I never know what "reality" means: but Lilian smoking a pipe to me is real, and Lilian merely coffee coloured and discreet is not nearly so real). What depresses me is that the workers seem to have taken on all the middle class re-

spectabilities which we—at any rate if we are any good at writing or painting—have faced and thrown out. Or am I quite wrong? (*L4* 228-9)

Here is a summary of the changes between the *Yale Review* and the *Life as We have Known It* versions. Firstly, in the *Yale Review* some place names are disguised, as are the names of Davies, Lilian Harris and Miss Kidd, but not of the women who contributed to the book. Secondly, much of the phrasing is different, presumably as Woolf strove to improve on the *Yale Review* version. The most significant change is: "If every reform they demand was granted this very instant it would not matter to me a single jot" became "…would not touch one hair of my comfortable capitalistic head." Thirdly, some corrections are pretty obviously Davies's. For example: "I am the wife of a miner. He comes back thick with coal grime. First he must have his bath. Then he must have his dinner. But there is only a wash tub" became "…Then he must have his supper. But there is only a copper." It also seems likely that the Co-operative women who were previously asking for "peace and disarmament and the sisterhood of nations" were later, thanks to Davies, demanding "peace and disarmament and the spread of Co-operative principles, not only among the working people of Great Britain, but among the nations of the world." Fourthly, some changes were mistakes that were picked up: Middlesbrough had been spelt incorrectly; and one of the contributors to the book, Mrs Scott, had been called a "midwife", then she correctly became a "felt hat worker." Fifthly, as Woolf indicated she would, she made some concessions. While the fictional Janet Erskine "may have been smoking a pipe—there was one on the table. She may have been reading a detective story—there was a book of that kind on the table," the real Lilian Harris, "whether it was due to her dress which was coffee coloured, or to her smile which was serene, or to the ash-tray in which many cigarettes had come amiably to an end, seemed the image of detachment and equanimity." And writing was no longer "an impure art;" it was "a complex art." However, although Woolf changed her phrasing, she still kept the working women's "thick-set and muscular" bodies.

But let the last word on this be Margaret's. In an unpublished letter, she wrote to Leonard after Virginia's death, on 9 June 1941: "How well I remember…how she encouraged the publication of the women's lives & wrote so beautifully her impressions in her Letter to me, making the book so specially dear to me. We should never have printed… but for you both, & I cannot tell you what your support of 'the Guild' has been to me" (Leonard Woolf Papers, III).

This discussion has been limited to Woolf's biographical essays. What she said about herself applies to them too: "I find that scene making is my natural way of marking the past. A scene always comes to the top; arranged; representative" (*MOB* 142). In "The New Biography" (1927), Woolf famously characterized "the whole problem of biography" as she saw it: "On the one hand there is truth; on the other is personality. And if we think of truth as something of granite-like solidity and of personality as something of rainbow-like intangibility and reflect that the aim of biography is to weld these two into one seamless whole, we shall admit that the problem is a stiff one" (*E4* 473). In January 1929 she wrote to Vita Sackville-West:

> I do nothing but try, vainly, to finish off a year's journalism in a week…. There are dates to look up. One can't simply invent the whole of Chelsea and King

George the 3rd and Johnson, and Mrs Thrale I suppose. Yet after all, thats the way to write; and if I had time to prove it, the truth of one's sensations is not in the fact, but in the reverberation. When I have read three lines, I re-make them entirely, if they're prose, and not poetry; and it is this which is the truth. (*L4* 5)

When Woolf published an anonymous article on John Evelyn in the *TLS* in 1920, in part a review of a book on Evelyn with a commentary by H. Maynard Smith, Smith wrote in to complain. "Your Reviewer" (i.e. Woolf) replied:

"Mr. Maynard Smith's letter appears to be intended to accuse me of inaccuracies and of misinterpretation in my review... He has, I admit, succeeded in discovering three slips in four columns, and for these I am willing to offer...my apologies.... But while I plead guilty to these chronological errors, I maintain my interpretation of Evelyn's character as against Mr. Smith's." (*E3* 267)

Thus the scenes that Woolf creates are not necessarily literally true. Sometimes she confesses to this in her published work—that is what she did in effect in "Beau Brummell" with the note about Berry Bros. There are other examples, such as this one in *Flush*: "He was stolen" (*F* 71). Woolf's endnote explains: "As a matter of fact, Flush was stolen three times; but the unities seem to require that the three stealings shall be compressed into one" (154). And there are a couple of examples in *Three Guineas* where she admits to changing port to claret (*TG* 161, 306) and "a large silver plaque in the form of a Reich eagle" to "ink-pots" (207, 315).

Woolf's view may be symbolized by her question to Margaret Llewelyn Davies about the introductory letter to *Life as We have Known It*: "I brought in a few cigarettes in Lilians ash tray—do they matter? A little blue cloud of smoke seemed to me aesthetically desirable at that point" (*L4* 287).

Works Cited

Coustillas, Pierre. "'A Voice that Spoke Straight and Shapely Words': Gissing in the Works and Papers of Virginia Woolf." *Gissing Newsletter* 23.2 (July 1987): 1-30.
Dudley, O. H. T.; Morley, Edith J.; Dixon, Ella Hepworth; Hutton, W. H. "Correspondence: Geraldine and Jane." *Times Literary Supplement* (March 7, 1929): 185.
Gissing, A. C. "Correspondence: Gissing's 'By the Ionian Sea'." *Times Literary Supplement* (April 27, 1933): 295.
Gissing, George. *Letters of George Gissing to Members of his Family*. Ed. Algernon and Ellen Gissing. London: Constable, 1927.
Jewsbury, Geraldine. *Selections from the Letters of Geraldine Jewsbury*. Ed. Mrs Alexander Ireland. London: Longmans, Green, and Co., 1892.
Leonard Woolf Papers. Sx Ms 13. University of Sussex, Lewis, UK.
Woodruff, E. H. "Correspondence: Geraldine and Jane." *Times Literary Supplement* (April 4, 1929): 276.
Woolf, Virginia. "Beau Brummell." *Listener* (November 27, 1929): 720-1.
—. *Beau Brummell*. New York: Rimington & Hooper, 1930.
—. *The Common Reader: Second Series*. London: Hogarth, 1932.
—. "Correspondence: Gissing's 'By the Ionian Sea'." *Times Literary Supplement* (May 4, 1933): 312.
—. *The Death of the Moth and other essays*. Ed. Leonard Woolf. London: Hogarth, 1942.

—. *The Diary of Virginia Woolf.* Ed. Anne Olivier Bell with Andrew McNeillie. 5 vols. London: Hogarth, 1977-84.
—. *The Essays of Virginia Woolf.* Ed. Andrew McNeillie. 4 vols. London: Hogarth, 1986-94.
—. *Flush: A Biography.* London: Hogarth Press, 1933.
—. "Geraldine and Jane." *Times Literary Supplement* (February 28, 1929): 149-50.
—. "Introduction." *By the Ionian Sea: Notes of a Ramble in Southern Italy.* By George Gissing. London: Jonathan Cape, 1933.
—. "Introductory Letter to Margaret Llewelyn Davies." *Life as We have Known It.* Ed. Margaret Llewelyn Davies. London: Hogarth, 1931.
—. *The Letters of Virginia Woolf.* Ed. Nigel Nicolson with Joanne Trautmann. 6 vols. London: Hogarth, 1975-80.
—. "Memories of a Working Women's Guild." *Yale Review* 20.1 (September 1930): 121-38.
—. *Moments of Being.* Ed. Jeanne Schulkind. 2nd ed. London: Hogarth, 1985.
—. *Three Guineas.* London: Hogarth, 1938.

WHO IS MR. RAMSAY? WHERE IS THE LIGHTHOUSE?: THE POLITICS AND PRAGMATICS OF SCHOLARLY ANNOTATION

by Jane Goldman

Before turning to my work as editor of *To the Lighthouse*, I will begin with some of the observations made by Susan Sellers and myself in the General Editors' Preface to the forthcoming Cambridge University Press Edition of the Writings of Virginia Woolf. We begin this with Woolf's own advice to readers in her essay, "How Should One Read a Book?", "The only advice, indeed, that one person can give another about reading is to take no advice, to follow your own instincts, to use your own reason, to come to your own conclusions. (*CR2* 258)" How should we read the writings of Virginia Woolf? This is not so much a question of interpretation as of practice. How are we to read this writer for whom reading is an activity that requires almost the same talents and energies as the activity of writing itself? Woolf understands the reader to be the "fellow-worker and accomplice"of the writer. The "quickest way to understand […] what a novelist is doing is not to read," she suggests, "but to write; to make your own experiment with the dangers and difficulties of words" (*CR2* 259). My fellow General Editor, Susan Sellers, is indeed making *her* "own experiment with the dangers and difficulties of words," in that she is launching her first novel, *Vanessa and Virginia* (published by Two Ravens Press in the UK, and Harcourt in the U.S.).

The "time to read poetry," Woolf recognizes, is "when we are almost able to write it." (*CR2* 264). If we are going to read Woolf creatively and critically, if we are to follow our own instincts, use our own reason, and come to our own conclusions, as she herself advises, we need to read her works in a form that provides us with the fullest means possible to exercise these powers, in a form that gives us as much unmediated access as possible to the record of these processes. This is the goal of the Cambridge edition of Woolf's writings.

EDITING WOOLF

So, how should we edit the writings of Virginia Woolf? Already the danger and difficulties of words are upon us. "We," that is Susan Sellers and I, as editors cannot forget that we are already committed and diverse readers of Woolf. Asking ourselves questions about how to edit Woolf, "we," as General Editors (and also as editors of individual volumes), very soon recognized the need to respond as "we," two active and different readers of Woolf. Yet, whatever our own often very different instincts, reasonings, and conclusions, we nevertheless share a recognition of the intense attention to the text that Woolf's writing demands of all her readers. This is the case in respect of its textual genesis, structure and variants, as well as in its possible—and its manifest—cultural and historical referencing, and regardless of our own individual interpretations. In our role as editors we conceive of ourselves as readers in need of access to a transparent record of textual process, rather than as readers who arrive at interpretative conclusions.

However, we would be foolish to ignore the fact that the act of editing is always and already bound up with reading precisely as an interpretative act. Cherishing our differences as critics, we also cherish the opportunity to engage as closely with the processes of Woolf's writing as any active reader could wish, and to make these processes available to fellow readers as fully and transparently as possible. It is also hard to ignore Woolf's scorn of institutionalized academic literary authority: "To admit authorities, however heavily furred and gowned, into our libraries and let them tell us how to read, what to read, what value to place upon what we read, is to destroy the spirit of freedom which is the breath of those sanctuaries. Everywhere else we may be bound by laws and conventions—there we have none" (*CR2* 258). Naked, transparency, not fur and gowns, is our editorial ideal, and we are guided, as clearly Woolf has been, by King Lear: "Through tattered clothes great vices do appear: / Robes and furred gowns hide all" (*Lear* 4.6.).

ANNOTATING WOOLF

How should we annotate Woolf? We have been guided too by Woolf's own recorded thoughts on editorial achievements. For example, reviewing as a lay reader a new scholarly edition of Walpole's letters, Woolf "assert[s], though not with entire confidence, that books after all exist to be read—even the most learned of editors would to some extent at least agree with that." ("Two Antiquaries: Walpole and Cole" [n.d.], *DM* 64). And as editors, we do indeed agree with that. We cannot ignore Woolf's inclusion of the common reader as part of a true scholarly community: "Aeschylus, Shakespeare, Virgil, and Dante [...] if they could speak—and after all they can—would say, 'Don't leave me to the wigged and gowned. Read me, read me for yourselves.'" Woolf worries that the weighty apparatus of scholarly editions hampers readers.

> But how [...] can we read this magnificent instalment [...] of our old friend Horace Walpole's letters? Ought not the presses to have issued in a supplementary pocket a supplementary pair of eyes? Then, with the usual pair fixed upon the text, the additional pair could range the notes, thus sweeping together into one haul not only what Horace is saying to Cole and what Cole is saying to Horace, but a multitude of minor men and matters. (*DM* 45)

In *Night and Day*, Mr Hilbery prepares an edition of Shelley that "scrupulously observe[s] the poet's system of punctuation" (*ND* 108-109). Woolf's novelist's sensitivity to the comedy of this undertaking does not wholly undermine his endeavour: Mr Hilbery, the narrator tells us, "saw the humour of these researches, but that did not prevent him from carrying them out with the utmost scrupulosity" (*ND* 109).

As editors, we share Woolf's concerns for the readability of books. Resisting the temptation to issue "in a supplementary pocket a supplementary pair of eyes," we have devised ways of alerting the reader, on the page, to the relevant parts of the textual apparatus. But if Woolf worries about "how great a strain the new method of editing lays upon the eye," she does come to acknowledge that "if the brain is at first inclined to jib at such perpetual solicitations, and to beg to be allowed to read the text in peace, it adjusts itself by degrees; grudgingly admits that many of these little facts are to the point; and finally becomes not merely a convert but a suppliant—asks not for less but for more and more and more" (*DM* 45-46). As editors, we also respond to this spur to feed the insatiable wants of the enquiring reader, once roused.

Sharing Woolf's own readerly desire for "more and more and more," and recognizing the same urgency in our fellow readers, we have made this refrain one of our guiding principles. But, we know too that while the scholarly scope afforded by a Cambridge edition can certainly give more, no edition can ever give all. The concept of such a totality is meaningless. The work of the editor is to engage the reader in a process of informed exploration and interpretation that continues beyond the edition. We understand the readers of this edition, then, to be accomplices in a process that can impose no finite interpretation on Woolf's writings. It is our hope that our work enables and enriches the continuing process of readerly collaboration. Another refrain taken from Woolf has also frequently sounded to us, particularly during the preparation of explanatory notes: "nothing [is] simply one thing" (*TL* 286). We would emphasize the open-endedness of all such annotation, and we have conceived ours in dialogue with the work of past and present readers and scholars of Woolf, with the hope of enabling and continuing the dialogues of the future.

It is nevertheless worth considering the extreme attention now extended by critics to every minor detail of Woolf's writing, including street and shop names, as David Bradshaw urges, and comparing this with some earlier critical approaches that tended to assume her otherworldliness as a writer remote from the fabric of things in the real world, and possessed of a vague, visionary aesthetics considered factually inaccurate and even deliberately careless. The attribution of factual indifference and "essential feminineness of [...] mind" (Bennett 13) initially deflected interest from the fine detail and precision of Woolf's cultural and intellectual referencing that scholars now investigate with considerable care. It was not so long ago that critics felt able to presume, for example, Woolf's lack of classical scholarship, rather than acknowledge her satirical characterization, in her account of Mrs. Dalloway's mistaken assignation, in *The Voyage Out*, of Clytemnestra to *Antigone*. (Woolf's own translation of the *Agamemnon*, languishing in the archives, points clearly to her knowledge of which classical play Clytemnestra actually graces.) Explanatory notes must also address the inevitable receding of Woolf's social and political references into an historical period and cultural context now becoming distant enough from many of today's readers to require elucidation. The research undertaken for the explanatory notes to the edition draws on the new wealth of scholarly work engaged in the detailed exploration of the myriad and sparklingly allusive surfaces of Woolf's texts as well as their deeper layering of cultural referencing and valences. We would also emphasize that where critical works are cited in the explanatory notes it is to point out the information they yield on Woolf's rich weaving of literary, cultural, historical and other allusions, rather than with regard to how these allusions and references are interpreted in those works. We have fiercely debated that boundary between editorial explanation and critical interpretation.

Reading is a sacred and infectious pleasure for Woolf, and an end in itself. So much so that she celebrates, in "How Should One Read a Book," its power even to dispense with the mythic Day of Judgement itself: "the Almighty will turn to Peter and will say, not without a certain envy when he sees us coming with our books under our arms, 'Look, these need no reward. We have nothing to give them here. They have loved reading'" (*CR2* 220). A declared atheist, Woolf resisted all notions of final judgement, religious, literary or political. We understand our edition to be continuing, and not capping, the on-going processes of reading and re-reading her work. We hope our fellow readers will recognize, in making use of it, the shifting processes and conditions that are implicit in following instincts, using reason and coming to conclusions about Woolf's work. For "who reads to bring about an end, however desirable? Are there not some pursuits that we practise because they are good in themselves, and some pleasures that are final? And is not this among them?" (*CR2* 220).

To The Lighthouse

Woolf claimed, in retrospect, to have made up *To the Lighthouse* all in one go. It simply came to her "one day [...] in a great, apparently involuntary, rush," while, in the manner of a perambulating visionary poet, she was 'walking around Tavistock Square,'" London, in 1926 (*MB* 81). Woolf's own emphasis on the sudden occurrence of the originating conception of the novel in the heart of metropolitan London provides an ironic enough sense of a start for a book that is ostensibly set in the remote Western Islands of Scotland, a place its author never visited until a good decade after publication. Indeed, this novel so archly conceived in Tavistock Square hardly mentions at all Woolf's native and familiar London, yet it quite openly flirts with the Cornwall of her childhood holidays while at the same time managing never actually to name it. As the opening pages of *Jacob's Room* show, Woolf was capable of naming Cornwall in her fiction just as several other of her works name and are often predominantly set quite overtly in London. But the flirtation with semi-autobiographical, familial landscapes in *To the Lighthouse* has proved so powerful that the Hebridean setting has been almost entirely overlooked, reduced to a mere Cornish cipher, by generations of its readers. Such biographical readings have drawn strength from Woolf's retrospective claims to have exorcised the ghosts of her parents through writing this novel.

The dislocating impact of the novel's juxtaposition of acknowledged autobiographical origins and invented, composite setting, presents questions for the editor and reader that require careful consideration of Woolf's broader possible sources. The explanatory notes to *To the Lighthouse* take up the task of the cultural, historical, and intellectual mapping of the text. My edition attempts, among other things to mend the past deficit of serious attention to its numerous and significant allusions to its Scottish setting—without in turn setting or fixing it too dogmatically or simply in any one place. "I'm so glad that you like some of the Lighthouse," Woolf wrote to her friend Violet Dickinson, mischievously adding: "Is it Cornwall? I'm not as sure as you are" (*L3* 389).

The cryptic, emblematic origin of *To the Lighthouse* in Woolf's own holographic hieroglyph, the "two blocks joined by a corridor" (*HTL* 3) may come to be understood hermeneutically as the work's very alpha and omega, this inscrutable sphinx-like diagram winking at us from the archives. A diagram of the textual form and temporal movement of Woolf's Hebridean novel, it has since been decoded as the toppling of the signifier of patriarchal subjectivity, the dark bar that overshadows the reader Phoebe in *A Room of One's Own*. But might it also be a map of Tavistock Square and environs, the primal scene, perhaps, of its own conception? On the other hand, Woolf may have taken partial inspiration from a diagram in J. Sands' guide to the Hebridean island of St. Kilda, which was in her library, where "the form of St. Kilda," Sands says, consists "of a number of steep hills, arranged like the figure 4 as it is written, or, if we include the island called Dun, like the letter H roughly formed. [...] The space below the bar of the H is the bay, and the space above it Glen Mòr." Sands' *Out of the World; or, Life in St. Kilda* (1878) opens with a chapter on his stay in Dunvegan, at the McLeod Clan's seat, in Skye, from where he began the last leg of his journey to the more remote island of St. Kilda. It is one of a number of works on Woolf's shelves that offer accounts of Skye, the Hebrides and Scotland, and which she may have plundered. Woolf herself enjoyed the hospitality of a member of the Macleod Clan from Dunvegan, when in April, 1923 she and Leonard were travelling in Grenada, Spain. She wrote to her sister with anecdotes of her hosts, Charles and Olive Temple. He was former Governor of Nigeria, and she was the second daughter of Sir Reginald Macleod, 27th Chief and Baron of Dunvegan, Skye. Olive Temple, she reports, "is a Scottish gentlewoman, clean, discreet, shabby, with blue eyes like poor Marny's [Margaret Vaughan], but is a woman of character" adding "Mrs Temple is of course a cousin of the Vaughans" (*L3* 26), thereby connecting the blue-eyed "Miss McLeod, lord of the Scottish Isles" (*L3* 26), albeit somewhat tenuously, to her own family tree: Marny Vaughan was *her* cousin too. So, just prior to writing *To the Lighthouse*, Woolf was in Spain discussing Skye with expatriate veterans of colonial Africa.

I will limit myself to just a couple of examples of Explanatory Notes for *To the Lighthouse*. My note on the name Ramsay includes the following information on just *some* of the highly relevant 14 people, and a number of places, I have been researching—all with the name Ramsay. Ramsay may indeed suggest quite a number of historical, geographical and fictional sources, all plausible in relation to Woolf. There is the eighteenth century campaigner against slavery, the Aberdeen born, Reverend James Ramsay of Teston, Kent, author of numerous abolitionist pamphlets and of the *Essay on the Treatment and Conversion of the African Slaves in the British Sugar Colonies* (1784), who was admired by the African writer Olaudah Equiano. Reverend Ramsay was also known to, and supported by, Leslie Stephen's grandfather, James Stephen (1758-1832), the lawyer and abolitionist who went to the West Indies to verify Ramsay's account and "investigate the charges of Ramsay's enemies," reporting back to William Wilberforce. Wilberforce cites James Stephen, in his diary, on the death of Ramsay. There is the celebrated diarist, John Ramsay of Ochtertyre, Stirling, who was considered the model for Sir Walter Scott's eponymous antiquary, Jonathan Oldbuck, in his novel *The Antiquary* which is explicitly mentioned in *To the Lighthouse*. And there is his ancestor, Sir John Ramsay of "Ouchterhouse" [Ochtertyre], a prominent participant in the Scottish rebellion (1297-1303) led by William Wallace. He is mentioned in *The Actes and Deidis of the Illustre and Vallyeant Campion Schir William Wallace* (c.1477), by the bard, "Blind Willy," and in the hugely popular adapted translation by William Hamilton of Gilbertfield, *Blind Willy's Wallace* (1722), where he is called, in Book VII, "righteous born" and in war "right meikle for to prise,/ Busie and true, both sober, wight and wise," along with his son Alexander Ramsay "the flower of courtliness"; and in William Hamilton Drummond's poem, *Bruce's Invasion of Ireland* (1826) ("*There Ouchterhouse Ramsay is stalking in pride*"). Woolf read all about the courtly Sir Alexander Ramsay of Dalwolsey, Sheriff of Teviotdale (d.1342), in *A Group of Scottish Women* (1908) by Harry Graham, a book she reviewed for the *TLS* ("Scottish Women", 1908). See his second chapter, "Some Scottish Amazon—'Black Agnes of Dunbar' (1313-1369)."

There is a cameo appearance of another Mr. Ramsay (sans first name) in "Kabnis" (a story about lynching, set in Georgia), the final episode in *Cane* (1923), the experimental work by Harlem writer, Jean Toomer. Toomer was published in numerous international little magazines in the 1920s, and in 1923 both he and Woolf were featured in the *The Dial*. In her preliminary holograph notes for *To the Lighthouse* Woolf lists Toomer as one of the "names to be used." I have other Ramsays to consider too, but time does not permit me to pursue them here. However, I would like to add that the names of all characters, however "minor," in each of Woolf's novels are given serious attention in the Cambridge edition. For example, Mrs Moffat in *The Waves*, on whom Bernard relies to "sweep [...] up" after him (*W* 84), shares the surname of a prominent trade union activist, Abe Moffat (1896-1975), and merits the same sort of attention by readers, critics, and editors that Mrs McNab and Mrs Bast, in *To the Lighthouse*, have received now for some time.

Place names also receive close scrutiny. Returning to *To the Lighthouse,* my Explanatory Note for "the Pope's Nose" onto which Andrew wanders in the beach scene in Part One, "The Window," demonstrates the poignant, post-war significance of that name. Presumably "the Pope's Nose," in the beach scene, is an outcrop of rock but there is none of that name on Skye (nor Cornwall). The term is widely used to refer to the rump of a fowl (also called the Parson's Nose), as other editors of *To the Lighthouse* have explained in their notes. But it was also the name given by the Ulster Division of Irish Protestant Troops to a significant German strongpoint, a machine-gun post, on the Somme battlefield to the west of the Schwaben Redoubt at Thiepval. See the press report, "Official Story of Loos. Fine Fighting by British Troops," which describes "a point called 'The Pope's Nose,'" in *The Times*, Saturday 20 May, 1916; and it is mentioned again in "Givenchy, Hooge, and Loos. Story of British Attacks. Need of Reserves and Munitions," *The Times*, Monday 22 May, 1916. On 28 September, 1916, the 11th Battalion, The Lancashire Fusiliers, undertook a successful raid against this strongpoint. The writer J. R. R. Tolkein was the Battalion Signalling Officer during this action. So Andrew's sojourn to the Pope's Nose may be an augury of his death in the Great War reported in "Time Passes." Woolf uses the term only once elsewhere in her writings, in a letter to Molly MacCarthy, in March 1927, on proposing a holiday abroad for Molly and Desmond MacCarthy: "let me know what happens to you, whether you fall into a crater, or kiss the Pope's nose, or whatever it may be" (*L3* 354).

Woolf's writing is richly textured with such sharply significant (albeit tiny and passing) allusions. The editorial task of annotating such writing—so subtle and fugitive and fragmentary, but at the same time so potent—demands intensive research, and builds on the considerable and continuing achievements of colleagues in Woolf studies and modernist studies. It is a highly rewarding process. But it also demands a way of framing the Explanatory Notes themselves so that they assist us all as readers in following our own instincts, using our own reason, and coming to our own conclusions.

Works Cited

Graham, Harry. *A Group of Scottish Women*. London: Methuen, 1908.
Ramsay, James. *Essay on the Treatment and Conversion of the African Slaves in the British Sugar Colonies*, 1784,
Sands, J. *Out of the World; or, Life in St. Kilda*. Second Edition. Edinburgh: MacLachlan and Stewart, 1878.
Toomer, Jean. *Cane*. 1923. New York: Norton, 1988.

Woolf, Virginia. "How Should One Read a Book?". *The Common Reader: Second Series*. London: Hogarth, 1932.
—. "Two Antiquaries: Walpole and Cole." *The Death of the Moth*. Ed. Leonard Woolf. London: Hogarth, 1942.
—. *Night and Day*. London: Duckworth, 1919.
—. *To the Lighthouse*. London: Hogarth, 1927.
—. *To the Lighthouse. The Original Holograph Draft*. Ed. Susan Dick. London: Hogarth, 1982.
—. *Moments of Being: Unpublished Autobiographical Writings*. Second Edition. Ed. Jeanne Schulkind. London: Hogarth, 1985.
—. *The Letters of Virginia Woolf*. 6 vols. Ed. Nigel Nicolson and Joanne Trautmann. London: Hogarth, 1975-1980.
—. *The Waves*. London: Hogarth, 1931.
—. "Scottish Women." *The Essays of Virginia Woolf*. Vol. 1. Ed. Andrew McNeillie. London: Hogarth, 1986.

Semi-Colons and Major Changes: Editing *Mrs. Dalloway*

by Anne E. Fernald

What is textual editing?

The process of preparing a textual edition of *Mrs. Dalloway* has involved a steep learning curve for me, and one that has made me acutely aware of the double audience for the Cambridge University Press textual edition: while I tremble at the thought of other textual editors pouring over my work for errors and misjudgments, I remain committed to and most interested in those scholars and readers who are *not* engaged in the project of producing a textual edition but are, instead, consulting my edition as an aid to their own work. These readers, as Edward L. Bishop and others have noted, will have little time for the charts the making of which consumes my spare hours: they need an introduction to guide them. Textual editors talk about major and minor changes, and I want to borrow that rubric for this essay on some of the changes that Woolf made while correcting the proofs of *Mrs. Dalloway*.

Mrs. Dalloway was the first of Woolf's novels to have simultaneous American and British publication. So, in January of 1925, she received three sets of proofs: a British set for the Hogarth Press (this set has since been lost), an American set to be sent to Harcourt in New York (and now in the archives of the Lilly Library at Indiana University), and a personal set which she bound into a book and sent to her friend Jacques Raverat who was dying in France. (This set is now at UCLA.)

Most of the changes Woolf made at this stage are minor indeed. But, as I have learned, sometimes a single minor change is part of a larger pattern of revision with some significance.

Semi-colons: a minor change?

Take, for example, the changes to the scene in which Peter remembers the night that Richard fell in love with Clarissa. Taken singly, the changes seem simple enough: a period becomes a semi-colon; a capital letter thus must now be set in lower case. Altogether, however, we see Woolf changing the character of Peter's memory, eliminating details—about Clarissa herself, about the island, about the hen she startles—and focusing the prose on a single, flowing memory of an achingly beautiful moment, a moment in which he saw Clarissa's beauty at its most intense and, simultaneously, recognized that she would never marry him. Here is the list of changes. The text before the first square bracket reproduces the first British edition; the following text reproduces the text as it appeared in the uncorrected proofs (UP):

> 96.6adventurousness;] adventurousness--there was something about her that night wild, intoxicating, tender. *UP*]

Semi-Colons and Major Changes

96.6 she] She *UP*]
96.7 island;] island--a wretched little hump in the middle of the pond. *UP*]
96.7 she] She *UP*]
96.8 hen;] hen, or some heavy bird which flew up. *UP*]
96.8 she] She *UP*]
96.8 laughed;] laughed. *UP*]
96.8 she] She *UP*] *see textual note*
96.11 matter]matter. He was above himself, exalted. *UP*]

You can see the effect of this change more readily by reading the passage as it appeared in the proofs. To highlight the changes in sentence length, I have inserted hard returns at the end of each sentence. Furthermore, the phrases that disappear from the first edition are made bold in the proof's passage so you can see how Woolf streamlined the passage at the proof stage.

Uncorrected Proofs

Her voice, her laugh, her dress (something floating, white, crimson), her spirit, her adventurousness-- **there was something about her that night wild intoxicating, tender.**

She made them all disembark and explore the island—**a wretched little hump in the middle of the pond.**

She startled a hen, **or some heavy bird which flew up**.

She laughed.

She sang.

And all the time, he knew perfectly well, Dalloway was falling in love with her; she was falling in love with Dalloway; but it didn't seem to matter.

He was above himself, exalted.

Nothing mattered.

First British Edition

Her voice, her laugh, her dress (something floating, white, crimson), her spirit, her adventurousness; she made them all disembark and explore the island; she startled a hen; she laughed; she sang.

And all the time, he knew perfectly well, Dalloway was falling in love with her; she was falling in love with Dalloway; but it didn't seem to matter.

Nothing mattered.

A MAJOR CHANGE AT PROOF STAGE

The single most significant change at the proof stage is a change so major that I cannot claim to have discovered it—or even pretend for a moment to have noticed it first. The change is a single inserted typescript page in the proofs: it is pretty hard to miss. Morris Beja writes that, "Both it [the Raverat proofs] and the Harcourt set of proofs are corrected by Woolf in her favored purple ink, with a typescript (interestingly different in each case) inserted with revisions for the section on Septimus Warren Smith's death" (Beja 130). And

G. Patton Wright, in a more traditional bibliographic essay, slows down even more to note that:

> On 31 pages of the Raverat proofs (R), Woolf made over 50 emendations and inserted between pages 224 and 225 a typescript revision of the scene in which Septimus Smith commits suicide. All revises, except for this typescript and two pencil emendations on pages 175 and 184, are made in the same bright purple ink she used in correcting proofs for the first American edition (A1) and presumably for the first British edition (E1) as well. Given this evidence, we can conclude that all changes for Raverat were made after 6 February." (Wright 244)

Neither Beja nor Wright spend much more time than this on the change in their articles on editing *Mrs. Dalloway*. Appropriately enough, they do not offer readings of the scene; however, I differ strongly in my sense of the emphasis that this change warrants. It seems to me that Septimus' suicide is perhaps the single most important event in the novel and the fact that this scene is also the single scene to which Woolf made a substantive correction, one significant enough to entail inserting a new page, deserves some measured consideration, some rhetorical emphasis. Surely some Woolf readers and scholars interested in this novel would want to know that Woolf was rethinking Septimus' suicide in the very final stages of revision.

After all, we know from Woolf's diary that she struggled with writing the "mad scenes" in Regents Park: "I am now in the thick of the mad scene in Regents Park. I find I write it by clinging as tight to fact as I can, & write perhaps 50 words a morning" (*D2*.272; 15 October 1923; see also *D2*.321). And she wrote in 1928 that she had originally thought to have Clarissa kill herself: "in the first version Septimus, ... had no existence; and ... Mrs. Dalloway was originally to kill herself." ("Introduction" v). So, beyond the novel's plot—which is evidence enough—we have powerful documentation both of Woolf's sense of the suicide's centrality and of her struggle to write in the voice of madness..

Let me highlight the changes more clearly: what Woolf is doing here is narrating Septimus' thought process, humanizing him by having him consider all the available options. I have highlighted the most significant addition, but, as you can see, there are, in fact, many, many changes in the scene.

Uncorrected proofs
burst open the door. Holmes would say, "In a funk, eh?" Holmes would get him. But no; not Holmes; not Bradshaw.

There remained the window, the large Bloomsbury lodging-house window, the tiresome, the troublesome, and rather melodramatic business of opening the window and getting out on to the sill. It was their idea of tragedy, not his or Rezia's (for she was with him); Holmes and Bradshaw always insisted upon scenes like this. As for himself (he had raised himself on to the sill now--could see Mrs. Filmer's pots were down below) life was pleasant, the air cooler after the heat; he had no wish to die. But look at the old man in the house opposite, staring at him! Human nature--Here was Holmes. He flung himself vigorously violently down on to Mrs. Filmer's area railings.

First British edition
burst open the door. Holmes would say, "In a funk, eh?" Holmes would get him. But no; not Holmes ; not Bradshaw. **Getting up rather unsteadily, hopping indeed from foot to foot, he considered Mrs. Filmer's nice clean bread-knife with "Bread" carved on the handle. Ah, but one mustn't spoil that. The gas fire? But it was too late now. Holmes was coming. Razors he might have got, but Rezia, who always did that sort of thing, had packed them.** There remained only the window, the large Bloomsbury lodging-house window; the tiresome, the troublesome, and rather melodramatic business of opening the window and throwing himself out. It was their idea of tragedy, not his or Rezia's (for she was with him). Holmes and Bradshaw liked that sort of thing. (He sat on the sill.) But he would wait till the very last moment. He did not want to die. Life was good. The sun hot. Only human beings? Coming down the staircase opposite an old man stopped and stared at him. Holmes was at the door. "I'll give it you!" he cried, and flung himself vigorously, violently down on to Mrs. Filmer's area railings.

In bold is an addition of fifty-eight words which rejects three alternate methods of suicide before settling on jumping from the window. In thinking through his options, we also hear Septimus' consideration for his landlady, with her very ordinary attachment to a nice knife, and we learn another detail about his marriage to Rezia (not to mention his sense of intimacy with her in this last moment of life). In my estimation, this is a major change of very significant proportions and I have no intention of hiding my thesis in my introduction to the novel.

The task of a textual edition is *not* to make an argument about these changes, although possible arguments—about the significance of the flow of Peter's thoughts, about Woolf's sense that suicide can be a rational choice—spring to mind. Instead, the agreeable editorial challenge before me is to craft an introduction that helps readers decipher lists of minor changes without imposing a reading on them. Such an introduction can include a substantial discussion of the changes to the suicide scene, presented in a manner that invites future scholars' interpretations. With regard to the minor changes, too, the art of textual editing involves balancing guidance and minimal interpretation. I will strive to show future scholars what they might look for in those long lists of minor changes. My introduction must signal where patterns of changes lie, where Woolf focused her revisions at the proof stage, where the primary differences between the American and British editions appear. Certainly my interests and biases will emerge in this forthcoming edition, but, perhaps against the current of these narcissistic times, I continue to strive for that powerful combination of precision and restraint within the bounds of the edition itself. This said, none of this precludes my publishing my own emerging interpretations elsewhere, but that is an ambition for another day.

Works Cited

Beja, Morris, "Text and Counter-Text: Trying to Recover *Mrs. Dalloway.*" *Editing Virginia Woolf: Interpreting the Modernist Text.* Ed. James M. Haule and J. H. Stape. New York: Palgrave, 2002. 127-138.
Woolf, Virginia. *Diary.* Ed. Anne Olivier Bell. 5 vols. New York: Harcourt, 1977-84.
—.Introduction. *Mrs. Dalloway.* 1925. New York: Random House/The Modern Library, 1928. v-ix.
—. *Mrs. Dalloway.* American page proofs. Bloomington, IN: Lilly Library, Indiana University, 1925.
—. *Mrs. Dalloway.* Personal page proofs (Raverat proofs). Los Angeles: UCLA Library, 1925.
—. *Mrs. Dalloway.* London: Hogarth Press, 1925.
—. *Mrs. Dalloway.* G. Patton Wright, ed. London: Hogarth, 1990.
—. *Mrs. Dalloway.* Ed. Morris Beja. Shakespeare Head. Oxford: Blackwell, 1996.
Wright, G. Patton, "The Raverat Proofs of *Mrs. Dalloway.*" *Studies in Bibliography*, 39 (1986): 242-61.

Editing *Flush* and Woolf's Editing in *Flush*

by Linden Peach

This paper has a twin focus: my work preparing a scholarly edition of Virginia Woolf's *Flush* for Cambridge University Press and Woolf's own editing within the text. Woolf began writing *Flush*, the biography of Elizabeth Barrett Browning's spaniel, in June 1931. In a letter to Lady Ottoline Morrell, 23 February 1933, she admitted: "*Flush* is only by way of a joke. I was so tired after *The Waves*, that I lay in the garden and read the Browning love letters, and the figure of their dog made me laugh so I couldn't resist making him a Life" (*D5* 161-2). The first handwritten draft of *Flush*, which carried the title *The Life, Character and Opinions of Flush, the Spaniel*, was completed in April 1932. *Flush* was eventually printed as a serial in the American *Atlantic Monthly*, in four installments from July to October 1933, and as a book on October 5, 1933.

Although the editor of *Flush* does not have to deal with as many different versions as editors of some of the other novels, the work does give rise to issues which are unique to *Flush*. It is the only Woolf novel to have been published as a serial *and* a book, each of which has its own conventions and is written to specific reader expectations. In each case, the reading experience is a very different one; the reader of a serial has to wait for the next installment, but a reader of a book has only to turn a page to discover "what happened next."

In terms of content and organization, there are significant differences between the *Atlantic Monthly* and the book version of *Flush*. The first British edition is divided into five chapters: "Three Mile Cross," "The Back Bedroom," "The Hooded Man," "Whitechapel," "Italy," and "The End," together with illustrations and end pages consisting of "Authorities" and "Notes." The *Atlantic Monthly* version consists of four installments: "Flush A Biography by Virginia Woolf"; "Mr Browning in Wimpole Street"; "Wimpole Street and Whitechapel"; and "A Cocker Spaniel Recaptures His Youth." Clearly, the different chapter and installment titles will influence the reader's response. "The Hooded Man" carries different connotations from "Mr Browning in Wimpole Street" and "Wimpole Street and Whitechapel" invites readers to consider the comparison of the two areas in *Flush*.

The content of the four installments in the *Atlantic Monthly* does not correspond with the chapters in the first British edition. The first installment, divided into nine sections, concludes with the bond developing between Flush and Elizabeth Barrett and his memories, or ancestral memories, of being free in what seems a colonial Spanish landscape with "parrots and wild trumpeting elephants" ("Flush: A Biography" 12), which occurs toward the end of the second chapter in the first British edition. "Mr. Browning in Wimpole Street" includes material from Chapters Two and Three in the British edition: Flush's adjustment to being an invalid's companion, the change in Elizabeth which begins with her intimate correspondence with Robert Browning and Flush's theft. It concludes dramatically: "He was Stolen" ("Mr. Browning" 174). Although Chapter Three ends with the same cliff hanger, it has a different impact, for the reader simply has to turn the page to discover what happens next. The third installment is the first to have the same opening as a chapter in the novel. It is concerned with the attempts to retrieve Flush from the thieves and with Elizabeth and Robert's elopement. But whereas the chapter in the first British edition concludes dramatically with Elizabeth setting out to meet Robert at a London bookshop, the *Atlantic Monthly* installment concludes with their journey to, and arrival in, Italy which opens Chapter Five, "Italy," in the first British edition. The final *Atlantic Monthly* installment, "A Cocker Recaptures His Youth," constitutes the penultimate and final chapters of the first British edition.

However, it is not only the organization of material that is different in the magazine and book versions of *Flush*. *Flush* raises unique issues for the editor concerning paragraphing and punctuation. Paragraphing is a crucial factor in determining the reader's response to a text, but publication in a journal imposes a structure on a text which arises from page size and column inches. The installments of *Flush* are divided into shorter and more paragraphs than the book chapters and are further subdivided into sections. Punctuation is equally important in influencing a reader's response to a text, but the differences between the punctuation of *Flush* in the *Atlantic Monthly* and the British and American editions have not been noted in scholarly editions of *Flush*. The differences in punctuation in the British Hogarth edition compared with the *Atlantic Monthly* version are partly a result of the journal's own house style, partly a product of changes Woolf has made so that the punctuation better conforms to standard practice and partly changes which have been made to create new meanings or emphases within the text.

One of the most obvious typographical changes made to the *Atlantic Monthly* version in the book edition is the use of the hyphen. There are examples of words that are hyphenated in the *Atlantic Monthly* but not in the first British or American book editions, such as "well-groomed" and "wide-open." However, these are relatively few. By contrast a large number of words are hyphenated in the first British and the first American book editions but not in the *Atlantic Monthly* such as "to-day," "hide-and-seek," "flower-beds," "window-box," "top-hat," "swallow-tail," and "half-past." There are many examples of sentences in the first British and American book editions from which seemingly superfluous commas in the *Atlantic Monthly* version are removed and as many examples of sentences where punctuation is strategically added. For example, the description of Flush in the *Atlantic Monthly* as having "a face of a young animal instinct with health and energy" ("Flush: A Biography" 8) is changed significantly by the addition of a semi colon: "a young animal; instinct with …" (*F* 26; ch.1).

Some of these changes are rooted in Woolf's own editing aims for *Flush* to which she referred in her diary. On January 21, 1933, while working on the final version of *Flush*, Woolf admitted: "I always see something I could press tighter …" (*D4* 144). Certainly, there are places where the British edition is less wordy than the version in the *Atlantic Monthly*. For example, the account of Elizabeth Barrett Browning's visit to try to retrieve Flush from the thieves in the third installment of *Flush* in the *Atlantic Monthly* includes the following line: "After all, Miss Barrett had but glanced at the faces of those men for ten minutes from a cab and yet she remembered them all her life" ("Wimpole Street and Whitechapel" 334). But it is tightened in the first British edition: "After all, Miss Barrett had but glanced at the faces of those men and she remembered them all her life" (*F* 95; ch. 4). There are examples of occasions, too, when, in preparing the British edition, Woolf seems to have taken more care to be accurate. Thus, the "Heralds' Office" ("Flush: A Biography" 9) is replaced by the "Heralds' College" in the first British edition (*F* 11; ch.

1). The account of the thieves in the Whitechapel episode "plying their trade in the West End" ("Wimpole Street and Whitechapel" 327) is rendered more precisely in the first British edition: "plying their trade all day in the West End" (*F* 75; ch. 4). There are also examples of ambiguity in the *Atlantic Monthly* version that are removed in the first British and American editions. For example, in the account of American table rapping, the clause "of the tables" is added to the sentence "to decipher the messages conveyed by the legs" ("A Cocker Recaptures His Youth" 451) in order to make it explicit that the noun "legs" refers to the table legs and not the legs of the participants around the table (*F* 140; ch. 6). The account of Grand Ducal Court in the first British and American editions has an upper case "c" for "court" (*F* 109; ch. 5) removing an ambiguity created by the lower case "c" in the installment in the *Atlantic Monthly* version ("A Cocker Recaptures His Youth" 440) because "court" with a lower case "c" in Britain normally refers to courts of law.

For a work that began as a joke, Woolf engaged in a great deal of research and reading to which her list of authorities in the British and American editions testify. Thus, an important issue for any editor of *Flush* is the extent to which she works at the boundary between text and "intertext." An example is the way in which the Spaniel Club is used as a trope within the novel. At one point, drawing on Hugh Dalziel's *British Dogs*, Woolf declares with reference to the Spaniel Club: "No Club has any such jurisdiction upon the breed of man" (*F* 11; ch.1). The use of the word "jurisdiction" continues the judicial metaphor from the previous paragraph into speculation as to whether the Heralds' College might be seen as a human equivalent of the Spaniel Club. As Francis Galton's influential paper "The Possible Improvement of the Human Breed Under the Existing Conditions of Law and Sentiment" suggests, the word "breed" was used in the early twentieth century in relation to the human race in discourse about the degeneration of human genetic potential (as the Spaniel Club talked of preventing the degeneration of the breed).

Before considering further Woolf's editing of her sources in *Flush*, it is important to note that another textual boundary as far as *Flush* is concerned is the extent to which the installments in the *Atlantic Monthly* relate to other articles in the numbers in which they were published. The first installment of *Flush* was the first article in the number of the *Atlantic Monthly* in which it was published and the only installment to be allocated this prestigious position. It was followed by another mock biography, George J. Anderson's "The Big Pepper and Brine Man," a "biography" of Peter Piper of Piper's Pickled Peppers. Woolf complained about her biography of Elizabeth Barrett Browning's spaniel in her letter to Frederick B. Adams, March 14, 1933, that "in fact very little is known about him, and I have had to invent a great deal" (*L5* 167). Anderson suggests that he has had a similar problem, alleging that Peter Piper was secretive about "personal dates, such a birth, marriage, and the like" ("The Big Pepper and Brine Man" 4). There is no external evidence that these two articles were deliberately juxtaposed as spoof biographies. However, the readers of the *Atlantic Monthly* were offered two works in juxtaposition which challenged the conventions of biography.

As mentioned above, the first installment of *Flush* also highlighted the importance that the Kennel Club attached to dogs being "pure bred" and how the rules of the Kennel Club were designed to preserve the best strain of a particular breed in order to prevent its physical degeneracy over generations. The October 1933 *Atlantic Monthly* includes Alice Hamilton's review of the 1933 edition of Adolf Hitler's *Mein Kampf* which stresses its implicit comparison between the obligations of ensuring a pure German race and the necessity of maintaining a good breed in husbandry: "The pure German stock is superior to others, and it is the highest duty of the state to foster this stock and prevent its 'bastardization' by admixture with inferior stocks" ("Hitler Speaks" 405). This emphasis upon purity in National Socialist ideology resonates with the first page of the fourth installment of *Flush* about thirty pages later in the journal: "He was the only pure-bred cocker spaniel in the whole of Pisa" (Woolf, "A Cocker Recaptures His Youth" 439).

Since Woolf relied on a select range of sources to a considerable extent in writing *Flush*, a final issue which arises in regard to this text, which does not emerge in relation to Woolf's other works in as sustained a way, is her use of source material. The principal sources—Dazliel's *British Dogs*, Beames's *The Rookeries of London* and the love letters of Elizabeth Barrett and Robert Browning—are very different from each other and perhaps not the kind of works that Woolf generally read. Each is relied upon at different points in the text and there are numerous examples of Woolf creatively recasting material from her sources. For example, at one point in Elizabeth Barrett Browning's account in her correspondence with Robert Browning of going to find the thieves that had taken Flush, she observes that they are greeted as if their mission is already known, "mark that no name had been mentioned" (*L2* 526). In *Flush*, Woolf changes what Browning wrote in order to stress the vulnerability of two women in this area and to make more ominous the fact that they were expected: "a cab with two ladies could only come upon one errand and that errand was already known'" (*F* 90; ch. 4). In her letter to Robert Browning, Elizabeth Barrett Browning observes that "we got into obscure streets; and our cabman stopped at a public house to ask the way" (*Letters2* 526). Woolf changes Elizabeth Barrett Browning's "obscure streets" to a "region unknown to respectable cab-drivers" (*F* 89; ch. 4). The effect is to emphasise that Barrett Browning is entering an area that is more than "obscure"; it includes much of which a woman of Barrett Browning's class would have had no experience, and which poses a threat to "respectable" people who would immediately stand out as potential victims of crime.

Woolf's creative rewriting of her sources frequently extended to "retextualizing," by which I mean that source material was lifted out of its original context and placed in a context where it acquired new-found significance. For example, drawing on Dalziel's *British Dogs*, Woolf maintains that the spaniel's origins can be traced to a time when Spain was seething in creation. The reference in *Flush* to a time when "Spain seethed uneasily in the ferment of creation" (*F* 7; ch. 1) would have had a particular resonance in the early 1930s when the Second Spanish Republic was proclaimed in April 1931. Often, retextualizing involved a network of carefully employed allusions. For example, references to Flush being collared and led on a chain bring to mind Elizabeth Barrett Browning's family's slave plantations in the East Indies, mentioned in the text, and her poem about Hiram Powers' "Greek Slave," a sculpture in Florence of a naked female Greek slave in chains which became an abolitionist symbol.

Thus, *Flush* develops Woolf's interest, evident also in *Orlando*, in challenging the boundaries between "scholarly research," "fiction," and "biography." The text provides examples where sometimes sources are disclosed but at other times concealed, examples of verbatim quotation and examples of rewording. Moreover, sometimes materials from different sources are conflated and sometimes the chronology of the sequence of letters which she uses is ignored. Indeed, Woolf's own list of authorities in the novel is problematic and possibly deliberately provocative. It begins with Woolf's own qualification: "It must be admitted that there are very few authorities for the foregoing biography" (*F* 151; Authorities). Some of her sources are included such as Elizabeth Barrett Browning's own poem about Flush, the correspondence of Robert and Elizabeth Browning upon which she relied heavily, the various additional collections of Elizabeth's letters on which she also drew, the letters of Mary Russell Mitford and Thomas Beames's *The Rookeries of London*. Woolf's research notebook includes source material from Hugh Dalziel's *British Dogs* upon which Woolf relied extensively but did include in her list of Authorities. However, the research notebook omits Beames's *The Rookeries* which is included in her Authorities but listed differently from the other sources. It is included in a way which appears to belie her extensive use of it in the Whitechapel chapter: "For an account of London Rookeries, *The Rookeries of London*, by Thomas Beames, 1850, may be consulted"(*F* 151; Authorities). Mrs Sutherland Orr's *Life and Letters of Browning* is cited in her own notes to the text, referring to Robert Browning's yellow gloves, but is not included in her list of Authorities. Her account of the Mitfords is heavily dependent, occasionally verbatim, on A. G. L'Estrange's *The Life of Mary Russell Mitford* (1870) which is again omitted from the Authorities and is not cited in the text.

Although it has only been possible in a relatively short paper to suggest the importance of *Flush*, it is clearly a significant text in which Woolf's editing and retextualizing of her source material reveal the novel's cryptic engagement with serious themes, such as eugenics and slavery. It develops Woolf's interest in working at the boundaries of text and intertext and of biography, scholarly research and fiction. Published as a serial and in book form, it provides insights into the differences between these modes and offers further insights into Woolf's own "editing": her juxtaposition of source materials; her interleaving of verbatim material with paraphrase; and her creative adaptation of her sources.

Works Cited

Anderson, George J. "The Big Pepper and Brine Man." *Atlantic Monthly* 152 (July 1933): 13-25.
Beames, Thomas. *The Rookeries of London*. London: T. Bosworth, 1850.
Browning, Robert, and Elizabeth Barrett Browning. *Letters*. Ed Robert W. B. Browning. London: Smith, Elder, 1899.
Dalziel, Hugh. *British Dogs: Describing the History, Characteristics, Breeding, Management, and Exhibition of the Various Breeds, of Dogs Established in Great Britain*. 2 vols. London: L. Upcott Gill, 1888.
Galton, Francis. "The Possible Improvement of the Human Breed under the Existing Conditions of Law and Sentiment." *Nature* 64 (1901): 161-4.
Hamilton, Alice. "Hitler Speaks: His Book Reveals the Man." *Atlantic Monthly* 152 (Oct. 1933): 399-408.
Woolf, Virgina. *Flush*. London: Hogarth Press, 1933.
—. "Flush: A Biography." *Atlantic Monthly* 152 (July 1933): 1-12.
—. "Mr.Browning in Wimpole Street." *Atlantic Monthly* 152 (Aug. 1933): 163-174.
—. "Wimpole Street and Whitechapel." *Atlantic Monthly* 152 (Sept. 1933): 326-337.
—. "A Cocker Recaptures His Youth." *Atlantic Monthly* 152 (Oct. 1933): 439-453.
—. *The Letters of Virginia Woolf*. Eds. Nigel Nicolson and Joanne Trautmann. 6 vols. London: Hogarth, 1975-80.
—. *The Diary of Virginia Woolf*. Eds. Anne Olivier Bell and Andrew McNellie. 5 vols. Harmondsworth: Penguin, 1979 -85.

RE-VISIONING PHILANTHROPY AND WOMEN'S ROLES: VIRGINIA WOOLF, PROFESSIONALIZATION, AND THE PHILANTHROPY DEBATES

by Milena Radeva

Recent criticism has challenged the divide between high modernism and mass culture.[1] Michael Tratner's *Modernism and Mass Politics* and other recent critiques of the relationship of Virginia Woolf's fiction and class (such as Fuhito Endo's analysis of the middle-class "paranoiac fantasy" of working class violence in *To the Lighthouse*)[2] have focused on Woolf's insights into and anxieties about Labour and mass politics in Britain between the wars. Alex Zwerdling's earlier work, *Virginia Woolf and the Real World*, devotes a chapter to "Class and Money" and another to "*Mrs. Dalloway* and the Social System." Yet no studies to my knowledge have focused on the particular ways in which the discourse of philanthropy mediates women's relationship to the public sphere in Woolf's fiction.

In this paper, I discuss the prominence of philanthropy in Woolf's novel *Mrs. Dalloway, To the Lighthouse,* in her essay "Memories of a Working Women's Guild" (1930), and to a lesser extend in *The Years*. With the eclipse of the "Old Philanthropy" (private, unpaid, haphazard, and largely dominated by women) and its transformation into the "New Philanthropy" (professional, scientific, masculine, and state-governed), upper middle class women, once prominent within philanthropic activities, had to work to overcome a change in their status "from (unpaid) influence to (paid) oblivion" (Lewis, 203).[3] I argue that Virginia Woolf's portrayal of philanthropic women addresses these sweeping changes in women's private and public lives at the cusp of the twentieth century. Woolf's novels and essay powerfully assert both the increasing need for professionalization of women's work and the continuing cultural transformation of the idea of giving, an idea especially popular and contested at the moment of the birth of the British welfare state.

Many of Woolf's major novels present sympathetic portraits of upper-middle class women philanthropists. In *Mrs. Dalloway*, Clarissa strives to live up to the ideal of the philanthropic Lady Bexborough; Mrs. Ramsay from *To the Lighthouse* wants her charity to be more than "half a sop for her own indignation, half a relief to her own curiosity" (*TTL* 9); and in *The Years* a sarcastic onlooker characterizes Eleanor Pargiter as "a well-known type; with a bag; philanthropic; well nourished; a spinster; a virgin; like all the women of her class, cold; her passions had never been touched; yet not unattractive" (*TY* 102). On the other hand, Woolf's fiction envisions a new generation of professional women—women like Elizabeth Dalloway, Lily Briscoe and Peggy Pargiter—who abandon the values and strictures of their mothers' generation in favor of joining the professions (veterinary science, painting, and medicine), and who preserve, and redefine, the ability to give. These "New Women" carve out a space for women's individual gifts in the male domain of the professions.

The importance of the cultural shift from private to state-run welfare measures at the turn of the twentieth century, a transition that is continually inscribed and reworked in Woolf's women characters, cannot be underestimated as it continues to inspire our thinking about giving and philanthropy today. In his well-known 1991 essay on the gift *Given Time*, Jacques Derrida returns to the late nineteenth and the early twentieth century through his analysis of Baudelaire's story "Counterfeit Money" and Marcel Mauss's 1925 anthropological work *The Gift*. For Derrida, the gift excludes reciprocity, exchange, return, debt; it "is annulled each time there is restitution or countergift" (Derrida, *Given Time* 12). Furthermore, in order for this condition to be satisfied, the gift must be forgotten in an absolute way: "It is thus necessary, at the limit, that [the donor] not *recognize* the gift as gift" (Derrida 13). From this perspective, philanthropy is impossible, as well as any gift giving, or at least any giving, says Derrida, "where there is subject and object" (24). Virginia Woolf's early twentieth-century writing on philanthropy poses the same problem of the impossible yet always desirable gift in advance of Derrida's essay.

For Virginia Woolf, as well as for Derrida, neither the state-based economy of gift-giving nor philanthropy represents true giving. In Woolf's writing, a panoply of philanthropic endeavors (from Lady Bexborough's bazaars to Richard Dalloway's Acts of Parliament to Miss Kilman's contributions to charitable causes) suggests that philanthropy is at best a transcendental illusion, a bestowing of privileges that entails obligations, and at worst a thinly-disguised and self-serving attempt to wield power and exercise control. Yet Woolf's repeated accounts of the (im)possibility of sympathy—for example in Woolf's uneasiness about class alliances in "Memories of a Working Women's Guild"—bear witness to the importance of the transformation of private charity into professional social work for early twentieth-century women. Woolf's "New Women" refashion philanthropy so that it is not simply "philanthropy up-to-date" but perhaps a true gift, one that hides its own origin and intent from the giver and that blurs the boundaries between self-seeking and sympathy to others.[4]

WOOLF'S WOMEN AND THE SYMPATHETIC IMAGINATION

Woolf's "philanthropic" upper middle class women offer an insider's criticism of philanthropy as class privilege. According to nineteenth century historians Martha Vicinus and Frank Prochaska, philanthropy provided privileged women with a convenient venue into the public world and enabled them to develop the skills they needed to join the professions.[5] However, in Woolf's fiction Mrs. Ramsay, Mrs. Dalloway, and even minor characters such as Lady Bruton acutely feel their lack of skills and formal training. Many of Woolf's "philanthropic women" either question the class privilege their philanthropy implies or themselves serve as a criticism of patronage and the "new," scientific philanthropy. In earlier versions of Clarissa and Richard in Woolf's first novel *The Voyage Out* and in "Mrs. Dalloway in Bond Street," Woolf depicts the Dalloways as a hypocritical and self-deceiving upper middle class couple. Rachel Vinrace, the inexperienced protagonist of *The Voyage Out*, is shocked by the sudden and passionate kiss of Richard Dalloway, a married man she knows as a respectable Conservative MP, "a battered martyr, parting every day with some of the finest gold, in the service of mankind" (*VO* 35). Rachel learns that upper-class philanthropists like Richard Dalloway are "humbugs" and "second-rate" (*VO* 47), and their charming accomplished wives (Clarissa) are superficial and vacuous.

In "Mrs. Dalloway in Bond Street" philanthropy or service to others is the stated reason for the existence of a dying class that has cut itself off from the realities of politics and the trauma of war (*Party* 21-22). Mrs. Dalloway in Bond Street explicitly opposes women's suffrage[6] (*Party* 13) and admires the Queen (a "thoroughly nice woman" [*Party* 13]), "the excellent policeman" (*Party* 17), and Lady Bexborough. Even though Clarissa and Miss Anstruther claim class superiority and character, in the end Clarissa is self-centered, and Miss Anstruther is bossy with the shop attendant, a "grey-headed woman" (*Party* 19, 22). Clarissa, who addresses the "girl" with "exquisite friendliness" (18), and sympathizes with her about her long hours behind the counter (20), is so impatient to finish her transaction that she "play[s] her finger on the counter" and thinks with voiceless sarcasm, "My dear slowcoach, [...] do you think I can sit here the whole morning? Now you'll take twenty-five minutes to bring me my change!" (*Party* 23).[7]

Despite the harsh indictments of the "public-spirit" of the British upper middle class in these earlier versions of Richard and Clarissa, the novel *Mrs. Dalloway* holds by far the most sympathetic portrait of Clarissa. Even though Clarissa shocks readers with her indifference to the Armenian genocide of 1914-1918, she has the intellectual honesty to admit this, an honesty that the two earlier Clarissas (in *The Voyage Out* and "Mrs. Dalloway in Bond Street") lack: "She cared much more for her roses than for the Armenians. Hunted out of existence, maimed, frozen, the victims of cruelty and injustice ... no, she could feel nothing for the Albanians, or was it the Armenians? But she loved her roses" (*MD* 120).[8] She also is able to sympathize (and possibly make alliances) with countrymen far removed from her class, experience, and even gender—from "the veriest frumps, the most dejected of miseries sitting on doorsteps (drink their downfall)" (*MD* 4) to the World War One veteran Septimus Smith, suffering from shell shock. In the climax of the novel, Clarissa has an emotional response to and an almost bodily experience of Septimus' suicide: "Always her body went through it first, when she was told, suddenly, of an accident; her dress flamed, her body burnt. He had thrown himself from a window. Up had flashed the ground; through him, blundering, bruising, went the rusty spikes. There he lay with a thud, thud, thud in his brain, and then a suffocation of blackness" (*MD* 184). As critics have noted, Septimus and Clarissa share a marginal status of being excluded from power, the power that Sir Bradshaw, the eminent psychiatrist, wields in order to preserve the status quo. *Mrs. Dalloway* suggests that Woolf privileges the sympathetic imagination over the philanthropic pretensions of the British ruling class and over the institutions and practices intent on preserving the privileges of this ruling class, such as psychiatry.

Between Old Philanthropy and the New

According to many historians, the British of the early twentieth century perceived themselves as a *laissez faire* society with a long-standing tradition "of political skepticism and social self-sufficiency, a continuing belief that, for better or worse, there were limits to what governments could do to alter the state of the world" (Harris 84). Yet at the same time, the early twentieth century saw the entrance of the masses in politics and the nascent welfare state. Between 1906 and 1915 the liberal administrations of Campbell-Bannerman and Asquith passed a number of proto-welfare measures such as the National Insurance Act (1911), the Education (Provision of Meals) Acts (1906 and 1914), Education (Administrative Provisions) Act (1907), Notification of Births Acts (1907 and 1915), Probation Act (1907), Children Act (1908), Old Age Pensions Act (1908), Housing and Town Planning Act (1909), and the Trade Board Act (1909). Contemporaries perceived this evolution of social policy and the heightened interest in charity organization as a "New Philanthropy."

An article published by Samuel Barnett in *The Contemporary Review* in 1911 sums up this new vision of systematic social policy: "Charity up-do-date, whether it be from person to person or through some society or fund, must be such as is approved by the same close thinking as business men give to their business, or politicians to their policy" (Barnett 225). Barnett compares philanthropists to physicians, who "must get the facts for a right diagnosis, and bring to the cure all the resources of civilization" (Barnett 225).[9] While Wyndham Lewis feared that such "effeminizing" social policies would put us back in the nursery,[10] Virginia Woolf's fiction examined the conflict between old philanthropy and the new in the private lives of middle-class women.

Almost all of the characters in Virginia Woolf's second modernist novel, *Mrs. Dalloway*, are involved in some form of philanthropic activity. Clarissa's husband Richard Dalloway, a Conservative MP, sits on numerous parliamentary committees designed to redress social ills; every walk in London reminds him of the London traffic, the malpractices of the police, costermongers in the streets, prostitutes, and the poor who all need his intervention. Lady Bexborough and Lady Millicent Bruton, Miss Kilman, Peter Walsh, Doctor and Lady Bradshaw, Hugh Whitbread and others are concerned with a great number of philanthropic projects: emigration to Canada, immigration from the third world, child welfare, the after care of the epileptic, prostitution, poverty, public morality, protection of birds in Norfolk, female vagrancy, the malpractices of the police, charitable bazaars, a Bill concerning shell-shocked soldiers from the War, and undernourished children in military training. Richard and Hugh go to help Lady Bruton write a letter to further the cause of emigration to Canada; and so on. This variety of projects suggests the immense significance of the philanthropic projects for the doomed ruling class in *Mrs. Dalloway* seeking to preserve its social position and swept by the ideas of the rising British welfare state and Labour politics.

Mrs. Dalloway and *To the Lighthouse* register both the upper middle class discomfort with the new, working-class, perspiring philanthropists like Miss Kilman and Charles Tanseley and their nostalgia for the rarified ideal of *noblesse oblige*.[11] *Mrs. Dalloway* dwells favorably on the charity of upper-class men and women such as Lady Bexborough and Richard Dalloway, M.P., and it marginalizes shabby philanthropists such as Miss Kilman. The Dalloways admire "these great swells, these Duchesses, these hoary old Countesses" and "the publicspirited, British Empire, tariff-reform, governing-class spirit" that they represent (*MD* 76). Clarissa idealizes Lady Bexborough and wants to be Lady Bexborough: "She would have been, in the first place, dark like Lady Bexborough, with a skin of crumpled leather and beautiful eyes. She would have been, like Lady Bexborough, slow and stately, rather large; interested in politics like a man; with a country house; very dignified, very sincere" (*MD* 10). In a revealing passage at the end of the novel Clarissa identifies Lady Bexborough with success: "She had wanted success. Lady Bexborough and the rest of it" (*M D* 185). The image of Lady Bexborough mourning for her favourite son's death in the war, her "perfectly right and stoical bearing" (*MD* 10) as she opens a bazaar with the telegram announcing his death in her hand, becomes fused with Clarissa's idealization of and nostalgia for *noblesse oblige*. For Clarissa as well as for Mrs. Ramsay, such power seems unattainable because of the rigidity that defines the barrier between the classes in the British system.

In contrast to Lady Bexborough stand working class philanthropists such as Doris Kilman and Charles Tansley. Tansley and Kilman, I would argue, stand for the anxieties that surrounded the birth of redistributive social policies in Britain and the rise to power of the Labour party, the same formidable party that will put Richard Dalloway out of parliamentary work (*MD* 111).[12] With her old mackintosh coat and her self-denial (she spares money from her meager income for causes she believes in), Miss Kilman challenges the philanthropy of establishment ladies who "did nothing, believed nothing" (*MD* 125). Clarissa criticizes Miss Kilman's self-righteous philanthropy as power-grabbing and a form of conversion, yet the very description of Miss Kilman calls forth class stereotypes and suggests the turn of the twentieth-century uneasiness about the claim of the working classes to political power: "Year after year she wore that coat; she perspired; she was never in the room five minutes without making you feel her superiority, your inferiority; how poor she was; how rich you were…—poor embittered unfortunate creature!" (*MD* 12).

Woolf's next novel, *To the Lighthouse,* presents a slightly more palatable version of a working class philanthropist in the character of Charles Tansley. Mr. Ramsay's philosophy student, Tansley is a working class intellectual who dreams about "settlements, and teaching, and working men, and helping his own class, and lectures" (*TTL* 12). Like Miss Kilman, Tansley is awkward, poor, and abrasive, especially in his interactions with upper middle class women; Lily Briscoe exposes Tansley's male chauvinism, his "[standing] behind her smoking shag ... and making it his business to tell her women can't write, women can't paint" (*TTL* 197). When Lily sees Charles "preaching brotherly love" from a platform, she satirizes the discrepancy between his insensitive private self and his philanthropic public persona: her reminds her of "the red, energetic, shiny ants" among the plantains. At the same time, however, Lily finally realizes that the Charles Tansley she detests is to some extent a construction of her own imagination, her "whipping boy" (*TTL* 197). Lily's feminist anger has partially dissolved in the general feeling of loss and dislocation after the First World War: "'Shag tobacco,' he said, 'fivepence an ounce,' parading his poverty, his principles. (But the war had drawn the sting of her femininity. Poor devils, one thought, of both sexes.)" (*TTL* 159).

The completion of Lily's painting in the end of the novel illustrates the importance of the Old and the New Philanhropy for the professional self-fashioning of Woolf's women characters. Though she is hindered by Charles's prejudice, Lily might be also partially inspired by his assertiveness. Lily's first flash of inspiration about the painting occurs during the dinner scene in *To the Lighthouse* when she resolves to "put the tree further in the middle" (*TTL* 84); this resolve immediately becomes associated with Charles and his obnoxious self-assertiveness: "he sat opposite to her with his back to the window precisely in the middle of the view," setting "his spoon precisely in the middle of the plate" and "[e]verything about him ha[s] that meagre fixity, that bare unloveliness" (*TTL* 85). Just before she puts the final strokes on her picture, Lily thinks again how "at dinner [Charles] would sit right in the middle of the view" (*TTL* 159). I would argue that despite the evident middle class anxiety about the New Philanthropy and Labour politics in Woolf's novels, Woolf's independent women such as Lily Briscoe follow the example of successful antagonists like Charles Tansley into the public sphere of the professions.

Lily's painting of Mrs. Ramsay also marks the resolution of her struggle with feminine compassion and philanthropy. After Mrs. Ramsay's death, Lily revisits the summer house of the Ramsay family and finds Mr. Ramsay's demands for sympathy and attention destructive of her concentration as an artist: "he permeated, he prevailed, he imposed himself. He changed everything. She could not see the colour; she could not see the lines" (*TTL* 149). Fearful of Mr. Ramsay's need for sympathy, and unable to express her compassion when it really comes (*TTL* 170), Lily grapples with the memory of the late Mrs. Ramsay: Mrs. Ramsay had given. Giving, giving, giving, she had died—and had left all this. Really, she was angry with Mrs. Ramsay" (*TTL* 149). Lily thinks that "it was all Mrs. Ramsay's fault" (150). Lily needs to vanquish the spirit of her symbolic mother, the womanly, maternal Mrs. Ramsay, in order to finish her painting.

Yet in the process of painting, Lily "re-fashions" her memories of Mrs. Ramsay and Charles. She comes to recognize Mrs. Ramsay's compassion as an artistic endeavor and to see Mrs. Ramsay as an artist as well: she creates by "making of the moment something permanent (as in another sphere Lily herself tried to make the moment permanent)." In this moment of Mrs. Ramsay's making, Lily and Charles leave behind their "squabbling, sparring, …silly and spiteful" and become friends and allies: "this scene on the beach for example, this moment of friendship and liking—which survived, after all these years complete, so that [Lily] dipped into it to re-fashion her memory of [Charles], and there it stayed in the mind affecting one almost like a work of art" (*TTL* 160). Lily returns to Mrs. Ramsay's moment as to an "illumination," her one "revelation" about the meaning of life: "herself and Charles Tansley and the breaking wave." Instead of anger, she now feels gratitude for Mrs. Ramsay: "She owed it all to her" (*TTL* 161).

Woolf evokes the language of gratitude and giving also in her description of Lily's creative process. Lily's painting beckons her with the anguish that Mr. Ramsay's demands and Mrs. Ramsay's gives: "Why always be drawn out and haled away? Why not left in peace…?" Painting Mrs. Ramsay reading a story to James makes Lily feel "like an unborn soul, a soul reft of body, hesitating on some windy pinnacle and exposed without protection to all the blasts of doubt" (*TTL* 158). Finally, Lily (like Mrs. Ramsay on another occasion) feels "extreme fatigue" (Woolf, *Lighthouse* 209). When she finishes the painting, Lily feels that she has somehow given Mr. Ramsay sympathy: "Whatever she had wanted to give him, when he left her that morning, she had given him at last" (*TTL* 208). In the anguish and rapture of creation, Lily calls out a vision of Mrs. Ramsay on the empty steps of the house, and draws that last line in the center of her painting that finally completes her work of art. Like Mrs. Ramsay herself, the painting has brought together Lily's memories and given flesh to all of Lily's relationships to the Ramsays and their guests.

"Fictitious Sympathy" and "Memories of a Working Women's Guild"

Mrs. Dalloway, *To the Lighthouse*, and Woolf's later essay "Memories of a Working Women's Guild" (1930) share a concern with the limits and authenticity of sympathy which suggests Derrida's definition of the gift as a striving towards the impossible (*Given Time* 4-5). Woolf's analysis of the unbridgeable divide between working class women and their middle class highbrow counterparts, "Memories of a Working Women's Guild," revisits once again "the nature of fictitious sympathy and how it differs from real sympathy and how defective it is because it is not based upon sharing the same important emotions unconsciously" (142).[13] Even if philanthropy and sympathy for Woolf are problematic, her persistent reworking of the theme of women's relationship to philanthropy and sympathy follows Derrida's injunction, "*Know* still what giving *wants to say, know how to give,* know what you want and what to say when you give, know what you intended to give, know how the gift annuls itself, commit yourself [*engage-toi*] even if commitment is the destruction of the gift, give economy its chance" (*Given Time* 30).

When she wrote "Memories of a Working Women's Guild" Woolf had already problematized her difficulty with sympathy in *Mrs. Dalloway* and *To the Lighthouse*. Clarissa's preference for her roses over the Armenians parallels Lily Briscoe's, William Bankes' and Mrs. Ramsay's fear that their indifference to wages and unemployment will be exposed: "for each thought, 'The others are feeling this. They are outraged and indignant with the government about the fishermen. Whereas, I feel nothing at all'" (*TTL* 94). Similarly, the narrator in "Memories" is an upper middle class outsider critical of her own lack of emotional response to the working women's demands at the Congress of the Women's Co-operative Guild. She feels that her sympathy is "too much of a game" (137); it is "the sympathy of the eye and the imagination, not of the heart and the nerves; and such a sympathy is always physically uncomfortable" ("Memories" 140). This withholding of sympathy, I would argue, is not a sign of declining philanthropic interest, but a symptom of a better, more critical understanding of the elusive nature of the gift.

Woolf's essay on the women's guild suggests that the problem of sympathy lies in the embodied nature of experience and makes this problem appear, at least for the time being, insurmountable. On the one hand, the narrator's wishes that her sympathy for the working women be more than "fictious" (140), "merely altruistic" (136), and lacking in feeling and that the working women's speeches could change from "mist and blankness" to "blood and bone" ("Memories" 137). Yet even though authentic sympathy depends on such embodiment, it is this very embodiment that also makes the writer's sympathy for the women of the co-operative guild impossible: "One could not be Mrs.Giles because one's body had never stood at the wash-tub; one's hands had never wrung and scrubbed and chopped up whatever the meat may be that makes a miner's dinner" ("Memories" 137). Having thus defined the problem of sympathy as a problem of the embodied human being, the speaker nevertheless wishes for the "great liberation" that would follow if upper-class ladies could "meet" these working women outside of philanthropy, "not as sympathizers, as masters and mistresses with counters between us or kitchen tables, but casually and congenially as fellow beings with the same ends and wishes even if the dress and body are different" ("Memories" 141).

In "Memories of a Working Women's Guild" as well as in her novels, Woolf unmasks both philanthropy and sympathy as manifestations of power but affirms the desire for sympathy and communion with others. This desire is clear in her volcanic images of sisterhood between upper-class and working class women: "this force of [the working women], this smouldering heat which broke the crust now and then and licked the surface with a hot and fearless flame, is about to break through and melt us together …but only when we are dead" ("Memories" 142). Like Derrida, Woolf does not definitively deny the possibility of such authentic sympathy outside of philanthropy, but she locates it in the indefinite and remote future and beyond the earthly possibilities of our lifetimes.

Notes

1. After Michael Levenson's insightful study of modernist character and form, *Modernism and the Fate of Individuality* (1991), a number of scholars have helped reorient the discussion of modernism and mass

culture and establish modernist fiction in its cultural and historical context, or what Levenson calls "the crisis of liberalism, the challenge to Eurocentrism, the advance of bureaucracy, the contest between men and women" (Levenson xiii). **Paul Peppis**, for instance, discusses the place of nationalism, empire, and reactionary politics in the formation of the English avant-garde. **Mark Morrisson** examines modernists' engagement with mass culture ("advertising practices, discourses of youth, education, and the purity of language in oral performance; the tactics of suffragist, anarchist, and socialist political movements; understanding of racial and ethnic difference in America; and the institutions of the publishing industry") and argues that early modernism was not a mere matter of coterie consumption but was engaged with the public sphere and with the commercial culture of the early twentieth century" (Morrisson 10). **Janet Lyon** investigates modernist manifestoes in their intersecting historical contexts; **Jennifer Wicke, Reginald Abbott, David Chinitz and Sebastian Knowles** query the connection of modernism to pop culture and consumption; and **Michael Tratner** challenges the critical commonplace about modernist individualism and claims that "modernism was an effort to escape the limitations of nineteenth century individualist conventions and write about distinctively 'collectivist' phenomena" (Tratner 3). These critical perspectives represent an emerging vision of modernism as deeply embedded in the political and social events of the time, at once shaping and being shaped by the turbulent early decades of the twentieth century.

2. Fuhito Endo. "Radical Violence Inside Out: Woolf, Klein, and Interwar Politics." *Twentieth Century Literature*, 52.2 (Summer 2006): 175-98.

3. Jane Lewis, "Women, social work and social welfare in twentieth-century Britain: from (unpaid) influence to (paid) oblivion." See Martin Daunton, *Charity, Self-Interest and Welfare in the English Past* (New York: St. Martin's P, 1996).

4. For Derrida, the gift excludes reciprocity, exchange, return, debt: "For there to be a gift, there must be no reciprocity, return, exchange, countergift, or debt. If the other *gives* me *back* or *owes* me or has to give me back what I give him or her, there will not have been a gift, whether this restitution is immediate or whether it is programmed by complex calculation of a long-term deferral or difference" (Derrida, *Given Time* 12). Thus, for Derrida, the gift "is annulled each time there is restitution or countergift" (*Given Time* 12). See Derrida, *Given Time,* 12-13.

5. Philanthropy helped women prove their capacity for holding a public office and in 1893, it was estimated that some 500,000 women worked "continuously and semi-professionally" in charities, 200,000 were "paid officials," 20,000 practiced as trained nurses, and at least 200,000 more worked part-time for charity (Prochaska, Women 224). The skills that women acquired in these associations were later applied to the suffrage movement and in acquiring positions in local government (Prochaska, Women 226). The more women entered the professions, the more "emotionalism, religiosity, and close domestic ties of traditional women had to be replaced with rationality, scientific knowledge, and corporate loyalties" (Vicinus 41). On the other hand, the success of women's professions depended also on the prosperity of women's colleges, on women's "canvassing for money, convincing parents and young women, and even testifying before government committees" (Vicinus 41).

6. Mrs. Dalloway on Bond Street thinks, "How then could women sit in Parliament? How could they do things with men? For there is this extraordinarily deep instinct, something inside one; you can't get over it; it's no use trying; and men like Hugh respect it without saying it" (*Party* 13).

7. In "Mrs. Dalloway in Bond Street" Clarissa justifies her life with service to others: "[f]or one doesn't live for oneself, thought Clarissa (*Party* 22). Although she does not believe any more in God (*Party* 21), she continues to emulate the virtues of her class: "like Lady Bexborough, who opened the bazaar, they say, with the telegram in her hand—Roden, he favorite, killed—she [Clarissa] would go on. But why, if one doesn't believe? For the sake of others, she thought taking the glove in her hand. The girl would be much more unhappy if she didn't believe" (*Party* 21-22).

8. This reference probably addresses the exodus and massacre of Armenians in the Ottoman empire in 1914-1918. Clarissa's response contrasts with William Gladstone's outrage at the similar Bulgarian massacres in the nineteenth century. In his article, "The Armenian Genocide: An Interpretation," Stephan Astourian establishes the intentional character of the Armenian deportations and their genocidal nature as precursors to the Nazi Holocaust. He states that "[a]t least a million and a half Armenians perished out of a total population of about two and a half million" and quotes Talât Paşha, the then Minister of the Interior, as saying that "the Porte wanted to take advantage of the world war to thoroughly get rid of its internal enemies, the indigenous Christians, without being disturbed by foreign diplomatic intervention." ("The Armenian Genocide: An Interpretation. *The History Teacher,* 23. 2, 1990: 114, 116).

9. [Philanthropists] must be students of personality and of the State. They must consider the individual who is in need or the charitable body which makes an appeal, as carefully as a physician considers his case; they must

get the facts for a right diagnosis, and bring to the cure all the resources of civilization ... Charity up-do-date, whether it be from person to person or through some society or fund, must be such as is approved by the same close thinking as business men give to their business, or politicians to their policy (Barnett 225).

10. In *The Art of Being Ruled* Lewis warned about a dystopian future when men and women would be reduced to the status of children in a nursery who "eat bread and jam dressed in short print frocks and bibs, sit in demure and silent rows, while one dressed as a martinet scolds them, and then administers shuddering fesseés" (Lewis, *Art* 136).

11. For a discussion of anxieties and mass politics in *To the Lighthouse,* see Fuhito Endo's article "Radical Violence Inside Out: Woolf, Klein, and Interwar Politics."

12. In his analysis of the "textual dialogues [of Woolf's *To the Lighthouse*] with Kleinian psychoanalysis," Fuhito Endo claims that the novel "critique[s] the very representation of the masses as a discursive product of the middle-class political paranoia in the 1920s" (Endo 193).

13. Ben Clarke notes that Woolf's analysis of class boundaries is "marked by contradictions and tensions," that it "attempts to sympathize with the aspirations of those who want 'baths and ovens and education and seventeen shillings instead of sixteen, and freedom and air'" and at the same time assigns the highest value on the members of the cultural elite, "ladies [who] desire Mozart and [sic] Einstein—that is, they desire things that are ends, not things that are means'" (Clarke 41).

Works Cited

Clarke, Ben. "'But the Barrier is Impassable': Virginia Woolf and Class." *Woolfian Boundaries; Selected Papers from the Sixteenth Annual International Conference on Virginia Woolf.* Clemson: Clemson U Digital P, 2006, 36-41.

Derrida, Jacques. *Given Time: I. Counterfeit Money.* Chicago and London: U of Chicago P, 1992.

Fuhito Endo. "Radical Violence Inside Out: Woolf, Klein, and Interwar Politics." *Twentieth Century Literature,* 52.2 (Summer 2006): 175-98.

Harris, Jose. *Private Lives, Public Spirit. A Social History of Britain, 1870-1914.* Oxford: Oxford UP, 1993.

—. "Society and the State in Twentieth-Century Britain." F.M.L. Thompson, Ed. *The Cambridge Social History of Britain 1750-1950.* Vol. 3. Cambridge: Cambridge UP, 1990: 63-119.

Lewis, Jane. "Women, social work and social welfare in twentieth-century Britain: from (unpaid) influence to (paid) oblivion." Martin Daunton, Ed., *Charity, Self-Interest and Welfare in the English Past.* New York: St. Martin's P, 1996.

Prochaska, F. K. "Philanthropy." In F.M.L. Thompson, Ed. *The Cambridge Social History of Britain 1750-1950.* Cambridge: Cambridge UP, 1990.

—. *Royal Bounty. The Making of a Welfare Monarchy.* New Haven: Yale UP 1995.

—. *Women and Philanthropy in Nineteenth-Century England.* Oxford: Clarendon P, 1980.

Tratner, Michael. *Modernism and Mass Politics. Joyce, Woolf, Eliot, Yeats.* Stanford, California: Stanford UP, 1995.

Vicinus, Martha. *Independent Women. Work and Community for Single Women, 1850-1920.* Chicago and London: U of Chicago P, 1985.

Woolf, Virginia. *Mrs. Dalloway.* 1925. London: Harcourt Brace, 1981.

—. "Mrs. Dalloway in Bond Street" In *Mrs. Dalloway's Party. A Short Story Sequence.* Ed. Stella McNichol. Orlando: Harcourt, 2001.

—. *To the Lighthouse.* 1927. New York: Harcourt, Brace Jovanovich, 1981.

—. "Memories of a Working Women's Guild." In Woolf, Virginia. *Collected Essays.* Volume IV. New York: Harcourt, Brace, and World, Inc., 1967.

—. *The Voyage Out.* (eLibrary)

Zwerdling, Alex. *Virginia Woolf and the Real World.* Berkeley: U of California P 1986.

The Artist / Intellectual as Politician

by Virginia Brackett

Virginia Woolf's artistic insecurity is well documented by both private and public comments in her diary and correspondence. While she achieved great success to counter that insecurity, she also confronted true failures, such as her biography of post-Impressionist artist, writer, critic and beloved Bloomsbury member Roger Fry. Woolf's comments regarding the writing of Fry's history reveals a gap between her youthful confidence that she could succeed in challenging the traditional approach to biography and the reality of her production. Her new biography blueprint lacked any "fixed scheme of the universe" and conformed to "no standard of courage or morality" ("New" 98). However, burdened with editing personal details of Fry's life and pressured to conform to public expectation, Woolf would indeed structure a traditional written life. She regained her unedited voice to produce "new biography" only in private interchanges with Benedict Nicolson.

Woolf adored Fry, describing him after his funeral as "Dignified & honest & large," one who "lived with such variety & generosity & curiosity" (*D4* 242). Later, she considers writing Fry's biography, declaring work the anecdote to depression. But the next day, she writes, "This time Roger makes it harder . . . Such a blank wall. Such a silence. Such a poverty. How he reverberated!" (*D4* 253). That reverberation is what she would regret being unable to capture in writing. Despite her early determination to write a biography demanding, according to Sir Sidney Lee, the "truth in its hardest, most obdurate form" ("New" 95), she would instead produce a work that did not at all reflect the traits she so valued in Fry. She could not meet the challenge to exercise her "right to independent judgment," moving away from the position of "chronicler" to that of "artist" (97), due to the personal nature of what would become a public document.

Following Helen Anrep's request in November 1934 that Woolf write Roger's biography, she responded by privately listing stages in Fry's life, reflecting upon those individuals best qualified to write about each. Her list reflects the influence of Fry not only on her view of historiography, but on her rhetorical style. That stylistic effect appears in Woolf's writing when, as Anne Banfield observes, "temporal relations connect moments as spatial ones," in a post-Impressionism approach. Fry believed that "each successive element is felt to have a fundamental and harmonious relationship with that which preceded it" (32-33). Woolf likely kept Fry's words in mind as she intellectually rejected the traditional approach to writing historical accounts. However, she did not achieve the harmony he proposed, a result of her deletion of crucial aspects of those temporal relations.

Woolf had early in her career described traditionally constructed history as inept at "capturing the reality of . . . . experience," finding history successful "only when the reader can re-experience the embodied subjectivity of individual impressions, as well as the material context of those impressions" (Westman 2) Thus, Woolf's idea for collaboration on the biography by a number of individuals reflected Fry's statement regarding the importance in art not only of impressions, but of an expression of the relationship among those impressions. Fry's statement also described Woolf's view of the proper expression of historical elements in a biographical framework.

In her collection *Essays* (1910), Woolf prioritized an *interesting* and *conceptual* approach to historiography above an objective approach that offered its audience a supposed "truth" ("Modes" 265). In Woolf's view, conventional historiography actually "impede[d] such truth-telling" because it "masquerade[d] as objective texts" (Westman 16). She bids readers "recognize" and accept their own "relationship" to history's narrative, inviting them to "add their voices to the dialogue" (Westman 16). She explained to Stephen Spender that while writing *The Years* she hoped to "envelop the whole in a changing temporal atmosphere," suggesting "there is no break, but a continuous development, possibly a recurrence of some pattern," a goal she felt a worthy one for historiography as well as fiction (*L6*, 116).

However, Woolf lacked confidence when writing Fry's history, noting, *if* free to write as she desired, this would be "a splendid, difficult chance" to construct biography (*D4*, 260). However, she quickly discovered she would not enjoy that freedom, due to Fry's affair with her sister Vanessa. The subjectivity Woolf deemed crucial to quality biography would threaten members of Fry's and her own circle. She would edit those details, fully knowing they would have made for a popular and more imaginative read. She had, after all, written in 1936 to Mrs. G.E. Easdale about Easdale's autobiography, "If you had used proper names, I daresay the public interest would have been excited. They like personalities, not ideas" (*L6* 25). She would find herself unable to shape Fry's true personality, due to devotion to family and friends and the potential backlash against them should she challenge cultural mores.

In 1937 Woolf stares at boxes containing Fry's records and wonders, "how anyone writes a real life. An imaginary one wouldn't so much bother me. But oh, the dates, the quotations!" (*L6* 135). She feels markedly pessimistic about writing any "truth" that would admit to artistry about a person whose family and friends still lived. Especially painful was the fact that "Roger was the most scornful of untruths of any man" (*L6*, 169); he would certainly have disapproved of her methods. To Vanessa almost a year later, Woolf confides, "writing lives is the devil. I shiver at the thought of Roger" (*L6*, 245) and two months later she tells Ethyl Smith, "Odd what a grind [writing] biography is," when it represented her "favourite reading" (*L6*, 262).

When the book's proofs arrived in October 1938, Woolf began what would become months of revision and editing, stating, "I am obsessed and quite futile" (*L6*, 293). In July 1939 she declared that she hated her typewriter (*L6*, 346) and later asked Vita Sackville-West, "How can one make a life out of Six Cardboard boxes full of tailor's bills love letters and old picture postcards?", labeling her book "so bad" (*L6*, 374). Pressured to comply with publisher requests, Woolf felt increasingly that she was producing something distasteful and abhorrent. By May 1940, she tells Smyth she is nearly blind from entering marginal comments on proofs, changing her own words to accept editorial revisions (*L6*, 399), and a month later she refers to her efforts as "my tethered and literal rubbish-heap grubbing in R. F." (*L6*, 404). The term "tethered" testifies to her feelings of restriction.

Woolf did avoid pain to family and friends in the writing of the book, made clear by a letter from Vanessa, now housed in the New York Public Library's Henry W. and Albert A. Berg collection. Woolf's biography had, in Vanessa's words, "brought him [Roger] back to me" (*L6*, fn 385). However, that victory proved bittersweet, as Woolf failed in her husband's estimation in crafting the biography. She recorded on March 20, 1940 Leonard

Woolf's anger when discussing her method as "merely analysis, not history. Austere repression... dull to the outsider. All those dead quotations..." (*L6* fn 385). She had succeeded in producing the exact brand of historical account that she had earlier denounced.

Woolf coped in part with her insecurities about the biography's quality by focusing in her private letters on attempts by Fry and other members of the group to shake their culture's tendency to cling to the past in terms of art and intellect. If she had failed to birth a new approach to history to offer her reading public, falling prey to pressure from that same public to edit her expression, she would succeed in defending Fry in her private writing. Free from editorial restriction in her correspondence, she wrote in passionate detail to Benedict Nicolson of Fry's and Bloomsbury's contribution to public debate regarding the proper role of intellectuals and the value of literary and artistic education. Nicolson was the son of Sackville-West and Harold Nicolson, whose *Some People* Woolf had reviewed as experimental biography that "succeeded remarkably" in blending the truth of biography with the "freedom, the artistry of fiction" ("New" 98). Woolf greatly admired that approach and predicted a future true biographer "whose art is subtle and bold enough to present that queer amalgamation of dream and reality" (100), but that would not be her. Her private defense of Fry came in response to Nicolson's accusation that members of Bloomsbury had been *too* intellectual to greatly affect society, that they had possibly ignored an opportunity to help prevent WWII. Benedict offered his comments partly in response to the heavily edited Fry biography.

Nicolson's description of Bloomsbury's outreach as "too sophisticated, too private" for a broad audience, echoed criticism Woolf had heard before from Herbert Read, among others. Read's review of the Fry biography for the *Spectator* praised it as "honest, sympathetic, understanding and ... objective in ... design and workmanship" (*L6*, fn 411), descriptors Woolf likely found distasteful in their support of the traditional approach that she had early on categorically rejected. However, Read did *not* view Fry favorably, writing that while Fry may have found great joy in his work and a stimulus to "endless intellectual research," his sensibilities could not "prevail ... against the pettiness and protectiveness of the Ivory Tower, against the benevolence of the Liberal outlook, against the intellect's pretensions to the final word" (fn 411). Unable sensibly to attack a positive review of her work, Woolf had to swallow the bitter pill of Read's opinion, no doubt blaming herself for not having effectively expressed her own view of Fry for others to share.

Woolf did, however, specifically counter Nicolson's charge by discussing Fry as the consummate artist who "did the best he could, given his education, given the society in which he was brought up" (*L6* 420). The caveats expressed her continued doubts regarding her ability to defend Fry against those who did not agree with her view as to the importance of his contributions to society. More importantly, they spoke to her acknowledgement that as his biographer, she had failed Fry.

But in a letter written in August of 1940 to Nicolson, Woolf at last found the liberated voice inherent to her formulation of a new biography, a voice she had previously to deny herself in the public space. She quotes from a letter she received from Nicolson that labeled Fry's life a "fools paradise," which Fry used in order to isolate himself from the disagreeable developments in the real world, "allow[ing] the spirit of Nazism to grow" (*L6* 413). Woolf rhetorically attempts to recall whether Roger deserved this charge, then begins both to instruct and correct Nicolson through a brilliant narrative turn. Within her letter, she composes an unedited Nicolson "biography" framed by her defense of Fry and the published book. Woolf dismisses Nicolson's charge that Fry avoided things disagreeable, adopting a third person narrative to best imitate the authorial voice. That objective voice counters that Fry had "faced insanity," a reference to the mental instability of his wife, "death, and every sort of disagreeable—," then cuts the voice off, as if musing. She adds for the benefit of her imaginary audience, "what can Ben mean?", questioning Nicolson's charge that Fry had enjoyed a completely agreeable existence (*L6* 413). She frames her defense within the detail of German raiders flying overhead, inviting Nicolson as reader to participate in her subjective point of view.

The creative biographer's voice relates of Nicolson, "After returning from a delightful tour in Italy, for which his expensive education at Eton and Oxford had well fitted him, he got a job as keeper of the King's pictures" (*L6* 413). Any astute reader would note the contrast between Nicolson's ideals and his actions. Ironically, as Woolf continues her brief "biography" of Nicolson, she fulfills her original desire to write biography by avoiding the self-imposed tone of objectivity encouraged by her publisher. Rather, she tells Nicolson's history in the context of his protesting certain aspects of Fry's history, valorizing each in relation to the other.

Woolf muses about family conflict Roger suffered when he rejected science for art and his supporting himself through odd jobs and "extension lecturing" when Ben's age. The contrast to Ben's pampered existence is clear. Next she reconstructs her memory of a party where Nicolson enthusiastically engaged other young people in intellectual discussion. Woolf notes the similarity of their conversation to interchanges during Bloomsbury gatherings, and then quotes Nicolson: "The intensely private world which Roger Fry cultivated could only be communicated to a few people as sensitive and intelligent as himself" (*L6*, 414). She debunks that charge by deftly holding up a rhetorical mirror in which Nicolson must see Fry's reflection. She abandons all pretense, guided by creative instinct rather than measured expression.

Woolf later quotes Nicolson's statement that society needs intellectual artists more at that moment than at any other. He makes clear that "stupidity and truth" will still prove abhorrent to such a person who will not retreat to any "tower," as he accuses Fry of doing. Rather, that individual must "persuade as many other people as possible to think and behave in the same way—and on his success and failure depends the future of the world" (*L6* 414). Woolf responds recounting Fry's work to persuade people, "more incessantly and successfully" than almost anyone else she could imagine. She queries Nicolson, "And wasn't that the best way of checking Nazism?" (414). In that moment, Woolf becomes the reader of historiography that she had early on declared proved essential to the interpretation of those facts, photos and dates that too often were left to stand alone in representation of a life. No "austere repression" strangles her expression.

Woolf shares a story from Sebastian Sprott who represents that individual reader she had desired to contribute to history's narrative. Sprott had explained that while "mooning" about the South Kensington Museum, he had encountered Roger, and within minutes dull museum objects "became vivid and intelligible." He mused there must exist many individuals like him, "people with scales on their eyes and wax in their ears" who could benefit from a Roger Fry to "remove the scales and dig out the wax" (*L6* 414). As Woolf nears the climax of her mixture of biography, history and apology, she admits to Nicolson that like everyone else, perhaps she, too, desires a scapegoat to blame for the war, but it certainly will not be Fry. She bemoans the fact that she has failed to do for Nicolson what she had earlier declared so crucial. The reader of the ideal history must re-experience the embodied subjectivity of individual impressions and their material context (*L6* 414). In bending to societal taboos against extra-marital sex and the public's mundane taste for traditional expression, she denied her readers all opportunity to try on the creative trappings of subjectivity. The desire she expressed in "The Art of Biography" to do "more to stimulate the imagination than any poet or novelist save the very greatest" (122) would not be fulfilled.

Woolf next interrogates the present in terms of the future, echoing Nicolson to ask, how does mankind prevent future wars? Stating she will be too old when that future comes, she asks of Nicolson whether he will sacrifice his art critic position to become a politician, as he declared members of Bloomsbury should have done. If Nicolson declines, then how precisely will he make art criticism "more public and less private than Roger did?" (*L6* 415). She later notes she was impressed by the historical knowledge inherent to Roger's Slade lectures. She concludes her interrogation of Nicolson, adding slyly, "But of course, I'm not an art critic; and have no right to express an opinion" (415). Hers is an intentionally disingenuous claim, and simple deconstruction reveals that she has every right, every individual has every right, to express any and all types of opinions. Perhaps their silence must become the scapegoat she sought (414), related in part to her own silence in matters of the truth where Roger was concerned.

The private venue inherent to personal correspondence emboldened Woolf to champion concern for public opinion and remain true to her value system when confronting Nicolson's charges. Woolf firmly believed that one's public activities could carry only so far, that those in the public eye risked becoming self-occupied, overly aware of self-image. That self-consciousness tainted the Fry biography and destroyed her opportunity to present the reading world a new model for biography. But in her private work she found herself elevated by that "little eminence" which the biographer's independence produces; she had "ceased to be the chronicler" and had "become an artist" ("New" 97).

Woolf once confided to Spender, "It's the thing we do in the dark that is more real; the thing we do because peoples eyes are on us seems to me histrionic, small boyish" (*L6*,122). By virtue of her own opinion, Woolf might have considered the Fry biography that something "histrionic, small boyish" that suffered due to its public nature and her resultant forced self-editing. However, her correspondence proved the "more real" thing. Written in the dark of isolation and unfettered by public input or opinion, it allowed Woolf at last to connect the temporal with the spatial through the practice of new biography.

Works Cited

Banfield, Anne. "Time Passes: Virginia Woolf, Post Impressionism, and Cambridge Time." *Poetics Today* 24.3 (Fall 2003): 471-516.

Bell, Anne Oliver, ed. *The Diary of Virginia Woolf*. Vol.4. New York: Harcourt Brace, 1982.

Fry, Roger. *Vision and Design*. London: Chatto and Windus, 1920.

Nicolson, Nigel, and Joanne Trautmann, eds. *The Letters of Virginia Woolf*. Vol. 6. New York: Harcourt, Brace, Jovanovich, 1980.

Westman, Karin E. "The Character in the House: Virginia Woolf in Dialogue with History's Audience." *Clio* 28.1 (Fall 1998):1-26. ProQuest. 4 Dec. 2007. <http://proquest.umi.com>.

Woolf, Virginia. *A Writer's Diary*. Ed. Leonard Woolf. New York: Harcourt, Brace, Jovanovich, 1954.

—. "The Art of Biography." *Virginia Woolf: Selected Essays*. Ed. David Bradshaw. New York: Oxford UP, 2008.
—. "Modes and Manners of the Nineteenth Century." *The Essays of Virginia Woolf*. Ed. Andrew McNellie. Vol. 1. New York: Harcourt Brace Jovanovich, 1987.
—. "The New Biography." *Virginia Woolf: Selected Essays*. Ed. David Bradshaw. New York: Oxford UP, 2008.

MODERNIST ARCHIVES AND ISSUES OF INTELLECTUAL PROPERTY

by Bonnie Kime Scott, Brenda Silver, Georgia Johnston, Vara Neverow and Merry Pawlowski

Scholars experienced with working in archives both have stories to tell and advice to give when it comes to issues of intellectual property. Like Georgia Johnston, one of the contributors to this discussion, many of us have a great fondness for A.S. Byatt's novel, *Possession,* and share the researcher's desire to possess a previously undiscovered work by a prized author. Her own recent discovery of Woolf's Rodmell lecture concerning the Dreadnought Hoax provided a learning experience of value to her, and to a wider group of archival scholars. Until she found the manuscript in the Women's Library, London Metropolitan University, only three pages of it had been available, published in an appendix to Quentin Bell's biography of Woolf. What did she have to do in order to publish some or all of it? This essay aims at preparing scholars for the array of problems that arise in working with archives and literary estates. It begins anecdotally, with the shared experiences of Georgia Johnston, Brenda Silver, Vara Neverow, Merry Pawlowski, and Bonnie Kime Scott. It ends with the expert opinion of Robert Spoo, a specialist in intellectual property issues, whose embedded essay deserves to enter the scholarly tool kit of Woolf scholars, as a form of legal assistance.

Unlike one of the characters in the Byatt novel, Georgia Johnston did not of course lift the manuscript itself, but she learned only later that she could have made a photographic copy, rather than hand copy the document laboriously on her first visit. Wishing to publish the Rodmell lecture together with her own analysis of it, Johnston appropriately contacted the Society of Authors, first stop on all permissions for Virginia Woolf. What surprised her at this stage was that another scholar was informed of the find by the Society of Authors and given the right to first publication of a corrected version of the text. Had she negotiated effectively? Was she shown professional courtesy in the matter? She has since been able to negotiate her own publication of an uncorrected "diplomatic" version of the lecture, and has permission to publish a report of the discovery in a major British newspaper simultaneously with the first publication. She may face some expenses. She has happily, as of this writing, found that the Society of Authors generously will not charge for permission, but is still waiting to hear from the library about possible fees for reproduction. Such fees often fall on the head of scholars, particularly where university presses are involved in their publications. There is some irony if the library charges a fee, since the manuscript was only on loan to Dame Frances Farrer, who failed to return it to Leonard Woolf, and so it remained with papers given to the library.

Brenda Silver made an "accidental discovery" of thirty-three of Virginia Woolf's reading notebooks in the Henry W. and Albert A. Berg Collection of the New York Public Library, Astor Lenox and Tilden Foundations. Once these claimed her attention, she went about studying thirty-three more housed in the Sussex University Library, and one in the Beinecke Rare Book and Manuscript Library at Yale University, her diligence resulting in *Virginia Woolf's Reading Notebooks,* published in 1983. She emphasizes the importance of working with librarians, both for their considerable knowledge of their collections, and in securing the library's permission to publish.

Later, when Silver wanted to publish passages from letters Woolf received after the publication of *Three Guineas,* she enlisted the help of Nigel Nicholson, who provided not only identifications, but where known, contact information. For letters, the copyright belongs to the writer, a difficult task when for the correspondents Nicholson couldn't identify she had only the 1938 address. Silver wrote to those addresses, receiving, surprisingly, several answers. Silver returned to the question of permissions for private communications when, drawing on her academic interest in literature and technology, she began incorporating posts on the VWOOLF email list, a substantial archive these days, into her writings. With email, as with letters, the copyright belongs to the sender, but email lists, Silver explained, are a grey area, falling between the public and private domains and presenting a number of quandaries concerning copyright and fair use. In the case of VWOOLF, she concluded, it is always better to err on the side of getting permissions.

In their paper, "Entering the Danger Zone: Archives, Intellectual Property Rights and Technology," Merry Pawlowski and Vara Neverow addressed a range of issues relating to publication of digitalized archival materials and to permissions relating to images. Regarding their work on the digital *Reading Notes for Three Guineas: An Edition and Archive* http://www.csub.edu/woolf_center, hosted by California State University at Bakersfield, Pawlowski and Neverow have been exceptionally fortunate to have enjoyed the full support of the University of Sussex library as well as that of the Society of Authors with Jeremy Crow as the representative of the Woolf Estate. In working with Bet Inglis, who was chief librarian of the Sussex manuscripts collection until 2000, Pawlowski and Neverow had free and full access to the fragile originals of the three invaluable scrapbook volumes for *Three Guineas,* Monks House Papers B16f. In their subsequent dealings with Dorothy Sheridan, the librarian who succeeded Bet Inglis following her retirement, they continued to have an excellent working relationship.

Pawlowski and Neverow were also very fortunate to have the support of Jeremy Crow when they first began to seek copyright permission to publish the Reading Notebooks online. Jeremy Crowe cautioned Pawlowski early on in the process that it was unlikely that the family would support online publication; however, Pawlowski had the opportunity to meet with Crowe in London and show him what she and Neverow had done, and he exhibited immediate interest and excitement about the project. He was able to secure the support of Olivier Bell, who represented the family, by showing her their work. Jeremy Crowe was key in helping to keep the cost of copyright permissions down for Pawlowski and Neverow, as he realized that they had limited financial support from their respective campuses, California State University at Bakersfield and Southern Connecticut State University for such fees.

While both Pawlowski and Neverow had received significant funding from their universities for their project for research and travel expenses as well as for a student assistant for Pawlowski, who was primarily responsible for developing the web site in consultation with the technology staff at CSU-Bakersfield, both were initially responsible for paying the permissions out of their own pockets. Jeremy Crowe's offer for renewal rights in 2008 was equally generous, and, as of this year, the International Virginia Woolf Society has kindly agreed to pay the modest permissions fee. Also, the Society is considering ways to grant wider access to this site for all of its members, as well as other website developments of an archival nature.

Neverow also spoke in regard to the issues related to accessing, acquiring and publishing images. As is the case with other archival material, there is no uniformity in the procedure for studying or acquiring images for publication. Each archive is unique in its provisions, constraints and quality of support for access and publication. Further, each archive has the authority to determine whether an image may be reproduced for private study or published at all as well as what that image's price might be—a decision typically based on the archive's own potentially arbitrary formula for its value. There are also situations in which the images or other materials belonging to the archive cannot be published without the permission of the estate or some other entity, as is the case with the Reading Notebooks at University of Sussex. Also daunting is that some images are of uncertain origin or indeterminate ownership. In such cases, using the image is problematic since one does not want to violate copyright or other legal constraints by reproducing the image for publication. Including wording to the effect that every effort has been made to contact copyright holders and that errors will be corrected if possible is well advised.

In addition to the excitement of finding something previously undiscovered and the frustration of navigating the mysterious labyrinths of permissions and access to actual images held in boxes and on shelves there is also the brave new world of digitization. Increasingly, one is now able to enter a vast virtual space where digital images are displayed electronically with seeming abandon and infinite accessibility. The pricey National Portrait Gallery, London, has a searchable web site displaying available images and an online form to order them. Depending on what one is trying to acquire, it is even possible to locate an image online and, just by an exchange of emails with a generous person who is willing to grant permission and cede any fees, publish an image gratis. In terms of online access of particular value to Woolfians, Neverow cited the Mortimer Rare Book Room at Smith College which has graciously made Leslie Stephen's photograph album available online (http://www.smith.edu/libraries/libs/rarebook/exhibitions/stephen/), allowing Woolfians to browse through these extraordinary images at their own leisure before selecting an image for publication at a modest fee. Neverow also noted that that Karen V. Kukil and her colleague Barbara Blumenthal at the Mortimer Rare Book Room at Smith College are both exceptionally helpful and attentive to the requests of those seeking images from their collections.

But digitization does not translate directly into access. At the Harvard Theater Library, where the Monks House photograph albums are held, the albums have now been digitized but are not online. Digitization certainly protects the fragile and portable images from damage and theft, but also limits the degree of close scrutiny for scholars. Neverow also observed that preserving the original format of materials is a challenge for the archive. With physical photo albums, photographs could easily be removed from an album and not replaced properly. Woolf's reading notebooks at Sussex were originally held together with metal rings; however, the rings were potentially damaging and had to be removed, somewhat altering the appearance of the archival material. However, the digitized version created by Pawlowski and Neverow makes access easy and affordable with a modest subscription fee, which should be especially appealing for those who cannot travel to Sussex.

Travel is not the only expense one can incur in pursuit of the archive. Maggie Humm was permitted to reproduce a significant number of images from the Harvard Theater Library as well as others from the Tate collection in her important *Snapshots of Bloomsbury*, but while it was very generous of these two archives to allow the reproduction, such a large project is also very expensive in terms of permissions. Thus, inevitably, there is also the question as to whether the publisher or the author will pay for the permissions. Neverow noted that *Virginia Woolf Miscellany* editorial policy is to pay for up to $50 of permissions per article, if possible. However, a weakening US dollar makes $50 look rather paltry if the purchase is made in Euros, and many permissions greatly exceed this amount. As far as the *Miscellany* is concerned (and this is typical of other publications as well), it is entirely the responsibility of the author to obtain the images and the permissions as well as the proper wording of the acknowledgement. Further, the publisher, of course, also has the right to reject an image that has not been properly acquired.

As both Pawlowski and Neverow have indicated, for the scholar dealing with the arcane world of archival material and intellectual property rights the challenges and frustrations are great but the rewards are potentially even greater. Throughout the presentation, Pawlowski and Neverow spoke enthusiastically of their positive experiences with the Woolf estate and with other archives having had the very good luck to work within an exceptionally supportive environment.

When Bonnie Kime Scott started working with modernist texts, she knew very little about copyright law, literary estates, and fair use. Her first book, *Joyce and Feminism*, involved archival work in Ireland, England, and the U.S., and even a 1977 interview with Joyce's daughter, Lucia, then living in a mental institution in England. In the seventies, the Joyce estate was handled by the Society of Authors and its major trustee was Jane Lidderdale, the godchild of Harriet Shaw Weaver, Joyce's publisher and original trustee. Miss Lidderdale served as Literary Trustee because she was the guardian of Lucia Joyce, succeeding Miss Weaver in that capacity.

Lidderdale exerted her own judgment as a guardian and an executor. Scott was permitted to interview Miss Joyce because she was interested in Lucia for herself—notably for her dance performances and her art work—decorative letters similar to the initial capitals in the Book of Kells, used for artistic publications of Chaucer and Joyce. A collection of Lucia's dance memorabilia housed at the University of Buffalo bore a note on its folder, supposedly in Sylvia Beach's handwriting, saying that Lucia had collected the items herself for preservation. This suggests that she had wanted her interest in the dance to be known and preserved and that she was aided in this by female friends. The interview itself suggested that dance had remained more important to her than the decorative letterines. Work of Margaret Morris, one of the choreographers in Lucia's files, now has a place in *Gender in Modernism*.

By the time *Joyce and Feminism* was published in 1984, Lucia Joyce had died and control of the estate had gone to Joyce's grandson, Stephen James Joyce. For the chapter "The Female Family of Joyce," Scott could present Lucia in her own terms, the interview being her own work. However, Scott was not permitted to quote from letters of Nora Joyce, even to demonstrate matters of syntax—her version of the psychological sentence of the feminine gender (to use a concept of Woolf's). Scott was so bold as to ask Stephen Joyce publicly why that permission was denied (this was at a Joyce Symposium, which he attended for several years, pontificating to the scholars about their defects). Joyce cited what he considered the personal violation to Nora of Richard Ellmann's *Selected Letters of*

James Joyce, which included for the first time erotic correspondence between James and Nora. The female family of Joyce had been reassigned to the 19th century private sphere. Quite recently Kevin Dettmar was denied permission to reprint Joyce's "Nausicaa" chapter from *Ulysses* for the Longman's Anthology of British Literature, showing the ongoing strictures of this estate.

An equal amount of intrigue, but a better result for the aspiring editor, comes in the case of Rebecca West, whose *Selected Letters* Scott edited in 2000. Unlike Joyce and Woolf, who died suddenly at 59, West lived to 90 and had ample time to decide about her literary trustees. West worked to control access to her private life—she wanted the story of her relationship to H.G. Wells to be presented in her own terms. The person least apt to do this was her only son, Anthony, a product of her 10 year liaison to Wells. He qualifies as another male relative wanting to control the story. But his aim was public devastation rather than protection of his mother, if *H.G. Wells: Aspects of a Life* is any indication. Scholars who ventured to the Beinecke Library, which houses West's early papers, found access closely controlled in the years immediately following West's death. This eased after Anthony's death, only four years after Rebecca's.

Michael Sisson, West's last literary agent at PFD, and West's nephew, Norman Macleod, have encouraged access for scholars and have approved the publication of a series of previously unpublished manuscripts, in addition to the letters. Scott had to establish herself as a critic and scholar of West, and she had to take PFD as her agent (the only one she has ever had). Norman Macleod's wife Marion and his daughter Helen contributed to the founding of the Rebecca West Society and its conferences, as has his sister Allison. Despite ambivalence about the mother-son relationship, Anthony West's first and second wives and two of her grandchildren saved and shared her letters to them. Scott has dozens of stories about the adventures of tracking down letters still in private hands, as do most editors of similar work. Merlin Holland (grandson of Oscar Wilde) blanked out some of West's least complimentary remarks about his mother in letters she wrote to his father, but gave the letters in their entirety as soon as she passed away. Concerning letters once in her possession, an elderly friend of West told Scott that she had "thrown them in the river," saying that she didn't want West's remarks about her sister to be in circulation. True or not, it made for a moment of drama in her elegant sitting room.

Scott's two hulking critical anthologies, *Gender in Modernism* (published 2007) and *The Gender of Modernism* (published 1990) reprinted whole or nearly whole works, and this created a serious need to negotiate, since this use was clearly out of the realm of "fair use." On a limited budget, cobbled together from university resources and a modest advance of royalties from the presses involved, Scott and her collaborators set about to make available obscure, forgotten and difficult to access modernist texts. The earliest, ones published before 1923, were generally safe, having fallen into the public domain. The least predictable were unpublished or recently published works recovered from archives, where revenues from first publication might still be expected. The adventure came in finding who really had the authority to grant permission, and how to ask. These encounters don't have nearly the depth of the West project, but they do reveal an array of attitudes and management styles by literary estates.

A typical route of inquiry started with a special collections library or a publisher, who could connect the editor with the Trustee or literary agent of a writer's estate. Scott's letter of inquiry did ask if they were an official trustee; if not could they kindly direct the inquiry elsewhere. It pleaded economic exigency—"This work is scholarly in purpose. It cannot be expected to do much more than recuperate the costs of its production." The most difficult estate was that of Edna St. Vincent Millay, who could be represented finally only by texts in the public domain. The custodian of the estate did not care to have the "modernist" label used in relation to Millay, perhaps an aftermath of dismissals of her work as "sentimental." The most expensive permission was from the Hemingway estate, reached via Simon and Schuster, which billed $1,400 for excerpts from *The Garden of Eden*. It was a recent publication that may have risked profits if too widely dispersed.

The trustee of the Hope Mirrlees estate could have presented difficulties. For that trustee is Valerie Eliot—well known for denying permissions related to her late husband. Mirrlees' fine poem "Paris," as hand set by Virginia Woolf for the Hogarth Press, came for free, probably thanks to the good rapport Julia Briggs had established with Mrs. Eliot. It is pleasing that Julia could complete her wonderful annotated edition of the poem for *Gender in Modernism,* months before her death.

Marianne Craig Moore, Literary Executor for her famous aunt, requested only a copy of the book for the estate file in return for permission to republish essays. She would not grant permission, however, for an archival item in the Rosenbach Museum, "Rat-Tail File," which would have fit well in the chapter on suffrage. This is a reminder that archival items are often more protected by literary estates. Descendants of less well known authors were delighted to have their relatives' work shared with a wider audience. Thus poetry on the political left by Ruth Lechlitner and Marie De. L. Welsh came free of charge.

Closer to home with Woolf, Henrietta Garnett wanted only copies of the paperback and hardback copies of the book for permission to publish an essay by Vanessa Bell, "Lecture Given at Leighton Park School." Woolf is represented by the following: "Reviewing" in a chapter titled "Journalism Meets Modernism," selections from the holograph of "The Prime Minister," a pre-text for *Mrs. Dalloway* in a chapter titled "Modernism, Trauma and Narrative Reformulation," and "The Cinema" in "Writing on Film in 1920s London." For this the Society of Authors, represented by Jeremy Crowe, asked what seemed a very reasonable combined total of two hundred pounds.

Preparatory to the conference panel on intellectual property, Scott e-mailed Jeremy Crowe to clarify procedures of the Society of Authors in granting permissions—responses she shared with Bob Spoo, the legal expert on the panel. These appear in his analysis, which follows. Scott's sense is that The Society of Authors does the routine work of handling permissions for the Woolf Estate, but that Anne Olivier Bell is still engaged in major decisions, as was Quentin Bell until his death. As readers of Quentin Bell's biography can attest, Quentin Bell had his own opinions about his aunt's politics and art, and at one stage opined that the "bottom of the barrel" had been reached in unpublished manuscripts. Jane Marcus engaged him in an exchange from which she emerged with the title "lupine" critic, which she embraced. But such opinions and exchanges have had little effect on permissions for archival items, which have continued to come. Throughout its history, the Virginia Woolf Estate can be placed on the benevolent end of the spectrum of literary estates, and we are all very fortunate in that.

"For God's sake, publish; only be sure of your rights":
Virginia Woolf, Copyright, and Scholarship

by Robert Spoo

In March 1928, Virginia Woolf wrote to Vita Sackville-West after learning that the latter wanted to translate Rainer Maria Rilke's *Duino Elegies* for the Hogarth Press: "For God's sake, translate Rilke: only be sure of your rights."[1] The legal triangle implied here is one with which modernist scholars are familiar: a *publisher* warning an *author* that, for a project to go forward, copyright permissions will have to be obtained from a *literary estate*. (Rilke had died in 1926.) Now that legislative extensions of copyright have ensured that modernism will remain "propertized" for some time to come, scholars must gird themselves for the continuing challenge of permissions-gathering. I offer here some thoughts, as a copyright lawyer and modernist scholar, about intellectual property and Woolf studies.[2] I will begin by making a few general observations about literary estates and then go on to discuss the Woolf copyrights in various contexts. Because permissions are necessary only when scholars cannot avail themselves of any privilege or exception recognized by law, I will stress aspects of the law that allow scholars (and publishers with a little knowledge and mettle) to bypass the permissions game.

Literary estates come in many flavors. Some encourage scholarship; some do not. On a spectrum stretching from scholar-friendly to downright difficult, the estates of Ezra Pound and H.D. would nestle in the friendly zone, while the James Joyce estate would be practically off the chart in the other direction. The Woolf estate appears to fall somewhere between these extremes, though closer to friendly than to difficult, at least in ordinary cases. This is no doubt partly due to the Woolf estate's use of the Society of Authors in London as an agent for handling routine scholarly requests. By "routine requests" I mean, chiefly, requests for permission to quote from Woolf's *published* works. Such requests are usually granted, and license fees are charged.

Use of the Society of Authors as a permissions clearinghouse is generally a good thing for scholarship. It reduces what legal analysts call "transaction costs"—the hassles and uncertainties of bargaining with a rights-holder—and prevents "market failure," where a use is refused altogether so that neither the scholar nor the estate benefits. One reason why the Joyce Estate has become a byword for intransigency among scholars is that some twenty years ago, the Estate stopped using the Society for routine academic requests and, gradually over time, came to insist that requests of all types be directed to the Estate's trustee and to the author's grandson. The result has been a loss of objectivity and efficiency in the processing of permissions requests, and a dramatic increase in uncertainty and anxiety among scholars. There is much to be said for a more dispassionate referee, like the Society, that treats requests largely as a business matter.

But there are drawbacks. Academics can become too dependent on the designated referee and forget that permissions are not always necessary. Quoting from copyrighted works for the purpose of criticism or scholarship is a core "fair use." In the U.S., fair use is especially likely to apply when a use is "transformative," that is, when it "adds something new, with a further purpose or different character, altering the [copyrighted work] with new expression, meaning, or message."[3] Reasonable quotations from *To the Lighthouse* to support an analysis of Lily Briscoe as an embodiment of modernism is the kind of transformative purpose for which the fair-use privilege was evolved. The U.S. Copyright Act stresses that fair use applies to both published *and* unpublished works, so that short, transformative quotations from an unpublished Woolf letter or manuscript would also be permissible, at least within the U.S.[4] (The parallel doctrine of "fair dealing" in Canada, the U.K., and other countries is somewhat more restrictive and is sometimes treated as *not* applying to unpublished writings.) Scholars should become familiar and comfortable with fair use, and academic publishers should not allow the privilege to atrophy through routine insistence on permissions-getting, even though requests can readily be referred to the Society of Authors. (The Society's website notes the validity of fair dealing and opines as to when—in terms of word counts—fair dealing might apply.[5] Bear in mind, though, that the law does not define fair use or fair dealing as a certain quantity of quoted words; fair use is not a numbers game, but rather a flexible doctrine that permits a range of uses in appropriate contexts.)

What types of requests, then, does the Society of Authors regard as *not* routine? Jeremy Crow of the Society has explained that the Society typically refers requests for "unusually substantial usages" or "unusual exploitations" to estates themselves.[6] These would include requests to prepare a new edition of a novel; to adapt a work for the stage or cinema; or to use a work in advertising or on merchandise. These uses are also ones that would not likely qualify as fair use or fair dealing. Another type of request that the Society often refers to estates concerns previously unpublished material. Sometimes "arrangements have already been made for initial publication elsewhere," or an estate believes that another project is "the most appropriate place for first publication."[7] In such cases, an estate is protecting what the law refers to as "the right of first publication," a concept that combines the right to decide where to publish a work first and the right to determine whether to divulge the work at all. It is understandable that an estate might want to invoke this right as a way of controlling the first appearance of a work. But I have seen the concept abused as a strategy for preventing *any* appearance of historically important documents created by famous, long-dead authors. A short quotation from an unpublished manuscript in a scholarly article or book should not interfere with the right of first publication.

Estates sometimes use copyrights to protect more than the right of first publication. Not infrequently, they use copyrights to ensure "respect for the known wishes of the deceased author, and the protection of the feelings and privacy of living persons mentioned in the works."[8] Here we enter controversial terrain. The "known wishes" of a dead author may be difficult to determine, and it is not always clear who is in a better position to know authors' wishes—estates or scholars—inasmuch as both groups are susceptible to self-serving bias. The issue becomes even more complicated when it is recalled that much of the unpublished material on which "privacy" claims are based is not private at all—in the sense of physically or legally unavailable—but rather held in archives to which the public has access. Scholars can learn the secrets buried in these documents; they just can't safely quote their findings in publications, for fear of copyright threats. They can kiss but not tell.

So when an estate purports to be using its copyrights to protect the privacy of the living or the dead, it is well to take a closer look. Copyright is a limited right, granted for a fixed term of years, subject to fair use and other exemptions, and powerless to prevent the disclosure of facts or ideas contained in a protected writing. Suppose that Virginia Woolf had confided the following to an unpublished scrap of paper dated September 1922 and held at the University of Sussex: "We saw Tom last night, dreadfully nervous over the coming reception of his poem. He had on again his marmoreal mask and manner, which always unnerve me. I think he had painted his lips and applied a cadaverous green powder to his cheeks and forehead." If a scholar encountered this (wholly invented) entry at Sussex, nothing in the law of copyright could prevent her from reporting the broadly-paraphrased facts or ideas in a published article. Fair use, in the U.S. at least, would allow her to state as well that Woolf had described Eliot as "marmoreal" and as wearing "cadaverous green powder." And, of course, once the copyright in the entry had expired, anyone could lawfully use the entry in its entirety, without any constraints.

So what does copyright have to do with protecting privacy? Very little, as a strict matter of law. Copyrights are primarily designed to safeguard economic rights, not privacy interests. The privacy of the deceased is something the law has little interest in anyway, and other areas of the law—such as defamation and the torts of "invasion of privacy" and "false light"—already offer protection to living persons in certain contexts. To use the ill-fitting machinery of copyright to try to stifle or discourage scholarly commentary is wrong and wrong-headed, in my opinion, yet the *in terrorem* effect of a copyright holder's threats, however unjustified, is often enough to cause a scholar or her publisher to omit quite reasonable quotations or paraphrased discussion, with the result that the documentary credibility of the scholar's claims is reduced.

In the U.S., courts are increasingly recognizing the problem of "copyright misuse," a term that generally refers to an attempt by a rights-holder to extend copyright protection beyond its appropriate sphere. Allegations of copyright misuse were a centerpiece of the lawsuit brought in 2006 by Professor Carol Loeb Shloss of Stanford University against the Estate of James Joyce.[9] (I have served as co-counsel for Shloss in this litigation.) Shloss had spent years researching a controversial subject—the sparsely-documented life of James Joyce's troubled daughter, Lucia—only to be forbidden by the Estate, for reasons of family privacy, to quote anything by Lucia, her father, or any Joyce family member, even though most of the documents the Estate declared off-limits were already published or held in collections open to the public. The case was settled—very favorably for Shloss— but not before the court had ruled that her claim of copyright misuse was an appropriate subject for litigation on the basis of the facts she had alleged.[10] Had the case continued, the court would have decided whether the Estate's aggressive attempts to deny scholarly fair use and other user rights in the name of "privacy" had crossed a legal line.

The public domain is the scholar's best friend, but when does a work fall into the public domain? The bad news is that copyright laws vary from country to country— copyright law is territorial—and the rules for when works enter the public domain are not uniform. The good news, for Woolf scholars, is that public-domain status of Woolf's works, including her currently unpublished writings, is not far off in some countries. Any work that Woolf published during her lifetime is now in the public domain in Canada and Australia, where copyrights of that vintage endure for the author's life plus fifty years. (Woolf died in 1941.) In the U.K., the Republic of Ireland, and many E.U. countries, copyrights last for the author's life plus seventy years, so works published during Woolf's lifetime should enter the public domain in those countries at the end of 2011—barring any further legislative extensions of copyright.

The U.S.—for many years a copyright self-exile from the rest of the world—has different rules for Woolf's lifetime-published works. Works published prior to 1923, in the U.S. or abroad, are generally in the U.S. public domain. Woolf's works published after 1922—unless they entered the public domain in some other way—generally will enjoy copyright in the U.S. for 95 years from the date of first publication.[11] Thus, the first edition of *Jacob's Room*, published in New York and London in 1922, is now in the public domain in the U.S., Canada, and Australia, but will remain in copyright in Britain and other countries until at least 2011. By contrast, *To the Lighthouse*, published in 1927, will remain in copyright in the U.S. until the end of 2022 and in Britain until the end of 2011, while it is in the public-domain now in Canada and Australia. It is difficult, accordingly, to make worldwide plans for texts when their copyrights do not expire uniformly. A complete study of the international copyright status of a given text should be made before embarking on any publication project.

You will notice that I have been using the term "lifetime-published works." What about works by Woolf that were published after her death? The rules for posthumously-published works are also complicated and difficult to encapsulate, since they, too, vary from country to country. In general, because many of Woolf's posthumously-published works were issued within the past few decades, they will likely enjoy copyright protection for some time to come in many countries. One more point about Woolf's lifetime-published works: the copyright in these works had expired in the U.K. at the end of 1991, but were "revived" in that country in 1996 when copyright terms were extended by twenty years in many countries of the European Union. To lessen the impact of revived copyrights, Britain enacted what are called "compulsory-license" provisions that permit anyone to make *any* use of a revived-copyright work *within the U.K.*, as long as the user gives reasonable advance notice to the copyright owner and agrees to pay a reasonable fee or remuneration at some point.[12] This means that anyone in the U.K. could re-edit and publish, within the U.K., a critical edition of the first printing of *Mrs. Dalloway*, after giving proper notice to the copyright holders and, at some point, paying a reasonable royalty or fee. Unfortunately, other E.U. countries in which Woolf's copyrights were revived, such as Ireland, lack such a compulsory license. This tends to limit the benefits of the U.K. compulsory license to the U.K., though it might be argued that the benefits could extend further in certain cases.

What about currently unpublished works by Woolf—letters, diary material, manuscripts? Here, too, the rules vary from country to country. In Canada, any work by Woolf that was unpublished as of 1997 entered the public domain there at the end of 2002.[13] This makes Canada the only major English-speaking country in which Woolf's currently unpublished works (and any works by her published for the first time after 1996 or so) are in the public domain. In the U.S., Woolf's currently unpublished works (and any works by her published for the first time after 2002) will enter the public domain at the end of 2011.[14] This means that, in the North American market, scholars will have a much freer hand with respect to Woolf's unpublished writings come 2012—though because copyright in Woolf's unpublished writings will remain in force longer in other countries, scholars will still have to seek permission for *worldwide* distribution.

Notes

1. *The Letters of Virginia Woolf*, vol. 3, ed. Nigel Nicolson and Joanne Trautmann (New York: Harcourt Brace Jovanovich, 1977), 469.
2. This essay does not constitute legal advice concerning any particular proposed use.
3. *Campbell v. Acuff-Rose Music, Inc.* 510 U.S. 569, 579 (1994).
4. See 107 U.S.C. § 107 (setting forth the definition of fair use and its factors).
5. See <http://www.societyofauthors.org/publications/quick_guide_permissions/>.
6. E-mail from Crow to Bonnie Kime Scott (June 10, 2008).
7. *Ibid.*
8. *Ibid.*
9. Threats from the Joyce Estate caused Shloss to delete much quoted material from her biography, *Lucia Joyce: To Dance in the Wake*, published by Farrar Straus & Giroux in 2003.
10. Two court opinions have been published in the case: *Shloss v. Sweeney*, 515 F. Supp. 2d 1068, 1077 (N.D. Cal. 2007); *Shloss v. Sweeney*, 515 F. Supp. 2d 1083, 1086 (N.D. Cal. 2007).
11. See U.S. Copyright Act, 17 U.S.C. § 304(b).
12. Duration of Copyright and Rights in Performances Regs., 1995 S.I. No. 3297, §§ 24, 25.
13. See Canadian Copyright Act, R.S., 1985, § 7(4), as amended.
14. See U.S. Copyright Act, 17 U.S.C. § 303(a).

Reading Dante, Misreading Woolf: New Evidence of Virginia Woolf's Revision of *The Years*

by James Haule

Virginia Woolf's *The Years* was a public triumph and a critical disaster. While it sold far more than her other books and became a number one best seller in the United States, many critics have followed the verdict of family and friends and declared it a failure. In *Downhill All the Way*, her husband Leonard said it was "much the most successful [book] of them all" but "the worst book she ever wrote" (145-46). Quentin Bell reports that Leonard lied to Virginia when he read the draft, declaring it "extraordinarily good," because "had he told her the truth he had very little doubt that she would kill herself" (196). Leonard told her that it had only one imperfection; it was far too long. She would have to cut it substantially before publication. Virginia Woolf was enormously relieved: "Miracles will never cease – L actually likes The Years! He thinks it so far [1908 Chapter] . . . as good as any of my books" (*D5* 28-29).

Less than a year earlier as Woolf completed her first draft of the novel, she was pleased with the result. She knew that "there still remains a great deal to do. I must still condense, & point" since it "needs sharpening, some bold cuts, & emphases." However, her "main feeling about this book is vitality, fruitfulness, energy. Never did I enjoy writing a book more . . ." (*D4* 361). Leonard's memory of the succeeding months were of "unending nightmare" (153) owing to Virginia's deteriorating mental condition. On July 9th, he insisted on a total break from revision and "we went down to Rodmell and stayed there for three and a half months. Virginia did not write at all, did not look at her proofs, and hardly ever moved out of Rodmell" (154). He remembered it as a harrowing, dangerous period of time, and he was deeply concerned that Virginia's delicate mental condition might lead to tragedy. Ultimately, the necessary deletions and revisions were completed and the novel published in April 1937. It came to 467 pages, some 328 pages shorter than Woolf's first draft.

Much of the material that Woolf cut from her novel has been presented elsewhere. The Winter 1977 Virginia Woolf Issue of the *Bulletin of the New York Public Library* and Mitchell A. Leaska's *The Pargiters: The Novel Essay Portion of THE YEARS* (1978) present what was removed from an early version of the novel and discuss its importance. Grace Radin's *Virginia Woolf's The Years: The Evolution of a Novel* (1981) expands her 1977 essay and explores the nature of Woolf's later revisions, demonstrating that the author proceeded with intelligence and care. Since then more evidence has come to light, including proof copies and the business records of R. & R. Clark and the Garden City Press. When this evidence is added to what we already know about Virginia Woolf's revisions of *The Years*, we can begin to construct a more reliable chronology of her changes, and a more detailed appreciation of her vision and artistry. Mitchell A. Leaska has said that in *The Years*, Woolf "was so possessed by her material that she no longer had dominion over it," concluding that "exactly what went wrong with the novel's growth, no one can tell with certainty" (191). We now have additional evidence that little if anything "went wrong." Woolf did not cut the novel in despair and desperation; she refashioned it in dramatic, subtle ways, turning it into what Michael Rosenthal has called "a richly organized fabric compounded of repetition, echo and allusion" (170). We can now appreciate all the more Virginia Woolf's own sense of accomplishment as she neared the end of her revision:

> There is no need whatever in my opinion to be unhappy about The Years. It seems to me to come off at the end. Anyhow to be a taut real strenuous book: with some beauty & poetry too. . . In fact I hand my complement to that terribly depressed woman, myself, whose head ached so often: who was so entirely convinced a failure; for in spite of everything I think she brought it off, & is to be congratulated. How she did it, with her head like an old cloth I don't know. (D5 38-39)

Our current understanding of clinical depression makes it difficult to assume that it necessarily limits achievement. We do know that the "treatment" for these conditions in the early part of the last century could contribute to a patient's distress, much as current medications may now. Woolf herself was aware of this, writing to Ethel Smyth in the midst of her revision of *The Years* to caution her, "Never trust a letter of mine not to exaggerate what's written after a night lying awake looking at a bottle of chloral and saying no, no, no, you shall not take it" (L6 44). We would do well to follow similar caution about the reports of others. Leonard Woolf's insistence that Virginia did not revise at all at Rodmell but spent "her time reading, drowsing, walking" (155) is contradicted by Virginia's letters at that time to Hugh Walpole, Ethel Smyth and Vita Sackville-West. There is now some new evidence to support her claim. In *Leonard and Virginia Woolf as Publishers*, J. H. Willis, Jr. often follows Leonard Woolf's recollection of the submission of manuscripts and the production of proofs, a reasonable procedure in the absence of other evidence. Business records now available alter the record somewhat and are important in the construction of a chronology of final revision. They cast some doubt on previous judgments about when and how Woolf made her revisions, and they allow us to us understand in more detail how she revised and the depth and beauty of her final construction. Since Grace Radin has begun the discussion of Woolf's revisions, it might be useful to summarize her findings before examining the new evidence.

Radin's article in the *The Bulletin of the New York Public Library* presented for the first time the complete text of two entire episodes that Woolf canceled from the galleys of *The Years*, what Leonard Woolf called "two enormous chunks."[1] There and in her book *Virginia Woolf's The Years: The Evolution of a Novel*, Radin makes a number of crucial points about Woolf's process of revision. There are four of particular importance.

Radin concludes that there was a far more continuous effort of revision than Leonard remembers. Checking the differences between the galley proofs then available and the "phenomenal" amount of work that Virginia did to produce the final text, Radin concludes that her husband's recollection presents a scenario that is "almost impossible" (114-15). She notes, too, that the brief descriptive passages before each chapter are not in the galleys and, by comparing the galleys to the published novel, she shows that VW worked to "sharpen and heighten the impact of her scenes" (118). She concludes, however, that this compression entailed some "loss of clarity" (118).²

Radin also shows that the deletion of two entire episodes, the wartime London scene and 1921, created problems in the novel, since links to them later in the text had to be changed. She concludes that Woolf appears to have "solved these problems practically rather than artistically" by inserting other memories that do not work as well as the originals. Radin sees in the preludes and interludes an attempt to provide structure. She notes that Woolf's diary comments "testify to her preoccupation with finding some means of providing a pattern and continuity for the amorphous mass of material she had compiled in her first draft" and that her ultimate goal was "a far more structured novel" (127).

One of the most valuable aspects of Radin's work on *The Years* is her ability to read the novel as Woolf wrote it, ignoring for the most part its critical history. She sees the "translucent beauty" of the opening of the "Present Day" chapter, the emphasis on the "aura of light from the setting sun" that "surrounds each object" and the atmosphere that becomes incandescent, "as if lit from within." She notices that Eleanor's name means "light" or "sun" and is "lighted from within by a spirit that has purified itself as she has learned to live without self-consciousness" (129-30).

Finally, Radin is careful with detail. She notes that Woolf used the words "proofs" and "galleys" synonymously, making it more difficult to understand the condition of the text she was revising. She notes, briefly but importantly, the quote from Dante that Eleanor encounters in "1911." In one instance Radin appears to agree with the critical history of the novel, that "Woolf's failure to unify *The Years* stems from her decision to avoid the use of extended interior monologues that characterized the novels of her middle period." Thus "in *The Years*, no such fluidity is possible" (152).²

Some records of Woolf's revisions have been available to scholars for some time. These include galley sheets at The Henry W. and Albert A. Berg Collection at the New York Public Library stamped "First proof" and "R. & R. Clark 15 December 1936" that Grace Radin used in her study. A close look at this material reveals that they are not from a full galley proof but were typeset independently. Although the text is designed to appear in the "1917" chapter of the novel, the pages are numbered sequentially 01 through 023. Thus they are not the first proofs of the novel but instead the "first" setting of this revised portion. Despite the handwritten label in ink on the upper right of page 013 that identifies this as a "Marked Proof," there are few "marks" on them: a question mark relating to quotation marks and two deletions and two small additions to the text. We also have had access through the Monks House Papers at the University of Sussex to four typewritten sheets, undated and corrected in Woolf's hand. Since they refer to a character named "Elvira" (who became Sara in the novel), they are certainly from 1933-34. In 1986 Frances Hooper donated two bound proofs of *The Years* to Smith College. They appeared to be a set prepared just before the first edition was printed, but a computer comparison between a proof copy and the first English edition reveals that these were not a final but the penultimate version of the novel. Woolf had not yet changed the chapter numbers to dates and there is no chapter "1918." They also differ from the published edition in numerous other ways, including punctuation, spelling, spacing and paragraphing. Many of the changes are substantive, including additions of words and sentences. Not counting the addition of chapter "1918," over 360 changes were made to these proofs before publication.

Since it was unlikely that any other drafts or proofs of the novel remained, business records were sought to see what they might reveal about the nature and the extent of Woolf's work. In time, ledgers and invoices from R. & R. Clark were discovered in the archives of the National Library of Scotland, and the University of Reading was found to hold a number of letters, work estimates and invoices from R. & R. Clark and the Garden City Press, the bindery used by the Hogarth Press. Among these was a particular surprise, a letter from an Alex McLachlan of 8 February 1936 to Virginia Woolf that accompanied his "duplication of scripts of your MS," indicating that he had made copies of her holographs of *The Years*. Also found there were letters between Leonard Woolf and William Maxwell (R. & R. Clark) that indicate both the scope and the pace of Woolf's revisions.

We learn that on 10 March 1936, Leonard Woolf sent 131 typescript pages to Maxwell with instructions to set immediately and return 5 galley proofs, the remainder of the pages of the novel to be sent "in batches" (Reading). Maxwell writes to Leonard 2 July 1936 to ask for instructions for handling confusing typewritten pages, noting specific problems of wording and paragraphing. On 18 December 1936 Leonard writes to order 12,000 copies of TY and an additional 5,000 for the Uniform Edition, since it would be "cheaper to do this." He notes that the novel "makes 464 pages if Mrs Woolf decides to include additional material sent to you recently" (Reading). Virginia Woolf was clearly working at a remarkable pace, sending "batches" of the novel, receiving proofs in turn and answering questions.

Invoices hint of other exchanges of this type. The most significant is an invoice from R. & R. Clark dated February 1937 listing work performed since the last billing (fourth quarter ending December 1936) which included a "comp of 32 pages" with "13 9/16 shs deleted" and "very extensive alterations." It also charges for "additional proofs (including 20 sets sewn in paper covers)," two copies of which are surely those at Smith College. Also included was a charge for "making up slips 14 ¾ shs of 32 pp" (Reading), probably indicating a charge for completing revisions that they could not initially execute with confidence. When this information is added to what we know from published sources, especially Woolf's letters and diaries, we are able to construct a fuller chronology of her revision.

On the 25 March 1935 Woolf was hard at work revising "in a rage" as she "wrote the whole of that d___d chapter again, in a spasm of desperation." She thinks she "got it right" by "breaking up, the use of thought skipping" and so cut "20 to 30 pages" (*D4* 290-91) Two days later she calls it the "the air raid chapter" ["1917"], a crucial section in the development of the structure of *The Years*. Here and throughout this period of revision, we learn that she is reading Dante's *Purgatorio*, which she finds hard to do with "half ones mind running on Eleanor & Kitty," a reference to "1917." Woolf worries that her chapter is "too thin" (*D4* 295).

By 16 October 1935 she thinks she has discovered how to use the "surface layer" of a scene while bringing in music and painting with her characters. "That is what I want to try for in the air raid scene." This is what she says she did in *The Waves*, using layers of experience "corresponding to the dimensions of the human being" so that the party ["Present Day"] is about the people at the same time it is about art. She is "doing Crosby – an upper air scene" (*D4* 347). This is a significant indication of her progress, since this scene becomes "1918," a chapter that we now know was added at the very end of the revision process.

Woolf notes with anguish on 10 December 1935 that she has promised to deliver the novel by the 15 February. The date was hopelessly optimistic. Her agreement to do this caused "a bad mornings work in consequence" (*D4* 356). The pressure is taking its toll.

On 29 December 1935, Woolf tells her diary that she has "just put the last words to The Years," though it is too long, some 797 pages. It needs sharpening with some "bold cuts & emphases," but she likes it and her "whole mind [is] in action," though "not as intensely as it was in *The Waves*" (*D4* 360-61).

By 8 February 1936 Woolf had received the duplicate scripts from McLachan and seventeen days later (25 February 1936) she is making changes to "that most accursed air raid scene," hoping to be done by 10 March. She appears to have been successful. Willis reports that on that date, 132 pages were sent to R. & R. Clark to be set. We know now that the correct number was 131 pages and that she expected galleys to be returned quickly while she worked on the additional "batches" of pages that would be sent to them for setting. Leonard Woolf has said that the reason for the unusual decision to produce galleys instead of page proofs was due to concerns about his wife's health: "Virginia was in despair about the book and wanted galleys so that she would be free to make any alternations she wished in proof" (153).

Willis reports that the last of these batches was sent to the printer on 8 March 1936, but Woolf's diary reveals that she is still working on the novel on 16 March and in "acute despair on re-reading" it. The day before she thought it might be her "best book," but now she is not so sure. She is typing and "only at the Kings death" ["1910"] (*D5* 17). She has done 250 pages of an estimated 700. Despite her anxiety about the novel and Leonard's concerns about her health, Woolf worked quickly. An unpublished letter of 14 April 1936 from The Garden City Press, LTD to the Hogarth Press provides an estimate for a book of 560 pages. This is also the date on the "galley proofs" of "1917" at the Berg. On 20 April Woolf tells Ethel Smyth from Rodmell that publication must be delayed, since she "shall probably have to cut and [revise] considerably" and the "the printers have only just sent the last lot" of proofs (*L6* 27).

Woolf, while desperate at night for sleep, continues to work during the day (*L5* 44, 46). Leonard says that she started on 12 June, "but almost at once it was clear that she had not really recovered" and must take a "complete rest" (154). If complete, the rest was short. Virginia Woolf tells Ethel Smyth on 25 June 1936 that she has "just done my first batch of proofs" (*L6* 49). This is supported Maxwell's letter of 2 July asking for clarification.

Seven days later on 9 July, the Woolfs go to Rodmell where Leonard says Virginia only rested. Her letters to Ethel Smyth, Hugh Walpole and Vita Sackville-West in July, August and September 1936 tell a different story. She is "living like a hermit till I've done my proofs" (*L6* 55; 14 July), keeping her "nose to the grindstone" (*L6* 61; 1 August) and that she is "trying to finish her proofs" in spite of headaches (*L6* 68; 27 August). She says that "every morning" she turns "wearily to my proofs" (*L6* 72; 15 Sept). These reports to friends contradict Leonard's insistence that revising began at "the end of October," and are born out by the fact that he was able to begin reading a draft of the novel soon after on 3 November. He had read to "1914" the next day. By 14 November 1936, Woolf tells her diary that she had reduced her 700 pages to 420 and on the 24th she says that she had learned in this book how to do "scenes" (*L6* 84). By the end of the month, Woolf likes the book, saying it is "taut real strenuous" (*D5* 38).

Willis reports that she finished the proofs on 30 November 1936, though a full month lapses before the galleys go off. What was sent when is not entirely clear. Willis says that ten pages were cut from "1917" and at least 25 pages from "1921" (289). In any event, we now have evidence that Leonard felt sufficiently confident in her progress to order the printing of 12,000 copies of a novel of 464 pages. It was 420 pages just a month earlier. Virginia Woolf's diary says that the final proofs were sent 30 December. Leonard says they were "returned to the printer" on the 31st.

Two unpublished letters from The Garden City Press, LTD to The Hogarth Press on January 5th and 6th seek to change an estimate based on "the decreased number of pages and the thickness of the paper," apologizing on the 6th for an original estimate of 368 pages that was due to "an oversight" at the printer's offices. Whether this was a polite way of altering the estimate due to authorial changes is unknown. We do know now, however, that R. & R. Clark billed for their work on 472 pages. *The Years* was published April 1937. It was 469 pages. The first American edition, entirely re-set by Harcourt Brace, was 435 pages.

This chronology establishes several things. Leonard and Virginia Woolf's memories about the revision process are markedly different. The time that Leonard allows for these massive revisions could not have been sufficient. Woolf must have worked on her novel almost as continuously as she claimed in order to have altered so large a novel as many times in so many ways. It is also clear that a number of unique elements entered the process, from duplicate manuscript sheets to several sets of galley proofs prepared for the author while she made extensive changes elsewhere in the novel. While Leonard accepted the extra cost of this radically modified process of revision with great patience, doubtless owing to his fears for her health, how Virginia Woolf put them to use is nothing short of remarkable. Perhaps the best indication of the brilliance of her technique can be found in the bound galley proofs at Smith College. The substantive revisions they contain and the major alterations that they lack indicate the scope and intensity of her efforts even at the eleventh hour.

The differences between the Smith Proofs and the published novel make it very clear that late in the revision process Virginia Woolf was making a large number of substantive changes. Perhaps the most important of these is the "1918" chapter. Its addition helps account for the page discrepancies in the proofs noted earlier, but it does far more than that. "1918" is the "Crosby—an upper air scene" that Woolf refers to as early as October 1935. It comes right after the "air raid" chapter ("1917") that caused her so much trouble for so long. This is not just a necessary transitional section that compensates for the removal of "two enormous chunks" or the desperate deletions and additions of a woman on the brink of madness. It is a calm, brilliant restructuring of *The Years* that makes it more subtle and finely constructed.

Virginia Woolf did much more than cut pages, take long walks and fight depression while she revised *The Years* for publication, though she herself contributed to this myth. Writing to Philippa Woolf two years after the novel was published (19 Sept 1939) she says that she had become "sick to death of *The Years*" and "took Leonards garden scissors and cut out patches and flung them on the bonfire" (*L6* 360). As we have seen, nothing could be further from the truth.

As Naomi Black reminds us, *The Years* was not the only claim on Woolf's attention. Its first version, called *The Pargiters*, was "closely connected to . . . the origins of *Three Guineas*" (61). Woolf worked on both at the same time while she watched the world slowly, inexorably descend into the darkness of total war. As she nears completion of her work on *The Years* in March 1936, Hitler invades the Rhineland. While a detailed discussion of all of Woolf's changes to the novel are beyond the scope of this study, we can begin to appreciate their nature and quality by looking closely at the chapters that caused her so much anxiety, "1917" ("the air-raid scene") and the "upper-air scene" that became "1918."

The "proofs" on which Radin based her conclusions were odd; they were from a late section of the novel and numbered independently. Never before had Woolf type-set a small amount of text in mid-revision. Her diary and letters show us that the "1917" chapter was causing her trouble. She refers to her changes as "scenes," something that she thinks later that she learned working on *The Waves*, and she worries if "they worth doing?" (*D5* 36). If we look at the structure of allusion in the novel and remember what she was reading in the spring of 1935, we can answer that question for her.

The diaries reveal that as Woolf worked on her revisions, she read Dante:

> I see I am becoming a regular diariser. The reason is that I cannot make the transition from Pargiters to Dante without some bridge. And this cools my mind. I am rather worried about the raid chapter ["1917"]: afraid if I compress & worry that I shall spoil. Never mind. Forge ahead, & see what comes next. (*D4* 291-92)

On 1 April she worries that she "shall never finish the Purgatorio. But whats the use of reading with half ones mind running on Eleanor & Kitty." She think that the scene is "too thin run" and needs "compacting" (*D4* 295).

Dante was integral to the structure of the novel, and Woolf was at some pains to reveal it. For example, in "1911" Eleanor opens a book that is sitting on a table:

> She read a few lines, here and there. But her Italian was rusty; the meaning escaped her. There was a meaning however; a hook seemed to scratch the surface of her mind.
>
> > chè per quanti si dice più lì nostro
> > tanto possiede più di ben ciascuno.
>
> What did that mean? She read the English translation.
>
> > For by so many more there are who say 'ours'
> > So much the more of good doth each possess.
>
> Brushed lightly by her mind that was watching the moths on the ceiling, and listening to the call of the owl as it looped from tree to tree with its liquid cry, the words did not give out their full meaning, but seemed to hold something furled up in the hard shell of the archaic Italian. (228)

Eleanor has read from *Purgatorio* XV. The rest of the passage, which she does not read, is important:

> And he [said] to me: 'Because you still
> have your mind fixed on earthly things,
> you harvest darkness from the light itself.

'That infinite and ineffable Good,
which dwells on high, speeds toward love
as a ray of sunlight to a shining body.

'It returns the love it finds in equal measure,
so that, if more of ardor is extended,
eternal Goodness will augment Its own.

'And the more souls there are who love on high,
the more there is to love, the more of loving,
for like a mirror each returns it to the other. (ll. 64-75)

Though Eleanor ("light") stops reading, we know the lesson of the canto: light attracts light. For Dante, God is light. For Woolf, light is a key to her purpose in the novel and a reply to the darkness of World War I.

The central event in "1917" is an air raid, during which Renny, Maggie and their dinner guests huddle in the cellar of "Number 30" near Westminster, the exact address where, at the beginning of the novel, Able Pargiter visits his mistress Mira. As the chapter opens, we are told that there is "no moon" and "darkness pressed on the windows; towns had merged themselves in open country. No light shone, save when a searchlight rayed round the sky" (301). This chapter is jeweled with allusions that guide us to the meaning of the text. Sitting in the "crypt-like" cellar with "stone walls" constructed when Westminster was built, the room had "a damp ecclesiastical look." Eleanor notices "the number on the box opposite was 1397. She noticed everything" (313). The box, like the others around it, holds wine bottles. She does not appear to know that 1397 is the year when construction of the roof of Westminster Hall begins under Richard II. They sit in its "shadow" (301). It is also the date for the first of Shakespeare's history plays, the beginning of English popular history:

> While historians today might argue about the significance of the end of Plantagenet rule in 1485, and whether terms such as the Hundred Years War and the Wars of the Roses serve any useful purpose, Shakespeare has dictated the most important cut-off date in English medieval history: 1397. Quite simply, that is the historical point at which his great cycle of history plays begins. It is therefore the start date for our collective familiarity with the leading characters from British history. (Mortimer 1)

Thus as the darkness of war rages about them, Woolf's characters sit in the middle of English history, waiting for the ultimate evil to triumph and all history to cease. It is hell.

"1918" is a bridge between the war years and "Present Day." It moves the novel from an inferno of war to the purgatory of the present. Crosby moves out of the house and into the open air to go shopping as the booming guns announce "that the war is over" (328). Old Crosby who had spent her life serving the Pargiter family "had aged greatly during the past four years" (325) of war and only now is able to resume domestic life above ground.

Woolf worked for some time on this chapter, finally adding it to the novel late in the revision process. The structure of her model, *The Divine Comedy*, reveals why: for Dante, heat and light are associated with the divine, cold and darkness with evil. Woolf saw the war as a descent into cold and darkness. Crosby's "open-air scene" is release. "Present Day" is modeled on *Purgatorio*, and as in Dante's poem, its most singular component is time. Unlike those who dwelled in the *Inferno* and in *Paradiso*, those in *Purgatorio* are time-bound until their penance is completed: "Inhabitants of the other two *cantiche* are in their eternal condition with one major exception: in both realms souls will receive their bodies to wear for eternity only at the Last Judgment. They are aware of time, but do not act in it (and those in hell are denied knowledge of the present)." Because there is a limit to how long souls remain in purgatory while they expiate their sins, they exist in a "real, present time" that ends with redemption (Hollander xxviii). This explains why Virginia Woolf added dates as chapter titles and called the last chapter "Present Day" after the Smith Proofs were set. She decides finally to use time as Dante did. The results are similar: Eleanor's "light" attracts light and counters the destructive power of sin, just as Dante's did in *Purgatorio*.

In the final chapter, "Present Day," Woolf does not allude to Dante but follows him closely. As Dante moves through *Purgatorio*, he has to be purified from the temptations of the seven deadly sins before he can ascend to Eden or "earthly paradise." As he begins the process, seven letter "P"s are placed on his forehead. As he banishes forever their power over him, the letters are removed, one by one. There is only one sin that is not removed in this way: Pride. It is the sin of the creator, the poet, the sin of the author. While Envy, Wrath, Sloth, Avarice (and Prodigality), Gluttony and Lust are clearly represented in "Present Day," the sin of Pride is not. Woolf aligns herself with Dante as if to include herself among the "poets" who are susceptible to this sin.[3]

Not only does Woolf refer to these sins in order, the devil himself makes an appearance: "Then curtains in the house opposite parted, and three heads appeared at the window. They looked at the heads outlined on the window opposite them. They were standing with their backs to the railings of the square. The trees hung dark showers of leaves over them" (391). In Dante, evil has three heads (Cerberus) and three faces (Satan).

The gathering of family and friends in "Present Day" lasts the night. When the party is nearly over, Eleanor imagines in the "mixture of lights" that is her family, a greater world to come:

> There must be another life, here and now, she repeated. This is too short, too broken. We know nothing, even about ourselves. We're only just beginning, she thought, to understand, here and there. She hollowed her hands in her lap, just as Rose had hollowed hers round her ears. She held her hands hollowed; she felt that she wanted to enclose the present moment; to make it stay; to fill it fuller and fuller, with the past, the present and the future, until it shone, whole, bright, deep with understanding. (461-62).

Then she remembers death: "For her too there would be the endless night; the endless dark. She looked ahead of her as though she saw opening in front of her a very long dark tunnel. But, thinking of the dark, something baffled her; in fact it was growing light. The blinds were white" (462). In the last scene of the novel, as light returns, Eleanor extends her hands to North as Beatrice does to Dante in the last canto of *Purgatorio*. The novel concludes with a hint of the Eden that Dante discovers: "The sun had risen, and the sky above the houses wore an air of extraordinary beauty, simplicity and peace" (469). The approaching light banishes fear and revives Eleanor. Like Dante, her "light" has been purged of human temptation and the darkness of war is over. Just as Dante insisted that hell, purgatory and heaven were not locations but states of being, Eleanor too "felt, or rather she saw, not a place, but a state of being, in which there was real laughter, real happiness, and this fractured world was whole; whole, and free" (420). She sees a better human existence which may now be within reach since the darkness of war, like the night itself, is finally over. This is an extraordinary conclusion from an author bravely battling depression as she watches the world slip inexorably back into the chaos her characters have at last overcome.[4]

On 15 March 1937 Virginia Woolf writes in her diary, considering what she might yet do with the "enormous chunks" deleted from her novel:

> Anyhow, being too tired to write, I've been thinking cd. I recast the rejected section of The Years for the Uniform Edition? Why do I bother? Only I rather suspect its needed for the whole argument impression. But there it is, safe; & I needn't consider this seriously at the moment. Keep it at the back of my mind, & judge from reviews—save that they're all so scatter brained—how far the book misses fire on that account. (*D5* 69)

Apparently, Woolf did not know that three months earlier, Leonard had ordered the Uniform Edition printed (Reading). Even after the terrible struggle to condense and revise, Virginia Woolf thought the rejected material might still belong in the novel. This final revision she did not live to begin.

The new information available from the letters, invoices and proofs changes our estimate of *The Years* while it puts to rest for good the assumption that, as she hovered on the brink of madness, she was cutting down a bad novel to make it suitable to print. Perhaps the most important lesson here is that the old evidence should have told us this without benefit of the new. We simply were not paying attention. The new evidence gives us more detail about how she worked, some of it surprising, and the proofs tell us that this incredible effort continued right up to the last moment, rendering the "final" proofs penultimate. But the rest of it was already before us: what she was reading when she was revising, the fact that she said she was working daily and continually and we just did not believe her, and the fact that extra galleys were struck to accommodate the multiple revisions necessary to so complicated a task. Ultimately there is *The Years* itself, which we have read as a novel that is not *To the Lighthouse*, *Mrs Dalloway* or *The Waves*, in other words, not a *real* Virginia Woolf novel but something less. We read what we expected: a desperate revision from a crazy woman saved only by condescending, reassuring lies from a family who misread the novel as badly as we did. We saw the experimental novels as the jewels of her life. The problem with this lapidary representation of her work is not the description; they *are* jewels. The problem is the message: these are "real" Virginia Woolf novels, that is not. Both are, and both are extraordinary.

Acknowledgements

I am indebted to Elva Louisa Baca and James Graham for their help in the complicated task of digitizing the Smith College proofs of The Years. I am also grateful for the assistance of several special collections and archive specialists. Ms. Karen V. Kukil, Associate Curator of Special Collections, William Allan Neilson Library Smith College Northampton, MA made the bound proofs of *The Years* available and offered invaluable help. The knowledge and kindness of Ms. Alison Metcalfe, Manuscripts Curator, National Library of Scotland and Ms. Karen Watson, Senior archive assistant, The Monks House Papers of Special Collections, the Library of The University of Sussex, Falmer, Brighton were indispensible. I have come to depend upon the encouragement and insight of Susan Dick, Naomi Black and S. P. Rosenbaum. They made the results of this study better in many ways, as usual. I am also especially grateful for S. P. Rosenbaum for allowing me to inspect his copy of documents from Archives of The Hogarth Press, Special Collections, Reading University Library, The University of Reading. What I owe Margaret Cyzeska is beyond acknowledgement.

A list of the textual variants between the Smith Proof and the first English edition of The Years, including references to the first American edition when helpful, is available in PDF format via email from jmhec3e@utpa.edu

Notes

1. Cf. "'I Am Not a Hero': Virginia Woolf and the First Version of *The Years*." Radin, *Massachusetts Review* 7.1 (Winter 1975): 195-208.
2. This follows Leonard Woolf who says that he "found it a good deal too long, particularly in the middle, and not really as good as *The Waves, To the Lighthouse*, and *Mrs. Dalloway*" (155).
3. References to the Seven Deadly sins in "Present Day." One each is listed here, though there are several instances of each in the chapter.

   Envy
   "I wish I'd done what you did," said a little man called Pickersgill. (332)

   Wrath
   "But there was one letter you wrote me," he continued as they waited. "An angry letter; a cruel letter."
   He looked at her. She had lifted her lip like a horse that is going to bite. That, too, he remembered.
   "Yes?" she said.
   "The night you came in from the Strand," he reminded her.. . . .
   "And I said to myself," she paused, "this is Hell. We are the damned?" (345)

   Sloth
   She held her finger between the pages of the book and looked up at him; a device, he knew, to put off the moment of action. He did not want to go either. (372)

   Avarice (& Prodigality)
   " . . . not to live; not to feel; to make money, always money...." (382)

   Gluttony
   That was what it came to--thirty years of being husband and wife--tut-tut-tut--and chew-chew-chew. It sounded like the half-inarticulate munchings of animals in a stall. Tut-tut-tut, and chew-chew-chew--as they trod out the soft steamy straw in the stable; as they wallowed in the primeval swamp, prolific, profuse, half-conscious, he thought; listening vaguely to the good-humoured patter, which suddenly fastened itself upon him. (404)

   Lust
   He opened the little book. Latin, was it? He broke off a sentence and let it swim in his mind. There the words lay, beautiful, yet meaningless, yet composed in a pattern--*nox est perpetua una dormienda* (424-25). This line is from Catullus 5, a public school staple:

Vivamus mea Lesbia, atque amemus,
rumoresque senum severiorum
omnes unius aestimemus assis!
soles occidere et redire possunt:
nobis cum semel occidit brevis lux,
nox est perpetua una dormienda.
da mi basia mille, deinde centum,
dein mille altera, dein secunda centum,
deinde usque altera mille, deinde centum.
dein, cum milia multa fecerimus,
conturbabimus illa, ne sciamus,
aut ne quis malus inuidere possit,
cum tantum sciat esse basiorum.

Let us live, my Lesbia, and let us love,
and let us judge all the rumors of the old men
to be worth just one penny!
The suns are able to fall and rise:
When that brief light has fallen for us,
we must sleep a never ending night.
Give me a thousand kisses, then another hundred,
then another thousand, then a second hundred,
then yet another thousand more, then another hundred.
Then, when we have made many thousands,
we will mix them all up so that we don't know,
and so that no one can be jealous of us when he finds out
how many kisses we have shared.

4. Dante is not the only author who influences the theme and structure of *The Years*. For example, in "1908" Martin comes to visit Eleanor after Abercorn Terrace is sold and before she has moved out. The brief scene ends as he picks up one of Eleanor's books: "'Renan,' he read. ''Why Renan?' he asked himself, beginning to read as he waited" (*TY* 160-61).

Ernest Renan (1823-1892) was a French theorist whose most famous essay is "Qu'est-ce qu'une nation?" (What is a Nation?). The argument of his essay and the argument of *The Years* have much in common:

> A nation is a soul, a spiritual principle. Two things, which in truth are but one, constitute this soul or spiritual principle. One lies in the past, one in the present. One is the possession in common of a rich legacy of memories; the other is present-day consent, the desire to live together . . . .

Renan, Ernest. "What is a Nation?" in Eley, Geoff and Suny, Ronald Grigor, ed. 1996. *Becoming National: A Reader*. New York and Oxford: Oxford UP, 1996, 41.

Works Cited

Alighieri, Dante. *The Inferno*. Trans. Robert & Jean Hollander. New York: Anchor Books, 2002.
—. *Pugatorio*. Trans. Robert & Jean Hollander. New York: Anchor Books, 2004.
Bell, Quentin. *Virginia Woolf: A Biography*. New York: Harcourt, 1972.
Black, Naomi. *Virginia Woolf as Feminist*. Ithaca: Cornell UP, 2004.
Brace, Donald. Four letters to Virginia Woolf. 1923-37. The Monks House Papers. Special Collections. The Library of The University of Sussex, Falmer, Brighton (UK).
Clark, R. & R. Unpublished Correspondence and Invoices to The Hogarth Press. 1936-37. *Archives of The Hogarth Press*, Special Collections, Reading University Library, The University of Reading (UK).
Clark, R. & R. Ledgers. January – June 1937. Entry for Hogarth Press 1937 February. *The Years*. National Library of Scotland, Edinburgh.

The Garden City Press, LTD. Unpublished letters to The Hogarth press. 5-6 January 1937. *Archives of The Hogarth Press*, Special Collections, Reading University Library, The University of Reading (UK).

McLachlan, Alex. unpublished letter to Virginia Woolf. 8 February 1936. *Archives of The Hogarth Press*, Special Collections, Reading University Library, The University of Reading (UK).

Maxwell, William and Leonard Woolf. Unpublished letters between R. & R. Clark and The Hogarth Press. 1936-37. *Archives of The Hogarth Press*, Special Collections, Reading University Library, The University of Reading (UK).

Mortimer, Ian. *The Fears of Henry IV: The Life of England's Self-Made King*. London: Jonathan Cape, 2007.

Radin, Grace. The *Years: The Evolution of a Novel*. Knoxville: U of Tennessee P, 1981.

—. "'Two enormous chunks': Episodes Excluded During the Final Revisions of *The Years*." *Bulletin of the New York Public Library* 80 (Winter 1977): 221-51.

Rosenthal, Michael. *Virginia Woolf*. New York: Columbia UP, 1979.

Willis, J. H., Jr. *Leonard and Virginia Woolf as Publishers: The Hogarth Press, 1917-41*. Charlottesville: UP of Virginia, 1992.

Woolf, Leonard. *Downhill All the Way: An Autobiography of the Years 1919 to 1939*. New York: Harcourt Brace Jovanovich, 1967.

Woolf, Virginia. *The Diary of Virginia Woolf*. Ed. Anne Olivier Bell, Assisted by Andrew McNeillie. Vols. 4 & 5. New York: Harcourt Brace Jovanovich, 1982 & 1984.

—. *The Letters of Virginia Woolf*. Ed. Nigel Nicolson and Joanne Trautmann. Vol. 6. New York: Harcourt, 1980.

—. The *Pargiters by Virginia Woolf: The Novel-Essay Portions of "The Years*. Ed. Mitchell A. Leaska. New York: New York Public Library, 1977

—. *The Years*. London: The Hogarth Press, 1937.

—. *The Years*. New York: Harcourt Brace, 1937.

—. *The Years*. Bound galley proofs. Special Collections William Allan Neilson Library, Smith College Northampton, MA.

—. *The Years*. Five pages ts, corrected. The Monks House Papers. Special Collections. The Library of The University of Sussex, Falmer, Brighton (UK).

Notes on Contributors

Elisa Bolchi is the author of *Il paese della bellezza* (Milan, I.S.U. Università Cattolica, 2007), which analyzes Virginia Woolf's reception within Italian cultural periodicals under Fascism. Other publications include an essay on the reception of Virginia Woolf and Katherine Mansfield. She currently teaches English Literature and Comparative Literature at Università Cattolica del Sacro Cuore, Milan.

Virginia Brackett teaches English and directs the Honors Program at Park University. Her 13 books include *Restless Genius: The Story of Virginia Woolf*, a recommended feminist book for youth by ALA Amelia Bloomer Project, 2005, and *The Facts on File Companion to British Poetry, 17th & 18th Centuries*, selected as a Booklist "Editor's Choice, Reference Sources, 2008."

Courtney Carter is a Professor of English at Hood College in Frederick, Maryland, where she teaches courses on nineteenth and twentieth century British literature. Her most recent publication is "Beyond the 'Trembling Instability of the Balance': The 'Quick' and the 'Quantum' in Lawrence's *Last Poems*." *D. H. Lawrence Studies* 15.2 (August 2007): 47-60.

Stuart N. Clarke has transcribed and edited Virginia Woolf's *Orlando: The Original Holograph Draft* (1993), was co-compiler with B. J. Kirkpatrick of the fourth edition of *A Bibliography of Virginia Woolf* (1997), and edited *Translations from the Russian* (2006), by Virginia Woolf and S. S. Koteliansky, and *The Essays of Virginia Woolf*, Vol. V (2009). He is a founding member of the Virginia Woolf Society of Great Britain and has edited its journal, the *Virginia Woolf Bulletin*, since its inception in 1999. He is currently editing Volume VI of *The Essays of Virginia Woolf* for publication in 2011.

Nephie Christodoulides (University of Cyprus) has published a book on Plath and motherhood (Rodopi 2005) and has two books forthcoming on H.D.: *H.D. and the Notion of the Rose* (Mellen) and the *H.D. Companion* (Cambridge University Press).

Nicole Coonradt is a PhD Student at the University of Denver focusing on Shakespeare and the Reformation. Other publications have appeared in *College Literature, Religion and the Arts, Cantaraville*, and *SHAW*.

Beth Rigel Daugherty Professor of English at Otterbein College, is working on a book-length project called *The Education of a Woman Writer: Virginia Woolf's Apprenticeship*. She has recently published an edition of letters to Virginia Woolf in *Woolf Studies Annual* and had essays included in *Trespassing Boundaries: Virginia Woolf's Short Fiction*, edited by Kathryn N. Benzel and Ruth Hoberman, and in the *Palgrave Advances in Virginia Woolf Studies*, edited by Anna Snaith.

Pamela Hall Evans is an independent scholar, lecturer, poet and biographer. She received her MA from the University of Denver and is currently writing a biography of the New Mexico artist Dorothy Eugenie Brett.

Anne Fernald is the author of *Virginia Woolf: Feminism and the Reader* (Palgrave 2006) and is currently editing *Mrs. Dalloway* for Cambridge University Press. She is an associate professor of English at Fordham University. She is the organizer for the nineteenth annual conference on Virginia Woolf, Forham University, 2009.

Luke Ferretter is Assistant Professor of English at Baylor University. He has published two books of critical theory and several articles on twentieth-century literature and critical theory, including essays on Derrida, Kristeva, Sylvia Plath, D. H Lawrence and Hanif Kureishi. He has recently completed a book on Sylvia Plath's fiction and is beginning a study of D. H. Lawrence's philosophy.

Meghan Fox is a writing instructor and doctoral student at SUNY, Stony Brook. She is specializing in Transatlantic Modernism.

Diane F. Gillespie, Professor Emerita of English at Washington State University, is author of *The Sisters' Arts: The Writing and Painting of Virginia Woolf and Vanessa Bell* and of numerous book chapters and articles. She is editor of Woolf's *Roger Fry: A Biography* and of *The Multiple Muses of Virginia Woolf* as well as co-editor of Julia Stephen's writings, *Virginia Woolf and the Arts*, and Cicely Hamilton's *Diana of Dobson's*.

Jane Goldman is Reader in English Literature at the University of Glasgow and General Editor of the Cambridge University Press Edition of the *Writings of Virginia Woolf*. She is author of number of works on Woolf and on Modernism, most recently *Modernism, 1910-1945, Image to Apocalypse*. She is editor of *To the Lighthouse* for Cambridge and is currently writing a book called *Virginia Woolf and the Signifying Dog*.

Evelyn Haller is Professor of English and Chair of the Fine Arts/Humanities Division at Doane College in Crete (near Lincoln), Nebraska. Her chapter on Virginia Woolf and dance will be published in *The Edinburgh Companion to Virginia Woolf and the Arts*.

Leslie Kathleen Hankins, professor of English at Cornell College, has presented at all of the annual Virginia Woolf conferences, often on the topic of Virginia Woolf and the cinema. She publishes regularly on Woolf and film of the twenties, most recently in Bonnie Kime Scott's 2007 *Gender of Modernism* anthology, the forthcoming Modern Language Association publication, *Approaches to Teaching Mrs. Dalloway*, edited by Eileen Barrett and Ruth Saxton, and Maggie Humm's forthcoming *Companion to Virginia Woolf and the Arts*.

James M. Haule is Professor of English at the University of Texas–Pan American. He is a member of the editorial committee of the *Shakespeare Head Press Edition of Virginia Woolf* and co-edited *The Waves* for that series. He is co-editor of *Editing Virginia Woolf: Interpreting the Modernist Text*. He has published numerous articles on Virginia Woolf, James Joyce, Edna O'Brien, Angus Wilson, Rosamund Lehmann and Elizabeth Bowen.

Brenda Helt completed her Ph.D. in English and Feminist Studies at the University of Minnesota in 2008. Her dissertation, *The Work of Bisexuality in Modernist Women's Writing: Sexual Epistemology, Modernist Aesthetics, Feminist Politics*, focuses primarily on

Virginia Woolf, H.D., and Rosamond Lehmann. She is currently working on a book titled *Neither/Nor: Bisexuality in Modernist Women's Writing.*"

Cheryl Hindrichs, an assistant professor of British Literature and Critical Theory at Boise State University, has published articles on Woolf, H.D., Walter Benjamin, and Germaine Dulac in *Studies in Short Fiction*, *The Space Between: Literature and Culture 1914-1945*, and *Feminist Studies*. Her current research focuses on lyric narrative in late modernism and the poetics of illness in modernism.

Maggie Humm is a Professor of Cultural Studies, University of East London UK. She has been a Distinguished Visiting Scholar and Professor at many universities including Massachusetts, San Diego State, Stanford, Rutgers, Queen's Belfast, and Karachi. Recent publications include *Snapshots of Bloomsbury: the Private Lives of Virginia Woolf and Vanessa Bell* (Rutgers and the Tate, 2006) and she is currently editing the *Edinburgh Companion to Virginia Woolf and the Arts* (Edinburgh University Press).

Erica Johnson teaches world literature at Wagner College in New York City. Recent scholarship includes *Home, Maison, Casa: The Politics of Location in Works by Jean Rhys, Marguerite Duras, and Erminia Dell'Oro* (Fairleigh Dickinson UP, 2003) and *Caribbean Ghostwriting* (also FDUP, forthcoming) as well as articles on Woolf, Rhys, Cixous, and Maryse Conde.

Joyce Kelley is an assistant professor of English at Auburn University, Montgomery. She joined the department there after a year as a postdoctoral fellow at Northwestern University. She is writing an article on Virginia Woolf and music for the forthcoming *Edinburgh Companion to Virginia Woolf and the Arts*, edited by Maggie Humm.

Danae Killian-O'Callaghan is a concert pianist whose work focusses on modernity and the interface between music and language. Currently a PhD candidate at the University of Melbourne, where she is the Helen Macpherson Smith Scholar, Danae is exploring the musicality of Woolf's writing in a thesis entitled "The Music of Wandering Stars: Viriginia Woolf's *The Waves* and the New Experience of the Spheres'-Harmony."

Justyna Kostkowska is Associate Professor of English at Middle Tennessee State University and author of *Virginia Woolf's Experiment with Genre and Politics 1926-1931: Visioning and Versioning* The Waves (2005). Her new interest is in the ecological imagination in the writing of Woolf, Winterson, and Ali Smith.

Karen Levenback, former Secretary-Treasurer and then President of the [International] Virginia Woolf Society, taught at George Washington University for more than fifteen years and is book review editor of the *Virginia Woolf Miscellany*. She dedicates this paper to Newt, who died on 2 July, and Kepler, who died on 10 November 2008.

Alice Lowe is an independent Woolf scholar and a freelance writer focusing on creative nonfiction. She has extensive experience in nonprofit management from which she recently retired; she currently consults with nonprofit organizations and is a contributing writer for community-based publications.

Linden Peach is Professor of English at Edge Hill University, near Liverpool, and is a Fellow of the English Association. He is the author of *Virginia Woolf* (Palgrave Macmillan), has contributed chapters to a number of key collections of new essays on Woolf, and is currently producing a scholarly edition of *Flush* for Cambridge University Press.

Milena Radeva teaches at Providence College. She has published articles on Virginia Woolf and Edith Wharton, and she is currently working on an article about Arthur Miller's reception in Bulgaria.

Roberta Rubenstein, Professor of Literature at American University in Washington, DC, is the author of *The Novelistic Vision of Doris Lessing: Breaking the Forms of Consciousness* (1979), *Boundaries of the Self: Gender, Culture, Fiction* (1987), and *Home Matters: Longing and Belonging, Nostalgia and Mourning in Women's Fiction* (2001) as well as a number of essays and book chapters on modern and contemporary women writers. Her new book, *Virginia Woolf and the Russian Point of View*—from which the essay in this volume is excerpted—is forthcoming from Palgrave Macmillan in Fall 2009.

Carol Samson holds a Ph.D. in English/Creative Writing. A Lecturer in the University of Denver Writing Program, she has published stories in several literary journals, including a story in the *Open Windows* 2006 anthology by Ghost Road Press which won the 2007 Colorado Book Award. Her play, *After Tea*, adapted from Virginia Woolf's *A Writer's Diary* was presented at the 18th International Conference on Virginia Woolf.

Bonnie Kime Scott is Professor and Chair of Women's Studies at San Diego State University. Recent works include the critical anthology, *Gender in Modernism: New Geographies, Complex Intersections* (2007), *Gender and Modernism,* a 4 volume set in the Routledge Critical Concepts in Literary and Cultural Studies series (2008), the annotated edition of *Mrs. Dalloway* for Harcourt Press (2005), and articles contributing to a greening of modernism, some related to her work in progress, *Virginia Woolf and Modernist Uses of Nature.*

Brenda R. Silver is Mary Brinsmead Wheelock Professor at Dartmouth College. She edited *Virginia Woolf's Reading Notebooks* (Princeton UP, 1983) and is the author of *Virginia Woolf Icon* (U of Chicago P, 1999). Her essay "Virginia Woolf Icon," an update of her book, is forthcoming in *Virginia Woolf and the Arts* (Edinburgh UP); she is currently writing an essay on popular fiction in the digital age for *The Cambridge Companion to Popular Fiction.*

Susan Solomon is a Ph.D. Candidate in Comparative Literature at Brown University. Her dissertation deals with international modernism, political violence, punctuation, and the inter-arts; she has contributed entries related to war in the *Encyclopedia of Sex and Gender* (Macmillan).

Elisa Kay Sparks is an Associate professor of English at Clemson University in South Carolina where she teaches seminars in Woolf and Eliot, Modernist London, and critical theory and science fiction, and she also directs the Women's Studies program. She has published articles about Woolf's connections to gardens and garden history, to the visual arts, and to the American painter, Georgia O'Keeffe—topics she also explores in the visual medium of printmaking.

Robert Spoo (Ph.D. English, Princeton University; J.D., Yale Law School) is Associate Professor of Law at The University of Tulsa College of Law and has served as legal counsel for numerous authors and academic clients. He has published widely on James Joyce, Ezra Pound, H.D., and other modernist authors, and currently focuses his research on the intersection between literary modernism and intellectual property.

Joanne Campbell Tidwell is the author of *Politics and Aesthetics in The Diary of Virginia Woolf* (Routledge, 2008), and earned her PhD at Auburn University in Auburn, AL. She is currently a lecturer at Peace College in Raleigh, NC.

Virginia Woolf. Diaries. Thursday, 20 June 1940 (Reel Three D35-1940). Reproduced by permission of the Society of Authors on behalf of the Virginia Woolf Estate and by the Henry W. and Albert A. Berg Collection of English and American Literature, New York Public Library (Astor, Lenox and Tilden Foundations). Cf. *The Diary of Virginia Woolf*, vol. 4, ed. Anne Olivier Bell (New York: Harcourt, 1982) 323.

www.ingramcontent.com/pod-product-compliance
Lightning Source LLC
Chambersburg PA
CBHW021348230426
43666CB00006B/444